Taking SIDES

Clashing Views on Controversial Issues in Business Ethics and Society

Fourth Edition

Taking SIDES

Clashing Views on Controversial Issues in Business Ethics and Society

Fourth Edition

Edited, Selected, and with Introductions by

Lisa H. Newton
Fairfield University
and
Maureen M. Ford
Fairfield University

Dushkin Publishing Group/Brown & Benchmark Publishers
A Times Mirror Higher Education Group Company

To our husbands—Victor J. Newton, Jr., and James H. L. Ford, Jr.

Photo Acknowledgments

Part 1   Pam Carley/DPG/B&B
Part 2   New York Stock Exchange
Part 3   Courtesy TRW
Part 4   E. Mandelmann/WHO
Part 5   Steve Delaney/EPA
Part 6   Milton Grant/UN Photo 155092

Cover Art Acknowledgment

Charles Vitelli

Manufactured in the United States of America

Fourth Edition

10   9   8   7   6   5   4   3   2   1

Library of Congress Cataloging-in-Publication Data

Main entry under title:
    Taking sides: clashing views on controversial issues in business ethics and society/edited,
    selected, and with introductions by Lisa H. Newton and Maureen M. Ford.—4th ed.
    Includes bibliographical references and index.
    1. Business ethics. I. Newton, Lisa H., *comp.* II. Ford, Maureen M., *comp.*

174.4
0-697-31291-7   95-83859

 Printed on Recycled Paper

PREFACE

From the very beginning of critical thought, we find the distinction between top-ics susceptible of certain knowledge and topics about which uncertain opinions are available. The dawn of this distinction, explicitly entertained, is the dawn of modern mentality. It introduces criticism.

—Alfred North Whitehead
Adventures of Ideas (1933)

This volume contains 40 selections, presented in a pro and con format, that debate a total of 20 different controversial issues in business ethics. In this book we ask you, the reader, to examine the accepted practices of business in light of justice, right, and human dignity. We ask you to consider what moral imperatives and values should be at work in the conduct of business.

This method of presenting opposing views on an issue grows out of the ancient learning method of *dialogue*. Two presumptions lead us to seek the truth in a dialogue between opposed positions: The first presumption is that the truth is really out there and that it is important to find it. The second is that no one of us has all of it (the truth). The way then to reach the truth is to form our initial opinions on a subject and give voice to them in public. Then we let others with differing opinions reply, and while they are doing so, we listen carefully. The truth that comes into being in the public space of the dialogue becomes part of your opinion—now a more informed opinion, and now based on the reasoning that emerged in the course of the airing of opposing views.

Each issue in this volume has an issue *introduction*, which sets the stage for the debate as it is argued in the YES and NO selections. Each issue concludes with a *postscript* that makes some final observations and points the way to other questions related to the issue. The introductions and postscripts do not preempt what is the reader's own task: to achieve a critical and informed view of the issue at stake. In reading an issue and forming your own opinion, you should not feel confined to adopt one or the other of the positions presented. There are positions in between the given views, or totally outside of them, and the *suggestions for further reading* that appear in each issue postscript should help you find resources to continue your study of the subject. At the back of the book is a listing of all the *contributors to this volume*, which will give you information on the philosophers, business professors, businesspeople, and business commentators whose views are debated here.

Changes to this edition   This edition represents a considerable revision. There are 6 completely new issues: *Classic Dialogue: Is Capitalism the Best Route to Human Happiness?* (Issue 1); *Should Casino Gambling Be Prohibited?*

i

(Issue 4); *Is Junk Bond Financing Advisable?* (Issue 6); *Are Financial Derivative Instruments Always a Gamble?* (Issue 7); *Does The Body Shop Misrepresent Itself and Its Products?* (Issue 16); and *Are Market Incentives Sufficient to Clean Up the Water?* (Issue 18). In addition, one or both of the YES and NO selections have been changed in the issues on business and medicine (Issue 2) and on tobacco advertising (Issue 15) to bring the debates up to date. In all, there are 15 new selections.

A word to the instructor   An *Instructor's Manual With Test Questions* (multiple-choice and essay) is available through the publisher for the instructor using *Taking Sides* in the classroom. And a general guidebook, *Using Taking Sides in the Classroom,* which discusses methods and techniques for integrating the pro-con approach into any classroom setting, is also available.

Acknowledgments   We were greatly assisted in this enterprise by Mimi Egan, publisher for the Taking Sides series, who was unstinting with her time, effort, and insight. Praise and thanks are also due to our families, without whose patience and support this volume would never have been completed. Special thanks go to those who responded to the questionnaire with specific suggestions for the fourth edition:

Ronald E. Berenbeim
New York University

Melvin J. Brandon
Spring Hill College

Henry W. Dmochowski
Pennsylvania State
  University–
  Great Valley

Stanley Flax
St. Thomas University

Timothy C. Fout
University of Louisville

Ronald R. Gauch
Marist College

Susan Helf
University of Washington

Rita C. Hinton
Mississippi University for
  Women

Grace Klinefelter
Art Institute of Fort
  Lauderdale

Paul Lansing
University of Illinois–
  Urbana-Champaign

Sherri L. Levin
Trinity College

Leon Levitt
Madonna University

Antonia Malone
Seton Hall University

Dan Marlin
Florida State University

Dennis R. McGrath
University of Baltimore

Thomas McGuire
University of Detroit
  Mercy–McNichols

Corinne Nicholson
St. Andrews Presbyterian
  College

Newman S. Peery
University of The Pacific

Howard R. Radest
University of South Carolina
  at Beaufort

Peter M. Shea
St. Leo College

Andrew Sikula, Sr.
California State
  University–Chico

Monica G. Thomas
California State
  University–Bakersfield

Michelle Tooley
Jefferson Community College

James T. Toomey
University of Idaho

John Trebnik
Marian College

Lisa H. Newton
Fairfield University

Maureen M. Ford
Fairfield University

CONTENTS IN BRIEF

CONTENTS

Free-market economist Adam Smith (1723–1790) argues that if self-interested people are left alone to seek their own economic advantage, the result, unintended by any one of them, will be greater advantage for all. German philosopher Karl Marx (1818–1883) and German sociologist Friedrich Engels (1820–1895) argue that if people are left to their own self-interested devices, those who own the means of production will rapidly reduce everyone else to virtual slaves.

Professor of medicine Arnold S. Relman argues that financial and technological pressures are forcing doctors to act like businessmen, with deleterious consequences for patients. Andrew C. Wicks, an assistant professor at the University of Washington School of Business, asserts that there are fundamental similarities between physician ethics and business ethics.

LaRue Tone Hosmer, a professor of corporate strategies, argues that codes of ethics are ineffective in bringing about more ethical behavior on the part of employees. Professor of philosophy Lisa H. Newton holds that the formation and adoption of corporate codes are valuable processes.

The Citizens' Research Education Network, formed to evaluate the effects of Connecticut's rapidly growing enthusiasm for casino gambling, concludes that casinos are harmful to cities. Professor of economics William R. Eadington argues that commercial gambling can promote the welfare of areas that host casinos.

Frank A. Olson, chief executive officer of the Hertz Corporation, argues that the unprecedented level of debt contracted by major U.S. corporations in the 1980s could lead to economic disaster. Michael T. Tucker, an associate professor of finance, argues that the increased indebtedness in the United States is simply an example of efficient markets at work.

Glenn Yago, a faculty fellow of the Rockefeller Institute of Government at the State University of New York at Stony Brook, argues that junk bonds have led to increases in jobs, productivity, and competitiveness in American industry. Ford S. Worthy, an associate editor for *Fortune* magazine, maintains that the promotion and sale of junk bonds reflect a dangerous exploitation of public ignorance and lack of foresight.

Associate professor of economics J. Patrick Raines and professor of economics Charles G. Leathers argue that trading in financial derivatives amounts to speculation and gambling in financial markets. Timothy Middleton, a contributing editor for *Nest Egg*, asserts that financial derivatives are regularly used by responsible investment professionals for a variety of risk-reducing purposes.

Professor of philosophy Lisa H. Newton argues that programs of preferential treatment represent reverse discrimination and are therefore unjust. Professor of philosophy Richard Wasserstrom argues that there is no inconsistency in objecting to discrimination while favoring preferential treatment.

Philosopher Sissela Bok asserts that blowing the whistle involves a breach of loyalty to the employer. Philosopher Robert A. Larmer argues that attempting to stop unethical company activities exemplifies company loyalty.

Michael A. Verespej, a writer for *Industry Week,* argues that a majority of employees are tolerant of drug testing. Jennifer Moore, a researcher of business ethics and business law, asserts that employers' concerns about drug abuse should not override employees' right to dignity and privacy.

George J. Annas, a professor of law and medicine, argues that women may not be legally excluded from traditionally male jobs without some real relation of gender to job performance. Hugh M. Finneran, former senior labor counsel for PPG Industries, Inc., holds that women should be excluded from industries involving substances that can deform or destroy a growing embryo.

Philosopher Richard A. Spinello argues that the pharmaceutical industry should regulate its prices in accordance with the principles of distributive justice. The Pharmaceutical Manufacturers Association, an association of 93 manufacturers of pharmaceutical and biological products, argues that price controls are counterproductive in providing scarce goods for the consumer.

Philosopher Roger Crisp argues that advertising removes decision-making power by manipulating consumers without their knowledge. John O'Toole, president of the American Association of Advertising Agencies, argues that advertising is no more coercive than an ordinary salesperson.

Investigative journalist Mark Dowie alleges that Ford Motor Company deliberately put an unsafe car—the Pinto—on the road, causing hundreds of people to suffer burn deaths and horrible disfigurement. James Neal, chief attorney for Ford Motor Company during the Pinto litigation, argues that there is no proof of criminal intent or negligence on the part of Ford.

Mark Green, the commissioner of Consumer Affairs in New York City, attacks a popular cigarette advertising campaign that seems to be aimed directly at children. Professor of philosophy John Luik argues that restricting the freedom of speech cannot be justified unless it is shown to be absolutely necessary to avoid certain harm, which has not been done in this case.

Investigative reporter Jon Entine argues that The Body Shop's claims to superior ethical standards in the conduct of business are hypocritical and false. Gordon Roddick, chairman and co-owner of The Body Shop, defends the integrity of the company and mounts a critique of Entine's reporting methods.

Professor of law Richard Epstein argues that if a law is passed that robs an individual's property of all value, he or she should be compensated for it. John Echeverria, a legal counsel to the National Audubon Society, argues that environmental regulations do not violate a right to one's property.

Robert W. Hahn, a resident scholar at the American Enterprise Institute, advocates a market-based approach to ending water pollution. Jeffery A. Foran, executive director of the Risk Science Institute, and Robert W. Adler, director of the Clean Water Project at the Natural Resources Defense Council, argue that only enforceable legislation—not the free market—can ensure clean water.

Doug Clement, formerly the coordinator of the National Infant Formula Action (INFACT) coalition, argues that Nestlé has caused the deaths of countless infants by marketing infant formula to the Third World. Maggie McComas et al. present Nestlé's response and the company's view of its present and future role in protecting infant nutrition in the Third World.

Professor of philosophy Michael Philips argues that there may be no *prima facie* reason to refuse the offer of a bribe. Professor of philosophy Thomas L. Carson argues that every acceptance of a bribe involves the violation of an implicit or explicit promise or understanding connected with one's office.

INTRODUCTION

The Study of Business Ethics: Ethics, Economics, Law and the Corporation

Lisa H. Newton
Maureen M. Ford

This book is aimed at an audience of students who expect to be in business, who know that there are knotty ethical problems out there, and who want a chance to confront them ahead of time. The method of confronting them is an invitation to join in a debate, a contest of contrary facts and conflicting values in many of the major issues of the day. This introductory essay should make it easier to join in the arguments. Managing ethical policy problems in a company requires a wide background—in ethics, economics, law, and the social sciences—which this book cannot hope to provide. But since some background assumptions in these fields are relevant to several of the problems we examine in this volume, we will sketch out very briefly the major understandings that control them. There is ultimately no substitute for thorough study of the rules of the game and years of experience and practice; but an overview of the playing field may at least make it easier for you to understand the object and limitations of the standard plays.

ETHICS

"Business ethics" is sometimes considered to be an oxymoron (a term that contradicts itself). Business and ethics have often been treated as mutually exclusive. But ethics is an issue of growing concern and importance to businesses, and we believe that many share our conviction that value questions are never absent from business decisions, that moral responsibility is the first characteristic demanded of a manager in any business, and that a thorough grounding in ethical reasoning is the best preparation for a career in business. The first imperative of business ethics is that it be taken seriously.

This book will not supply the substance of a course in ethics. For that you are directed to any of several excellent texts in business ethics or to any general text in ethics (see the list of suggested readings at the end of this introduction). *Taking Sides: Clashing Views on Controversial Issues in Business Ethics and Society* teaches ethics from the issue upward, rather than from the principle downward. You will, however, come upon much of the terminology of ethical reasoning in the course of considering these cases. For your reference, a brief summary of the ethical principles and forms of reasoning most used in this book is found in Table 1.

Table 1

Fundamental Duties

	Beneficence— promoting human welfare	Justice— acknowledging human equality	Respect for Persons— honoring individual freedom
Basic fact about human nature that grounds the duty	Humans are animals, with vulnerable bodies and urgent physical needs, capable of suffering.	Humans are social animals who must live in communities and therefore must adopt social structures to maintain communities.	Humans are rational, free—able to make their own choices, foresee the consequences, and take responsibility.
Value realized in performance of the duty	Human welfare; happiness.	Human equality.	Human dignity; autonomy.
Working out of the duty in ethical theory	Best modern example is utilitarianism, from Jeremy Bentham and John Stuart Mill, who saw morality as that which produced the greatest happiness for the greatest number. Reasoning is consequential, aimed at results.	Best modern example is John Rawls's theory of justice as "fairness"; maintaining equality unless inequality helps everyone. Reasoning is deontological: morality derived from duty, not consequences.	Best modern example is Immanuel Kant's formalism, where morality is seen as the working out of the categorical imperative. Reasoning is deontological.
Samples of implementation of the duty in business	Protecting safety of employees; maintaining pleasant working conditions; contributing funds to the local community.	Obedience to law; enforcing fair rules; nondiscrimination; no favoritism; giving credit where credit is due.	Respect for employee rights; treating employees as persons, not just as tools; respecting differences of opinion.

© 1988 Lisa Newton

ECONOMICS

Adam Smith

Capitalism as we know it is the product of the thought of Adam Smith (1723–1790), a Scottish philosopher and economist, and a small number of his European contemporaries. The fundamental capitalist act is the *voluntary exchange*: two adults, of sound mind and clear purposes, meet in the marketplace, to which each repairs in order to satisfy some felt need. They discover that each has that which will satisfy the other's need—the housewife needs flour, the miller needs cash—and they exchange at a price such that the exchange furthers the interest of each. To the participant in the free market, the *marginal utility* of the thing acquired must exceed that of the thing traded, or else why make the deal? So each party to the voluntary exchange walks away from it richer.

Adding to the value of the exchange is the *competition* of dealers and buyers; because there are many purveyors of each good in the marketplace, the customer is not forced to pay exorbitant prices for things needed. (It is a sad fact of economics that to the starving man, the marginal value of a loaf of bread is very large, and a single merchant could become unjustly rich.) Conversely, competition among the customers (typified by an auction) makes sure that the available goods end up in the hands of those to whom they are worth the most. So at the end of the market day, everyone goes home not only richer (in real terms) than when they came—the voluntariness of the exchange ensures that—but also as rich as they could possibly be, since each had available all possible options of goods or services to buy and all possible purchasers of the goods or services brought to the marketplace for sale.

Sellers and buyers win the competition through *efficiency*; that is, through producing the best quality goods at the lowest possible price or through allotting their scarce resources toward the most valuable of the choices presented to them. It is to the advantage of all participants in the market, then, to strive for efficiency (i.e., to keep the cost of goods for sale as low as possible while keeping the quality as high as possible). Adam Smith's most memorable accomplishment was to recognize that the general effect of all this self-interested scrambling would be to make the most possible goods of the best possible quality available at the least possible price. Meanwhile, sellers and buyers alike must keep an eye on the market as a whole, adjusting production and purchasing to take advantage of fluctuations in *supply and demand*. Short supply will make goods more valuable, raising the price, and that will bring more suppliers into the market, whose competition will lower the price to just above the cost of manufacture for the most efficient producers. Increased demand for any reason will have the same effect. Should supply exceed demand, the price will fall to a point where the goods will be bought. Putting this all together, Smith realized that in a system of free enterprise, you have demonstrably the best possible chance of finding for sale what you want, in good quantity and quality and at a reasonable price. Forget benevolent monarchs ordering things for our own good, Smith suggested; in this system, we are led as by an *invisible hand* of enlightened self-interest to achieve the common good, even as we think we are being most selfish.

Adam Smith's theory of economic enterprise emerged in the natural law tradition of the eighteenth century. As was the fashion for that period, Smith presented his conclusions as a series of laws: the law of supply and demand, which links supply, demand, and price; the law that links efficiency with success; and, ultimately, the laws that link the absolute freedom of the market with the absolute growth of the wealth of the free-market country.

To these laws were added others, specifying the conditions under which business enterprise would be conducted in capitalist countries. The laws of *population* formulated by English clergyman and economist Thomas Malthus (1766–1834) concluded that population would always outstrip food production, ensuring that the bulk of humanity would always live at the subsistence level. Since Smith had already postulated that employers would purchase labor at the lowest possible price, it was a one-step derivation for English economist David Ricardo (1772–1823) to conclude that workers' *wages* would never exceed the subsistence level, no matter how prosperous industrial enterprise should become. From these capitalist theorists proceeded the nineteenth-century assumption that society would inevitably divide into two classes, a minority of fabulous wealth and a majority of subsistence-level workers.

These laws, like the laws of physics advanced at that time by Sir Isaac Newton (1642–1727) and the laws of psychology and government advanced at that time by John Locke (1632–1704), were held to be immutable facts of nature, true forever and not subject to change. No concept of progress, or of the historical fitness of a system to society at a point in time, was contemplated.

Karl Marx

Only within the last century and a half have we learned to think "historically." The notion of progress, the vision of a better future, and even the very idea that we might modify that future, in part by the discernment of historical trends, were unknown to the ancients and of no interest to medieval chroniclers. For Western political philosophy, history emerged as a factor in our understanding only with the work of the nineteenth-century German philosopher G. W. F. Hegel (1770–1831), who traced the history of the Western world as an ordered series of ideal forms, evolving one from another in logical sequence toward an ideal future. A young German student of Hegel's, Karl Marx (1818–1883), concluded from his study of philosophy and economics that Hegel had to be wrong: the phases of history were ruled not by ideas but by the *material conditions* of life, and their evolution one from another came about as the ruling class of each age generated its own revolutionary overthrow.

Marx's theory, especially as it applies to the evolution of capitalism, is enormously complex; for the purposes of this unit, it can be summarized simply. According to Marx, the *ruling class* in every age is the group that *owns the means of production* of the age's product. Throughout the seventeenth century, the product was almost exclusively agricultural, and the means of production was almost exclusively agricultural land: landowners were the aristocrats and rulers. With the coming of commerce and industry, the owners of the factories joined the ruling class and eventually dominated it. It was in the nature of such capital-intensive industry to concentrate within itself more capital: as Adam Smith had proved, its greater efficiency would drive all smaller labor-intensive industry out of business, and its enormous income would be put to work as more capital, expanding the domain of the factory and the machine indefinitely (at the expense of the cottage and the human being). Thus would the wealth of society concentrate in fewer and fewer hands, as the owners of the factories expanded their enterprises without limit into mighty industrial empires, dominated by machines and by the greed of their owners.

Meanwhile, all this wealth was being produced by a new class of workers, the unskilled factory workers. Taken from the ranks of the obsolete peasantry, artisans, and craftsmen, this new working class, the *proletariat*, expanded in numbers with the gigantic mills, whose "hands" they were. Work on the assembly line demanded no education or skills, so the workers could never make themselves valuable enough to command a living wage on the open market. They survived as a vast underclass, interchangeable with the unemployed workers (recently displaced by more machines) who gathered around the factory gates looking for jobs—*their* jobs. As Ricardo had demonstrated, they could never bargain for any wage above the subsistence level—just enough to keep them alive. As capitalism and its factories expanded, the entire population, except the wealthy capitalist families, sank into this hopeless, pauperized class.

So Marx saw Western society under capitalism as one that ultimately would be divided into a small group of fabulously wealthy capitalists and a mass of paupers, mostly factory workers. The minority would keep the majority in strict control through its hired thugs (the state—the army and the police), control rendered easier by thought control (the schools and the churches). The purpose of the ideology taught by the schools and the churches—the value structure of capitalism—was to show both classes that the capitalists had a right to their wealth (through the sham of liberty, free enterprise, and the utilitarian benefits of the free market) and a perfect right to govern everyone else. Thus, the capitalists could enjoy their wealth in good conscience and the poor would understand their moral obligation to accept the oppression of the ruling class with good cheer.

Marx foresaw, and in his writings attempted to help bring about, the disillusionment of the workers: there would come a point when the workers would suddenly ask, *Why* should we accept oppression all our lives? Their search for answers to this question would show them the history of their situation, expose the falsehood of the ideology and the false consciousness of those who believe it, show them their own strength, and lead them directly to the solution that would usher in the new age of socialism—the revolutionary overthrow of the capitalist regime. Why, after all, should they not undertake such a revolution? People are restrained from violence against oppression only by the prospect of losing something valuable, and, as Marx concluded, the industrialized workers of the world had nothing to lose but their chains.

As feudalism had been swept away, then, by the "iron broom" of the French Revolution, so capitalism would be swept away by the revolt of the masses, the irresistible uprising of the vast majority of the people against the minority of industrial overlords and their terrified minions—the armed forces, the state, and the church. After the first rebellions, Marx foresaw no lengthy problem of divided loyalties in the industrialized countries of the world. Once the scales had fallen from their eyes, the working class hirelings of the army and police would quickly turn their guns on their masters and join their natural allies in the proletariat to create the new world.

After the revolution, Marx predicted, there would be a temporary "dictatorship of the proletariat," during which the last vestiges of capitalism would be eradicated and the authority to run the industrial establishment would be returned to the workers of each industry. Once the economy had been decentralized, to turn each factory into an industrial commune run by its own workers and each landed estate into an agricultural commune run by its farmers, the state as such would simply wither away. Some central authority would certainly continue to exist, to coordinate and facilitate the exchange of goods within the country (one imagines a giant computer, taking note of where goods are demanded, where goods are available, and where the railroad cars to take the goods from one place to the other are). But with no ruling class to serve and no oppression to carry out, there will be no need of the state to rule *people;* what is left will be confined to the administration of *things.*

Even as he wrote, just in time for the revolutions in Europe of 1848, Marx expected the end of capitalism as a system. Not that capitalism was evil in itself; Marx did not presume to make moral judgments on history. Indeed, capitalism was necessary as an economic system to concentrate the wealth of the country into the industries of the modern age. So, in Marx's judgment, capitalism had a respectable past and would still be necessary for awhile in the developing countries to launch their industries. But that task completed, it had no further role in history, and the longer it stayed around, the more the workers would suffer and the more violent the revolution would be when it came. The sooner the revolution, the better; the future belonged to communism.

As the collapse of the communist governments in Eastern Europe demonstrates (if demonstration were needed), the course of history has not proceeded quite as Marx predicted in 1848. In fairness, it might be pointed out that no other prophets of the time had any more luck with prognostications about the twentieth century. In any case, since Marx wrote, all participants in the debate on the nature and future of capitalism have had to respond to his judgments and predictions.

LAW: RECOVERING FOR DAMAGES SUSTAINED

Life is full of misfortune. Ordinarily, if you suffer misfortune, you must put up with it and find the resources to deal with it. If your misfortune is my fault, however, the law may step in and make me pay for those damages, one way or another.

Through *criminal law*, the public steps in and demands punishment for an offense that is serious enough to outrage public feeling and endanger public welfare. If I knock you on the head and take your wallet, the police will find me, restore your wallet to you, and imprison or otherwise punish me for the crime.

Through *civil law*, if I do you damage through some action of mine, you may take me to civil court and ask a judge (and jury) to determine whether or not I have damaged you, if so by how much, and how I should pay you back for that damage. There are a number of forms of action under which you may make your claim; the most common for business purposes are *contract* and *torts*. If you and I agree to (or "contract for") some undertaking, and I back out of it after you have relied on our agreement to commit your resources to the undertaking, you have a right to recover what you have lost. In torts, if I simply injure you in some way, hurting you in health, life, or limb, or destroying your property, I have done you a wrong (*tort*, in French), and I must pay for the damage I have done. How much I will have to pay will depend (as the jury will determine) on (1) the amount of the damage that has been caused, (2) the extent to which I knew or should have known that my action or neglect to act would cause damage (my *culpability*), and (3) the extent to which *you* contributed to the damage, beyond whatever I did (*contributory negligence*).

One of the debates that follow (on the Pinto automobile) has to do with a suit at law alleging *negligence,* a tort, on the part of a company, in that it made and put up for sale a product known to be defective and that the defect injured its users. To establish negligence, civil or criminal, four elements must be demonstrated: First, there must have been a *duty*—the party accused of negligence must have had a preexisting duty to the plaintiff. Second, there must have been a *breach of,* or failure to fulfill, that duty. Third, the plaintiff must have suffered an *injury*. And fourth, the breach of the duty must have been the *proximate cause* of the injury, or the thing that actually brought the injury about. Where negligence is alleged in a product liability case, it must be established that the manufacturer had a duty to make a product that could not do certain sorts of harm, that the duty was breached and the harm was caused, that nothing else was to blame, and that the manufacturer therefore must compensate the victim for the damage done.

Two other debates (on cigarette advertising and Nestlé infant formula) contain very similar allegations—although no lawsuit is at issue at this point. (Tobacco manufacturers have already been sued for negligence in deaths from lung cancer; the results are uncertain.) In all these cases, one set of claims amounts to an accusation of deliberately damaging innocent consumers, placing them in harm's way for the sake of profit; the other set counters that the company did not know and could not have known that the product was dangerous and/or that the freely chosen behavior of the consumers contributed in some way to the damage that was done, so the company cannot be held totally responsible. In all cases, *risk* and *responsibility* are the central issues: when a small car explodes and burns when hit by a much larger van, to what extent is the company responsible for the flimsiness of the car and to what extent did the consumer assume the risk of that happening when she bought a small, economical car? When infants sicken and die because their mothers misuse an infant formula, to what extent are the mothers at fault for failing to read and follow the directions, and to what extent should the company have foreseen that the directions would be unreadable and unworkable in the contexts of the product's sale and use?

Should companies ultimately be responsible for any harm that comes from the use of the products they so profitably marketed and sold? Or should consumers be content to bear the responsibility for risks they have freely accepted? Our ambivalence on this question as a society mirrors, and proceeds from, the ambivalence of the individual at the two poles of materialization of risk: when we are in a hurry, short of cash, or in need of a cigarette, then risky behavior looks to us to be our right, and we are resentful of the busybodies who would always have us play it safe. But when the risk materializes—when the accident or the disease happens—the perception of that risk (and the direction of that resentment) changes drastically. From the perspective of the hospital bed, it is crystal clear that the behavior was not worth the risk, that we never realized the behavior was risky, that we should have been warned, and that it was someone's duty to warn us. In that instantaneous change of perspective, three elements of negligence come into view: duty, breach, and injury. No wonder product liability suits are so common.

Yet the suit is a relatively recent phenomenon because of a peculiarity in the law. Until the twentieth century, a judge faced with a consumer who had been injured by a product (physically or financially) applied the principle of *caveat emptor*—"let the buyer beware"—and could ask the seller to pay damages only to the original buyer, and only if the exact defect in the product could be proven. For example, a defective kerosene lamp might explode and burn five people, but the exact defect (broken seam or shoddy wick) had to be brought into court or the case would be thrown out. In addition, the buyer could sue only the seller, not the manufacturer or designer, because the right to collect damages rested on the law of *contract*, not torts, and on the warrant of merchantability implied in the contractual relationship between buyer and seller. The cause of the action was understood to be a breach in that contract.

There matters stood until 1916, when an American judge allowed a buyer to sue the manufacturer of a product. A Mr. MacPherson had been injured when his car collapsed under him due to a defect in the wood used to build one of the wheels, and MacPherson went to court against the Buick Motor Company. The judge reasoned that the action was in torts, specifically "negligence," and not in contract, for a manufacturer is under a duty to make carefully any product that could be expected to endanger life, and this duty existed irrespective of any contract. So if MacPherson, or any future user of the product, was injured because the product was badly made, he could collect damages even if he had never dealt with the manufacturer in any way.

In the 1960s the automobile was still center stage in the arguments over the duties of manufacturers. Consumer advocate Ralph Nader's book *Unsafe at Any Speed* (1966) spearheaded the consumer rights movement with its scathing attack on General Motors and its exposé of the dangerous design of the Corvair. In response to the consumer activism resulting from that movement, Congress passed the Consumer Product Safety Act in 1972 and empowered the Consumer Product Safety Commission, an independent federal agency, to set safety standards, require warning labels, and order recalls of hazardous products. When three girls died in a Ford Pinto in 1978, the foundations of consumer rights against careless manufacturers were well established. What was new in the Ford Motor Company case was the allegation of *criminal* negligence—in effect, criminal homicide.

At present, product liability suits are major uncharted reefs in the navigational plans of American business. If a number of people die in a fire in a hotel, for instance, their families will often sue not only the hotel, for culpable negligence, but the manufacturers of the furniture that burned, alleging that it should have been fire-retardant; the manufacturers of the cushions on the furniture, alleging that they gave off toxic fumes in the fire; and the manufacturers of the chemicals that went into those cushions, alleging that there was no warning to the consumers on the toxicity of those chemicals in fire conditions. The settlements that can be obtained are used to finance the suit and the law firm that is managing it for the years that it will take to exhaust all the appeals. This phenomenon of unlimited litigation is relatively new on the American scene, and we are not quite sure how to respond to it.

THE CORPORATION

The human being is a social animal. We exist in the herd and depend for our lives on the cooperation of those around us. Who are they? Anthropologists tell us that originally we traveled in extended families, then settled down into villages of intensely interlocked groups of families. With the advent of the modern era, we have found our identities in family, village, church, and nation. Yet, in the great transformation of the obligations of the Western world (see Henry Maine [1822–1888], *From Status to Contract*), we have abandoned the old family-oriented care systems and thrown ourselves upon the mercy of secondary organizations: club, corporation, and state. The French sociologist Emile Durkheim (1858–1917), in his classic work *Suicide*, suggested that following the collapse of the family and the church, the corporation would be the association in the future that would supply the social support that every individual needs to maintain a moral life.

Can the corporation do that? Or is the corporation merely the organization that implements Adam Smith's self-interested pursuit of the dollar, with no purpose but to maximize return on investment to the investors while protecting them from unlimited liability?

On the other hand, once formed, and having become a major community figure and employer, does the corporation have a right to exist that transcends at least the immediate pursuit of money? The issue of so-called hostile takeovers sends us back to the purpose and foundation of business enterprise in America. Let us review: When an entrepreneur gets a bright idea for how to make money, he or she secures the capital necessary to run the business from investors (venture capitalists), uses that capital to buy the land, buildings, and machinery needed to see the project through, hires the labor needed to do the work, and goes into production. As the income from the enterprise comes in, the entrepreneur pays the suppliers of raw materials, pays the workers, pays the taxes, rent, mortgages and utility bills, keeps some of the money for him- or herself (salary), and then divides up the rest of the income (profit) among the investors (probably including him- or herself) in proportion to the capital they invested. Motives of all parties are presupposed: the entrepreneur wants money, the laborers and the landlords want money, and the investors, who are the shareholders in the company, want money. The investors thought that this enterprise would yield them a higher return on their capital than any other investment available to them at the time; that is why they invested. However, this is a free country, and people can move around. If the workers see better jobs, they will take them; if a landlord can rent for more, the lease will be terminated; and if the investors see a better place to put their capital, they will move it. The determiner of the flow of capital is the rate of return, no more and no less. Loyalty to the company, faithfulness to the corporation for the sake of the association itself, is not on anyone's agenda—not on the worker's, certainly not on the landlord's, and *most* certainly not on the shareholder's.

The shareholders are represented by a board of directors elected by them to see that the company is run efficiently; that is, that costs are kept down and income up to yield the highest possible return. The board of directors hires management—the cadre of corporate officers headed by the president and/or chief executive officer to do the actual running of the company. The corporate officers thus stand in a *fiduciary* relationship to the shareholders; that is, they are forbidden by the understandings on which the corporation is founded to do anything at all except that which will protect and enhance the interests of the shareholders. That goes for all the normal business decisions made by the management; even the decision not to break the law can be seen as a prudent estimate of the financial costs of lawbreaking.

Yet our dealings with the business world, as citizens and as consumers, have always turned on recognition and support of the huge reliable corporations in established industries; not just coal and steel, which had certain natural limitations built into their consumption of natural resources, but the automobile companies, the airlines, the consumer products companies, and even the banks. Companies had "reputations" and "integrity," and they cultivated (and bought and sold) "good will." Consumers cooperated with the companies that catered to them in developing "brand loyalty." And, most important, those working in business cooperated with their employers in developing "company loyalty," which became a part of their lives, just as loyalty to one's tribe or nation was part of the lives of their ancestors. Is the company that sought our loyalty—and got it—just a scrap of paper, to disappear as soon as return on investment falls below the nearest competition? What part do we want corporations to play in our associative lives? If we want them to be any more than profit maximizers for the investors, what sorts of protections would we have to offer them, and what sorts of limitations should we put on their extra-profit-making activities?

CURRENT ISSUES

Business ethics ultimately rests on a base of political philosophy, economics, and philosophical ethics. As these underlying fields change, new topics and approaches will surface in business ethics. For example, hostile takeovers did not take place very often in the regulatory climate that existed prior to the Reagan administration. The change in political philosophy introduced by his administration resulted in new business practices, which resulted in new ethical problems. Also, the work of John Rawls, a professor of philosophy at Harvard University, profoundly influenced our understanding of distributive justice and, therefore, our understanding of acceptable economic distribution in the society. The work currently being done in postmodern philosophy will change the way we see human beings generally and, hence, the activity of business.

No single work can cover all the issues of ethical practice in business in all their range and particularity, especially since, as above, we are dealing with a moving target. Our task here is much more limited. The purpose of this book is to allow you to grapple with some of the ethical issues of current business practice in the safety of the classroom, before they come up on the job where human rights and careers are at stake and legal action looms outside the boardroom or factory door. We think that rational consideration of these issues now will help you prepare for a lifetime of the types of problems that naturally arise in a complex and pluralistic society. You will find here no dogmas, no settled solutions to memorize. These problems do not have preset answers but require that you use your mind to balance the values in conflict and to work out acceptable policies in each issue. To employ business ethics, you must learn to think critically, to look beyond short-term advantages and traditional ways of doing things, and to become an innovator. The exercise provided by these debates should help you in this learning.

There is no doubt that businesspeople think that ethics is important. Sometimes the reasons why they think ethics is important have to do only with the long-run profitability of business enterprise. There is no doubt that greater employee honesty and diligence would improve the bottom line or that strict attention to environmental and employee health laws is necessary to protect the company from expensive lawsuits and fines. But ethics goes well beyond profitability, to the lives that we live and the persons we want to be. What the bottom line has taught us is that the working day is not apart from life. We must bring the same integrity and care to the contexts of factory and office that we are used to showing at home and among our friends. An imperative of business ethics is to make of your business life an opportunity to become, and remain, the person that you know you ought to be—and as far as it is within your capability, to extend that opportunity to others.

We attempt, in this book, to present in good debatable form some of the issues that raise the big questions—of justice, of rights, of the common good —in order to build bridges between the workaday world of employment and the ageless world of morality. If you will enter into these dialogues with an open mind, a willingness to have it changed, and a determination to master the skills of critical thinking that will enable you to make responsible decisions in difficult situations, you may be able to help build the bridges for the new ethical issues that will emerge in the next century. At the least, that is our hope.

SUGGESTED READINGS

Tom L. Beauchamp and Norman E. Bowie, *Ethical Theory and Business*, 3d ed. (Prentice Hall, 1988).

John Matthews, Kenneth Goodpaster, and Laura Nash, *Policies and Persons: A Casebook in Business Ethics*, 2d ed. (McGraw-Hill, 1991).

Manuel Velasquez, *Business Ethics: Concepts and Cases*, 2d ed. (Prentice Hall, 1987).

PART 1

Capitalism and Corporations in Theory and Practice

The nations of the Western European tradition tend to regard business as central to their citizens' lives and the meaning of their national life. But does business always represent what we want our countries to be about? This first section initially explores business theory. Should societies choose capitalism over other economic systems? This section also explores three relatively new enterprises for business: the rapidly expanding medical field, the efforts of business to develop codes of ethics to handle growing problems, and the proliferation of casino gambling.

- Classic Dialogue: Is Capitalism the
  Best Route to Human Happiness?

- Are Business and Medicine Ethically
  Incompatible?

- Are Corporate Codes of Ethics Just
  for Show?

- Should Casino Gambling Be Prohibited?

ISSUE 1

Classic Dialogue: Is Capitalism the Best Route to Human Happiness?

YES: Adam Smith, from *An Inquiry into the Nature and Causes of the Wealth of Nations, vols. 1 and 2* (1869)

NO: Karl Marx and Friedrich Engels, from *The Communist Manifesto* (1848)

ISSUE SUMMARY

YES: Free-market economist Adam Smith (1723–1790) argues that if self-interested people are left alone to seek their own economic advantage, the result, unintended by any one of them, will be greater advantage for all. He maintains that government interference is not necessary to protect the general welfare.

NO: German philosopher Karl Marx (1818–1883) and German sociologist Friedrich Engels (1820–1895) argue that if people are left to their own self-interested devices, those who own the means of production will rapidly reduce everyone else to virtual slaves. Although the few may be fabulously happy, all others would live in misery.

The rationale of capitalism is that an unintended coordination of self-interested actions will lead to the production of the greatest welfare of the whole. The logic procedes thusly: As a natural result of free competition in a free market, quality will improve and prices will decline without limit, thereby raising the real standard of living of every buyer; to protect themselves in competition, sellers will be forced to innovate by discovering new products and new markets, thereby raising the real wealth of the society as a whole. Products improve without limit, wealth increases without limit, and society prospers.

But how does the common man—the "least advantaged" member of society—fare under capitalism? Not very well. The most efficient factories are those that hire workers at the lowest cost. And if all industry is accomplished by essentially unskilled labor and every worker can therefore be replaced by any other, then there is no reason to pay any worker beyond the subsistence wage. Therefore, only when free competition *fails* because the economy is expanding so rapidly that it runs out of labor can the working man's wages rise in a free market. According to capitalist theory, however, such a market imbalance—too few workers and therefore "artificially" high wages—will rapidly disappear because greater prosperity allows more of the working-class babies to survive to adulthood and enter into the workforce. Eighteenth-century economists Adam Smith, Thomas Malthus, and David Ricardo all agreed that as the society as a whole approaches maximum efficiency, all except the capitalists (the owners) approach the subsistence level of survival. So most of the accumulated wealth of the nation actually ends up in the hands of the employers, who enjoy the low prices of bread themselves while saving the money they would need to spend to keep their workers alive if the bread were more expensive.

This is where Karl Marx comes in. He focused not on the making of the wealth but on how the wealth is distributed—who gets it and who gets to enjoy it when it has been generated by the capitalist process. Marx found it unreasonable for the bulk of society's wealth to be languishing in the bank accounts of the super-rich. He argued that the welfare of the nation as a whole would be vastly increased if it could be shared systematically with the workers, which would allow them to join their employers as consumers of the manufactured goods of society. Lord John Maynard Keynes would later point out that such distribution would be an enormous spur to the economy; Marx, however, was more concerned that it would be a great gain in justice.

One empirical question that surrounds the issue of social justice in a free-market society is this: If the controllers of the wealth—the capitalists—are required to share it with the workers who produced it, will they not lose motivation to put their money at risk in productive enterprises? Other questions concern entitlement (aren't those who control the capital entitled to the entire return on it?) and the relative importance of liberty and equality as political values. As you read the following selections by Adam Smith and by Marx and Friedrich Engels, keep in mind that the debate is not bound by the historical controversies of Marx and his opponents; it goes to the core of contemporary notions of entitlement and justice.

YES

Adam Smith

AN INQUIRY INTO THE NATURE AND CAUSES OF THE WEALTH OF NATIONS

OF THE DIVISION OF LABOUR

The greatest improvement in the productive powers of labour, and the greater part of the skill, dexterity, and judgment with which it is anywhere directed or applied, seem to have been the effect of the division of labour.

The effects of the division of labour, in the general business of society, will be more easily understood by considering in what manner it operates in some particular manufactures. It is commonly supposed to be carried furthest in some very trifling ones; not perhaps that it really is carried further in them than in others of more importance: but in those trifling manufactures which are destined to supply the small wants of but a small number of people, the whole number of workmen must necessarily be small; and those employed in every different branch of the work can often be collected into the same workhouse, and placed at once under the view of the spectator. In those great manufactures, on the contrary, which are destined to supply the great wants of the great body of the people, every different branch of the work employs so great a number of workmen, that it is impossible to collect them all into the same workhouse. We can seldom see more, at one time, than those employed in one single branch. Though in such manufactures, therefore, the work may really be divided into a much greater number of parts than in those of a more trifling nature, the division is not near so obvious, and has accordingly been much less observed.

To take an example, therefore, from a very trifling manufacture, but one in which the division of labour has been very often taken notice of, the trade of the pin-maker; a workman not educated to this business (which the division of labour has rendered a distinct trade), nor acquainted with the use of the machinery employed in it (to the invention of which the same division of labour has probably given occasion), could scarce, perhaps, with his utmost industry, make one pin in a day, and certainly could not make twenty. But

From Adam Smith, *An Inquiry into the Nature and Causes of the Wealth of Nations, vols 1 and 2* (1869). Notes omitted.

in the way in which this business is now carried on, not only the whole work is a peculiar trade, but it is divided into a number of branches, of which the greater part are likewise peculiar trades. One man draws out the wire, another straights it, a third cuts it, a fourth points it, a fifth grinds it at the top for receiving the head; to make the head requires two or three distinct operations; to put it on is a peculiar business, to whiten the pins is another; it is even a trade by itself to put them into the paper; and the important business of making a pin is, in this manner, divided into about eighteen distinct operations, which in some manufactories are all performed by distinct hands, though in others the same man will sometimes perform two or three of them. I have seen a small manufactory of this kind where ten men only were employed, and where some of them consequently performed two or three distinct operations. But though they were very poor, and therefore but indifferently accommodated with the necessary machinery, they could, when they exerted themselves, make among them about twelve pounds of pins in a day. There are in a pound upwards of four thousand pins of a middling size. Those ten persons, therefore, could make among them upwards of forty-eight thousand pins in a day. Each person, therefore, making a tenth part of forty-eight thousand pins, might be considered as making four thousand eight hundred pins in a day. But if they had all wrought separately and independently, and without any of them having been educated to this peculiar business, they certainly could not each of them have made twenty, perhaps not one pin in a day; that is, certainly, not the two hundred and fortieth, perhaps not the four thousand eight hundredth part of what they are at present capable of performing, in consequence of a proper division and combination of their different operations....

This great increase of the quantity of work, which, in consequence of the division of labour, the same number of people are capable of performing, is owing to three different circumstances: first, to the increase of dexterity in every particular workman; secondly, to the saving of the time which is commonly lost in passing from one species of work to another; and lastly, to the invention of a great number of machines which facilitate and abridge labour, and enable one man to do the work of many....

It is the great multiplication of the productions of all the different arts, in consequence of the division of labour, which occasions, in a well-governed society, that universal opulence which extends itself to the lowest ranks of the people. Every workman has a great quantity of his own work to dispose of beyond what he himself has occasion for: and every other workman being exactly in the same situation, he is enabled to exchange a great quantity of his own goods for a great quantity, or, what comes to the same thing, for the price of a great quantity of theirs. He supplies them abundantly with what they have occasion for, and they accommodate him as amply with what he has occasion for, and a general plenty diffuses itself through all the different ranks of the society.

Observe the accommodation of the most common artificer or day-labourer in a civilised and thriving country, and you will perceive that the number of people of whose industry a part, though but a small part, has been employed in procuring him this accommodation exceeds all computation. The woollen coat, for example, which covers the day-labourer, as coarse and rough as it may appear, is the produce of the joint labour of a great multitude of workmen. The shepherd, the sorter of the wool, the wool-comber or carder, the dyer, the scribbler, the spinner, the weaver, the fuller, the dresser, with many others, must all join their different arts in order to complete even this homely production. How many merchants and carriers, besides, must have been employed in transporting the materials from some of those workmen to others who often live in a very distant part of the country! How much commerce and navigation in particular, how many ship-builders, sailors, sail-makers, rope-makers, must have been employed in order to bring together the different drugs made use of by the dyer, which often come from the remotest corners of the world! What a variety of labour too is necessary in order to produce the tools of the meanest of those workmen! To say nothing of such complicated machines as the ship of the sailor, the mill of the fuller, or even the loom of the weaver, let us consider only what a variety of labour is requisite in order to form that very simple machine, the shears with which the shepherd clips the wool. The miner, the builder of the furnace for smelting the ore, the feller of the timber, the burner of the charcoal to be made use of in the smelting-house, the brickmaker, the bricklayer, the workmen who attend the furnace, the mill-wright, the forger, the smith, must all of them join their different arts in order to produce them. Were we to examine, in the same manner, all the different parts of his dress and household furniture, the coarse linen shirt which he wears next his skin, the shoes which cover his feet, the bed which he lies on, and all the different parts which compose it, the kitchen-grate at which he prepares his victuals, the coals which he makes use of for that purpose, dug from the bowels of the earth, and brought to him perhaps by a long sea and a long land carriage, all the other utensils of his kitchen, all the furniture of his table, the knives and forks, the earthen or pewter plates upon which he serves up and divides his victuals, the different hands employed in preparing his bread and his beer, the glass window which lets in the heat and the light and keeps out the wind and the rain, with all the knowledge and art requisite for preparing that beautiful and happy invention, without which these northern parts of the world could scarce have afforded a very comfortable habitation, together with the tools of all the different workmen employed in producing those different conveniences; if we examine, I say, all these things, and consider what a variety of labour is employed about each of them, we shall be sensible that without the assistance and co-operation of many thousands, the very meanest person in a civilised country could not be provided, even according to, what we very falsely imagine, the easy and simple manner in which he is commonly accommodated. Compared, indeed, with the more extravagant luxury of the great, his accommodation must no doubt appear extremely simple and easy; and yet it may be true, perhaps, that the accommodation of an European prince does not always so much exceed that of an industrious and frugal peasant, as the accommodation of the latter exceeds that of many an African king, the absolute master of the lives and liberties of ten thousand naked savages.

OF THE PRINCIPLE WHICH GIVES OCCASION TO THE DIVISION OF LABOUR

This division of labour, from which so many advantages are derived, is not originally the effect of any human wisdom, which foresees and intends that general opulence to which it gives occasion. It is the necessary, though very slow and gradual consequence of a certain propensity in human nature which has in view no such extensive utility; the propensity to truck, barter, and exchange one thing for another.

Whether this propensity be one of those original principles in human nature, of which no further account can be given; or whether, as seems more probable, it be the necessary consequence of the faculties of reason and speech, it belongs not to our present subject to inquire. It is common to all men, and to be found in no other race of animals, which seem to know neither this nor any other species of contracts.... But man has almost constant occasion for the help of his brethren, and it is in vain for him to expect it from their benevolence only. He will be more likely to prevail if he can interest their self-love in his favour, and show them that it is for their own advantage to do for him what he requires of them. Whoever offers to another a bargain of any kind, proposes to do this. Give me that which I want, and you shall have this which you want, is the meaning of every such offer; and it is in this manner that we obtain from one another the far greater part of those good offices which we stand in need of. It is not from the benevolence of the butcher, the brewer, or the baker, that we expect our dinner, but from their regard to their own interest. We address ourselves, not to their humanity but to their self-love, and never talk to them of our own necessities but of their advantages. Nobody but a beggar chooses to depend chiefly upon the benevolence of his fellow-citizens. Even a beggar does not depend upon it entirely. The charity of well-disposed people, indeed, supplies him with the whole fund of his subsistence. But though this principle ultimately provides him with all the necessaries of life which he has occasion for, it neither does nor can provide him with them as he has occasion for them. The greater part of his occasional wants are supplied in the same manner as those of other people, by treaty, by barter, and by purchase. With the money which one man gives him he purchases food. The old clothes which another bestows upon him he exchanges for other old clothes which suit him better, or for lodging, or for food, or for money, with which he can buy either food, clothes, or lodging, as he has occasion.

... Each animal is still obliged to support and defend itself, separately and independently, and derives no sort of advantage from that variety of talents with which nature has distinguished its fellows. Among men, on the contrary, the most dissimilar geniuses are of use to one another; the different produces of their respective talents, by the general disposition to truck, barter, and exchange, being brought, as it were, into a common stock, where every man may purchase whatever part of the produce of other men's talents he has occasion for....

OF RESTRAINTS UPON THE IMPORTATION FROM FOREIGN COUNTRIES OF SUCH GOODS AS CAN BE PRODUCED AT HOME

... The general industry of the society never can exceed what the capital of the society can employ. As the number of workmen that can be kept in employment by any particular person must bear a certain proportion to his capital, so the number of those that can be continually employed by all the members of a great society, must bear a certain proportion to the whole capital of that society, and never can exceed that proportion. No regulation of commerce can increase the quantity of industry in any society beyond what its capital can maintain. It can only divert a part of it into a direction into which it might not otherwise have gone; and it is by no means certain that this artificial direction is likely to be more advantageous to the society than that into which it would have gone of its own accord.

Every individual is continually exerting himself to find out the most advantageous employment for whatever capital he can demand. It is his own advantage, indeed, and not that of the society, which he has in view. But the study of his own advantage naturally, or rather necessarily, leads him to prefer that employment which is most advantageous to the society.

First, every individual endeavours to employ his capital as near home as he can, and consequently as much as he can in the support of domestic industry; provided always that he can thereby obtain the ordinary, or not a great deal less than the ordinary, profits of stock.

Thus, upon equal or nearly equal profits, every wholesale merchant naturally prefers the home trade to the foreign trade of consumption, and the foreign trade of consumption to the carrying trade. In the home trade his capital is never so long out of his sight as it frequently is in the foreign trade of consumption. He can know better the char-

acter and situation of the persons whom he trusts, and, if he should happen to be deceived, he knows better the laws of the country from which he must seek redress. In the carrying trade, the capital of the merchant is, as it were, divided between two foreign countries, and no part of it is ever necessarily brought home, or placed under his own immediate view and command. The capital which an Amsterdam merchant employs in carrying corn from Konigsberg to Lisbon, and fruit and wine from Lisbon to Konigsberg, must generally be the one half of it at Konigsberg and the other half at Lisbon. No part of it need ever come to Amsterdam. The natural residence of such a merchant should either be at Konigsberg or Lisbon, and it can only be some very particular circumstance which can make him prefer the residence of Amsterdam. The uneasiness, however, which he feels at being separated so far from his capital, generally determines him to bring part both of the Konigsberg goods which he destines for the market of Lisbon, and of the Lisbon goods which he destines for that of Konigsberg, to Amsterdam; and though this necessarily subjects him to a double charge of loading and unloading, as well as to the payment of some duties and customs, yet for the sake of having some part of his capital always under his own view and command, he willingly submits to this extraordinary charge; and it is in this manner that every country which has any considerable share of the carrying trade, becomes always the emporium, or general market, for the goods of all the different countries whose trade it carries on. The merchant, in order to save a second loading and unloading, endeavours always to sell in the home market as much of the goods of all those different countries as he can, and thus, so far as he can, to convert his carrying trade into a foreign trade of consumption. A merchant, in the same manner, who is engaged in the foreign trade of consumption, when he collects goods for foreign markets, will always be glad, upon equal or nearly equal profits, to sell as great a part of them at home as he can. He saves himself the risk and trouble of exportation, when, so far as he can, he thus converts his foreign trade of consumption into a home trade. Home is in this manner the centre, if I may say so, round which the capitals of the inhabitants of every country are continually circulating, and towards which they are always tending, though by particular causes they may sometimes be driven off and repelled from it towards more distant employments. But a capital employed in the home trade, it has already been shown, necessarily puts into motion a greater quantity of domestic industry, and gives revenue and employment to a greater number of the inhabitants of the country, than an equal capital employed in the foreign trade of consumption; and one employed in the foreign trade of consumption has the same advantage over an equal capital employed in the carrying trade. Upon equal, or only nearly equal profits, therefore, every individual naturally inclines to employ his capital in the manner in which it is likely to afford the greatest support to domestic industry, and to give revenue and employment to the greatest number of people of his own country.

Secondly, every individual who employs his capital in the support of domestic industry, necessarily endeavours so to direct that industry, that its produce may be of the greatest possible value.

The produce of industry is what it adds to the subject or materials upon which it is employed. In proportion as the value of this produce is great or small, so will likewise be the profits of the employer. But it is only for the sake of profit that any man employs a capital in the support of industry; and he will always, therefore, endeavour to employ it in the support of that industry of which the produce is likely to be of the greatest value, or to exchange for the greatest quantity either of money or of other goods.

But the annual revenue of every society is always precisely equal to the exchangeable value of the whole annual produce of its industry, or rather is precisely the same thing with that exchangeable value. As every individual, therefore, endeavours as much as he can both to employ his capital in the support of domestic industry, and so to direct that industry that its produce may be of the greatest value, every individual necessarily labours to render the annual revenue of the society as great as he can. He generally, indeed, neither intends to promote the public interest, nor knows how much he is promoting it. By preferring the support of domestic to that of foreign industry, he intends only his own security; and by directing that industry in such a manner as its produce may be of the greatest value, he intends only his own gain, and he is in this, as in many other cases, led by an invisible hand to promote an end which was no part of his intention. Nor is it always the worse for the society that it was no part of it. By pursuing his own interest he frequently promotes that of the society more effectually than when he really intends to promote it. I have never known much good done by those who affected to trade for the public good. It is an affectation, indeed, not very common among merchants, and very few words need be employed in dissuading them from it.

What is the species of domestic industry which his capital can employ, and of which the produce is likely to be of the greatest value, every individual, it is evident, can, in his local situation, judge much better than any statesman or lawgiver can do for him. The statesman, who should attempt to direct private people in what manner they ought to employ their capitals, would not only load himself with a most unnecessary attention, but assume an authority which could safely be trusted, not only to no single person, but to no council or senate whatever, and which would nowhere be so dangerous as in the hands of a man who had folly and presumption enough to fancy himself fit to exercise it.

To give the monopoly of the home market to the produce of domestic industry, in any particular art or manufacture, is in some measure to direct private people in what manner they ought to employ their capitals, and must, in almost all cases, be either a useless or a hurtful regulation. If the produce of domestic can be brought there as cheap as that of foreign industry, the regulation is evidently useless. If it cannot, it must generally be hurtful. It is the maxim of every prudent master of a family, never to attempt to make at home what it will cost him more to make than to buy. The tailor does not attempt to make his own shoes, but buys them of the shoemaker. The shoemaker does not attempt to make his own clothes, but employs a tailor. The farmer attempts to make neither the one nor the other, but employs those different artificers. All of them find it for their interest to employ their whole industry in a way in which they have some advantage over their neighbours, and to purchase with a part of its produce, or, what is the same thing, with the price of a part of it, whatever else they have occasion for.

What is prudence in the conduct of every private family, can scarce be folly in that of a great kingdom. If a foreign country can supply us with a commodity cheaper than we ourselves can make it, better buy it of them with some part of the produce of our own industry, employed in a way in which we have some advantage. The general industry of the country, being always in proportion to the capital which employs it, will not thereby be diminished, no more than that of the above-mentioned artificers, but only left to find out the way in which it can be employed with the greatest advantage. It is certainly not employed to the greatest advantage, when it is thus directed towards an object which it can buy cheaper than it can make. The value of its annual produce is certainly more or less diminished, when it is thus turned away from producing commodities evidently of more value than the commodity which it is directed to produce. According to the supposition, that commodity could be purchased from foreign countries cheaper than it can be made at home. It could, therefore, have been purchased with a part only of the commodities, or, what is the same thing, with a part only of the price of the commodities, which the industry employed by an equal capital would have produced at home, had it been left to follow its natural course. The industry of the country, therefore, is thus turned away from a more to a less advantageous employment, and the exchangeable value of its annual produce, instead of being increased, according to the intention of the lawgiver, must necessarily be diminished by every such regulation.

By means of such regulations, indeed, a particular manufacture may sometimes be acquired sooner than it could have been otherwise, and after a certain time may be made at home as cheap or cheaper than in the foreign country. But though the industry of the society may be thus carried with advantage into a particular channel sooner than it could have been otherwise, it will by no means follow that the sum total, either of its industry or of its revenue, can ever be augmented by any such regulation. The industry of the society can augment only in proportion as its capital augments, and its capital can augment only in proportion to what can be gradually saved out of its revenue. But the immediate effect of every such regulation is to diminish its revenue, and what diminishes its revenue is certainly not very likely to augment its capital faster than it would have augmented of its own accord, had both capital and industry been left to find out their natural employments.

Though for want of such regulations the society should never acquire the proposed manufacture, it would not, upon that account, necessarily be the poorer in any one period of its duration. In every period of its duration its whole capital and industry might still have been employed, though upon different objects, in the manner that was most advantageous at the time. In every period its revenue might have been the greatest which its capital could afford, and both capital and revenue might have been augmented with the greatest possible rapidity.

The natural advantages which one country has over another in producing particular commodities are sometimes so great, that it is acknowledged by all the world to be in vain to struggle with them. By means of glasses, hot-beds, and hot-walls, very good grapes can be raised in Scotland, and very good wine too can be made of them, at about thirty times the expense for which at least equally good can be brought from foreign countries. Would it be a reasonable law to prohibit the importation of all foreign wines, merely to encourage the making of claret and burgundy in Scotland? But if there would be a manifest absurdity in turning towards any employment thirty times more of the capital and industry of the country than would be necessary to purchase from foreign countries an equal quantity of the commodities wanted, there must be an absurdity, though not altogether so glaring, yet exactly of the same kind, in turning towards any such employment a thirtieth or even a three-hundredth part more of either. Whether the advantages which one country has over another be natural or acquired, is in this respect of no consequence. As long as the one country has those advantages and the other wants them, it will always be more advantageous for the latter rather to buy of the former than to make. It is an acquired advantage only which one artificer has over his neighbour who exercises another trade; and yet they both find it more advantageous to buy of one another than to make what does not belong to their particular trades.

NO

Karl Marx and Friedrich Engels

MANIFESTO OF THE COMMUNIST PARTY

A spectre is haunting Europe—the spectre of Communism. All the powers of old Europe have entered into a holy alliance to exorcise this spectre; Pope and Czar, Metternich and Guizot, French Radicals and German police-spies.

Where is the party in opposition that has not been decried as communistic by its opponents in power? Where the opposition that has not hurled back the branding reproach of Communism, against the more advanced opposition parties, as well as against its reactionary adversaries?

Two things result from this fact.

I. Communism is already acknowledged by all European Powers to be itself a Power.

II. It is high time that Communists should openly, in the face of the whole world, publish their views, their aims, their tendencies, and meet this nursery tale of the Spectre of Communism with a Manifesto of the party itself.

To this end, Communists of various nationalities have assembled in London, and sketched the following manifesto, to be published in the English, French, German, Italian, Flemish and Danish languages.

BOURGEOIS AND PROLETARIANS

The history of all hitherto existing society is the history of class struggles.

Freeman and slave, patrician and plebeian, lord and serf, guild-master and journeyman, in a word; oppressor and oppressed, stood in constant opposition to one another, carried on an uninterrupted, now hidden, now open fight, a fight that each time ended, either in a revolutionary re-constitution of society at large, or in the common ruin of the contending classes.

In the early epochs of history, we find almost everywhere a complicated arrangement of society into various orders, a manifold graduation of social rank. In ancient Rome we have patricians, knights, plebeians, slaves; in the Middle Ages, feudal lords, vassals, guild-masters, journeymen, apprentices, serfs; in almost all of these classes, again, subordinate gradations.

The modern bourgeois society that has sprouted from the ruins of feudal society, has not done away with class antagonisms. It has but established new

From Karl Marx and Friedrich Engels, *The Communist Manifesto* (1848).

classes, new conditions of oppression, new forms of struggle in place of the old ones.

Our epoch, the epoch of the bourgeoisie, possesses, however, this distinctive feature; it has simplified the class antagonisms. Society as a whole is more and more splitting up into two great hostile camps, into two great classes directly facing each other: Bourgeoisie and Proletariat.

From the serfs of the Middle Ages sprang the chartered burghers of the earliest towns. From this burgesses the first elements of the bourgeoisie were developed.

The discovery of America, the rounding of the Cape, opened up fresh ground for the rising bourgeoisie. The East-Indian and Chinese markets, the colonization of America, trade with the colonies, the increase in the means of exchange in commodities, generally, gave to commerce, to navigation, to industry, an impulse never before known, and thereby, to the revolutionary element in the tottering feudal society, a rapid development.

The feudal system of industry, under which industrial production was monopolized by closed guilds, now no longer sufficed for the growing wants of the new markets. The manufacturing system took its place. The guild-masters were pushed on one side by the manufacturing middle-class; division of labor between the different corporate guilds vanished in the face of division of labor in each single workshop.

Meantime the markets kept ever growing, the demand, ever rising. Even manufacturing no longer sufficed. Thereupon, steam and machinery revolutionized industrial production. The place of manufacture was taken by the giant, Modern Industry, the place of the industrial middle-class, by industrial millionaires, the leaders of whole industrial armies, the modern bourgeoisie.

Modern Industry has established the world-market, for which the discovery of America paved the way. This market has given an immense development to commerce, to navigation, to communication by land. This development has, in its turn, reacted on the extension of industry; and in proportion as industry, commerce, navigation, railways extended in the same proportion the bourgeoisie developed, increased its capital, and pushed into the background every class handed down from the Middle Ages.

We see, therefore, how the modern bourgeoisie is itself the product of a long course of development, of a series of revolutions in the modes of production and of exchange.

Each step in the development of the bourgeoisie was accompanied by a corresponding political advance of that class. An oppressed class under the sway of the feudal nobility, an armed and self-governing association in the medieval commune, here independent urban republic (as in Italy and Germany), there taxable "third estate" of the monarchy (as in France), afterwards, in the period of manufacturing proper, serving either the semi-feudal or the absolute monarchy as a counterpoise against the nobility, and in fact, cornerstone of the great monarchies in general, the bourgeoisie has at last, since the establishment of Modern Industry and of the world-market, conquered for itself, in a modern representative State, exclusive political sway. The executive of the modern State is but a committee for managing the common affairs of the whole bourgeoisie.

The bourgeoisie, historically, has played a most revolutionary part.

The bourgeoisie, wherever it has got the upper hand, has put an end to all feudal, patriarchal, idyllic relations. It has pitilessly torn asunder the motley feudal ties that bound man to his "natural superiors," and has left remaining no other nexus between man and man than naked self-interest, than callous "cash payment." It has drowned the most heavenly ecstasies of religious fervor, of chivalrous enthusiasm, of philistine sentimentalism, in the icy water of egotistical calculation. It has resolved personal worth into exchange value, and in place of the numberless indefeasible chartered freedoms, has set up that single, unconscionable freedom—Free Trade. In one word, for exploitation, veiled by religious and political illusions, it has substituted naked, shameless, direct, brutal exploitation.

The bourgeoisie has stripped of its halo every occupation hitherto honored and looked up to with reverent awe. It has converted the physician, the lawyer, the priest, the poet, the man of science, into its paid wage-laborers.

The bourgeoisie has torn away from the family its sentimental veil, and has reduced the family relation to a mere money relation.

The bourgeoisie has disclosed how it came to pass that the brutal display of vigor in the Middle Ages, which Reactionists so much admire, found its fitting complement in the most slothful indolence. It has been the first to show what man's activity can bring about. It has accomplished wonders far surpassing Egyptian pyramids, Roman aqueducts, and Gothic cathedrals; it has conducted expeditions that put in the shade all former Exoduses of nations and crusades.

The bourgeoisie cannot exist without constantly revolutionizing the instruments of production, and thereby the relations of production, and with them the whole relations of society. Conservation of the old modes of production in unaltered form, was, on the contrary, the first condition of existence for all earlier industrial classes. Constant revolutionizing of production, uninterrupted disturbance of all social conditions, everlasting uncertainty and agitation distinguish the bourgeois epoch from all earlier ones. All fixed, fast-frozen relations, with their train of ancient and venerable prejudices and opinions, are swept away, all newly-formed ones become antiquated before they can ossify. All that is solid melts into air, all that is holy is profaned, and man is at last compelled to face with sober senses, his real conditions of life, and his relations with his kind.

The need of a constantly expanding market for its products chases the bourgeoisie over the whole surface of the globe. It must nestle everywhere, settle everywhere, establish connections everywhere.

The bourgeoisie has through its exploitation of the world-market given a cosmopolitan character to production and consumption in every country. To the great chagrin of Reactionists, it has drawn from under the feet of industry the national ground on which it stood. All old-established national industries have been destroyed or are daily being destroyed. They are dislodged by new industries, whose introduction becomes a life and death question for all civilized nations, by industries that no longer work up indigenous raw material, but raw material drawn from the remotest zones; industries whose products are consumed, not only at home, but in every quarter of the globe. In place of the old wants, satisfied by the productions of the country, we find new wants, requiring for their satisfaction the products of distant lands and climes. In place of the old local and national seclusion and self-sufficiency, we have intercourse in every direction, universal inter-dependence of nations. And as in material, so also in intellectual production. The intellectual creations of individual nations become common property. National one-sidedness and narrow-mindedness become more and more impossible, and from the numerous national and local literatures there arises a world-literature.

The bourgeoisie, by the rapid improvement of all instruments of production, by the immensely facilitated means of communication, draws all, even the most barbarian, nations into civilization. The cheap prices of its commodities are the heavy artillery with which it batters down all Chinese walls, with which it forces the barbarians' intensely obstinate hatred of foreigners to capitulate. It compels all nations, on pain of extinction, to adopt the bourgeois mode of production; it compels them to introduce what it calls civilization into their midst, i.e., to become bourgeois themselves. In a word, it creates a world after its own image.

The bourgeoisie has subjected the country to the rule of the towns. It has created enormous cities, has greatly increased the urban population as compared with the rural, and has thus rescued a considerable part of the population from the idiocy of rural life. Just as it has made the country dependent on the towns, so it has made barbarian and semibarbarian countries dependent on the civilized ones, nations of peasants on nations of bourgeois, the East on the West.

The bourgeoisie keeps more and more doing away with the scattered state of the population, of the means of production, and of property. It has agglomerated population, centralized means of production, and has concentrated property in a few hands. The necessary consequence of this was political centralization. Independent, or but loosely connected provinces, with separate interests, laws, governments and systems of taxation, became lumped together in one nation, with one government, one code of laws, one national class-interest, one frontier and one customs-tariff.

The bourgeoisie, during its rule of scarce one hundred years, has created more massive and more colossal productive forces than have all preceding generations together. Subjection of Nature's forces to man, machinery, application of chemistry to industry and agriculture, steam-navigation, railways, electric telegraphs, clearing of whole continents for cultivation, canalization of rivers, whole populations conjured out of the ground— what earlier century had even a presentiment that such productive forces slumbered in the lap of social labor?

We see then: the means of production and of exchange on whose foundations the bourgeoisie built itself up, were generated in feudal society. At a certain stage in the development of these means of production and of exchange, the conditions under which feudal society produced and exchanged, the feudal organization of agriculture and manufacturing industry, in one word, the feudal relations of property became no longer compatible with the already developed productive forces; they became so many fetters. They had to be burst asunder; they were burst asunder.

Into their places stepped free competition, accompanied by a social and political constitution adapted to it, and by the economical and political sway of the bourgeois class.

A similar movement is going on before our own eyes. Modern bourgeois society with its relations of production, of exchange and of property, a society that has conjured up such gigantic means of production and of exchange, is like the sorcerer, who is no longer able to control the powers of the nether world whom he has called up by his spells. For many a decade past the history of industry and commerce is but the history of the revolt of modern productive forces against modern conditions of production, against the property relations that are the condition for the existence of the bourgeoisie and of its rule. It is enough to mention the commercial crises that by their periodical return put on trial, each time more threateningly, the existence of the entire bourgeois society. In these crises a great part not only of the existing products, but also of the previously created productive forces, are periodically destroyed. In these crises there breaks out an epidemic that, in all earlier epochs, would have seemed an absurdity—the epidemic of overproduction. Society suddenly finds itself put back into a state of momentary barbarism; it appears as if a famine, a universal war of devastation had cut off the supply of every means of subsistence; industry and commerce seem to be destroyed; and why? Because there is too much civilization, too much means of subsistence, too much industry, too much commerce. The productive forces at the disposal of society no longer tend to further the development of the conditions of bourgeois property; on the contrary, they have become too powerful for these conditions, by which they are fettered, and so soon as they overcome these fetters, they bring disorder into the whole of bourgeois society, endangering the existence of bourgeois property. The conditions of bourgeois society are too narrow to comprise the wealth created by them. And how does the bourgeoisie get over these crises? On the one hand by enforced destruction of a mass of productive forces; on the other, by the conquest of new markets, and by the more thorough exploitation of the old ones. That is to say, by paving the way for more extensive and more destructive crises, and by diminishing the means whereby crises are prevented.

The weapons with which the bourgeoisie felled feudalism to the ground are now turned against the bourgeoisie itself.

But not only has the bourgeoisie forged the weapons that bring death to itself; it has also called into existence the men who are to wield those weapons—the modern working-class—the proletarians.

In proportion as the bourgeoisie, i.e., capital, is developed, in the same proportion is the proletariat, the modern working-class, developed, a class of laborers, who live only so long as they find work, and who find work only so long as their labor increases capital. These laborers, who must sell themselves piecemeal, are a commodity, like every other article of commerce, and are consequently exposed to all the vicissitudes of competition, to all the fluctuations of the market.

Owing to the extensive use of machinery and to division of labor, the work of the proletarians has lost all individual character, and, consequently, all charm for the workman. He becomes an appendage of the machine, and it is only the most simple, most monotonous, and most easily acquired knack that is required of him. Hence, the cost of production of a workman is restricted, almost entirely, to the means of subsistence that he requires for his maintenance, and for the propagation of his race. But the price of a commodity, and also of labor, is equal to its cost of production. In proportion, therefore, as the repulsiveness of the work increases, the wage decreases. Nay more, in proportion as the use of machinery and division of labor increases, in the same proportion the burden of toil also increases, whether by prolongation of the working hours, by increase of the work enacted in a given time, or by increased speed of the machinery, etc.

Modern Industry has converted the little workshop of the patriarchal master into the great factory of the industrial capitalist. Masses of laborers, crowded into the factory, are organized like soldiers. As privates of the industrial army they are placed under the command of a perfect hierarchy of officers and sergeants. Not only are they the slaves of the bourgeois class, and of the bourgeois State, they are daily and hourly enslaved by the machine, by the over-looker, and, above all, by the individual bourgeois manufacturer himself. The more openly this despotism proclaims gain to be its end and aim, the more petty, the more hateful and the more embittering it is.

The less the skill and exertion or strength implied in manual labor, in other words, the more modern industry becomes developed, the more is the labor of men superseded by that of women. Differences of age and sex have no longer any distinctive social validity for the working class. All are instruments of labor, more or less expensive to use, according to their age and sex.

No sooner is the exploitation of the laborer by the manufacturer so far at an end, that he receives his wages in cash, than he is set upon by the other portions of the bourgeoisie, the landlord, the shopkeeper, the pawnbroker, etc.

The low strata of the middle class —the small trades-people, shopkeepers, and retired tradesmen generally, the handicraftsmen and peasants—all these sink gradually into the proletariat, partly because their diminutive capital does not suffice for the scale on which Modern Industry is carried on, and is swamped in the competition with the large capitalists, partly because their specialized skill is rendered worthless by new methods of production. Thus the proletariat is recruited from all classes of the population.

The proletariat goes through various stages of development. With its birth begins its struggle with the bourgeoisie. At first the contest is carried on by individual laborers, then by the workpeople of a factory, then by the operatives of one trade, in one locality, against the individual bourgeois who directly exploits them. They direct their attacks not against the bourgeois conditions of production, but against the instruments of production themselves; they destroy imported wares that compete with their labor, they smash to pieces machinery, they set factories ablaze, they seek to restore by force the vanished status of the workman of the Middle Ages.

At this stage the laborers still form an incoherent mass scattered over the whole country, and broken up by their mutual competition. If anywhere they unite to form more compact bodies, this is not yet the consequence of their own active union, but of the union of bourgeoisie, which class, in order to attain its own political ends, is compelled to set the whole proletariat in motion, and is moreover yet, for a time, able to do so. At this stage, therefore, the proletarians do not fight their enemies, but the enemies of their enemies, the remnants of absolute monarchy, the landowners, the non-industrial bourgeoisie, the petty bourgeoisie. Thus the whole historical movement is concentrated in the hands of the bourgeoisie; every victory so obtained is a victory for the bourgeoisie.

But with the development of industry the proletariat not only increases in number, it becomes concentrated in great masses, its strength grows, and it feels that strength more. The various interests and conditions of life within the ranks of the proletariat are more and more equalized, in proportion as machinery obliterates all distinction of labor, and nearly everywhere reduces wages to the same low level. The growing competition among the bourgeoisie, and the resulting commercial crises, make the wages of the worker ever more fluctuating. The unceasing improvement of machinery, ever more rapidly developing, makes their livelihood more and more precarious, the collisions between individual workmen and individual bourgeois take more and more the character of collision between two classes. Thereupon the workers begin to form combinations (Trades Unions) against the bourgeoisie; they club together in order to keep up the rate of wages; they found permanent associations in order to make provision beforehand for these occasional revolts. Here and there the contest breaks out into riots.

Now and then the workers are victorious, but only for a time. The real fruits of their battles lie, not in the immediate result, but in the ever expanding union of the workers. This union is helped on by the improved means of communication that are created by modern industry, and that place the workers of different localities in contact with one another. It was just this contact that was needed to centralize the numerous local struggles, all of the same character, into one national struggle between classes. But every class struggle is a political struggle. And that union, to attain which the burghers of the Middle Ages, with their miserable highways, required centuries, the modern proletarians, thanks to railways, achieve in a few years.

This organization of the proletarians into a class, and consequently into a political party, is continually being upset again by the competition between the workers themselves. But it ever rises up again, stronger, firmer, mightier. It compels legislative recognition of particular interests of the workers, by taking advantage of the divisions among the bourgeoisie itself. Thus the ten-hour bill in England was carried.

Altogether collisions between the classes of the old society further, in many ways, the course of development of the proletariat. The bourgeoisie finds itself involved in a constant battle. At first with the aristocracy; later on, with those portions of the bourgeoisie itself, whose interests have become antagonistic to the progress of industry; at all times, with the bourgeoisie of foreign countries. In all these battles it sees itself compelled to appeal to the proletariat, to ask for its help, and thus, to drag it into the political arena. The bourgeoisie itself, therefore, supplies the proletariat with its own elements of political and general education, in other words, it furnishes the proletariat with weapons for fighting the bourgeoisie.

Further, as we have already seen, entire sections of the ruling classes are, by the advance of industry, precipitated into the proletariat, or are at least threatened in their conditions of existence. These also supply the proletariat with fresh elements of enlightenment and progress.

Finally, in times when the class-struggle nears the decisive hour, the process of dissolution going on within the ruling class, in fact, within the whole range of old society, assumes such a violent, glaring character, that a small section of the ruling class cuts itself adrift, and joins the revolutionary class, the class that holds the future in its hands. Just as, therefore, at an earlier period, a section of the nobility went over to the bourgeoisie, so now a portion of the bourgeoisie goes over to the proletariat, and in particular, a portion of the bourgeois ideologists, who have raised themselves to the level of comprehending theoretically the historical movements as a whole.

Of all the classes that stand face to face with the bourgeoisie today, the proletariat alone is a really revolutionary class. The other classes decay and finally disappear in the face of Modern Industry; the proletariat is its special and essential product....

In the conditions of the proletariat, those of old society at large are already virtually swamped. The proletarian is without property; his relation to his wife and children has no longer anything in common with the bourgeois family-relations; modern industrial labor, modern subjugation to capital, the same in England as in France, in America as in Germany, has stripped him of every trace of national character. Law, morality, religion, are to him so many bourgeois prejudices, behind which lurk in ambush just as many bourgeois interests.

All the preceding classes that got the upper hand, sought to fortify their already acquired status by subjecting society at large to their conditions of appropriation. The proletarians cannot become masters of the productive forces of society, except by abolishing their own previous mode of appropriation, and thereby also every other previous mode of appropriation. They have nothing of their own to secure and to fortify; their mission is to destroy all previous securities for, and insurances of, individual property.

All previous historical movements were movements of minorities, or in the interests of minorities. The proletarian movement is the self-conscious, independent movement of the immense majority, in the interest of the immense majority. The proletariat, the lowest stratum of our present society, cannot stir, cannot raise itself up, without the whole superincumbent strata of official society being sprung into the air.

Though not in substance, yet in form, the struggle of the proletariat with the bourgeoisie is at first a national struggle. The proletariat of each country must, of course, first of all settle matters with its own bourgeoisie.

In depicting the most general phases of the development of the proletariat, we traced the more or less veiled civil war, raging within existing society, up to the point where that war breaks out into open revolution, and where the violent overthrow of the bourgeoisie lays the foundation for the sway of the proletariat.

Hitherto, every form of society has been based, as we have already seen, on the antagonism of oppressing and oppressed classes. But in order to oppress a class, certain conditions must be assured to it under which it can, at least, continue its slavish existence. The serf, in the period of serfdom, raised himself to membership in the commune, just as the petty bourgeois, under the yoke of feudal absolutism, managed to develop into a bourgeois.

The modern laborer, on the contrary, instead of rising with the progress of industry, sinks deeper and deeper below the conditions of existence of his own class. He becomes a pauper, and pauperism develops more rapidly than population and wealth. And here it becomes evident that the bourgeoisie is unfit any longer to be the ruling class in society, and to impose its conditions of existence upon society as an overriding law. It is unfit to rule, because it is incompetent to assure an existence to its slave within his slavery, because it cannot help letting him sink into such a state that it has to feed him, instead of being fed by him. Society can no longer live under this bourgeoisie, in other words, its existence is no longer compatible with society.

The essential condition for the existence, and for the sway of the bourgeois class, is the formation and augmentation of capital; the condition for capital is wage-labor. Wage-labor rests exclusively on competition between the laborers. The advance of industry, whose involuntary promoter is the bourgeoisie, replaces the isolation of the laborers, due to competition, by their revolutionary combination, due to association. The development of Modern Industry, therefore, cuts from under its feet the very foundation on which the bourgeoisie produces and appropriates products. What the bourgeoisie therefore produces, above all, are its own grave-diggers. Its fall and the victory of the proletariat are equally inevitable.

POSTSCRIPT

Classic Dialogue: Is Capitalism the Best Route to Human Happiness?

As a society, Americans have always prized liberty over equality. The attitude within the United States seems to be that the wealth of the society as a whole is the only legitimate goal of economic enterprise and that distribution for the sake of equity or charity is a side issue best left to churches and private charities. Americans have resisted attempts to socialize such basic needs as medicine, communications (e.g., the telephone companies), and economic security for the old, young, and infirm. In promoting capitalism, economists point to the failures of socialism in England and Sweden, and they cite the fall of communism in Eastern Europe and Russia.

The United States has built some safety nets: Social Security, Medicare and Medicaid, Aid to Dependent Children, and the like. But these and other elements of the welfare system have become a major political issue. People in the welfare system complain about its failure to provide adequately for those who need the most—babies and the infirm elderly, for example. Meanwhile, conservative members of Congress argue that welfare subsidies are costing the taxpayers too much. Can it be said that capitalism is "working" for people on welfare?

What about the "invisible hand" of Smith's free market; is it operating in the United States? Does America have true capitalism?

The last two decades of economic reform have seen the richest persons in America absorbing more and more of the wealth and income while the poorest people have been becoming poorer. Should society strive to redistribute the productive assets of the country?

SUGGESTED READINGS

Adam Smith, *The Wealth of Nations* (Clarendon Press, 1976).

Richard John Neuhaus, "The Pope Affirms the 'New Capitalism,'" *The Wall Street Journal* (May 2, 1991).

"The Search for Keynes: Was He a Keynesian?" *The Economist* (December 26, 1992).

David Schweickart, *Against Capitalism*, rev. ed. (Cambridge University Press, 1993).

Keith Bradsher, "As U.S. Urges Free Markets, Its Trade Barriers Are Many," *The New York Times* (February 7, 1992), A1.

John D. Bishop, "Adam Smith's Invisible Hand Argument," *Journal of Business Ethics* (March 1995).

ISSUE 2

Are Business and Medicine Ethically Incompatible?

YES: Arnold S. Relman, from "What Market Values Are Doing to Medicine," *The Atlantic Monthly* (March 1992)

NO: Andrew C. Wicks, from "Albert Schweitzer or Ivan Boesky? Why We Should Reject the Dichotomy Between Medicine and Business," *Journal of Business Ethics* (vol. 14, 1995)

ISSUE SUMMARY

YES: Professor of medicine Arnold S. Relman argues that although doctors should not be businessmen, financial and technological pressures are forcing them to act like businessmen, with deleterious consequences for patients and for society as a whole.

NO: Andrew C. Wicks, an assistant professor at the University of Washington School of Business, challenges the perceived contrast between physician ethics and business ethics and suggests that a closer look will reveal fundamental similarities.

The heart of this issue may lie with the confusion between the two types of ethics involved: the *professional ethic* and the *market ethic*. the *professional,* or *fiduciary,* ethic, applicable to all professional-client relationships and all commercial fiduciary-beneficiary relationships, requires that the active party (professional or trustee) act *only in the interests of the other.* For example, doctors must act only in the interests of their patients, lawyers for their clients, pastors for their congregations (individually and collectively), and the managers of funds and trusts for those who have entrusted funds to them. By this ethic, boards of directors of publicly owned corporations must act only in the interests of the shareholders in the corporation.

The *market* ethic, on the contrary, requires that each party protect *its own interests,* abstaining only from force and fraud as means to achieving an agreement. This adversarial ethic, best seen in labor negotiations and proceedings in a court of law, underlies the "voluntary transaction" on which the free market is based. The free market assumes a universe of rational free agents, each acting to maximize self-interest within a legal framework designed to protect the rights of all. Not all people fit that assumption—especially the very young, very old, sick, or disabled, or simply those who are very far away from the dealings—which is why there are fiduciary relationships.

The professional ethic of the physician is brief and simple, and it is reflected in the Hippocratic oath that is generally taken by those about to begin a medical practice:

> In whatsoever houses I enter, I will enter to help the sick, and I will abstain from all intentional wrongdoing and harm. . . . And whatsoever I shall see or hear in the course of my profession in my intercourse with men, if it be what should not be published abroad, I will never divulge, holding such things to be holy secrets. Now if I carry out this oath, and break it not, may I gain forever reputation among all men for my life and for my art.

There is much more to the oath than this, but the essence of the oath is as applicable now as it was 2,500 years ago when Hippocrates first established it; the essence is that the physician acts only for the benefit of the patient, attending to the patient's illnesses, comforting and reassuring him or her, tailoring diets and advice to the patient's particular case, and keep her or his secrets in absolute confidence.

The relationship between the physician and the patient remained the same in the period between 500 B.C. and A.D. 1900. Sick people sought out healers, trusted their advice, often were helped by their ministrations, and, to the extent the patients were able, paid them for their services. In the twentieth century however, medicine began to be "professionalized": Licensing laws were established to eliminate quacks; legislation was enacted requiring licensed professionals to supervise a required professional education; professional organizations active in advancing the state of the art and protecting the professional image surfaced; and, generally, higher rates of reimbursement were charged by the physicians. Rapid advances in medical technology at mid-century sent medical costs beyond the reach of people with ordinary incomes and savings; third-party reimbursement—first from private insurers and then from the federal government (in the form of Medicare and Medicaid)—was introduced at the third quarter of the century and helped relieve the extraordinary burden on patients, but it also allowed the medical profession to prescribe ever more expensive technological cures, which sent health care costs through the roof.

As twentieth century draws to a close, the consequences of these costs for the economy as a whole are becoming clear. "Cost-containment" measures that take medical care decisions out of the physician's private office and put them into the hands of corporate boards of Health Maintenance Organizations (HMOs) and hospitals dominate medical progress at this point. But how does this affect the privacy aspect of the patient-physician relationship?

As you read these selections, ask yourself whether or not business is incompatible with the physician's ethic, as Arnold S. Relman seems to understand it. Does the reformulation proposed by Andrew C. Wicks make sense? Or do both writers miss the point? What do you see in the future for medical care in America?

YES   Arnold S. Relman

WHAT MARKET VALUES ARE
DOING TO MEDICINE

From its earliest origins the profession of medicine has steadfastly held that physicians' responsibility to their patients takes precedence over their own economic interests. Thus the oath of Hippocrates enjoins physicians to serve only "for the benefit of the sick," and the oft-recited prayer attributed to Moses Maimonides, a revered physician of the twelfth century, asks God not to allow "thirst for profit" or "ambition for renown" to interfere with the physician's practice of his profession. In modern times this theme has figured prominently in many medical codes of ethics. The International Code of the World Medical Organization, for example, says that "a doctor must practice his profession uninfluenced by motives of profit." And in 1957, in its newly revised Principles of Medical Ethics, the American Medical Association [AMA] declared that "the principal objective of the medical profession is to render service to humanity." It went on to say, "In the practice of medicine a physician should limit the source of his professional income to medical services actually rendered by him, or under his supervision, to his patients."

Such lofty pronouncements notwithstanding, the medical profession has never been immune to knavery and profiteering. And, particularly in the days before biomedical science began to establish a rational basis for the practice of medicine, the profession has had its share of charlatans and quacks. Still, the highest aspiration of the medical profession—sometimes honored in the breach, to be sure—has always been to serve the needs of the sick. And that has been the basis of a de facto contract between modern society and the profession.

What are the terms of this contract? In this country, state governments grant physicians a licensed monopoly to practice their profession and allow them considerable autonomy in setting their educational and professional standards and their working conditions. The professional education of physicians is heavily subsidized, because tuition, even in the private medical schools, does not nearly cover the costs of educating medical students. Furthermore, the information, tools, and techniques that physicians use to practice their profession are usually developed through publicly supported research. Finally, hospitals provide physicians with the facilities and personnel and often even the specialized equipment they need to treat their hospitalized patients, thus relieving doctors of many of the kinds of overhead costs that businessmen must pay. Physicians have enjoyed a privileged position in our society, virtually assuring them of high social status and a good living. They have been accorded these privileges in the expectation that they will remain competent and trustworthy and will faithfully discharge the fiduciary responsibility to patients proclaimed in their ethical codes.

THE DISTINCTIONS BETWEEN MEDICAL PRACTICE AND COMMERCE

Now, if this description of a contract between society and the medical profession is even approximately correct, then clearly there are important distinctions to be made between what society has a right to expect of practicing physicians and what it expects of people in business. Both are expected to earn their living from their occupation, but the relation between physicians and patients is supposed to be quite different from that between businessmen and customers. Patients depend on their physicians to be altruistic and committed in advising them on their health-care needs and providing necessary medical services. Most patients do not have the expertise to evaluate their own need for medical care. The quality of life and sometimes life itself are at stake, and price is of relatively little importance, not only because of the unique value of the services rendered but also because patients usually do not pay out of pocket for services at the time they are received. Although most physicians

are paid (usually by the government or an insurance company) for each service they provide, the assumption is that they are acting in the best interests of patients rather than of themselves. A fact that underscores the centrality of the patient's interests is that advertising and marketing in medical practice were until very recently considered unethical.

In contrast, in a commercial market multiple providers of goods and services try to induce customers to buy. That's the whole point. Competing with one another, businesses rely heavily on marketing and advertising to generate demand for services or products, regardless of whether they are needed, because each provider's primary concern is to increase his sales and thereby maximize his income. Although commercial vendors have an obligation to produce a good product and advertise it without deception, they have no responsibility to consider the consumer's interests—to advise the consumer which product, if any, is really needed, or to worry about those who cannot afford to buy any of the vendors' products. Markets may be effective mechanisms for distributing goods and services according to consumers' desires and ability to pay, but they have no interest in consumers' needs, or in achieving universal access.

In a commercial market, consumers are expected to fend for themselves in judging what they can afford and want to buy. *"Caveat emptor"* ["Let the buyer beware"] is the rule. According to classical market theory, when well-informed consumers and competing suppliers are free to seek their own objectives, the best interests of both groups are likely to be served. Thus, in commerce, market competition is relied upon to protect the interests of consumers. This is quite different from the situation in health care, where the provider of services protects the patient's interests by acting as advocate and counselor. Unlike the independent shoppers envisioned by market theory, sick and worried patients cannot adequately look after their own interests, nor do they usually want to. Personal medical service does not come in standardized packages and in different grades for the consumer's comparison and selection. Moreover, a sick patient often does not have the option of deferring his purchase of medical care or shopping around for the best buy. A patient with seizures and severe headache who is told that he has a brain tumor requiring surgery, or a patient with intractable angina and high-grade obstruction of a coronary artery who is advised to have a coronary bypass, does not look for the "best buy" or consider whether he really needs "top-of-the-line" surgical quality. If he does not trust the judgment and competence of the first surgeon he consults, he may seek the opinion of another, but he will very shortly have to trust someone to act as his beneficent counselor, and he will surely want the best care available, regardless of how much or how little his insurance will pay the doctor.

Some skeptics have always looked askance at the physician's double role as purveyor of services and patients' advocate. They have questioned whether doctors paid on a fee-for-service basis can really give advice to patients that is free of economic self-interest. One of the most caustic critiques of private fee-for-service medical practice was written early in this century by George Bernard Shaw, in his preface to *The Doctor's Dilemma*. It begins,

> It is not the fault of our doctors that the medical service of the community, as at present provided for, is a murderous absurdity. That any sane nation, having observed that you could provide for the supply of bread by giving bakers a pecuniary interest in baking for you, should go on to give a surgeon a pecuniary interest in cutting off your leg, is enough to make one despair of political humanity. But that is precisely what we have done. And the more appalling the mutilation the more the mutilator is paid....
>
> Scandalized voices murmur that... operations are necessary. They may be. It may also be necessary to hang a man or pull down a house. But we take good care not to make the hangman and the housebreaker the judges of that. If we did, no man's neck would be safe and no man's house stable.

Some contemporary defenders of fee-for-service evidently see no need to answer attacks like Shaw's. They reject the distinctions I have drawn between business and medical practice, claiming that medicine is just another market —admittedly with more imperfections than most, but a market nevertheless. They profess not to see much difference between medical care and any other important economic commodity, such as food, clothing, or housing. Such critics dismiss the notion of a de facto social contract in medical care. They assert that physicians and private hospitals owe nothing to society and should be free to sell or otherwise dispose of their services in any lawful manner they choose.

THE MEDICAL-INDUSTRIAL COMPLEX

Until recently such views had little influence. Most people considered medical care to be a social good, not a commodity, and physicians usually acted as if they agreed. Physicians were not impervious to economic pressures, but the pressures were relatively weak and the tradition of professionalism was relatively strong.

This situation is now rapidly changing. In the past two decades or so health care has become commercialized as never before, and professionalism in medicine seems to be giving way to entrepreneurialism. The health-care system is now widely regarded as an industry, and medical practice as a competitive business. Let me try briefly to explain the origins and describe the scope of this transformation.

First, the past few decades have witnessed a rapid expansion of medical facilities and personnel, leading to an unprecedented degree of competition for paying patients. Our once too few and overcrowded hospitals are now too numerous and on average less than 70 percent occupied. Physicians, formerly in short supply and very busy, now abound everywhere (except in city slums and isolated rural areas), and many are not as busy as they would like to be. Professionalism among self-employed private practitioners thrives when there is more than enough to do. When there isn't, competition for patients and worry about income tend to undermine professional values and influence professional judgment. Many of today's young physicians have to worry not only about getting themselves established in practice but also about paying off the considerable debt they have accumulated in medical school. High tuition levels make new graduates feel that they have paid a lot for an education that must now begin to pay them back-handsomely. This undoubtedly influences the choice of specialty many graduates make and

conditions their attitudes toward the economics of medical practice.

Along with the expansion of health care has come a great increase in specialization and technological sophistication, which has raised the price of services and made the economic rewards of medicine far greater than before. With insurance available to pay the bills, physicians have powerful economic incentives to recruit patients and provide expensive services. In an earlier and less technologically sophisticated era most physicians were generalists rather than specialists. They had mainly their time and counsel to offer, commodities that commanded only modest prices. Now a multitude of tests and procedures provide lucrative opportunities for extra income. This inevitably encourages an entrepreneurial approach to medical practice and an overuse of services.

Another major factor in the transformation of the system has been the appearance of investor-owned health-care businesses. Attracted by opportunities for profit resulting from the expansion of private and public health insurance, these new businesses (which I call the medical-industrial complex) have built and operated chains of hospitals, clinics, nursing homes, diagnostic laboratories, and many other kinds of health facilities. Recent growth has been mainly in ambulatory and home services and in specialized inpatient facilities other than acute-care general hospitals, in part because most government efforts to control health-care costs and the construction of new facilities have been focused on hospitals. Nevertheless, the growth of the medical-industrial complex continues unabated. There are no reliable data, but I would guess that at least a third of all non-public health-care facilities are now operated by investor-owned businesses. For example, most nursing homes, private psychiatric hospitals, and free-standing therapeutic or diagnostic facilities are investor-owned. So are nearly two thirds of the so-called health-maintenance organizations, which now provide comprehensive prepaid medical care to nearly 35 million members.

EFFECTS ON PROVIDERS

This corporatization of health care, coupled with increasingly hostile and cost-conscious policies by private insurance companies and government, has had a powerful and pervasive effect on the attitudes of health-care providers— including those in the not-for-profit sector. Not-for-profit, nonpublic hospitals ("voluntary hospitals"), which constitute more than three quarters of the non-public acute-care general hospitals in the country, originally were philanthropic social institutions, with the primary mission of serving the health-care needs of their communities. Now, forced to compete with investor-owned hospitals and a rapidly growing number of for-profit ambulatory facilities, and struggling to maintain their economic viability in the face of sharp reductions in third-party payments, they increasingly see themselves as beleaguered businesses, and they act accordingly. Altruistic concerns are being distorted in many voluntary hospitals by a concern for the bottom line. Management decisions are now often based more on considerations of profit than on the health needs of the community. Many voluntary hospitals seek to avoid or to limit services to the poor. They actively promote their profitable services to insured patients, they advertise themselves, they establish health-related businesses, and they make deals with physicians to generate more revenue. Avoiding uninsured patients simply adds to the problems of our underserved indigent population and widens the gap in medical care between rich and poor. Promoting elective care for insured patients leads to overuse of medical services and runs up the national health-care bill.

Physicians are reacting similarly as they struggle to maintain their income in an increasingly competitive economic climate. Like hospitals, practicing physicians have begun to use advertising, marketing, and public-relations techniques to attract more patients. Until recently most medical professional societies considered self-promotion of this kind to be unethical, but attitudes have changed, and now competition among physicians is viewed as a necessary, even beneficial, feature of the new medical marketplace.

Many financially attractive opportunities now exist for physicians to invest in health-care facilities to which they can then refer their patients, and a growing number of doctors have become limited partners in such enterprises—for example, for-profit diagnostic laboratories and MRI [magnetic resonance imaging] centers, to which they refer their patients but over which they can exercise no professional supervision. Surgeons invest in ambulatory-surgery facilities that are owned and managed by businesses or hospitals, and in which they perform surgery on their patients. Thus they both are paid for their professional services and share in the profits resulting from the referral of their patients to a particular facility. A recent study in Florida revealed that approximately 40 percent of all physicians practicing in that state had financial interests in facilities to which they referred patients. The AMA, however, estimates that nationwide the figure is about 10 percent.

In other kinds of entrepreneurial arrangements, office-based practitioners make deals with wholesalers of prescription drugs and sell those drugs to their patients at a profit, or buy prostheses from manufacturers at reduced rates and sell them at a profit—in addition to the fees they receive for implanting the prostheses. In entering into these and similar business arrangements, physicians are trading on their patients' trust. This is a clear violation of the traditional ethical rule against earning professional income by referring patients to others or by investing in the goods and services recommended to patients. Such arrangements create conflicts of interest that go far beyond the economic conflict of interest in the fee-for-service system, and they blur the distinction between business and the medical profession.

Not only practitioners but also physicians doing clinical research at teaching hospitals are joining the entrepreneurial trend. Manufacturers of new drugs, devices, and clinical tests are entering into financial arrangements with clinicians engaged in testing their products—and the results of those studies may have an important effect on the commercial success of the product. Clinical investigators may own equity interest in the company that produces the product or may serve as paid consultants and scientific advisers, thus calling into question their ability to act as rigorously impartial evaluators. Harvard Medical School has wisely taken a stand against such arrangements, but unfortunately this obvious conflict of interest has so far been ignored, or at least tolerated, in many other institutions.

Business arrangements of this kind are also common in postgraduate education.

Respected academic clinicians are frequently hired by drug firms to give lectures or write articles about the manufacturers' new products. The assumption, of course, is that these experts are expressing honest and dispassionate opinions about the relative merits of competing products, but such an assumption is strained by the realization that an expert is being handsomely paid by the manufacturer of one particular product in a market that is often highly competitive.

Similarly, drug manufacturers offer inducements to practicing physicians to attend seminars at which their products are touted, and even to institute treatment with a particular drug. In the former case the ostensible justification is furtherance of postgraduate education; in the latter it is the gathering of post-marketing information about a new drug. The embarrassing transparency of these subterfuges has recently caused pharmaceutical manufacturers to agree with the AMA that such practices should be curtailed.

In short, at every turn in the road physicians both in practice and in academic institutions are being attracted by financial arrangements that can compromise their professional independence.

ANTITRUST MEDICINE

The courts have significantly contributed to the change in atmosphere. For many years the legal and medical professions enjoyed immunity from antitrust law because it was generally believed that they were not engaged in the kind of commercial activity that the Sherman Act and the Federal Trade Commission Act were designed to regulate. In 1975 the Supreme Court ended this immunity (*Goldfarb v. Virginia State Bar*). It decided that the reach of antitrust law extended to the professions. Since then numerous legal actions have been taken against individual physicians or physicians' organizations to curb what government has perceived to be "anti-competitive" practices. Thus the courts and the Federal Trade Commission have prevented medical societies in recent years from prohibiting commercial advertising or marketing and from taking any action that might influence professional fees or legal business ventures by physicians.

Concerns about possible antitrust liability have caused the AMA to retreat from many of the anti-commercial recommendations in its 1957 code of ethics. The latest revisions of the ethical code say that advertising is permissible so long as it is not deceptive. Investments in healthcare facilities are also permissible, provided that they are allowed by law and disclosed to patients, and provided also that they do not interfere with the physician's primary duty to his or her patients. Reflecting the new economic spirit, a statement has been added that competition is "not only ethical but is encouraged." Indeed, the AMA goes even further, declaring that "ethical medical practice thrives best under free market conditions when prospective patients have adequate information and opportunity to choose freely between and among competing physicians and alternate systems of medical care." Thus an earlier forthright stand by organized medicine against the commercialization of medical practice has now been replaced by an uneasy ambivalence.

Very recently, however, the AMA seems to have reconsidered its position, at least with respect to some kinds of entrepreneurial activity. At its last meeting it adopted a resolution advising physicians not to refer patients to an outside facility in which the physician has an ownership interest—except when the facility was built in response to a demonstrated need and alternative financing for its construction was not available. It remains to be seen whether this advice will be heeded and whether the AMA will take a similar position on other commercial practices. It will also be interesting to see what response this modest stand in defense of professional ethics will elicit from the Federal Trade Commission.

THE GOVERNMENT'S RESPONSE

Government policy has also been ambivalent. The Reagan and Bush Administrations have staunchly supported competition and free markets in medicine under the delusion that this is a way to limit expenditures. The White House has therefore supported the Federal Trade Commission's antitrust policies and until recently has resisted all proposals for curbing entrepreneurial initiatives in health care. But expenditures are not likely to be limited in a market lacking the restraints ordinarily imposed by cost-conscious consumers who must pay for what they want and can afford. And if the competing providers in such a market have great power to determine what is to be purchased, then their competition inevitably drives up expenditures and the total size of the market. In business, success is measured in terms of increasing sales volume and revenues —the last thing we want to see in the health-care system. Despite its preference for market mechanisms, however, the Bush Administration recently abandoned ideology and supported legislation to regulate physicians' fees and to prevent physicians from referring their Medicare patients to diagnostic laboratories in which they have a financial interest. Regulations and new legislation to provide even stricter limits on physicians' investments in health-care facilities are currently under consideration in several states—not for ethical reasons but simply as measures to limit health-care spending. Clearly, cost control is now the highest priority in public policy.

Despite its recent willingness to intervene in limited ways to control costs generated by some of the entrepreneurial activities of physicians, the government has as yet shown little interest in interfering with the spreading commercialization of our health-care system. That should not be surprising, because private enterprise is now widely heralded as the answer to most economic problems. We hear much these days about the privatization of schools, highways, airports, jails, national parks, the postal service, and many other aspects of our society—and by this is meant not simply removal from government control but transfer to investor ownership. Business, it is said, can do a much better job of running most of these things than government, so why not turn them over to private enterprise? I do not want to debate this general proposition here, but medical care, I suggest, is in many ways uniquely unsuited to private enterprise. It is an essential social service, requiring the involvement of the community and the commitment of health-care professionals. It flourishes best in the private sector but it needs public support, and it cannot meet its responsibilities to society if it is dominated by business interests.

WHY SHOULD THE PUBLIC CARE?

If government is not concerned about the loss of social and professional values in our health-care system, should the American public care? I think it must. The quality and effectiveness of our medical care depend critically on the values and the behavior of its providers. If health care is not a business, then we should encourage our physicians to stand by their traditional fiduciary obligations, and we should enable, if not require, our voluntary hospitals to honor their commitments to the community.

If most of our physicians become entrepreneurs and most of our hospitals and health-care facilities become businesses, paying patients will get more care than they need and poor patients will get less. In a commercialized system the cost of health care will continue to escalate and yet we will not be assured of getting the kind of care we really need. In such a system we will no longer be able to trust our physicians, because the bond of fiduciary responsibility will have been broken. To control costs, government will be driven to adopt increasingly stringent regulations. Ultimately health care will have to be regulated like a public utility, and much greater constraints will be placed on physicians and hospitals than are now in place or even contemplated.

Our health-care system is inequitable, inefficient, and too expensive. It badly needs reform. The task will be arduous and the solution is far from clear, but I believe that the first step must be to gain a firm consensus on what we value in health care and what kind of a medical profession we want. The medical profession has held a privileged position in American society, based on the expectation that it will serve society's needs first of all. How can it hope to continue in that position if it loses the trust of the public? We cannot expect to solve our health-care problems unless we can count on the basic altruism of the profession and its sense of responsibility to patients and the general public welfare. American society and the medical profession need to reaffirm their de facto contract, because they will have to depend on each other as the United States painfully gropes its way toward a better system of health care.

Physicians have the power to make health-care reform possible. They know the system better than anyone, and if they want to, they can use its resources more prudently than they do now without any loss of medical effectiveness. It is primarily their decisions that determine what medical services will be provided in each case, and therefore what the aggregate expenditure for health care will be. If physicians remain free of conflicting economic ties, and if they act in a truly professional manner, medical facilities will probably be used more appropriately, regardless of their ownership or organization. In any case, no proposed reforms in the health-care system can ultimately be successful without a properly motivated medical profession. But if physicians continue to allow themselves to be drawn along the path of private entrepreneurship, they will increasingly be seen as self-interested businessmen and will lose many of the privileges they now enjoy as fiduciaries and trusted professionals. They will also lose the opportunity to play a constructive role in shaping the major reforms that are surely coming.

The medical profession is not likely to change its direction without help. The incentives that now encourage—indeed, in many cases require—physicians to act primarily as businessmen will have to be changed, and probably so will the configurations in which most physicians practice. In my opinion, a greater reliance on group practice and more emphasis on medical insurance that prepays providers at a fixed annual rate offer the best chance of solving the economic problems of health care, because these arrangements put physicians in the most favorable position to act as prudent advocates for their patients, rather than as entrepreneurial vendors of services. However, regardless of what structural changes in the health-care system are ultimately adopted, physicians hold the key. The sooner they join with government and the public in reaffirming the medical profession's ethical contract with society, the easier will be the task of reform and the greater the chance of its success.

NO

Andrew C. Wicks

ALBERT SCHWEITZER OR IVAN BOESKY? WHY WE SHOULD REJECT THE DICHOTOMY BETWEEN MEDICINE AND BUSINESS

As we contemplate the profound changes the Clinton administration will propose for health care, it is not surprising that numerous passionate and conflicting views exist on what direction to take. While investigating the full range of such perspectives is a task nearly as imposing as restructuring our ailing health care system, I do want to explore some key assumptions that frame how many people think about health care reform. These assumptions are tied to a broader sense that medicine and business are, and should remain, polar opposites—things which ought never to be mixed together or confused for fear that the results could be disastrous. More specifically, many scholars in medicine and medical ethics lament that medicine is increasingly becoming a business, and that the ethos of business will inevitably erode the moral identity of health care workers and dominate the physician-patient relationship.

. . . While I share much of the concern that is raised here, I will argue that this conceptualization of the issues is overly simplistic and that a more nuanced analysis is necessary. To make my argument I want to explore three questions:

1. What specific changes in medicine reflect the introduction of "business" thinking and are these changes desirable from an ethical standpoint?
2. How substantial are the differences between the ethics of medicine and the ethics of business?
3. Can the two ethical models, or aspects of them, be combined in a positive way?

As a vehicle to address these questions, I will focus on how we think about the models of medicine and business, specifically the ways in which ethical imperatives shape the activities of their respective practitioners and the missions of their institutions. . . .

From Andrew C. Wicks, "Albert Schweitzer or Ivan Boesky? Why We Should Reject the Dichotomy Between Medicine and Business," *Journal of Business Ethics*, vol. 14 (1995), pp. 339–349. Copyright © 1995 by D. Reidel Publishing Co., Dordrecht, Holland, and Boston, U.S.A. Reprinted by permission of Kluwer Academic Publishers. Notes omitted.

My approach to these issues will be that of an ethicist, trained to reflect on normative issues. I will not offer or defend specific policies or institutional arrangements, although my arguments will have direct relevance to the sorts of practical proposals that are being considered for health care. My underlying goal is to help reconceptualize how we think about both medicine and business, and in so doing, reshape how we approach the "American health care crisis."

THE COSTS OF COMMERCIALISM

Among the more significant concerns that the commercialization of medicine raises are the following:

1. The market model doesn't "fit" medicine. Patients are vulnerable, they lack the knowledge to operate as effective consumers under a "caveat emptor" ["let the buyer beware"] model, and health care is an overridingly important good whose availability ought not to be determined by one's income or ability to pay.
2. The business model creates conflicts of interest in medicine, particularly between physicians and patients.
3. Allowing the market model to direct consumption is unacceptable: care would be focused on what pays rather than what is needed; market-thinking validates and supports the idea of "creating" needs rather than just meeting them; there would be incentive to overconsume which could possibly increase overall health care costs.
4. Thinking about health care as a business erodes the basis of a right to health care. That is, by thinking about

health care as a commodity, rather than as a basic human right or special set of goods, it becomes more fitting to leave allocation and purchasing to market forces and individual ability to pay.
5. The growing ethos of commercialism erodes, or perhaps even renders inept, the Hippocratic tradition. By teaching physicians that they are business people we legitimate their self-interested aspirations, make patients equivalent to "customers" and, in so doing, undermine the sacred moral calling of physicians.

While I highlight these concerns and suggest they have merit, I also will argue that they create an overly simplistic picture. My strategy will be to expose some dubious assumptions which cloud our thinking on these matters. Among the assumptions embedded in the thinking of critics, such as Relman and Dougherty, are the following:

1. Medicine and business are ethically opposed and incompatible.
2. There can be no substantial mixture and/or balancing of the ethics of medicine and business [opening the door to commercialism and business will inevitably lead to its dominance over medicine].
3. The ethical problems associated with "medicine as a business" can be remedied only by rejecting the business framework.

The conceptions of business and medicine that are tied to these assumptions depict medicine as fundamentally about caring and healing. Physicians and other health care workers are compassionate, put the interests of their patients above their own, and are altruistic—i.e. there is a clear moral, perhaps even an "ultra" moral, content which defines their identity and shapes their activity. In contrast, business people are thought of as self-interested to the point of excluding any concern other than profit in their activities—i.e. they pursue only activities which serve their interest and maximize profits. The quintessential business person is greedy and driven by bottom line "business" considerations. Talk of concern for others or morality would, at best, be an after-thought, and at worst, only confuse the pursuit of their larger raison d'etre. As such, business activity is fundamentally amoral.

Let us examine these assumptions in turn. I will condense my critique of this reading of the two fields into four separate arguments.

Overestimating charity and altruism in health care workers.

This position makes too much of the charitable and altruistic nature of health care professionals. My purpose in saying this is not to question the integrity of the profession, or the extremely valuable moral traditions of medicine, but rather to temper the level of esteem in which we hold physicians. Due to the nature of the physician-patient relationship under a fee-for-service arrangement, it is in the self-interest of the physician not only to apply beneficial therapies, but to be overzealous. Providing aggressive and even excessive care to patients actually benefits the physician financially—to this extent, the well-being of the patient and the self-interest of the physician point generally in the same direction. One can also look to the stance of the majority of physicians and the AMA [American Medical Association] on such issues as HMO's, Medicare and

Medicaid, and wholesale reform of the health care system to provide access for more patients as further evidence to question the degree to which physicians are self-effacing and charitable. Finally, one can point to the relatively high and rising salaries of physicians, the growth of medical specialists, the decline in indigent care, and the geographic maldistribution of physicians towards wealthier areas as further confirmation that we should be skeptical of imagining Albert Schweitzer or Mother Teresa when we call to mind the ordinary physician. Again, this is not to malign physicians or question their moral charge, rather, it is to give it a more sober and balanced interpretation.

The moral problems of introducing "business" into medicine aren't qualitatively different from those that currently exist in the "medical" model.

As I have already argued, the conflicts of interest which have been attached to the business model as areas of great concern, are present in the current system of health care delivery. The only difference is that while the "medical" model creates incentives to overtreat, the "business" model would lead physicians to undertreat. Even though both scenarios contain obvious conflicts many would argue that the former arrangement is clearly preferable to the latter. Yet, it has been persuasively argued that such a conclusion is far from obvious. First of all, there are substantial risks and harms which go along with overtreatment. Extra office visits may only hurt one's pocketbook, but unnecessary surgery, x-rays, or other invasive procedures can pose more serious physical harms to patients with little or no benefit. A recent report on the periodic use of unnecessary cesarean sections provides a disturbing reminder of just how common a phenomenon this may be. In addition, there are costs to society and third parties from overtreatment in the form of higher overall medical costs and fewer resources to offer more beneficial treatments to patients with clear and compelling needs. Finally, in this era of de facto rationing and fiscal scarcity, there is an implicit and indirect trade-off being made. When treatments are offered, others are being denied such that we must remember the harms of overtreatment are not simply to the patient and to society, but to other particular patients who have pressing medical needs that may not be met....

Talking in grand metaphors/paradigms oversimplifies the problem.

Although I direct the next criticism at the commentators whom I challenge, it is also a criticism of my paper. By talking about "medicine" and "business" in global and unified models, we risk imposing a singular framework or paradigm onto a complex set of institutions and relationships. "Health care" and "medicine" include the interaction of patients with physicians, nurses, and nurse practitioners; it refers to interactions which take place in free clinics,—emergency rooms, private hospitals, public teaching hospitals, individual physician practices and HMO's; and it also connects with medical supply companies, pharmaceutical companies, insurance companies, and a range of other public and private institutions which play a variety of direct and indirect roles in the availability and delivery of health care. Talk of models is important and helps clarify a range of problems, yet it can also create new and less visible ones. The oppositional model of medicine and business tends to rein-

force the idea of a singularity of norms and ideals, of context and organizational structure. Without tempering this image and accounting for the subtle and significant differences across these realms, such modeling can create arrangements which are not only inappropriate but dangerous. Indeed, I would argue that the differences that are encompassed between the various relationships and levels provides evidence that we need a more nuanced and balanced approach. The range of institutions, and the degree to which they are tied to the moral imperatives of medicine, should reinforce the idea that we are better off seeing the two models as on a continuum rather than as opposites.

Practical realities may force a marriage/ combination.

Finally, if we are to construct a health care system which best fulfills the range of purposes we have for it, then it must be able to encompass a variety of objectives. A number of these objectives seem to require applying to medicine the skills, wisdom, and reflection of "business." There is a need to cut costs, reduce bureaucratic waste, spur innovation, recognize scarcity and turn what are now defacto trade-offs into conscious choices. We need to avoid the replication of services and expensive technologies across hospitals and research centers in close proximity; we need to educate physicians—at some level—to be more active gate-keepers of health services; and finally, we not only want to create greater access with reasonable cost, we want to temper public expectations and consumptive behavior—a key factor in the increased use and overall cost of health care. While this list is far from exhaustive, it illustrates the need for combining and perhaps even integrating the two models as well as the skills, wisdom, and imperatives of each. There are a number of ways to realize the ethical goals in practice, and we may be able to continue to keep the "business" and "medical" tasks distinct, but it seems clear that the two activities (and the ethics which emerge from them) can no longer be separated to the degree that they have been. In fact, one could argue that one of the key sources of this health care crisis is a failure to connect these two models, and more specifically, to ask the hard questions raised by fiscal scarcity.

IN SEARCH OF A BETTER MODEL FOR BUSINESS

So far I have challenged the validity of the oppositional model based on practical limitations and reasons internal to the model itself. I want next to extend the argument by offering an alternative way of conceptualizing the ethics of medicine and business. I begin with a reconsideration and reconstruction of business ethics. In so doing, I seek to challenge how we think about the content of the terms "business" and "ethics", and as a result, how we think about medical ethics.

I take the description of business in the oppositional model outlined above as an accurate description of how many, and perhaps most, Americans approach the subject of business ethics. It is a model that economists have done a great deal to create and perpetuate. Business is about the pursuit of profit and self-interest—or more accurately, any form of self-beneficial activity that allows one to make a profit. Egoism and the valorization of greed drive business activity such that ethical considerations have no meaningful place, except as outside constraints

placed on firms by consumers and the public (e.g. as boycotts, laws and regulations). This is not because people want businesses to ignore ethical issues, rather, it is due to the fact that competition, efficiency and the dynamics of the market leave no room for people to hold such ideals—those who do lose out. Why is this the case? In part, it has to do with assumptions about ethics. At its core, many assume ethics to be about altruism, about being kinder and gentler, about being charitable. Many associate ethical activity with looking out for others, putting their needs above one's own, doing the right thing for the right reasons. Ethics, we tend to think, requires denying self-interest. Thus, ethics and business cannot fit together: one activity upholds self-interest, while the other rejects it. In such a context, business ethics is necessarily an oxymoron and capitalism becomes all of the disturbing things that the movie *Wall Street* and the many narratives on the "Decade of Greed" made it out to be.

I want to challenge this viewpoint for a variety of reasons, many of which have been articulated by others. To do so, I will draw on examples of corporate activity, and specifically, one particular problem faced by Merck & Co., a prominent American pharmaceutical firm.

One obvious and common criticism is that this model gives us an extreme and unrealistic account of human beings. Few people are as greedy or purely self-interested as we assume Ivan Boesky, Michael Milken and others to have been. Human action stems from a variety of impulses and norms that have to do with our acculturation, sense of propriety, and other moral and social values. Self-interest is clearly one such impulse, and an important feature of human behavior, but its influence is far more complex as it is both shaped and balanced by a variety of other features. At the same time, few people are as pure of heart and single-mindedly self-effacing as Mother Teresa or Albert Schweitzer. Even when we perform the most apparently selfless acts, there is usually some element of "impure" motivation for selfish gain that accompanies it. Most human activity takes place in the realm in between, where there are a variety of motives and where practices have elements of both self-interest and regard for others. This is true for business as it is for other spheres or practices. The "self-interest" model should be rejected because it forces us to make crude and unrealistic assumptions about how people behave, glossing over the most interesting and complex part of life.

Second, the two realms problem sets the content of both ethics and business in ways which profoundly limit our ability to fit the two together. While economists have used some of Adam Smith's writings to argue for self-interest —better described as egoism or greed— as the crucial driving force of capitalism, their slant on the concept is defective. I have no argument against self-interest, but I would maintain that there is a vast difference between self-interest and selfishness or greed. The former allows room for consideration of the interests of others and competing moral interests (indeed, when it is constrained by other relevant moral values and virtues, we may call self-interest a moral concept). The same cannot be said for greed or selfishness, as the content of these notions is premised on rejecting any moral limits and competing norms. Thus, on this rehabilitated account, we can agree that self-interest has a prominent role in business, but only when it is constructed as a moral value which is shaped and limited by a variety of other moral considerations. Indeed, on this view, there is nothing odd about connecting or integrating self-interest with a range of other moral purposes for the organization or the individual.

It is equally important that we offer a more compelling account of ethics. Rather than highlighting altruism and charity, it would be more appropriate to focus on aspects of the moral life as respect for others, decency, trust, and justice or fair play. These concepts are arguably more relevant and appropriate concepts to use for interaction among strangers or for public and professional life. They are also less directly opposed to self-interest (particularly in the context of my rehabilitated definition). Indeed, on my redescription, not only is there nothing morally illegitimate about the pursuit of self-interest or financial gain, it may be described as a limited virtue. Thus, by taking a closer look at the content of both business and ethics it is apparent that how the terms are defined has a lot to do with the account of business ethics which emerges. When we use a more balanced and careful approach, ethics and business seem to fit together quite well.

Finally, I draw attention to particular corporations to illustrate the differences generated by this revised interpretation of business ethics. Consider the much publicized dilemma faced by Merck & Co. as they decided whether or not to develop and distribute a treatment for river blindness, a horrible illness which afflicted scores of people in the third world (particularly in parts of Africa, Central and South America).

A Merck scientist discovered that a drug the company had developed to fight parasites in farm animals could possibly be adapted to kill the parasite which caused river blindness. The parasites, which grew to almost two feet in length once they entered the body via an insect bite, began as a relatively benign but offensive presence in nodules just under the skin. However, once they reproduced, creating millions of microscopic worms, victims experienced severe suffering that started with itching so terrible that some victims opted to commit suicide rather than continue to endure the pain. As the organisms spread, they often infiltrate the eyes, causing blindness. The idea of creating a drug to treat an illness that was so awful and affected so many was wonderful, except for the fact that none of the potential customers could pay for the drug. Merck faced the dilemma of whether to invest millions of dollars to develop the drug when there was little in the way of potential financial return. Its best case scenario involved gaining financial support from various private and public sources to help offset costs and to deliver the drugs, but such assistance had not been obtained. A key component of this situation is Merck's corporate philosophy:

> We try never to forget that medicine is for the people. It is not for the profits. The profits follow, and if we have remembered that, they have never failed to appear. The better we have remembered it, the larger they have been.

The company had assembled a world-class collection of scientists and workers who were not only among the most technically capable, but who were highly motivated. This motivation can be traced to their commitment to Merck's corporate philosophy, a credo which they took quite seriously and which they believed the company did as well. The drug development proved a success, but Merck's extensive efforts to get support for development and distribution failed. Transporting the drug was a further problem—sufferers lived in the bush where there were no established transportation networks. Thus, even if they opted to give the drug away, it would cost them roughly $20 million per year to get it to those in need. What should Merck do? Merck decided to give the drug away and pay to transport it to all countries who wanted the drug—forever.

While this is an extraordinary decision in itself, what is more important for our purposes is how we describe or interpret the situation. Under the "self-interest" model, the dilemma becomes a question of charity. Merck either pursues its larger goal of profit maximization and refuses to develop the drug because it won't generate enough income or good will to pay for the costs, or it decides to undertake a charitable activity. I would argue that this is a poor way to look at this case. A more constructive (and probably more accurate) way to look at it is as a test of Merck's mission statement. Just as their corporate mission statement exploded the dichotomy between business and ethics, so too was their decision a question of whether the company stood for the particular mixture of ethical and business imperatives that made up that philosophy. This is my final reason for dropping the "self-interest" model —because firms like Merck, and many others, reject it. These firms are finding ways to mix values and self-interest: starting with a commitment to serving a moral goal (e.g. patients, customers, or a variety of other "stakeholder" groups, i.e. those groups who can affect or who are affected by the activities of the corporation). Firms are finding that they can shape their guiding philosophy in terms of moral commitments, what many are calling value-driven management, and still have financially successful firms.

... Organizations don't have to be "charitable" or non-profit to undertake important communal projects or to serve moral ends. Ethics doesn't have to be about altruism or a singularity of intention to "do the right thing." Scientists at Merck and physicians in medical practice both display a moral commitment to a mission which we would be wrong to describe as largely "altruistic" or "charitable" because of the extent to which they benefit in the process, but it remains an important moral mission nonetheless. Indeed, I want to argue that it is vital that we distinguish this sort of activity (and the importance of the moral purposes served) from the endeavors of "greed" which the public has attributed to business's profit maximization philosophy. Within the prevailing profit maximization philosophy, moral concerns are, at best, seen as largely irrelevant to the purposes and activities of the firm and at worst, opposed to pursuing their "business" interests. Failure to draw such distinctions reinforces the idea that moral concerns are the domain of government or private citizens and have no place in "business". It leads us to perpetuate a world where corporations focus exclusively on one goal—the wealth, the material gain of its economic activity—while excluding virtually all others. It turns business into an activity which is more destructive and oppressive than creative and uplifting....

FROM OPPOSITION TO CONTINUUM: THE CORE SIMILARITIES OF BUSINESS ETHICS AND MEDICAL ETHICS

I have now set the groundwork for pressing a larger argument about the similarity of business and medical ethics: both in terms of a larger mission or strategic statement of purpose, as well as the moral requirements of practitioners (i.e. physicians and managers respectively). While some have emphasized the altruism of physicians, I have argued that physicians have operated in a system where they can adopt the mantle of altruism without sacrificing their self-interest. Physicians make a good living caring for their patients, and although many have raised questions about the extent of their compensation, no one has questioned that physicians be well paid for serving their patients. Few people hold many illusions about the "altruism" of corporations, although many have provided vital support to charities, local communities, and other important causes. Thus, while altruism is more typically associated with physicians, it is hard to make a persuasive case for this being a prominent feature of either profession.

At the same time, I have argued that we should reject the other end of the spectrum, the model of business as driven by pure egoism and the unbridled pursuit of self-interest. As stakeholder firms and total quality management firms have found, doing so does not mean sacrificing financial success and firm survival, but can be seen as a key to securing both. A balanced reading of the business model and the content of "business" also lead us to want to reject this extreme as well. Insofar as this problem is not associated with medicine, except to the extent that it has been dominated by "business" thinking, I shall assume that my rejection of the greed model for business is sufficient to discredit this other pole of the oppositional model.

The common ground that emerges by closing off these two extremes and accepting the model I have articulated for business ethics is quite substantial. It is clear that physicians serve important moral goals by proclaiming their allegiance to the interests of patients and the general health of the community. Yet, while this is their "mission" statement, it is also not opposed to financial success and a reasonable standard of living. We argue about whether physicians are doing enough to help the poor, are being paid too much, or are sacrificing certain health needs of the community for their own benefit, but few reject that any viable picture of medicine contains elements of both models. Doctors are not about maximizing profits, but about serving patients—yet, like Merck, they recognize that in serving the patients, they will also be financially successful. The point is not to legitimize all self-regarding activities or collapse them into moral duties that are more other-regarding. Rather, it is to recognize that self-interest is a concept different from selfishness and greed, and that the former is perfectly compatible with serving other moral ends while the latter is not. Combining ethics and self-interest together is also about rehabilitating our view of medical (as well as business) ethics, moving away from the extreme of altruism and charity, and toward a view that makes trust, respect for others, decency, and a sense of fair play central concepts. Embracing this model does not entail watering down our expectations, lowering our standards, or legitimizing unacceptable behavior. Instead,

it offers us a more complex view of the world and a more viable account of human activity that may well, ironically, allow us to have higher expectations of corporations and provide them with the means to meet those standards.

There are also important comparisons that some have drawn at the level of individual practitioners in medicine and business—between managers and physicians. It appears that there is a basic difference between the two fields in that physicians have one basic duty and serve one group, while managers have many duties and serve many groups. Whereas stakeholder theory has created obligations for managers to serve an array of interests, physicians have typically had one overriding duty: to serve the well-being of their patients. Yet, even in its prime, this dyadic model was over-simplistic. There have always been limits to this duty, particularly when there are compelling claims on behalf of communal health, legal constraints, the physician's own conscience, or the well-being of third parties. Further, if we accept Haavi Morreim's argument that the emergence of fiscal scarcity requires that we reject the dyadic model, and that the interests of a number of other groups and interests must be included, the role of physician begins to look a good deal more complex and more akin to that of the business manager in the stakeholder model. In practice, we may want to take steps to ensure that physicians focus primarily on the health and well-being of individual patients, yet they must also use the interests and claims of a wide variety of other stakeholder groups to shape and structure their activity. Just as managers used to think that it was enough to serve stockholders and operate in a role perhaps similar to physicians, the emergence of other compelling moral duties have pressed us to dramatically revise, if not disintegrate entirely, both models....

CONCLUSION

... While this discussion doesn't provide definitive answers, it seems possible to respond to my original three questions. *Is the introduction of "business" thinking creating drastic and/or dangerous changes in the practice of medicine?* First, based on the model I have defended and drawing on numerous scholarly sources and examples, it seems clear that "business" thinking and the business model need not be as corrosive as critics have made it out to be. Indeed, based on the reality of fiscal scarcity and the need to temper care for particular patients with a broader sense of justice, it seems evident that the influence of business may be a positive influence. *How substantial are the differences between the ethics of medicine and the ethics of business?* I have offered a sustained critique of the oppositional model which associated medicine with altruism and business with unmitigated self-interest, arguing that both are exaggerated and indefensible. In addition, I provided an alternative reconstruction of the two models ... which establishes core similarities between the two. This view explodes the oppositional image of medicine and business and places them on a continuum which is structured by these core similarities, but allows for significant differences between them. *Can the two models, or aspects of them, be molded together in a constructive way?* Not only can they be connected, but given the goals we have for health care, it seems essential that they be combined to construct a more useful system.

... [W]hile I suggest that we should continue to be skeptical about the effects of strict corporate control over the health care system and the willingness of companies to accept the sorts of ethical arguments I have articulated, health care institutions may be an ideal context in which to forge such a marriage. Medicine is an area where such interfaces of business and ethics—concerns about costs, innovation, and economics as well as the needs of particular patients and broader human welfare—can, and perhaps must, be connected in terms of the basic strategic identity of health care institutions if they are to serve our large goals. We may be able to draw on the ethics of medicine and the ethics of business to find a way out of the American health care crisis which avoids the pitfalls of the two "extreme" models with which we began.

Regardless of what one thinks of business ethics, or the ethos that pervades much of corporate America, it is clear that we can no longer entertain such global and simplistic dichotomies between medicine and business. Further discourse and the effort to create a promising direction for our health care system requires a more balanced and complex view of the situation, and acknowledgment that whatever directions we take must have substantial elements of both.

POSTSCRIPT

Are Business and Medicine Ethically Incompatible?

There is no end in sight to the growth of health care costs in the United States: as the population ages and needs more medical care, and as the technology continues to advance, costs will continue to rise. Under the heading of "respect for liberty," or contractual freedom, there is no natural limit on what an individual might medically "need," or, more accurately, what an individual might be permitted to buy in the medical marketplace—and, therefore, what a physician might prescribe for personal patients. Under the heading of "distributive justice," any necessary medical treatment that is available to the rich ought also to be available to the poor, which places an incredibly large demand on the public coffers. Nowhere else in the economy is there this fatal combination of an *essential* service (necessary for life), a strong history of *private* allotment (through physicians and their individual patients), and a *public* responsibility for payment.

It can be argued, and Wicks occasionally does argue, that the market ethic will protect the health care consumer because the for-profit hospitals and HMOs want to retain their customer bases. However, because the oldest and sickest patients (the ones who need medical care the most) cost the most to treat, the HMOs do not want them as customers. In a hospital or HMO that is a publicly owned corporation, management is responsible to the directors, who are responsible to the shareholders and therefore have a fiduciary responsibility to maximize the financial position of the institution. As a result, the physicians who are the employees of the corporation may very well be held to *financial* standards of performance as well as—or instead of—*medical* standards.

SUGGESTED READINGS

Adrienne C. Locke, "Doctors View Ethics of Cost Control," *Business Insurance* (February 25, 1991).

Chris Messina, "The Heart Attack Business," *High Technology* (March 1989).

Michael Schachner, "On-Site Medical Center Touts: Employer-Owned Facilities Can Reduce Costs, Improve Quality," *Business Insurance* (May 11, 1992).

Matthew Schwartz, "Self-Referrals Pump Up Health Care Costs," *National Underwriter* (October 26, 1992).

ISSUE 3

Are Corporate Codes of Ethics Just for Show?

YES: LaRue Tone Hosmer, from *The Ethics of Management* (Irwin Press, 1987)

NO: Lisa H. Newton, from "The Many Faces of the Corporate Code," in *The Corporate Code of Ethics: The Perspective of the Humanities,* proceedings of the Conference on Corporate Visions and Values (Fairfield University, 1992)

ISSUE SUMMARY

YES: LaRue Tone Hosmer, a professor of corporate strategies, argues that codes of ethics are really only for show and that they are ineffective in bringing about more ethical behavior on the part of employees.

NO: Professor of philosophy Lisa H. Newton holds that the formation and adoption of corporate codes are valuable processes because they raise corporate awareness of ethical issues and because they can be a valuable part of the corporate action review process.

Business ethics, as an academic discipline and a corporate concern, is the product of the combination of two unlikely companions. Early in the twentieth century, what was called "business ethics" was in reality a set of agreements, created for and by businessmen, concerning the way they did business, and for the most part they were highly *un*ethical. These agreements demanded that you keep your salesman off the other guy's turf; that you refrain from introducing new products in direct competition with other members of the club; that you hire only white males, or at least make sure that only white males made it to the upper echelons of the company; and that you keep secret whatever you might know about your fellow businessmen's adulterated products or fictional tax returns. In short, like the "ethics" of any profession of the period, business ethics were the rules of the in-group— self-protective and self-serving.

Meanwhile, the ethics taught in colleges was linguistic and analytic. Professors taught only terms and their meanings, conversed only with themselves and their students, and were well aware that their teachings were of little use in the real world of business. Business ethics was not seen as a serious discipline.

However, starting in the late 1950s, scandals began to surface: price-fixing, unsafe products, and foreign bribes, for example. In response, the "social responsibility" movement, led primarily by the churches and a few crusading consumer advocates such as Ralph Nader, attempted to make business accountable to the general public for its practices. Businesses were told to get out of South Africa because of apartheid, to ensure product quality and safety, and to take responsibility for the environment. Although the business community's first response was to ignore the activists, some severe consequences —such as jail terms for some very respectable corporate officers, demonstrations, and hostile regulatory legislation—made it clear that some attention would have to be paid to ethics or at least to the *appearance* of ethics.

Businesspeople started thinking seriously about public accountability around the time when the armed conflict in Vietnam brought the ethics professors out of their classrooms and into the public arena. Philosophy developed a new, socially relevant branch of ethics, soon to be called "applied ethics," and by the early 1970s the ethicists of the applied branch were in dialogue with physicians over medical ethics, lawyers on legal ethics, and businesspeople on business ethics. Some familiarity with ethics is now required of most undergraduate business majors.

But does writing and teaching about ethics do any good? LaRue Tone Hosmer says no. He sees a fundamental problem with codes of ethics in that "ethics in management represents a conflict between the economic and the social performance of an organization." Accordingly, codes of ethics must be exercises in futility because they direct the corporation away from its primary function. Lisa H. Newton, arguing the contrary, asserts that the actual code is the least important element in the development of the corporate culture. She argues that the process of code development—principled, comprehensive, and participative—is the most valuable part of the development exercise.

Ask yourself, as you read these selections, is there a conflict between economic and social performance—that is, between business and ethics? Is *business ethics* an oxymoron?

YES

LaRue Tone Hosmer

ETHICAL CODES

Ethical codes are statements of the norms and beliefs of an organization. These norms and beliefs are generally proposed, discussed, and defined by the senior executives in the firm and then published and distributed to all of the members. Norms, of course, are standards of behavior; they are the ways the senior people in the organization want the others to act when confronted with a given situation. An example of a norm in a code of ethics would be, "Employees of this company will not accept personal gifts with a monetary value over $25 in total from any business friend or associate, and they are expected to pay their full share of the costs for meals or other entertainment (concerts, the theatre, sporting events, etc.) that have a value above $25 per person." The norms in an ethical code are generally expressed as a series of negative statements, for it is easier to list the things a person should not do than to be precise about the things a person should do.

The beliefs in an ethical code are standards of thought; they are the ways that the senior people in the organization want others to think. This is not censorship. Instead, the intent is to encourage ways of thinking and patterns of attitudes that will lead towards the wanted behavior. Consequently, the beliefs in an ethical code are generally expressed in a positive form. "Our first responsibility is to our customer" is an example of a positive belief that commonly appears in codes of ethics; another would be "We wish to be good citizens of every community in which we operate." Some company codes of ethics appear in [the two boxes that follow].

Do ethical codes work? Are they helpful in conveying to all employees the moral standards selected by the board of directors and president? Not really. The problem is that it is not possible to state the norms and beliefs of an organization relative to the various constituent groups—employees, customers, suppliers, distributors, stockholders, and the general public—clearly and explicitly, without offending at least one of those groups. It is not possible to say, for example, that a company considers its employees to be more important to the success of the firm than its stockholders, without putting the stockholders on notice that profits and dividends come second. Stockholders, and their agents at trust departments and mutual funds, tend to resent that, just as the employees would if the conditions were reversed. Consequently codes of ethics are usually written in general terms, noting obligations to each of the groups but not stating which takes precedence in any given situation.

The basic difficulty with codes of ethics is that they do not establish priorities between the norms and beliefs. The priorities are the true values of a firm, and they are not included. As an example, let us say that one division in a firm is faced with declining sales and profits; the question is whether to reduce middle-management employment and cut overhead costs—the classic downsizing decision—but the code of ethics says in one section that we respect our employees and in another section that we expect "fair" profits. How do we decide? What is "fair" in this instance? The code of ethics does not tell us.

Let us look at two other examples very briefly. Another division in our company is in a market that has grown very rapidly and has now reached such a large size that direct distribution from the factory to the retail outlets would be much more economical. Our code of ethics says that we will "work closely with our suppliers and distributors, for they too deserve a profit," but perhaps we can reduce our prices to our customers, and gain a competitive advantage for ourselves, if we eliminate the wholesalers and ship directly. The code does not tell us how to choose between our distributors, our customers, and ourselves.

As a last example, we are fortunate in having within our company another division that also is growing rapidly; it needs to build a new manufacturing plant, but a town in an adjoining state has offered much more substantial tax concessions than the town in which we have operated for 60 years, and in which, let us assume, there is substantial unemployment and need for additional tax revenues. Our code of ethics says that we will be "good citizens" in every community in which we operate, but it does not explain how to choose between communities, or what being a "good citizen" really means.

Ethical dilemmas are conflicts between economic performance and social performance, with the social performance being expressed as obligations to employees, customers, suppliers, distributors, and the general public. Ethical codes can express a general sense of the obligation members of senior management feel towards those groups, but the codes cannot help a middle- or lower-level manager choose between the groups, or between economic and social performance. Should we reduce employment and increase our profits? Should we eliminate our wholesalers and cut our prices? Should we build in another city and reduce our taxes? Should we—and this is the reason I have included the code of ethics of Johnson and Johnson, Inc.—spend over $100 million removing Tylenol from the shelves of every store in the country after the nonprescription drug was found to have been deliberately poisoned in the Chicago area during 1982, causing the deaths of four individuals. James Burke, chairman of Johnson and Johnson, credits that code

THE ETHICS CODE OF JOHNSON AND JOHNSON, "OUR CREDO"

We believe our first responsibility is to the doctors, nurses and patients, to mothers and all others who use our products and services.

In meeting their needs everything we do must be of high quality.

We must constantly strive to reduce our costs in order to maintain reasonable prices.

Customers' orders must be serviced promptly and accurately.

Our suppliers and distributors must have an opportunity to make a fair profit.

We are responsible to our employees, the men and women who work with us throughout the world.

Everyone must be considered as an individual.

We must respect their dignity and recognize their merit.

They must have a sense of security in their jobs.

Compensation must be fair and adequate, and working conditions clean, orderly and safe.

Employees must feel free to make suggestions and complaints.

There must be equal opportunity for employment, development and advancement for those qualified.

We must provide competent management, and their actions must be just and ethical.

We are responsible to the communities in which we live and work and to the world community as well.

We must be good citizens—support good works and charities and bear our fair share of taxes.

We must encourage civic improvements and better health and education.

We must maintain in good order the property we are privileged to use, protecting the environment and natural resources.

Our final responsibility is to our stockholders.

Business must make a sound profit.

We must experiment with new ideas.

Research must be carried on, innovative programs developed and mistakes paid for.

New equipment must be purchased, new facilities provided and new products launched.

Reserves must be created to provide for adverse times.

When we operate according to these principles, the stockholders should realize a fair return.

Source: Company annual report for 1982, p. 5.

THE ETHICS CODE OF BORG-WARNER CORPORATION, "TO REACH BEYOND THE MINIMAL"

Any business is a member of a social system, entitled to the rights and bound by the responsibilities of that membership. Its freedom to pursue economic goals is constrained by law and channeled by the forces of a free market. But these demands are minimal, requiring only that a business provide wanted goods and services, compete fairly, and cause no obvious harm.

For some companies that is enough. It is not enough for Borg-Warner. We impose upon ourselves an obligation to reach beyond the minimal. We do so convinced that by making a larger contribution to the society that sustains us, we best assure not only its future vitality, but our own.

This is what we believe. . . .

We believe in the dignity of the individual. However large and complex a business may be, its work is still done by people dealing with people. Each person involved is a unique human being, with pride, needs, values and innate personal worth. For Borg-Warner to succeed we must operate in a climate of openness and trust, in which each of us freely grants others the same respect, cooperation and decency we seek for ourselves.

We believe in our responsibility to the common good. Because Borg-Warner is both an economic and social force, our responsibilities to the public are large. The spur of competition and the sanctions of the law give strong guidance to our behavior, but alone do not inspire our best. For that we must heed the voice of our natural concern for others. Our challenge is to supply goods and services that are of superior value to those who use them; to create jobs that provide meaning for those who do them; to honor and enhance human life, and to offer our talents and our wealth to help improve the world we share.

Box continued on next page.

with guiding the actions of his company. "This document (the code of ethics) spells out our responsibilities to all our constituencies: consumers, employees, community, and stockholders. It served to guide all of us during the crisis, when hard decisions had to be made in what were often excruciatingly brief periods of time. All of our employees worldwide were able to watch the process of the Tylenol withdrawal and subsequent reintroduction in tamper-resistant packaging, confident of the way in which the decisions would be made. There was a great sense of shared pride in the knowledge that the Credo was being tested... and it worked!" I think that we can agree that the employees of Johnson and Johnson should be proud of the response of their firm, which put consumer safety

We believe in the endless quest for excellence. Though we may be better today than we were yesterday, we are not as good as we must become. Borg-Warner chooses to be a leader—in serving our customers, advancing our technologies, and rewarding all who invest in us their time, money, and trust. None of us can settle for doing less than our best, and we can never stop trying to surpass what already have been achieved.

We believe in continuous renewal. A corporation endures and prospers only by moving forward. The past has given us the present to build on. But to follow our visions to the future, we must see the difference between traditions that give us continuity and strength, and conventions that no longer serve us—and have the course to act on that knowledge. Most can adapt after change has occurred; we must be among the few who anticipate change, shape it to our purpose, and act as its agents.

We believe in the commonwealth of Borg-Warner and its people. Borg-Warner is both a federation of businesses and a community of people. Our goal is to preserve the freedom each of us needs to find personal satisfaction while building the strength that comes from unity. True unity is more than a melding of self-interests; it results when values and ideals are also shared. Some of ours are spelled out in these statements of belief. Others include faith in our political, economic and spiritual heritage; pride in our work and our company; the knowledge that loyalty must flow in many directions; and a conviction that ownership is strongest when shared. We look to the unifying force of these beliefs as a source of energy to brighten the future of our company and all who depend on it.

Source: Company booklet, published 1982.

ahead of company profits, but we also have to agree that that response, and that priority ranking, is not unequivocally indicated in the Credo of the company.

NO

Lisa H. Newton

THE MANY FACES OF THE
CORPORATE CODE

We seem to be in another of our code-writing phases. Interest in the development of corporate codes of ethics—by which term we encompass corporate Aspirations, Beliefs, Creeds, Guidelines and so on through the alphabet—has continued to rise since the 1970's, in tandem with the interest in the teaching and taking of ethics, in colleges and workplaces alike. In what follows, I take on some of the dominant themes in the codes of ethics literature, in an attempt to give a partial overview of the state of the art in the formulation of the corporate code.

The attempt turns out to be a study in multiple function. The much-recommended "corporate code of ethics" serves a diversity of functions, and must avoid a similar diversity of pitfalls. Some of these we will survey; to anticipate the end, we will discover that for maximum effectiveness and ethical validity, each code ought to meet three specifications:

1. In its *development and promulgation*, the code must enjoy the maximum participation of the officers and employees of the corporation (the principle of *participation*);
2. In its *content*, the code must be coherent with general ethical principles and the dictates of conscience (the principle of *validity*);
3. In its *implementation*, the code must be, and must be seen to be, coherent with the lived commitments of the company's officers (the principle of *authenticity*).

CLEAR AND PRESENT NEED

Businesses ought to have codes of ethics, if for no other reason than to allay real doubts that businessmen are capable of morality at all. Leonard Brooks has recently taken note of the " . . . crisis of confidence about corporate activity. Many corporate representations or claims have low credibility, including those made regarding financial dealings and disclosure, environmental protection, health and safety disclosures related to both employees and customers, and questionable payments." That is quite a list of things to be distrusted about. If we were looking for a blanket indictment of business, that one ought to cover the ballpark.[1] Or as Michael Hoffman and Jennifer Moore put it somewhat more concisely, it is the opinion of many of our wiser heads that "... business faces a true crisis of legitimacy."[2]

We cannot, *pace* Milton Friedman, leave the governance of the corporation to the forces of the market. While the market may bring about economic efficiency, Gerald Cavanagh points out, it cannot guarantee that corporate performance will be ethically and socially sensitive. Here the responsibility lies with the Board of Directors and top management, and it is "essential that board and management step up to the task," ascertain the ethical climate already prevailing and guide policy and decision in ethical directions. He adds as a final qualification that "while codes, structures and monitoring can encourage ethical decisions, it is even more important to have ethical people in the firm who want to make ethical judgments, know how to, and are not afraid to do so."[3] This is surely true: there is no structure or device in the universe, let alone within the capability of the American business community, that will keep people moral if they are determined to be immoral. But most people, at least most businesspeople, it seems are really neither one nor the other; they are prepared to be either, depending on the prevailing culture, and that is where the code can help.

There is nothing new in the aspiration to ethical codes. As early as 1961, Fr. Raymond Baumhart's survey of 2,000 business managers showed two-thirds of them interested in developing codes of ethics, which they thought would improve the ethical level of business practice.[4] By the seventies, public attention reinforced that view. George Benson traces the current effort on codes to the revelations on foreign and domestic bribery in government investigations 1973–1976, leading to the Foreign Corrupt Practices Act of 1977.[5] In the mid-seventies, W. Michael Blumenthal, then CEO of Bendix, went so far as to propose that the business executives of America organize a professional association to develop a comprehensive code of ethics for business with a review panel to enforce it. The idea died at the time, but might be worth following up at some point.[6] To this day, the most highly placed businessmen support the development of codes of ethics. In a survey conducted by Touche Ross in October, 1987, 1,082 respondents concluded that the most effective way to encourage ethical business behavior was the adoption of a code of ethics—outscoring the adoption of further legislation by 19%.[7] Nor is this support surprising. Ethics pays, not just in public relations but in company work. As the Business Roundtable, an association of Chief Executive Officers of major U.S. companies, concluded in 1988,

> It may come as a surprise to some that... corporate ethics programs are not mounted primarily to improve the reputation of business. Instead, many executives believe that a culture in which ethical concern permeates the whole organization is necessary to the self-interest of the company.... In the view of the top executives represented in this study, there is no conflict between ethical practices and acceptable profits. Indeed, the first is a necessary precondition for the second.[8]

To be sure, we can, at least in theory, behave like saints without a code to describe how we are behaving. But a written document reinforces an intention to be ethical—as a reminder, as a guide, and as a focus for the solidarity of the corporate officers in their attempts to run the company along the lines it lays down. And beyond this, there is the first concern mentioned: that the public is, probably justifiably, concerned over the proclivities of the business community and interested in seeing tangible proof of its intention to behave.

So a public commitment to ethics serves at least two functions: it addresses the concerns of the public and it reinforces (and clarifies) a bottom-line-justified interest in ethical behavior on the part of the officers. A third reason to take ethics seriously, address the subject explicitly, and articulate provisions to enforce it, is simple realism. As Freeman and Gilbert point out, as long as organizations are composed of human beings, no organizational task can proceed, nor can any cogent corporate strategy be formulated, without recognizing that these human beings have values. Their "First Axiom of Corporate Strategy," "Corporate strategy must reflect an understanding of the values of organizational members and stakeholders," is derived directly from the discovery that the human players in the corporate enterprise very often act in accordance with personal and cultural ethical imperatives, and that the corporation relegates itself to irrelevance if it fails to recognize this fact. Their second Axiom, "Corporate strategy must reflect an understanding of the ethical nature of strategic choice," acknowledges the interaction between corporate direction and private value. It is essential that the choices made by management in strategic planning meet the ethical standards implicit in the stakeholders' values.[9] The authors note the current fashion for describing strategy formulation as if persons did not exist, and point out at some length the errors of such attempts.[10]

WHY CODES FAIL

We sometimes take note of "widespread skepticism" as to the effectiveness of codes and the motivation behind their development. That skepticism bears some examination. Oddly, the doubts do not seem to have their roots in the business community, whose opinions are captured above. It seems to originate in the academic community of the business schools, possibly due to misunderstandings on the nature of valid corporate codes. LaRue Tone Hosmer states well the prevailing error:

> Ethical codes are statements of the norms and beliefs of an organization. These norms and beliefs are generally proposed, discussed, and defined by the senior executives in the firm and then published and distributed to all of the members. Norms, of course, are standards of behavior; they are the ways the senior people in the organization want the others to act when confronted with a given situation.[11]

Again,

> The beliefs in an ethical code are standards of thought; they are the ways that the senior people in the organization want others to think.[12]

With that understanding, no wonder that he must immediately insist that "[t]his is not censorship"! Although that insistence is hardly reinforced with his following, "the intent is to encourage ways of thinking and patterns of attitudes that will lead towards the wanted behavior."

And with both of those understandings in place, again it is not surprising that his evaluation of codes is negative: "Do ethical codes work? Are they helpful in conveying to all employees the moral standards selected by the board of directors and president? Not really."[13] The problem with the code he describes is not only that it is not effective—taking no essential account of the nature of the business, let alone the pre-existing commitments of the people to whom it is supposed to apply, how could it be? —but that it is not ethical. The basis for its norms is, it appears, completely subjective, founded on the whim of whoever happens to be in the executive offices the day that it occurs to a CEO to write a code of ethics; its application is coercive, being conceived by a more powerful group to apply to a less powerful group (but not to themselves); and there is no built-in check to see that it will actually help the company and its employees achieve the ends of the business. In short, it fails by any standards of reasonableness, and why on earth any firm would be interested in such a code is puzzling beyond the norm for such writings. (As Richard DeGeorge points out, we are occasionally willing to allow short lists of rules to be simply imposed on us, as long as the author is reliably known to be God. Senior officers, even CEO's, are not God.)[14]

While we have Hosmer's example before us, we may take the opportunity to extract some more general ethical principles from the critique. The code he describes was brought into existence by a few people in a few remote offices, enlisting the energies of none of the lower-ranking employees of the company. For this reason it fails on any measure of democracy, that understanding of governance that holds participation in policy formulation to be a part of justice; and it fails on any estimate of likely relevance to the situation of those excluded employees. The temptations that beset the stockman and secretary are best known to them, and it is inherently unwise to draw up rules without drawing on their experience. To avoid both sets of failures, it is essential to include as many employees as possible in the development process. This imperative we may call the *principle of participation*.

Second, the content of the code is completely unspecified save by reference to its authors—its provisions are those that strike the CEO and his golfing buddies as good, at the time they write it. Given their understandings of justice (see above and below), we are not inspired to confidence in their intuitions, but that is quite beside the point. Subjective presentations of this type can never qualify as imperatives with the authority of ethics. The provisions of a code must be reasoned, logically consistent, defended by reasoned argument, and coherent with the usual understandings of ethics: they must demonstrate respect for the individual, a commitment to justice, and sensitivity to the rights and interests of all parties affected by corporate action. We may call this requirement the *principle of validity*.

Third, it is assumed that the code is written by the senior officers, but that they themselves are not bound by it, and are therefore by implication perfectly free to ignore it or defy it if that is what they want to do. No liberty could be more destructive. People will do not as they are told, but as it is modeled to them; the company's values are trumpeted in the acts of the highest ranking employees, and need appear nowhere else. Again there is a violation of justice, in the development of a set of rules from which a privileged few shall be exempt, and again there is gross inattention to effectiveness. Whatever we may not know about codes, we know for sure that the real culture of a corporation will be embodied in the behavior of the senior officers, especially the CEO, and that it is imperative to secure the allegiance and the compliance of those persons for a code to be taken seriously; we may call this imperative the *principle of authenticity*. Hosmer's understanding of a corporate code violates all three principles, and condemns itself to ineffectiveness through its violations.

In the limiting case, then, a purported "code" can be no more than some authority's attempt to impose whimsical rules, which are bound to fail. A second type of code that is doomed to failure is the oracular code, confined to bare rules or ideals, no matter how derived or promulgated, with no commentary or explanation grounding the rule in experience.

> The difficulty with many codes is not that they prescribe what is immoral, but that they fail to be truly effective in helping members of the profession or company to act morally. To be moral means not only doing what someone says is right, but also knowing *why* what one does is right, and assuming moral responsibility for the action. How were the provisions of the code arrived at? On what moral bases do the injunctions stand?[15]

The standard instruction at the end of such codes, to discuss any dilemmas with the legal office, won't do it; they don't know morality. Implicit in this objection is a strong suggestion that the code must serve an educational function. This is correct; we will come back to this point.

A third and common way for codes to fail is through failure of the highest executives to take the provisions seriously, not only as they apply to themselves (the principle of authenticity, above), but as they apply to the company's management policies (especially "management by objectives") and other standard procedures. If the CEO honestly believes in the provisions, and takes the lead in modeling and enforcing them, if top management follows suit, and if the company's reward and punishment structure reinforces those provisions consistently, the code may well achieve its purpose even if it fails as a model of logical coherence. If they do not [do] so, there is very little chance that anyone else will either, at least when no one is watching. "Management needs to understand the real dynamics of its own organization. For example, how do people get ahead in the company? What conduct is actually rewarded, what values are really being instilled in employees?"[16] And the modeling and enforcement must be spread throughout the company. As Andy Sigler, CEO of Champion International and initiator of one of the best corporate codes in existence, put it, "Making speeches and sending letters just doesn't do it. You need a culture and peer pressure that spells out what is acceptable and isn't and why. It involves training, education, and follow-up."[17] For example, the institutionalization of any code must include protection from retaliation by supervisors against whistleblowers.[18] Kenneth Arrow would go further, arguing that any effective code must not only be fused into the corporate culture, but "accepted by the significant operating institutions and transmitted from one generation of executives to the next through standard operating procedures [and] through education in business schools."[19]

HOW CODES SUCCEED

The first condition for success is a commitment to the promotion of ethical behavior in a company—not to better public relations, nor to more certain deterrence of Federal inspectors, nor to the terror of an occasional bad apple, but to make the whole company a better and finer employer, producer, resident and citizen. For starters, the business community must take a leaf from the book of the professions, who have seen themselves as moral communities from the outset.[20] Like the professions, the corporation must take its status as a moral agent seriously. (There is almost a note of surprise in Leonard Brooks' observation that nowadays, there is a public expectation that if managers are caught *in flagrante delicto* [in the act of committing a misdeed], as they sometimes are, they will be punished. "This is a significant change because it is signalling that our society no longer regards the interests of the corporation or its shareholders to be paramount in importance. Neither corporate executives nor professionals can operate with impunity any longer, because society now expects them to be accountable.")[21] It certainly does.

From that basic commitment should follow a commitment to a process aimed at gathering that ethos from, and infusing it throughout, the entire company. Our first and third specifications, the principle of participation and the principle of authenticity, are two phases of that process commitment. The whole company (starting from the top) must commit itself to the development of the corporate code; the whole company (including the most junior members) must contribute to the process of deliberation; and the whole company (again, especially the top) must be, and feel, bound to obey and to exemplify it.

The imperative of validity is no more than a remote test of the coherence of the content. In accordance with the examples set by the professions, it is not essential for a cede to be a model of academic ethics. The requirement that the code be in conformity with theory does not mean that the code must explicitly signal the kind of reasoning that validates it. Earlier in this enterprise academicians were perhaps too insistent, and codecrafters too self-conscious, on this point; earlier discussions of the issue of corporate and professional codes were known to break down on the issue of "consequentialist vs. deontological moral reasoning." Both are necessarily included in the development of a corporate ethic. As Robin and Reidenbach point out, maintaining a certain kind of "ethical profile" (e.g. strong customer orientation for a sales-driven industry) is absolutely essential for the bottom line—there is no more utilitarian requirement. Yet the "core values" extracted from that profile (e.g. "Treat customers with respect and honesty,... the way you would want your family treated") can be derived from any system of primary duties, and are deontological in form and function. Any good formulation of a company's creed should be subject to verification by both kinds of moral reasoning.[22]

As Robin and Reidenbach emphasize, the code must be drawn to reflect the aims of the particular set of business practices with which the company is concerned. The ruling ideal of the code might equally be integrity of the practitioners, the excellence of craftsmanship, or the dedication to serve the client/customer, depending on the type of business it is. One of the first principles of "excellence" in the running of any company—the imperative to "stick to the knitting"—entails that a code for one industry, or one kind of company, need not apply with equal force to any others.

Along that line, be it noted that there are many reasons why a code cannot be all things to all people. Critics with certain key areas of interest, for instance, will often discover limits in codes that might not occur to the rest of us. Pat Werhane, for instance, complains that codes "usually tell the employee what he or she is not permitted to do, but they seldom spell out worker rights."[23] She goes on to argue that they tend to turn employees into legalists, obedient to the letter of the regulation but ignorant of its moral spirit.

The solution to both problems may lie in the shift of focus from dead rule to living dialogue. I am inclined to argue that the real value of the code does not lie in the finished product, rules with explanations that all must obey, but in the process by which it came to be. The first call for participation is an invitation to the employee to look into his conscience, discover his own moral commitments, and attempt to prioritize and formulate them. This may be the first time he has ever been asked to take on that job, and the educational value is enormous. The second phase of the participatory process includes the discovery of community consensus, a dialogue in which the employee must test his perceptions against those of others, re-examine and perhaps replace those that do not meet the test, and discover the defenses of those that do. However the code emerges, we will have much more articulate employees at the end of the process than we had at the beginning. And in this articulation is implicit genuine self-awareness: the employee now has his moral beliefs where he can see and get at them, and can be educated to apply them in new and creative ways should the situation around him change.

And it will change. Change was always a fact in the American business community, and very rapid, almost chaotic, change an occasional reality. Now, as Tom Peters points out, partly at his instigation, it has become a conscious policy. The continuation of that dialogue is needed especially as firms radically reorganize themselves, destroying the traditional departmental divisions and job descriptions. In the absence of traditional guides, all members of the corporation will need new and extraordinary norms to govern practice, and there is no substitute for a dialogical process in place as the change happens.[24]

NOTES

1. Leonard J. Brooks, "Corporate Codes of Ethics," *Journal of Business Ethics* 8 (1989):117–129, p. 119.

2. W. Michael Hoffman and Jennifer Mills Moore, *Business Ethics*, second edition. New York: McGraw Hill, 1990, p. 2.

3. Gerald F. Cavanagh, *American Business Values*, second edition. Englewood Cliffs, New Jersey: Prentice-Hall, 1984, p. 159.

4. Raymond C. Baumhart, S. J., "How Ethical Are Businessmen?" *Harvard Business Review* 39 (July–August 1961):166–71.

5. George C. S. Benson, "Codes of Ethics," *Journal of Business* 8 (1989):305–319, p. 306.

6. W. Michael Blumenthal, "New Business Watchdog Needed," *The New York Times*, May 25, 1975, F1; and "R_x for Reducing the Occasion of Corporate Sin," *Advanced Management Journal* 42 (Winter 1977):4–13.

7. Touche Ross, *Ethics in American Business: An Opinion Survey of Key Business Leaders on Ethical Standards and Behavior*. New York: Touche Ross, 1988, p. 14. The sample included only chief

executive officers of companies with S500 million or more in annual sales, deans of business schools and members of Congress.

8. *Corporate Ethics: A Prime Business Asset*. New York: The Business Roundtable, 1988, p. 9.

9. R. Edward Freeman and Daniel R. Gilbert, Jr., *Corporate Strategy and the Search for Ethics*. Englewood Cliffs, New Jersey: Prentice-Hall, 1988, pp. 6–7.

10. *Loc. cit*. See also p. 138, and p. 197, n.25.

11. LaRue Tone Hosmer, *The Ethics of Management*. Homewood, Illinois: Irwin, 1987, p. 153.

12. *Ibid*. p. 154.

13. *Loc. cit*. p. 154.

14. Richard T. DeGeorge, *Business Ethics*, third edition. New York, Macmillan, 1990, p. 390.

15. DeGeorge, *op. cit*. p. 391.

16. William H. Shaw, *Business Ethics*. Belmont, California: Wadsworth Publishing Company, 1991, p. 175.

17. Andrew Sigler, CEO of Champion International, cited in "Businesses Are Signing Up for Ethics 101," *Business Week*, February 15, 1988, p. 56.

18. Leonard J. Brooks, "Corporate Codes of Ethics," *Journal of Business Ethics* 8 (1989):117–129, p. 124.

19. Kenneth J. Arrow, "Social Responsibility and Economic Efficiency," *Public Policy* 21 (Summer 1973):42.

20. Mark S. Frankel, "Professional Codes: Why, How, and With What Impact?" *Journal of Business Ethics* 8 (1989):109–115, p. 110.

21. Brooks, *op. cit*. p. 119.

22. Donald P. Robin and R. Eric Reidenbach, *Business Ethics: Where Profits Meet Value Systems*. Englewood Cliffs, New Jersey: Prentice-Hall, 1989, pp. 94–95.

23. Patricia H. Werhane, *Persons, Rights and Corporations*. Englewood Cliffs, New Jersey: Prentice-Hall, Inc. 1985, p. 159.

24. See Tom Peters, "Get Innovative or Get Dead (part one)," *California Management Review* 33 (Fall 1990):9–26.

POSTSCRIPT

Are Corporate Codes of Ethics Just for Show?

Why might a corporation's management decide to develop a corporate code of ethics, to sponsor or join lectures and workshops on ethics, or to hire consultants to run "ethics training programs" for their middle managers? There are numerous possible answers to this question: The company may be in the headlines again for falsifying time sheets for government projects, and management wishes to project a righteous image before sentencing; employees may be stealing supplies and the employers want to make their people more moral in order to cut costs; or managers may simply believe that ethics as a principle is important to the company.

There may be no single answer to that question in any given case. Surely, given the fiduciary obligations of management to the shareholders, and given the expectations of the community, the managers will stress different motivations for community service at shareholders' meetings. This is probably as it should be; people are complex beings and operate from mixed motivations in most areas of life. There may be no need to insist on purity of motive before an ethics project begins. Motives, after all, come immediately under scrutiny in any consideration of ethics, and it is natural to search for ulterior ones. Whatever the motivation, are efforts to improve corporate behavior often successful? Should we promote the adoption of corporate codes of ethics in all, some, or no companies?

SUGGESTED READINGS

Peter Drucker, "What is Business Ethics?" *The Public Interest* (Spring 1981).

Catherine C. Langlois and Bodo B. Schlegelmilch, "Do Corporate Codes of Ethics Reflect National Character? Evidence from Europe and the United States," *Journal of International Business Studies* (November 1990).

Maurica Lefebvre and Jang B. Singh, "The Content and Focus of Canadian Corporate Codes of Ethics," *Journal of Business Ethics* (October 1992).

Robert Solomon and Kristine Hanson, *It's Good Business* (Atheneum, 1985).

ISSUE 4

Should Casino Gambling Be Prohibited?

YES: Citizens' Research Education Network, from *The Other Side of the Coin: A Casino's Impact in Hartford* (December 16, 1992)

NO: William R. Eadington, from "The Proliferation of Commercial Gaming in America," *The Sovereign Citizen* (Fall 1994)

ISSUE SUMMARY

YES: The Citizens' Research Education Network, formed to evaluate the effects of Connecticut's rapidly growing enthusiasm for casino gambling, concludes that casinos are harmful to cities and that other avenues to urban revival should be pursued.

NO: Professor of economics William R. Eadington argues that gambling is a normal extension of commercial activity and that it can promote the welfare of areas that host casinos.

Cities in the United States grew to wealth and splendor with the expansion of heavy manufacturing and America's domination of the world markets following World War II. The cities attracted hundreds of thousands of immigrants in search of jobs, education, and a better life for themselves and their families. While the good times lasted, waves of immigrants educated their children and watched them move up into the mobile middle class and adopt a suburban lifestyle. When the bad times came, the last of those waves (notably the African Americans and Hispanics from the South and from the Caribbean) were left stranded in a city without jobs, without ways up or out, and with little hope for improvement.

In times of growth, the rich cities created and offered to the public an enormous variety of expensive services—medical, cultural, and social support—that were not available in the smaller towns. These services were funded by the high tax revenues from the manufacturers, who were forced to stay in the cities by their need for raw materials and labor—they could only operate where the railroads converged, the ships could dock, and very large numbers of people lived within walking distance of the plants.

Beginning in the 1950s, technological advance led to new forms of transportation for raw materials and made possible new types of factories that employed a fraction of the workforce demanded by the old ones. No longer did the factories have to stay in the cities, and taxes were much lower elsewhere, so they left. The educated middle class also left; they moved to the new suburbs, where they created new country villages with pleasant vistas and low property taxes, and where they could still use the city's resources if they wanted. Left behind, however, were the workers who could not move; the expensive services—the hospitals and universities; and various people who had drifted to the city because they needed those services but had no means by which to leave. The cities were left without a tax base and without any clear direction for an economic future.

Present initiatives to introduce casino gambling to cities, and the issue before us in this debate, result from two facts. First, traditional economic remedies are unlikely to help the cities. The services that the public demands from the cities are too expensive to support with any available enterprise that might choose to locate in a city. Manufacturing has been lost to technology and foreign competition, and the new information industries will not employ the city's poor and undereducated, feed its hungry, or care for its sick.

Second, casino gambling has shown itself to be a highly profitable enterprise. No coercive collection mechanisms are needed to transfer money from private pockets to the public good; people choose freely and happily to spend their money at the gaming tables. Costs are low and revenues are spectacular. For instance, the Mashantucket Pequot Indians in Connecticut set up a casino on their reservation in 1992. The casino now supports and educates every member of the once-destitute tribe with its income; it contributes handsomely to Native American cultural foundations; it employs hundreds of non-Indian residents of the state; and, in addition to what it contributes to the state in taxes, it transfers $130 million each year to Connecticut as quid pro quo for the casino's monopoly on slot machines.

Inner cities are dying for lack of jobs and money; casinos supply both, without adding to the tax burden of the marginal industries and dwindling middle class that remains within the city boundaries. The argument to bring casino gambling into the cities seems compelling. However, critics have expressed concern about the possible relationship between casinos and crime, especially organized crime. Critics also cite the many problems associated with compulsive gambling and the additional drain that impoverished gamblers put on social services.

As you read the following selections, remember that no one can really know for certain how far the market for gaming will continue to expand or what effects casinos will have on aging urban centers.

THE OTHER SIDE OF THE COIN:
A CASINO'S IMPACT IN HARTFORD

HUMAN COSTS SUMMARY

Casino Supporters' Claims vs. Reality

Neighborhoods

Claims: Casinos will revitalize Hartford.

Reality: Casinos created land speculation in Atlantic City that led to the mass destruction of homes and businesses that served local residents. Nevada has a higher rate of poverty than Connecticut. While jobs are being created in Las Vegas at a high rate, older central neighborhoods do not appear to benefit. Rather, new neighborhoods are being built on the outskirts of the city to house workers who move into Las Vegas from other areas. Las Vegas is not just the exciting, prosperous town casino supporters would have us believe. Riots broke out in sections of Las Vegas following the Rodney King verdict, indicating a high level of frustration and anger in some Las Vegas neighborhoods. There is no evidence that casinos will bring anything to Hartford neighborhoods but dislocation, crime, and traffic.

Gambling Addiction

Claims: Addicted gambling is a small problem.

Reality: Connecticut already has one of the highest levels of gambling addiction measured and studies have shown that casinos are especially inviting to addicted gamblers. Pathological gambling is a growing problem that affects about 160,000 people in Connecticut. Furthermore, it is estimated that for each addicted gambler, 10 to 17 other people (family members, employers, employees, crime victims, creditors) are negatively affected by the addicted gambler's behavior. Addicted gamblers often commit crimes for money to continue gambling and by the time they seek treatment, many

From Citizens' Research Education Network, *The Other Side of the Coin: A Casino's Impact in Hartford* (December 16, 1992). Notes omitted.

have no money, no job, and no insurance. Therefore, the public costs to treat gambling addiction are much higher than other addictions. In addition to crime and addiction treatment, it has been estimated that each addicted gambler costs society $30,000 in "abused money" and lost productivity. It is believed that almost 25% of addicted gamblers attempt suicide.

Youth

Claims: The complex will provide family entertainment. Under-age persons will not be allowed in the casino.

Reality: Gambling addiction is twice as high among youths as adults and casinos have poor records for keeping out underage gamblers. One study of underage college students near Atlantic City found that 40% of them had gambled in a nearby casino. Nearly one-third of high school students in New Jersey reported gambling weekly or more in 1987, more than three times the rate in other states. Among the adult population, problem gamblers are more likely than other gamblers to have started gambling before they were 15 years old. The marketing of casinos as part of a family entertainment complex exposes more children to gambling who may later develop gambling addiction.

HUMAN COSTS OF CASINOS

Residents of Hartford are facing multiple crises in the 1990s. Drug abuse continues to outpace efforts to discourage it; unemployment is high; the schools are struggling to educate children with too little money and support; child abuse and neglect is commonplace; and alcoholism still destroys families. As businesses close or move away, hope grows dimmer. There is no place for residents to buy groceries at a fair and reasonable price. Child care is difficult to find. Is a casino going to meet any of the real needs of Hartford residents?

CASINOS AND THE NEIGHBORHOODS

While all of Hartford would be affected in some way by the presence of a casino, the proposed location of the casino complex makes its impact especially important to people living in Hartford's north end. The preliminary proposal by Steve Wynn would require the demolition of Barnard-Brown School and the Hartford Graduate Center. Right near the site lie several offices, social service agencies, and apartments. Those will all be affected by the casino complex. The next concern is what kind of development will tend to spring up around the casino and how will that affect the people who live and work in the neighboring community?

The impact of the casino on the nearby neighborhood would depend largely on the legislation controlling its operation. One possibility is that speculative investment in Hartford real estate could destroy residential areas and force businesses that serve Hartford residents to close. This was the case in Atlantic City in large part because the city government gave the impression that it would allow casinos in any part of the city. Although a plan was adopted that limited casinos to specific areas, the city regularly granted exemptions to that restriction. The result was that developers bought property all over the city in hopes that someone else may eventually buy it from them (at a much higher price) to build a casino.

Once speculators owned land, they found it easier to tear down the existing buildings while they waited for a casino developer to come along. By tearing down the buildings, they saved money on property taxes. Needed housing for residents of Atlantic City was thus destroyed, although few of the sites ever became casinos.

The issue comes down to what speculators *believe* is the attitude of city officials regarding further development, not what their attitudes really are. If government leaders appear divided on this issue or speculators believe that new leaders will be elected who will favor further casino development, land speculation and displacement of city residents could result.

Even if speculators believe that no more casinos will ever be allowed in Hartford, the construction of the casino complex and supporting facilities will affect the neighboring area. Virtually all of the visitors to the casino will be arriving by car or bus. Many will use the highways; many may seek short-cuts through the surrounding streets. (Since casinos are generally a 24-hour business, the effect of cars and buses at all hours could be very disturbing to nearby residents.) Roads may have to be widened. Perhaps parking garages will be added. All we really know is that the area will be affected, probably in a way that does not preserve the unique architecture of that neighborhood or benefit the residents or small businesses owners.

The exact location of a Hartford casino is not set in stone, but the question for the people in the neighborhoods near any casino site has to be whether they trust the political process enough to believe that it will prevent destructive speculation and development that displaces current residents and businesses. Hartford has experience with that kind of development: Constitution Plaza replaced a thriving neighborhood that had supported generations of Hartford immigrants; I-84 was built where other neighborhoods had once been, causing the city to lose some wonderful old buildings. True community development happens when people in an area have better housing, better job opportunities, and chances to start their own businesses. The steam-roller style development of Las Vegas casino developers won't benefit the people who live in our communities.

PROBLEM AND PATHOLOGICAL GAMBLING

It is estimated that there are between 43,000 and 94,000 pathological gamblers in Connecticut, plus between 61,000 and 121,000 problem gamblers. Together, that represents about 6.3% of the adult population of Connecticut.

Gambling addiction is a real problem that needs to be carefully considered and addressed. Addicted gamblers are split into two groups by mental health experts. People with the addiction are problem gamblers; those with severe addictions are pathological gamblers.

Pathological gambling has symptoms similar to those of addictions to alcohol or other drugs. Increasing amounts of money are gambled; the gambler becomes obsessed with betting and acts without concern for the impact on himself or others. (Three out of four addicted gamblers are male.) He borrows money to gamble beyond his ability to repay it in hopes that he will get lucky. Many begin to commit crimes in order to get money for gambling. Families suffer as gamblers use money that should be used to pay the rent or buy food. By the time an addicted gambler seeks treatment, he is often unemployed and/or uninsured. Therefore, the costs of treatment need to be paid by the public. Addicted gamblers also have no money to hire attorneys, so if an addicted gambler is charged with a crime, the public defender's office often must provide legal defense. The financial strain on the addicted gambler's family is often severe and the family may need public assistance. The public and personal costs of gambling addiction are, therefore, very high.

Experts on gambling addictions say that the social stigma that was once associated with gambling has been removed. At the same time, while people are bombarded with messages about the dangers of drug or alcohol abuse, no widespread effort exists to educate them about the dangers of gambling. As the State of Connecticut has progressed from charity bingo to the state lottery to pari-mutuel wagering to the daily lotto to casinos, the message is clear that gambling is now an acceptable form of recreation. Thus, more people are more likely to try gambling. Of those who try gambling, a certain percentage will be likely to develop a gambling addiction.

The only national study of gambling concluded that the availability of gambling in Nevada had caused an increase in gambling addiction. In that study, 0.77% of the adult population nationally scored as "probable compulsive gamblers" while 2.62% of Nevada residents scored as such. (People who had moved to Nevada recently or specifically for the gambling opportunities were not counted.) According to the State of Connecticut's consultant regarding gam-

bling, "All subsequent studies of the prevalence of problem gambling, regardless of the methods used, indicate that *casino gambling* is especially appealing to problem and pathological gamblers."

Gambling addiction does not strike all people equally. Rachel Volberg, a specialist in the study of problem gambling, has said, "Certain groups appear to be at greater risk for developing gambling related problems. Minority individuals, African Americans and Hispanics, seem to be at a somewhat greater risk; also, individuals under the age of 30, individuals with low income and low levels of education." ...

Financial Costs of Gambling Addiction
In addition to the pure social impact of gambling addiction, there are financial costs. While the exact costs associated with the high number of addicted gamblers in Connecticut are impossible to measure, estimates can be made. The Task Force on Gambling Addiction in Maryland estimated that the 50,000 pathological gamblers in that state cost "$1.5 billion annually in lost work productivity and embezzled, stolen or otherwise abused dollars." If that cost estimate holds true for Connecticut, **the cost of *pathological* gambling in this state is between $1.3 and $2.8 billion annually.** (This does not include similar costs for problem gamblers.)

Looked at another way, the cost for each addicted gambler is $30,000 per year in lost productivity and "abused" (i.e., embezzelled or stolen) money. (This estimate does not include the costs of law enforcement, medical treatment, or family support.) Thus, if 1,000 people develop a gambling addiction as a result of the great access and temptation of a downtown casino, it will cost society $30 million, plus the costs of law enforcement and addiction treatment, which are substantial. Much of this expense will have to be borne by Connecticut taxpayers.

Problem and pathological gambling should not be dismissed lightly. It is an expensive social problem that affects hundreds of thousands of people. Nationally, rates of addictive gambling have increased dramatically over the past two decades, growing right along with the increase in legal gambling options.

CASINOS AND YOUTH

Addictive gambling among high-school age persons is becoming a widely recognized crisis nationally. Although students are constantly exposed to messages about the dangers of drugs and alcohol, they are also told that gambling is a respectable form of entertainment. State sponsored gambling (i.e. the state lottery) strongly sends the message that gambling is acceptable. It is even presented as a virtue because revenues often go to good causes like education or the elderly. Advertising for state lotteries is widespread, misleading, and effective. More kids, therefore, try gambling and more become addicted.

It is estimated that about 5% of high school students have gambling addictions. Many have no trouble buying lottery tickets from careless vendors, and illegal bookies have been known to develop a large business from students. In 1987, almost one-third of the high school students in north, central, and south New Jersey stated that they gambled weekly or more. This is 3–5 times the rate in other states. It is estimated that at least one million minors gamble in Atlantic City casinos each year. One survey of college students at a New

Jersey campus near Atlantic City found that 40% of the under-21 students had illegally gambled at a nearby casino.

The cynical view of the current move to "family entertainment" centers in Las Vegas (as well as the complex proposed for Hartford) is that the gamblers of tomorrow are being groomed today. Gambling has left the smoke-filled back room and has become more widely accepted. Casinos are now being marketed as appropriate family vacation destinations. It is not yet known how that will affect the attitudes of children who grow up surrounded by this kind of gambling. Barriers to gambling that traditionally existed are being destroyed and it can be safely assumed that, in the future, more of today's children will gamble more money more often.

CRIME SUMMARY

Casino Supporters' Claims vs. Reality

Regular Crime

Claims: Casinos do not attract crime any more than would a Disney theme park.

Reality: Analysts have concluded that two-thirds of the crime increase expected from a new casino in New Orleans is because it is a casino, not because of the number of new visitors to the city. Casinos simply attract a different kind of customer (and criminal) than would a children's theme park. It is estimated that a 100,000-square foot casino in New Orleans that attracts 5 million visitors a year will cost the city about $5 million in law enforcement and court cost.

Organized Crime

Claims: Casino operators have no connection to organized crime.

Reality:

- Any business that creates the huge cash profits of the casino industry has a tendency to attract organized crime.
- Links between the most respected casino operators and organized crime have been exposed repeatedly. For example, early in 1992, the Las Vegas Police Department released a list of the associates of Charles Meyerson, a long-time friend and employee of Steve Wynn, who have ties to organized crime families. Meyerson's work card was revoked by the city for arranging a free five-night stay at the Mirage for three high-ranking members of the Genovese crime family in July of 1991 and Mr. Meyerson was accused by Las Vegas police of being an associate of Genovese crime boss Anthony "Fat Tony" Solerno. (A vice president and director of Wynn's company resigned his position in 1984 after he was seen by investigators visiting Solerno's headquarters in New York.)
- Traditionally, casinos have been used by organized crime to launder cash. The best way to prevent this is to report large cash transactions to authorities, but the IRS stated in August, 1992, that despite tough new reporting requirements, casino employees are still lax in reporting large cash transactions.
- Law enforcement experts say that organized crime infiltration of casino-related businesses and labor unions

is a very real problem. The United States Senate Permanent Subcommittee on Investigations found in 1984 that organized crime actively involved with the Hotel Employees and Restaurant Employees International Union. The Subcommittee concluded that the union locals in Las Vegas and Atlantic City were controlled by organized crime. In December 1990, the U.S. Justice Department brought a civil action against the Las Vegas local, alleging that it was controlled by the Bruno/Scarfo family of organized crime.

POTENTIAL IMPACT ON CRIME IN HARTFORD

It's a question as old as the casino business itself. Will the introduction of casinos increase the level of crime in the community? Everyone, including casino supporters, will agree that a casino will cause the crime rate to increase. But, the casino supporters also argue that *any attraction* that brings visitors to a city will cause crime. Crime is no more a reason to stop casinos, they argue, than any other tourist development.

Casinos vs. Disney World

Recently, a casino executive stated that the crime rate in Orlando—the home of Disney World—is higher than the crime rate in Atlantic City, even though they both have about 30 million visitors per year. The executive concluded that there is nothing about casinos themselves that attracts criminals.

A common sense way to compare the impact of casinos in Atlantic City with the impact of Disney in Orlando is to look at their reported crimes before and after the opening of these entertainment developments. While Orlando has experienced a disturbing increase in crime over the past 25 years, there is no noticeable jump in criminal activity immediately following the opening of Disney World. Between 1977 [when the first casino opened] and 1982 in Atlantic City, however, crime increased 237% and has stayed high since.

Furthermore, the crime rate increase or decrease each year in Orlando closely mirrors those of all of Florida. The increase in the crime rate in Atlantic City, however, jumped much higher than the crime rate seen in all of New Jersey in 1977.

Casino Crime Separated from Tourist Crime

Analysts at the University of New Orleans, Division of Business and Economic Research, did a study of casino crime to separate the effect of increased visitors from the effect of casino gambling per se.

They compiled data from 80 cities, large and small, and factored into their analysis of crime:

- number of visitors
- personal income
- poverty rates
- racial composition
- unemployment rates
- population density
- police expenditures

By accounting for all these factors that influence crime rates, they were able to separate the impact casino gambling has on crime *from the effect of increased tourism*. What they concluded was that in New Orleans, a 100,000 square foot casino with 4.9 million visitors a year would mean 3,802 additional crimes within the city. *More than two-thirds of those crimes (2,625)*

would be due to gambling, less than one-third (1,177) would be due to increased visitors to the city. They calculated that the new crime caused by the casino would cost the city almost $5 million per year in police and corrections spending, district attorney costs, and court costs. The State of Louisiana would also face the costs of housing additional convicted criminals in prison.

Clearly, casinos are different than other tourist attractions. They create an atmosphere that attracts a different group of people than does a Disney theme park. Hartford needs to take this certain increase in crime into consideration before allowing a casino in the city.

CASINOS AND ORGANIZED CRIME

Experts disagree over the extent that organized crime is involved in the casino gambling industry. Many believe that tight regulation of casinos has driven organized crime away over the past 30 years or so.

Links to the Mob

An in-depth analysis of organized crime and its involvement with casinos is beyond the scope of this analysis. Of particular interest to Hartford, however, may be the legal troubles of Mirage Resorts employees over the years. The *Las Vegas Review-Journal* has published stories detailing links between one long-time Mirage Resorts employee and organized crime. His history of association with organized crime figures (he claims to have not known about their criminal ties) shows the kind of "innocent" trouble casino operators can get into.

Corruption of the unions that staff casinos is also a major problem. The U.S. Senate Permanent Subcommittee on Investigations found in 1984 that organized crime was active in the Hotel Employees and Restaurant Employees International Union and concluded that the union locals in Las Vegas and Atlantic City were controlled by organized crime. In December 1990, the U.S. Justice Department brought a civil action against the Las Vegas local, alleging that it was controlled by the Bruno/Scarfo family of organized crime.

Political Corruption

Any industry with as much wealth as the casino business opens the door to inappropriate political influence. Political corruption has been a problem in Atlantic City both before and after the arrival of the casinos. Three mayors have been convicted of corruption since 1977 and three more have been forced to resign. Political corruption limits any government's ability to regulate or act in the community's best interest. The casino also presents an opportunity to build political patronage. Government officials may have the temptation to use their influence (gained from casino operators in exchange for their legislative support) to get jobs for friends, thereby giving the casino even more power to influence policy decisions.

Money Laundering

Another major drawback of the casino business is some of the customers it attracts. People who make a lot of money and operate on a cash basis (i.e. drug dealers or "mobsters") make excellent casino patrons because they have money to spare and are limited in how they can spend it. Federal regulations have been tightened over the years so that very large cash transactions through casinos have to be reported much as they are through banks, but the casino industry has a long history of looking the other way.

There have been repeated incidents of organized crime figures being associated with major casino hotel executives who claim ignorance of the mob ties.

Organized crime is a serious problem and law enforcement professionals around the country say that the threat of organized crime infiltration of casino-related businesses must be fully considered before allowing a casino in the city.

CONCLUSION

Public officials must look beyond personal gain or even state budget needs to make a determination of what is truly in the public's best interest. Urban casinos do not contribute to the public good, would ultimately harm the city, and should, therefore, not be allowed in Hartford.

Although the casino industry has already entered Connecticut through the Mashantucket Pequot reservation, bringing casinos to the cities of the state will create far more problems than it will solve.

Among the problems identified are:

- casino associated costs (law enforcement, gambling addiction, traffic) that exceed the casino generated public revenue;
- replacement of existing jobs with casino jobs;
- negative impact on non-casino businesses;
- failure to develop a convention or tourism industry in Hartford;
- increased levels of gambling addiction, especially among Hartford residents;
- the creation of a gambling environment in Connecticut that may act to discourage investment by other industries;

- negative influence on Hartford's youth, especially the unmistakable message that gambling is acceptable in light of the high rates of addicted teenage gamblers;
- higher rates of crime; and
- likely attraction of organized crime to Hartford.

Hartford would be best served by devoting its resources to developing and implementing a comprehensive economic development plan designed to create a diversified economy. Dependence on only one or two industries is not in Hartford's best interest.

NO

William R. Eadington

THE PROLIFERATION OF COMMERCIAL GAMING IN AMERICA

Commercial gaming has arrived in America in the 1990s. To understand this, it is worthwhile to begin by examining the phenomenal success of the Foxwood's Casino and High Stakes Bingo in Ledyard, Connecticut. This is an Indian casino, owned by the 260 tribal members of the Mashantuckett Pequot Indian tribe, which opened in February, 1992. The amount of revenue generated by the casino in gaming winnings—customer expenditures on table games—in its first year of operation exceeded $200 million. In their second year of operation, after they negotiated with the Governor of Connecticut for the right to have slot machines and an exclusive franchise on casinos in Connecticut in exchange for a minimum $100 million payment to the State, their gaming winnings will approach $500 million. In their third year of operation—1994—when they have doubled their size, their gross gaming revenues could approach $700 million. At that point, they will be generating almost as much revenue as all the casinos in Reno, Nevada.

For another comparison, if you were to take all the movie theaters in America, the Foxwood's Casino is already generating about 10% as much in revenue as is generated in all ticket sales to all movie theaters in this country. Furthermore, because of its monopoly status in New England, the casino's profit margins are likely to be approximately 50%. That is for a tribe that ten years ago only had three people living on the reservation.

The gaming industry in America is going through an unprecedented proliferation and expansion that carries with it some amazing stories, of which the Ledyard situation is one. It also poses some fascinating and quite complex challenges to public policy, with regard to the impact that gambling is likely to have on society.

We are in the midst of a near total reversal of legal commercial gaming opportunities for American citizens in terms of their presence and accessibility. We are actually in the midst of a phenomenon that is occurring world wide.

local convenience store and purchase a lottery ticket. In 1992 lottery sales in America were over $21 billion, and after payment of prizes to winners, lotteries generated gross revenues of about $10 billion to the various states that had them. Casinos, as late as 1989 still could only be found in two places in the United States, in Nevada and in Atlantic City. Yet only four years later, one could gamble legally casino style in Nevada and Atlantic City, New Jersey; in mining town small stakes casinos in South Dakota and Colorado; on riverboats in Iowa, Illinois and Mississippi, and soon Louisiana, Missouri and Indiana. Or one could go [to] Indian casinos in Connecticut, Michigan, Minnesota, Wisconsin, South Dakota, Washington, Arizona, California, Colorado, New York, and soon in Mississippi, Louisiana, Texas and Rhode Island. All of this has transpired in a period of four years.

There has also been an expansion of non-casino casino style gambling, in the form of slot machines, video poker machines, or—in the euphemistically more acceptable name—video lottery terminals. The spread of gaming devices has been quite rapid, with their introduction into bars and taverns or other age restricted locations in the states of Montana, South Carolina, South Dakota, Oregon, Louisiana, West Virginia and Rhode Island. It has also recently been considered by the legislature of the state of Massachusetts, among others.

What does the casino industry do? How big an industry is casino gaming? And how does it affect peoples lives?

In 1992, the gross winnings for the various gaming industries in the United States, including lotteries, casinos, race tracks, charitable gambling and Indian gaming, were nearly $30 billion. That is the total expenditure of all customers on various gambling products. This also reflects total player losses after payment of winnings, as well as gross revenues on gaming to the various operators and purveyors of gambling services. This is approximately 0.6% of disposable income in the United States; roughly one-dollar out of every $150 spent in America is spent on gambling. This represents about five times as much money as Americans spend on going out to the movies: it represents about the same amount of income that is earned by all stock brokerages and securities firms in America; it represents approximately one-fourth of the gross revenues of all attorneys in America. Gambling is not a small business, it is substantial in its revenues and in its presence in society, and it is in the midst of a phenomenal expansion.

What has happened to social attitudes concerning gambling, and why are we seeing this phenomenon occurring now, at this very point in time?

There have historically been three main arguments in opposition to gambling. All of these arguments have been undermined by trends in the past three decades. The arguments are as follows:

1. *Gambling leads to political corruption and brings organized crime into the mainstream of society.*

However, as has been discovered time and again, political corruption and the infiltration of organized crime into gambling occurs more often when gambling is illegal, or where it is set up legally with considerable discretion given to public officials who can essentially sell the economic rents from gambling to the highest bidders. Gambling, especially when it is presented with a high degree of competent and professional regulation, can be

3. Gambling creates compulsive gamblers.

The third argument against gambling, compulsive gambling, is a real issue. Society is gaining greater understanding over time of this phenomenon. Among those factors that have improved our understanding of compulsive gambling in recent years is that it is an affliction that affects only a small percentage of the population, estimated at between one and five percent of the adult population. It is unclear whether compulsive gambling is a psychological or a physiological phenomenon. It is also unclear whether it is truly an addiction or merely an irresponsibility, an immaturity, on the part of those who are so cursed. But society has chosen more and more to take the attitude that if most people want to gamble, and if most people can do so responsibly, than gambling should not be prohibited for the majority, just to protect a small minority who might be at fault anyway, and for whom prohibition of gambling might not stop them from destroying themselves through gambling or some other vice anyway.

In summary, society has changed its attitude from "gambling is wrong, gambling is a sin", to one of saying "It's ok to gamble". The policy questions have shifted from "Should we gamble or not?" to "Who gets to benefit by being the purveyors of gambling services?" With regard to this point, we have seen the various claimants come forward. The claimants on gambling are the following groups, all of whom are well deserving. Governments have said that they should be the purveyors of gambling services because clearly they must deal with the fiscal crisis that is pervasive throughout this country, and clearly the demands for public services cannot be met through continuing tax increases on the middle class and the poor. So if government gets to run gambling, they can generate important tax revenues, and turn around and spend it in a fashion that is beneficial for society.

A second group of claimants—charities —respond to this argument with the claim that, if we allow government to take the revenues from gambling, it is like throwing it into a black hole. Nothing good seems to come out of government. They can absorb as much income as they can without resolving their crises. Rather, society should let charities be the purveyors of gambling services. Charities throughout Canada, and charities in certain states in the United States such as North Dakota or Minnesota, have become major purveyors of gambling services. In Minnesota, for example—a state of about four million people—charitable organizations and not-for-profit organizations in 1990 grossed about $250 million from their legal charitable gambling, after payment of prizes. They certainly are in the gambling business, and their argument is, "Let us have the revenues from gambling because we will spend them directly on things of definite and distinct value for the community; as charities, we know how to do good things."

Another set of groups who are purporting to be the legitimate claimants to the right to offer gambling are cities, or regions, in partnership with private sector gambling corporations. We have seen a bit of this in Connecticut, with attempts to legalize casinos in Hartford and Bridgeport, and we have seen legalization of a number of casinos in the Midwest, on the basis that their communities need jobs; their communities need investments; their communities need to stimulate economic development and tourism.

The way they do this is to try to capture the same kinds of economic benefits that have accrued to Nevada and—to a lesser extent—New Jersey. The argument is, if the state would authorize a casino or casinos, private sector firms in partnership with political jurisdictions will create jobs; they will create investments; they will bring in tourists to the area; and everybody will benefit.

The fourth group of claimants are the Indian tribes in America. There is little doubt that, among all the minorities who have been treated in various ways by government programs over time, Indians have probably been the least effectively treated. The worst of the welfare cases in America have been Indian stories. After a combination of the emergence of Indian sovereignty as a well-defined right and a quirky law—the Indian Gaming Regulatory Act of 1988—along with some quite opportunistic situations that evolved for certain tribes, Indian gaming has become the most powerful economic development tool ever to develop for Indian tribes in America. Some tribes—such as the Mashantuckett Pequot of Connecticut—are becoming wealthy beyond their wildest expectations because of being at the right place at the right time with a set of circumstances that could be fully exploited.

Of the various claimants, one should probably concentrate on private sector casino development in league with cities, which is probably going to be the most important one over time. What are the jurisdictions who are legalizing casinos trying to do, and how effective are they likely to be? The motivation for places such as New Orleans, Kansas City, St. Louis, Davenport, Biloxi/Gulfport, Chicago, Bridgeport, Hartford and in Canada, Windsor and Montreal and Winnipeg have been to attempt to capture the economic benefits from casinos in the same manner as Nevada has done. These cities have looked at Las Vegas, which is a very interesting city for a number of reasons. They argue that they should be able to achieve the same successes.

Las Vegas is a city that most people would have claimed in 1960 was "all mobbed up". The common perception outside of Nevada was that Las Vegas was a city run for mobsters, by mobsters, in a very corrupt political system. However, Las Vegas is a city that for each of the last three decades has been among the five fastest growing metropolitan areas in the United States. It is a city that now has the ten largest hotels in the world. In terms of number of rooms, Las Vegas has more hotel rooms than both New York and London. Las Vegas is probably the best large convention city in the world today. They have the ability to accommodate over 100,000 visitors at one time. Las Vegas is also evolving in the same general direction as Orlando, Florida, with the construction of major amusement parks at a number of destination resort casino properties. In fact, the term "Las Orlando", has been used more and more commonly in recent years, and the term is actually getting to the point where one wonders whether the term Las Orlando, is an attempt to describe Las Vegas as a variant of Orlando, or an attempt to describe Orlando as a variant of Las Vegas.

The process of a rush to legalization of gambling has pointed out some very interesting patterns, and indeed, weaknesses in the American system. The first such weakness is that the American political system can be very myopic. It tends to concentrate on a single issue and run with that issue as long as it can. With regard to gambling, the dominant policy consideration used to be organized crime. That was the only point of debate: the concern that gambling inevitably led to involvement by organized crime and consequent political corruption.

If one examines the way that New Jersey wrote its Casino Control Act in 1977, and tries to see what their concerns were as embodied in the Act, it becomes very clear. The concerns of the Casino Control Act were to keep organized crime out of the casino gaming business, because that is its natural tendency. And that was the dominant way of thinking about commercial gaming until the late 1980s, especially with regard to casinos. And then —all of a sudden—concerns about organized crime diminished; they seemed to pass into posterity, into nostalgia. What replaced it was the primacy of economic benefits to be derived from gaming. Gambling's greatest social value is in creating economic benefits; thus, state after state has moved toward the legalization of gambling to capture those economic benefits.

There is a second weakness inherent in the American political system. This is the belief that if legislation works well in one place, it can work just as well in another jurisdiction, even though the safeguards may be slightly more relaxed and the circumstances somewhat different. There has been a very interesting and clear evolution in the legalization of casino style gambling in America. If we examine the third jurisdiction to legalize casinos, after Nevada and Atlantic City, we find it in a little place called Deadwood, South Dakota. Deadwood is about thirty miles from Mount Rushmore, and its population is about 1600 people. It is a small, remote, rural area. Deadwood peaked economically in the 1890s as a mining town, and it has not had much economic stimulus ever since. It is most famous for being the town where Wild Bill Hickock was shot in the back while playing poker, holding a hand of aces and eights, now known as the "dead man's" hand. The tourist attraction of Deadwood was the tomb of Wild Bill in Boot Hill, buried next to Calamity Jane.

In the 1980s, the town of Deadwood was literally falling apart. The city fathers argued the only way Deadwood could be saved would be to create a revenue source that will allow them to put some money aside for historic preservation of Deadwood. They were able to convince the voters of South Dakota in the 1988 election to authorize small stakes limited casino gambling in Deadwood. Five dollar maximum wagers were allowed, and no license could have more than thirty slot machines or table games. In November, 1989, Deadwood opened its first casinos and became the third jurisdiction in America to have casinos. Within a year every business in Deadwood had become a casino, and every other business was pushed out. In one sense, it was phenomenally successful; in another sense it was a disaster. People would travel six or eight hours to get to the slot machines of Deadwood.

Shortly thereafter, Iowa set up constrained riverboat gaming legislation that would allow no more than five dollar maximum wagers, and a person could lose no more than $200 per excursion. There was a belief among the good people of Iowa that the evils of gambling would show up if large wagers were allowed and if people were allowed to lose too much money in any given visit. Therefore, they legislated against it. They also allocated three percent of the gross winnings from their casinos for compulsive treatment programs, so that any social damage created by the casinos would be taken care of. They also mandated that —at least when the river was not frozen —gambling would have to take place on the riverboats while they were floating on the water. The belief—or symbolism —was that if all the sinning from gambling was taking place on the Mississippi River, then those sins, as they work their way back to shore, would be washed pure by the time they reached shore so as to not infect the good people of Iowa.

So Iowa and South Dakota set the tone for responsible, remote, small stakes gambling. But what happened next? Illinois is right across the river from Iowa and so they decided they did not want Iowa to get all the gaming revenues from their citizens, so they passed a riverboat gaming bill as well. However, they failed to put in the maximum wager limitation, or the maximum loss limitation, and they even allowed casino credit about which Iowa would shudder at the thought. Within nine months after Iowa passed its legislation, Illinois had copied it.

Further down the Mississippi River, in the state of Mississippi, the legislature argued that they also should have riverboat gambling; but they carried it one step further. They legislated that their riverboats did not have to go out and sail on the river. Indeed, after the law was passed, the Attorney General of Mississippi offered an opinion that Mississippi gaming boats do not even need to have motors on the boats. Indeed, they did not even have to be boats. A license holder in Mississippi can build a casino as long as it sits over the water. So, in an analogy to Darwinian evolution, we have seen casinos crawl out of the rivers and position themselves on the banks of rivers to become land-based casinos.

By the time riverboats worked their way into Louisiana, not only were the riverboats getting closer to the shore; they were getting closer to the cities. Louisiana, over a period of a little over a year, passed legislation that authorized riverboats within New Orleans, a major metropolitan area. They also passed non-casino gaming legislation that allowed video lottery terminals in bars, taverns, truck stops and off-track betting parlors throughout the state. Then in 1992, they passed legislation for a land-based monopoly casino in the center of New Orleans, right in the heart of its tourism area.

Thus, there has been a very rapid evolution from harmless, distant, remote gambling, to wide-open urban style gambling, bringing for the first time casinos to where many people live. This has been part of a process that has moved very quickly. It is also being copied in a lot of other jurisdictions. Every new jurisdiction, in order to be competitive, takes the position that they have to be more aggressive than the previous competing jurisdiction which legalized. So as legislation has moved one step further each time, casinos and their presence have become less constrained, less remote, less socially responsible.

The Indian gaming issue—which has been more influenced through the courts —accelerates the process of legalization. If Indians have casinos in particular jurisdictions, the entire public policy debate changes, because once Indians have casinos, the debate in the state, as has already occurred in Connecticut, is no longer, "Should we have casinos?" Rather, the important questions shift to "Who should have the casinos?", "Who should benefit from them?", and "Where should they be located?"

So, at this point in time, America confronts a situation where the momentum for the spread of gambling is, in my opinion, still just beginning. The United States casino and gaming market could be characterized as being terribly undersupplied. That under-supply is being addressed in a variety of ways, and at a very rapid pace.

How much growth remains in the gaming industry in America? In the United States, as mentioned earlier, commercial gaming is nearly a $30 billion a year industry. That represents an expenditure of about $110 per capita.

How much can such expenditures grow? To gain some insight into that question, we can examine the experience of New South Wales, Australia, the largest Australian state, home of Sydney, the country's largest city. In many respects, Australia is similar to America. With regard to gambling, there is generally widely available and accessible gambling in New South Wales. Per capita expenditures in New South Wales are about $570, about four times that of America when corrected for exchange rate differences.

How large can the American gaming industry get? It is not unreasonable to project an industry with gross revenues of $100 billion to $125 billion at maturity with current population and current real income. It can expand by a factor of about four or five just by addressing the question of under-supply of gaming facilities in America. If this process continues unconstrained, we could go from about 300,000 slot machines in America, to about three million, within a decade or so.

One of the issues with this type of projection is, could this really occur? The one thing that is working to bring it about is, if one examines the reasons why politicians are legalizing gaming, especially casino style gaming, one sees the rationale shrouded in economic justifications. Legislatures legalize casinos because of jobs. As Mayor Richard Daly of Chicago said, "Why do we want casinos in Chicago? Jobs, jobs, jobs."

POSTSCRIPT

Should Casino Gambling Be Prohibited?

By the end of 1995, the possible introduction of casino gambling into two major cities in Connecticut—Hartford and Bridgeport—had become a hotly debated issue. Thirty-seven states and the District of Columbia currently have lotteries. In 1993 those lotteries sold $25.1 billion in tickets. Many regions have instituted or are considering instituting riverboat casinos or other restricted gaming establishments. Nonprofit institutions have long supported themselves with gambling. Can the private sector be far behind?

Underlying the entire debate is the tension of passing time; the market for gambling cannot be infinite, and each casino that opens draws revenue that the next cannot tap. And video lotteries—essentially, casinos on the Internet—which bring income to no location whatsoever, threaten gambling establishments of all kinds.

Life is a gamble, and risk is a part of daily life. In that sense, the questions before us are not new. But they are certainly more complex, and they will demand attention in the next decade. Cities in the United States need help, and casinos may be the solution. But is this solution worth the potential problems of gambling?

SUGGESTED READINGS

"Canada: A Gamble," *The Economist* (June 18–24, 1994).

Francis X. Clines, "Gambling, Pariah No More, Is Booming Across America," *The New York Times* (December 5, 1993).

"Gambling May Yield Revenue Windfall," *Aviation Week and Space Technology* (August 15, 1994).

Susan B. Garland, "Clinton vs. the Sin Lobby: All Bark," *Business Week* (July 18, 1994).

Robert Goodman, "Legalized Gambling as a Strategy for Economic Development," *United States Gambling Study* (March 1994).

Dan Parker, "Night Moves—When an Industry Runs Around the Clock (Weekends and Holidays) It Leaves Workers and Families Run-down and Stressed Out," *The Atlantic City Press* (June 14, 1993).

Timothy P. Ryan, Patricia J. Connor, and Janet F. Speyerer, *The Impact of Casino Gambling in New Orleans* (Division of Business and Economic Research, University of New Orleans, LA, May 1990).

Gerald Slusher, *The Casino Industry and Its Impact on Southern New Jersey* (Division of Economic Development, Atlantic City, NJ, January 1991).

Frank Wolfe, "Inherited Talents," *Forbes Four Hundred* (October 17, 1994).

PART 2

Ethics in Financial Areas

Not too long ago, the popular image of Wall Street was of respectable, staid men who quietly and conservatively managed the pensions, funds, and general economic affairs of the nation. In recent times, this image has become tarnished. A proliferation of corporate takeovers, savings and loan crises, and what many see as reckless investment practices have led to widespread public distrust of the players on Wall Street and their methods. Is this suspicion justified, or are most buyers and sellers conducting business as usual? This section examines three practices that are currently under debate: leveraged buyouts, junk bond financing, and financial derivative instruments.

- Are Leveraged Buyouts Bad for the Bottom Line?
- Is Junk Bond Financing Advisable?
- Are Financial Derivative Instruments Always a Gamble?

ISSUE 5

Are Leveraged Buyouts Bad for the Bottom Line?

YES: Frank A. Olson, from "Twilight of the LBOs," *Fairfield Business Review* (Spring 1991)

NO: Michael T. Tucker, from "LBOs May Not Be Dead Yet—A Response to Frank Olson," *Fairfield Business Review* (Spring 1991)

ISSUE SUMMARY

YES: Frank A. Olson, chief executive officer of the Hertz Corporation, argues that the unprecedented level of debt contracted by major U.S. corporations in the 1980s could lead to bankruptcies, unemployment, and widespread corporate inflexibility in the face of change.

NO: Michael T. Tucker, an associate professor of finance, argues that the increased indebtedness in the United States is simply an example of efficient markets at work within the rules of the game, satisfying shareholders' desire for a higher return on investment.

The issue of leveraged buyouts (LBOs) centers on the purpose and foundation of business enterprise in America, or at least the legal and financial foundation for the corporation. The directors of the corporation are elected by the stockholders and have no right to do anything except for the greater profit of the investors; all the business of the corporation is conducted to this end.

But what if the decision to maximize shareholder gain is also a decision to severely weaken or terminate the company? At issue here is not bankruptcy—the condition in which the business simply cannot bring in enough income to cover its costs. At issue here is the decision to liquidate or cripple a company because some individual or investment group—often including managers of the company—offers a price for a controlling portion of the shares that is much higher than any projection of reasonable yield from operation would predict. Why such a price would be offered (by anyone) is one of the topics at issue in the debate that follows.

On one side, Frank A. Olson claims that the buyout results in large profits for the shareholders of record who tender their shares at the right time and in very large profits for the buyout group. However, the members of the buyout group spend very little of their own money in bringing off this type of deal. Most of the money to buy shares comes from loans, with the company's assets and future operating profits as collateral (which provides the "leverage" for the buyout). Therefore, the executives and deal makers who orchestrate a buyout take little financial risk in the face of tremendous benefits, while the company itself and its employees (as the collateral) risk total collapse. The rest who profit are the lawyers and bankers, leaving nothing of the accumulated investment for later owners.

Michael T. Tucker argues that an extraordinarily high price for shares can be offered only when the company is badly mismanaged and when a better management system could make the same assets yield a much higher return. Tucker's formula says, in effect, that if your objective is to increase present shareholder wealth (and it should be), then, given the current tax structure, your best bet is to reduce equity and get yourself as far into debt as possible while subtracting the costs of possible bankruptcy.

From a consequential perspective, the dispute sets up the ethical evaluation of the leveraged buyout as follows: If it succeeds in producing more efficient and more effective corporate operations, then the buyout is justified; if it succeeds only in increasing the wealth of the buyout engineers and destroying an American enterprise, then it is criminally wrong.

What is the board of directors to do when faced with a tender offer (offer for all shares of stock tendered, or presented, to the buyer) at an unimaginably high price, given the market history of the stock? If the return to the shareholder would be higher than the shareholder would otherwise expect from that stock, does the board have any right to resist the offer? But if a perfectly good company that makes a profit, provides jobs, and pays taxes to the community would be killed by this deal, does the board have any right *not* to resist it? One problem with this kind of offer is the number of conflicting interests faced by the board of directors. For example, members of the board are from the company itself; usually at least half the board are also corporate officers. Consequently, they will likely lose their jobs if the deal goes through. Some members of the board are also in management and may be in the group engineering the buyout. Under normal circumstances, all of the directors are also shareholders and stand to improve their personal fortunes substantially if the buyout succeeds.

Under the circumstances, what should the board do? Protect the individuals? Protect the company itself? Is a company valuable in and of itself for the products it makes and for its contributions to the economy? As you read the following selections, ask yourself if the purpose of the corporation ever does, or can, or should go beyond the return on investment for the investor, such as to take on a social role in the nation as a whole. Should the public be concerned about protecting corporations from leveraged buyouts?

YES

Frank A. Olson

TWILIGHT OF THE LBOs

It is a real privilege for me to have this opportunity to participate in the Olin Fellow lectures. I compliment you on the high standards you have set by this lecture series. They present me with quite a challenge today.

I would like to share with you the introduction to a recent article in *Forbes* Magazine by James Grant:

> "Trammell Crow, the king of the surviving Dallas real estate developers and a charter Forbes Four Hundred member, is credited with a number of pithy business sayings. Builders are leveraged and optimistic fellows, and some of Crow's remarks are inspirational, e.g., "The way to wealth is debt." However, recent goings-on in the credit markets may force a revision in that epigram. The updated version may read, less pithily, "The way to oblivion in a bear market is also debt, and nobody rings a bell."

Debt is the original fair-weather friend. It is with you on the upside and against you on the downside. So long has the financial sun been shining that it seems—especially—to the bulls on Wall Street—as though the skies will never darken. But if you can acknowledge the possibility of even one inclement business session, you will want to reflect on the leveraged American condition, and on many of the private American fortunes that constitute the Forbes Four Hundred. You will want to consider that debt may become just as unpopular one day as it now is popular.

Financially speaking, the story of the 20th century has been the mellowing of the American lender. At the turn of the century, it was hard to get a loan. In 1989, if you have a mailbox into which a credit card can be dropped, it is almost impossible not to get one. Consumers, governments and businesses have borrowed as never before. It is the decade of the Five-Year Yugo Loan, the leveraged buyout loan, the unsecured bridge loan, the teaser-rate adjustable-rate mortgage loan, the rescheduled Brazilian or Mexican loan, the Sotheby's Art-Quality Loan and the liposuction and breast-enlargement loan. It is the decade of retractable facsimile bonds, subordinated primary capital perpetual floating rate notes and collateralized fixed-rate multi-tranche tap notes. All in all, the 1980s are to debt what the 1960s were to sex.

Therefore I have chosen as my subject today one of the most controversial economic phenomena of recent times: the madcap LBO binge that has been restructuring corporate America. Most people speaking and writing on this subject have a substantial vested interest in it. I refer of course to the investment bankers and dealers, commercial bankers, legal and financial mergers and acquisitions experts and other buyout players, including many corporate executives. Many of these people have made fortunes by playing this high-stakes game.

My own direct exposure to this subject derives from my experience as a member of the Board of UAL Corporation, parent of United Airlines. As you know, the management and pilots of UAL initially launched a $6.8 billion tender offer for the company, to be paid for mostly by $7.2 billion in loans.

Since this particular buyout case is still in development and has raised some complex, unresolved issues as well as controversy, I shall refrain from commenting upon it today. But my interest in the whole leveraged buyout phenomenon that has swept American industry extends beyond my immediate concerns with UAL.

From my own vantage point, I shall attempt to do four things today:

- give you my views on the nature and magnitude of the LBO phenomenon;
- focus on some of the good and the bad elements in it;
- step back and consider some of the serious dangers developing for our economy as a whole as a result of the torrent of LBO-induced changes that have been flowing through corporate America;
- and, finally, suggest to you some measures I believe must be taken to curb the excesses and potential dangers developing in the most recent wave of leveraged financing.

As most of you know, the leveraged buyout, or LBO as it is called, has been used increasingly in recent years in two ways. It has been used as an aggressive move by corporate managers or financial experts who stand to make enormous profits for themselves. And it has been used as a defensive tactic by managements seeking to protect their companies from takeovers.

In both cases, investors take advantage of the fact that the value put on a company's assets in the public markets is less than the "true value" of those assets if they were better managed or sold to others. LBO investors also take advantage of GAAP accounting, which penalizes public companies, particularly goodwill accounting.

In an LBO, a group of investors that often includes company management buys a publicly-owned company or a division of such a company with mostly borrowed money, taking the company private. Using little of their own funds, the investors borrow against the assets and expected cash flow of the target company. That is how they get their leverage.

Frequently the money is raised through the sale of high-risk, high-yield securities popularly known as junk bonds. The risks of such leveraging fall on the lenders who advance the money and the employees of the company who are asked to make sacrifices, not on the dealmakers and executives. The capital structure of a typical LBO has been senior debt 50–60%, junior debt 20–30% and equity 10%.

Investors repay LBO loans from the company's cash flow or from the sale of its assets, which could be anything from a division or subsidiary to the company's planes or manufacturing facilities or equipment. To increase cash flow and service the heavy debt load, management usually takes an ax to the company's costs, often including its personnel.

The big argument in favor of LBOs has been that they force managements to make more productive use of assets. They are supposed to give managers more incentive to make tough decisions, such as selling off some assets. No one who believes in free markets could argue against that. If a company sells off a mediocre division to a buyout group led by the division's management, the managers become owners with more stake in success than they have ever had before.

The most convincing argument for junk bonds is that they provide financing for entrepreneurs who otherwise might not get it. The ex-king of junk bonds, Michael Milken, recently noted that there are 20,000 to 30,000 U.S. companies that are not investment grade but need and deserve capital to build their businesses. Milken made the case that these companies play a vital role in U.S. economic growth.

Investors who have participated in the leveraged buyout binge have reaped enormous rewards. In the heydays of LBOs, until the last few years, their returns very often were more than 40% a year, sometimes more than 50% or 60% a year, returns that not many of us achieve with our more mundane investments. The quick money earned by short-term players in these games is no small change. Arbitrageurs, the short-term investors who have a major influence on equity prices, encourage buyouts and stir up the equity markets with their speculative activity. Investment and commercial bankers pull down huge financial and advisory fees, typically totaling four percent of a company's purchase price.

The number of LBOs rose from 99 in 1981 to 316 in 1988, an increase of over 300%. The dollar value of these transactions exploded from about $10 billion in 1980 to something between $52 billion and $67 billion in 1988, depending upon which estimate is used. There are about $200 billion or more worth of junk bonds now outstanding.

By the end of 1988, one estimate put total debt of U.S. corporations (excluding financial institutions) at $1.8 trillion, with interest payments of these corporations amounting to an all-time high approaching 30% of their internal cash flow, and roughly half their taxable income, as compared with 25% a decade ago. Corporate borrowing increased at a 15.4% annual rate during the last economic cycle versus an average 8.4% for the previous six cycles, according to economist Henry Kaufman, causing a severe drop in credit ratings. Corporate borrowing amounted to some 43% of gross national product last year, up from 32% five years earlier.

To keep all this in perspective, we must acknowledge that, while banks have been the biggest buyout lenders (and this has been one of their most lucrative businesses in recent times), LBO loans made up only about 10% of total commercial loans by big banks last year, and some 55% at smaller banks. Nevertheless, the growth of this debt should raise anxieties, not least among lenders such as those who are already wrestling with the problems of Latin American loans gone bad. At one New York bank LBO loans accounted for more than 11% of all outstanding loans a year ago and have increased since then.

Naturally the banks and other financial experts who serve as advisers and buyout fund managers earn higher fees when higher prices are paid for LBO targets. This tends to make the LBO phenomenon a fee-driven binge, unrelated, for instance, to the use of debt for greater corporate productivity.

Needless to say, the restructuring and radical surgery precipitated by LBOs can, and does, create a great amount of turmoil and tension in the corporate world. Whether the result of aggregate LBO transactions is good or bad for the American economy is not an easy question to answer. Many academics and others are still trying to answer it.

I believe the answer to this question was more positive in the early days of LBOs than it is today. The first buyout targets were companies with either poor management that simply was not delivering the returns on assets that shareholders had a right to expect, or with cash flows that could not be plowed back into the business because of the dearth of attractive internal investment opportunities. Typically they were companies in relatively non-cyclical industries, companies with fairly steady cash flows that could finance the debt incurred in the buyouts.

For companies that generated a lot of cash, but did not have any exciting opportunities to reinvest in their own operations, LBOs made sense as a way to get cash out without paying it in dividends, which are taxed twice under one of the most misguided provisions of our tax code.

The basic objectives of the "good," old LBOs was to improve management of assets. Another objective was to increase returns on shareholder equity through financial leverage and, in some cases, simply to get rid of unpromising businesses by taking the cash out of them for more productive use. By and large the LBOs occurred in industries that could best afford to support them with strong, assured cash flows.

No one could object to the good intentions reflected by most of these early buyouts. Many of them helped companies operate more efficiently. Often they kindled new entrepreneurial sparks by giving management, and often their employees also, an ownership interest. Just the mere scare of LBOs undoubtedly has caused corporate managements to pay more attention to how they utilize their assets.

However, many buyouts in the recent headlines have less to do with improving management than with financial gymnastics. In my view the buyout craze can lead to unhealthy extremes when the smart-money crowd looks upon businesses simply as cash machines. Focusing on cash generation is fine, but it is not the whole function of management. If management makes decisions solely for short-term cash generation, it is likely to neglect a lot of other things that make for long-term business success.

Perhaps most worrisome of all, the buyout binge has moved into industries and companies that are more volatile or cyclical than early buyout targets. In some cases these latest corporate targets are intimately involved with basic public concerns like transportation and safety.

Take the case of the recent $7.5 billion bid for American Airlines made, and then withdrawn, by real estate investor-promoter Donald Trump. With this attack, American became the third of the nation's major airlines to be engaged in takeover or buyout battles featuring massive borrowing.

Investors jumped at the possibilities for making quick gains in this industry where management may have done many things right but perhaps have not translated the full value of their assets into the price of their stock. The battle for American would have pitted a financial promoter, who has been in and out of other companies before for short-term profits when takeover rumors drove their prices up, against AMR Chairman Robert Crandall, the man who built American into the nation's leading airline. Crandall has an unequaled reputation for topnotch airline management and has argued against leveraging of companies in his industry.

Taking on massive debt in the airline industry is different from doing so in most of the traditional LBO situations. The industry is fiercely competitive and volatile. A heavy debt load could disadvantage an airline when it needs to lower fares or buy new aircraft, and could reduce its flexibility to react to problems such as rising fuel or wage costs, or a drop in traffic.

This kind of situation raises the question of what effect the LBO binge has had across American industry. When CEOs are more preoccupied with short-term takeover strategies than they are with long-range planning to improve performance and service to their customers, there is good cause for alarm.

Perhaps most repugnant is the spectacle of well-heeled investors reaping enormous quick profits just by stock buyups that send takeover rumors flying, and then selling their shares when someone else moves in. That is what happened when Beverly Hills billionaire Marvin Davis made his bid for NWA, the parent of Northwest Airlines, and then walked away with a profit variously estimated at $50 to $100 million by selling his appreciated shares.

Similarly, one has to worry about the public and congressional reaction to a management-led buyout where a corporate officer who stands to make many millions on the sale of his stock asks wage and salary concessions of employees down the line, who are making very modest salaries, to help make the deal go through. One cannot help wondering how much damage such stories have done to the image of business and financial executives in the mind of the American public.

The takeover of NWA and the bid for UAL spread takeover fever through the whole U.S. airline industry and fueled the fires of speculators. This drove up the prices of still-independent Delta Air Lines and USAir, in fact the whole Dow Jones transportation average, and stirred members of Congress into action. When Congress is aroused, the specter rises of new government controls on this industry that has gained so much from deregulation.

The Trump bid for American Airlines was one signal that the LBO era is entering the twilight zone, insofar as the willingness of responsible people to tolerate it is concerned. But this and other airline industry fracases are not the only indications that the buyout binge may have peaked. LBO companies are turning out to be a mixed bag, some good, some bad, including those engineered by the most successful buyout firm, Kohlberg, Kravis, and Roberts [KKR].

We have heard mostly about KKR's success stories. RJR Nabisco paid down its debt easily and has announced new product drives and other initiatives. KKR's studies of its LBOs in general found increases in employment, research and development spending and capital spending by 17 LBOs in which the firm still had an equity stake in January 1989.

However, the number of highly leveraged companies running into trouble in paying their creditors appears to be increasing steadily. Some of KKR's buyouts have gotten into difficulties recently that could result in losses for investors, or even bankruptcies, instead of the big returns that investors expected.

SCI Television of Nashville, for example, formerly part of Storer Broadcasting, failed to make a September debt payment and saw its junk bonds plunge in value. Seaman Furniture ran into trouble meeting interest and principal payments. Rumors of possible troubles also have floated over other KKR buyout companies including Beatrice, Jim Walter and Owens-Illinois.

In retailing, Campeau Corporation, which bought the two biggest department store chains in America, saw its leveraged empire head into a cash-flow crisis that wreaked havoc with such prestigious stores as New York's Bloomingdales and Boston's Jordan Marsh. In the financial services field, Integrated Resources failed to make interest payments on nearly $1 billion of debt, raising fears of bankruptcy among its creditors.

Some companies that undertook management-led buyouts to avert hostile takeovers have been casualties in the buyout game. Trailer-maker Fruehauf Corporation, for instance, was forced to sell most of its businesses to pay for its $1.5 billion LBO to thwart investor Asher Edelman.

All of these situations are signs that the financial extremes of the 1980s, the leveraging of corporate America, are already causing pain in many quarters. Yet despite the clear warning signs, there is still plenty of money around to bankroll LBOs, as recent oversubscribed takeovers such as Warner Communications and NWA have indicated. KKR alone is reported to have access to a $30 billion "war chest," ready for more action, based on $3 to $4 billion subscribed but uncommitted money for equity investments leveraged at 8 to 1.

But if the LBO scares and casualties I have mentioned can occur in the heady atmosphere of our recent bullish markets, what would happen to all the firms leveraged with unprecedented debt in the crunch of a serious recession? You can be sure that the severity of any such recession would be accentuated by the rush of defaults and bankruptcies that could occur.

Federal Reserve Chairman Alan Greenspan noted, in testimony before the House Ways and Means Committee earlier this year, that greater use of debt makes the corporate sector more vulnerable to an economic downturn or a rise in interest rates. Would LBO companies go bankrupt when they lacked the cash flow to service their debt and were unable to restructure their indebtedness? What would be the consequences for many thousands of investors who have put money into junk bonds? What would be the consequences for the banks that hold large quantities of LBO debt in their loan portfolios? What would happen to the workers employed by LBOs that might be forced into bankruptcy? To what extent would the Federal Reserve Board be forced to ease monetary policy to avoid financial calamity, risking renewed inflation?

Defaults of junk bonds in the first half of this year already were double those of the previous year, at some $3.2 billion. Downgrades of corporate debt by at least one major rating service currently are exceeding upgrades two-to-one because of restructurings and takeovers. As Federal Reserve Vice Chairman Manuel Johnson has pointed out, in the event of recession companies could be forced to sell assets at a time when there was little demand for corporate assets. High debt levels, he warned, could bring a series of bankruptcies that could cause a crisis of confidence.

Instead of focusing on these scary possibilities, however, I want you to think with me today about some of the lessons of the LBO era, lessons that put this whole phenomenon into historical perspective. I think these lessons point the way to some public policy imperatives.

Our great free market system has its excesses, and the LBO craze is one of them. These are among the prices we pay for freedom. They are typically followed by some kind of government regulation that puts limits of one kind or another on our freedoms. Let us be sure this time that any government intervention strengthens the system, rather than weakens it.

Congress, however, has looked at the challenge presented by the LBO binge and reacted in a piecemeal manner rather than focusing on the root causes of the abusive fee-driven deals. They have proposed new rules which could restrict the deductibility of interest incurred in financing acquisitions. This is a mistake. In its efforts to create an appearance of political action, Congress has closed its eyes to the fact that these restrictions could very well have the opposite effect.

The limitations on the interest deduction would impact all financings, whether driven by fees or sound business judgment. In addition, such limits would merely make financings more costly. Fi-nally, they would only serve to lead the buyout brokers to create new, and, depending on your perspective, innovative or junk financing vehicles.

This band-aid approach by Congress is bad public policy. Instead of patchwork restrictions, Congress should encourage what is needed most: the infusion of equity into the financing of America's growth. The excesses of the LBO revolve around its very name, the "leveraged" part of the buyout.

Congress has, in fact, encouraged this leverage up to now by providing powerful incentives for corporate debt as opposed to equity. These incentives are provided through our tax laws. Equity investors have had to pay a tax twice on their return on equity: once through the corporate tax and again on the tax they pay on dividends. Lenders, on the other hand, face no such double tax in that interest is deductible at the corporate level. This has led to junk bonds replacing what would otherwise be equity investment.

Fed Chairman Greenspan has recognized this and warned in recent testimony before Congress that double-taxation of earnings from corporate equity capital has encouraged leveraging, causing debt levels to be higher than they should be. So long as equity securities are handicapped in this way, we will not provide the incentives for the broadest public participation in ownership of our enterprises. The critics who say that abolishing this discrimination against equity financing is unthinkable in these times of big budget deficits simply have not thought this through.

One, the deficit impact of allowing companies to deduct dividends as well as interest payments could be minimized. The goal should be to equalize treatment of dividends and interest, and this need not add to deficits. If the same percentage of each were deductible by corporations, as proposed in June by Congress's Joint Committee on Taxation, equity would have a chance, and the budgetary effect would be neutral.

Second, there has been much recent focus on lowering the tax on capital gains as a means of generating investment in the economy. A far more powerful incentive would result with the phase out of the double tax penalty. Equity capital has many advantages over debt, and as a nation we have every reason to encourage it.

A company weathering hard times can cut dividends on stock instead of laying off workers and closing plants. If it cuts payment on its debt, cutbacks and layoffs and even bankruptcy are much more likely, exacerbating an economic downturn. A company with lower debt and higher equity has more ability to invest in research and development and in more efficient production equipment. This is hardly a new theme for American business. It is a very old theme. But it needs to be played over and over again, until people outside the business world understand it.

If the rules of the game are skewed to favor debt, naturally there will be an accumulation of debt. And naturally there will be people finding ways to use the leverage of debt for their own quick profit. If the rules of the game encourage the public to own, not just loan to, American business, corporate management will act from a longer-term perspective which will be in the best long-term interests of the U.S. economy.

It probably would be helpful also to increase the capital requirements of lending by the banks and others who finance these leveraged deals. Efforts are under way in some areas, such as the savings and loan bailout law, which prohibits thrifts from owning junk bonds.

Another possible solution, recommended by Dr. Albert Wojnilower of First Boston, is to impose mandatory capital standards on large corporations such as those already imposed on banks and savings and loan associations. Small firms would be exempt, since they do not contribute materially to the systemic problem. He has in mind a financial ratio approach similar to that already applied by lenders and bond rating agencies. The equity requirement would be satisfiable only by pure equity.

The required ratios would have to be set at different levels for different firms, depending on their size and industry. It has long been known that debt-equity and other financial ratios differ according to industry and size of firm. A certain arbitrariness is unavoidable, but it would hardly be greater than that already involved in the setting of bond ratings by the private rating agencies.

The twofold penalty for noncompliance would be simple and automatic. The lesser penalty would be the withdrawal of the tax advantage for the excess debt. Interest would be treated as though it were dividends. This would limit the tax incentive for equity retirement without radically revising our tax system. But in many cases this would not be an adequate deterrent. The more potent penalty to be applied would be the compulsory dismissal of senior management, with forfeiture of equity entitlements, golden parachutes and such benefits.

Those of us who cherish and understand our free market economy will not stand by forever and see fortunes made overnight by the buying and selling of our companies instead of the building of our companies. For these times, we need builders more than we need master jugglers of corporate assets. We must not tolerate a system that provides richer rewards for purely financial driven transactions than for efforts to increase manufacturing and marketing productivity and industrial creativity.

We must not tolerate forever an American tax code that penalizes management for seeking public participation in ownership over financial institutions' participation in loading companies with debt. We must not allow American companies to load themselves with so much debt as to make them vulnerable when the economy turns down. These are big imperatives as we head into the 1990s and the fierce global competition that is going to characterize the next decade.

NO
Michael T. Tucker

LBOs MAY NOT BE DEAD YET—
A RESPONSE TO FRANK OLSON

News of the death of LBOs is likely to be as premature as that of the early reported demise of Mark Twain. Mr. Frank A. Olson might wish LBOs would go away because of the problems they cause for corporate management, but the underlying rationale that has driven LBOs has not vanished with the inability of United Airlines to raise sufficient debt capital to consummate the deal to which Mr. Olson is so strongly opposed.

During the 1980s, U.S. companies retired $500 billion in equities while piling up $1 trillion in new debt. Merrill Lynch estimates that meeting the obligations to all those bondholders garners as much as 30% of corporate cash flow, a greater percentage allocated to interest than in either of the two worst postwar recessions.

Yet the merger and acquisition tidal wave of the 1980s characterized by corporations amassing debt while retiring equity has a strong foundation in financial theory. Its philosophical origins can be traced to the 1958 Modigliani and Miller (MM) pioneering work on corporate capital structure published in the *American Economic Review*. At the time of the paper's appearance, corporate America heavily favored equity over debt. The generation that made financing decisions had all too current memories of the Depression. Balance sheets with zero long-term liabilities were not unusual. All-equity companies were deemed prudent instead of ripe for takeover. Fiscal conservatism was the rule rather than the exception.

The premise of MM's paper was that leveraged firms are worth more than firms without debt. An unleveraged firm is defined as having a worth equivalent to the present value of its after tax cash flows in perpetuity:

$$V_u = \frac{EBIT(1 - t)}{k_c}$$

V_u = value of a firm without debt

k_c = the required rate of return on equity capital

EBIT = earnings before interest and taxes

t = the firm's tax rate.

The above example assumes no growth in the firm's earnings stream. The formula can be easily adjusted to account for growth without impact on its basic implications.

MM define the value of a leveraged firm in terms V_u:

$$V_L = V_u + tD$$

V_L = value of a leveraged firm

tD = tax shield on debt.

Firms with debt have the ability to deduct interest payments. That deductibility protects a proportion of earnings from taxes, resulting in a tax shield. Although there is a cost associated with debt, tax deductibility is a form of government subsidization of debt financing, making it a less costly form of financing than equity.

Dividends, lacking tax deductibility, cost a firm more than debt. In addition, shareholders receiving the dividends pay taxes on them. Equity financing does, however, have advantages. Failure to make an expected dividend payment will not result in the firm being in default. Defaulting on interest or principal payments may cause bankruptcy, with creditors suddenly becoming owners of the firm. Equity holders, as former owners of the firm, lose all value. In the 1980s, with the help of junk bond messiah Mike Milken, the tax advantages of deducting interest payments, together with the threat of others borrowing and buying up the company, convinced financial officers that bonds were the safest route for financing their growth needs while insuring their employment.

As debt replaced equity, stock prices soared until that fateful day in October 1987. In the halcyon days of early 1987, a $500 million firm could peddle 10% of itself for $50 million. In the winter of 1987–88, 18% of corporate control would have to be surrendered to raise the same $50 million. Further tilting the scales toward debt was the 9% interest-rate on benchmark long-term Treasury bonds.

While debt has inherent bankruptcy risk, failure to have some debt could imply overly cautious management under MM's Proposition I. A firm with no debt is undervalued when compared to a similar firm with leverage. The benefits of the tax shield are lost. Issuance of debt increases firm value and also gives management the opportunity to repurchase shares at a premium from current shareholders. Repurchasing shares offers a better alternative for shareholder gain than dividends. Because share repurchases are not taxed twice like dividends, firms can offer a premium to shareholders. The only tax due is paid by the shareholders based on capital gains.

Management that fails to keep shareholders financially satisfied may find itself prey to takeover attempts by groups offering shareholders the opportunity to sell their shares at prices considerably higher than current valuations. In the early 1980s, companies in noncyclical industries, i.e., businesses unaffected by the business cycle, became the favored targets of leveraged buyout artists. Companies with low debt to equity ratios had large amounts of unused debt capacity. Kohlberg, Kravis and Roberts (KKR), premier takeover artists of the 1980s, employed the purchased companies' own assets to engineer takeovers. By borrowing heavily they were able to buy back all shares of these companies at substantial premiums. Shareholders were happy, and the newly constituted companies paid off handsomely. Creditors received high interest payments on "junk bonds." New equity investors reaped large returns when the company was subsequently broken up and went public as a new entity some years later.

T. Boone Pickens of Mesa Petroleum, a major buyout player, described himself as a champion of neglected shareholders. By borrowing large amounts of money and buying firms, Pickens and his ilk promised full value. They blamed management for squandering the firm's assets. Of course, all those involved in consummating these deals did not labor out of charity.

Agency theory is the philosophical underpinning of Pickens' rhetoric. According to agency theory, management, acting as agents of the shareholders, does not necessarily maximize shareholder utility. Managers are out to maximize their own utility. Rather than take greater investment risks through borrowing and financing new projects in order to give shareholders maximum payouts, management may elect a more conservative course that protects their interests. Debt also tends to restrict free cash flow, channeling it into interest payments. The more fixed payment obligations, e.g., interest, that a firm has to meet, the less spending flexibility management retains. Agency theorists, ever suspicious of management misappropriation of funds, view limiting free cash flow as a way to control management actions. Companies with less cash flow will have to do more with what they do have. This is sometimes described as becoming "lean and mean." The implication is that these aggressive, slimmed-down firms have fewer layers of middle management, and fewer country club memberships and corporate jets.

Cutting costs too much can be bad for business. Mr. Olson argues that firms with too much debt are severely constrained and at risk of bankruptcy. While some debt may be beneficial, overdoing it can be harmful. A corollary to MM Proposition I adds a third term to the formula, taking Mr. Olson's objections into account. The present value of bankruptcy costs serves as a check against balance sheets too heavily weighted in favor of debt:

$$V_L = V_u + tD - PV(\text{Bankruptcy Cost})*(\text{Probability of Bankruptcy})$$

Bankruptcy, in a perfectly functioning market, would imply a smooth and costless transmission of the corporation's assets from shareholders to creditors. Given our efficient but less than perfect markets, bankruptcy has costs such as litigation, lost operational efficiency, and lost investment opportunities. As the debt of a firm increases, the probability of insolvency also rises. At some point the present value of bankruptcy costs is greater than any gains from further debt. When that level of debt has been attained, the firm can be said to have reached its optimal capital structure.

Corporations in cyclical industries will have a lower optimal debt level than firms in noncyclical industries, because their cash flows are susceptible to greater variability. The airline industry, a very competitive and cyclical segment of the economy, has a lower optimal debt level than the food industry with its noncyclical cash flows. United Airlines, as Mr. Olson pointed out, if subjected to the leveraged buyout terms proposed in October 1989, would entail high debt service levels. Those debt service levels could supersede optimal level of debt, resulting in the restructured firm being worth less than it was prior to restructuring.

While this decline in value would be true if the newly constituted United Airlines were in all ways the same as the former firm, it may not be true if the nature of the firm itself has changed. Agency theory argues that when management and ownership are closely linked, maximizing corporate and managerial goals will imply the same actions. Waste is eliminated through self interest, and the firm functions more efficiently. Firm ownership by employees, as proposed by the United Airlines LBO, would have created such a situation. The deal did not collapse because of feared inability to service excess debt. The demise was reported to be due to an excess of greed on the part of management anxious to reap an immediate payout upon consummation. This does not preclude the success of a differently structured deal to accomplish a similar change in ownership.

The tilt of balance sheets toward more debt and away from equity is simply an example of efficient markets working within the confines of the current rules of the game. Firm valuation is enhanced with more debt, as pointed out by Modigliani and Miller. Management failing to restructure accordingly will be subject to replacement by others willing to use the firm's debt capacity to satisfy shareholder's desire for higher returns on investment.

The form of that restructuring has not been limited to traditional subordinated debenture* debt. Borrowing has undergone some dramatic changes under the

*[Debentures are bonds that are backed by the general good name of the issuing company in lieu of collateral.—Eds.]

creative tutelage of investment bankers eager to package new products. Some of the most original thinking has been done for oil and gas companies. A menagerie of quasi-debt, quasi-equity issues has emerged over the last few years with acronyms that speak more of the jungle than Wall Street. Triton Energy and Maxus were the first to use Liquid Yield Options Notes (LYONS), convertible zero coupon bonds. LYONS investors have the option of either holding the note to term, collecting interest, or converting to equity. This differs from traditional convertible bonds which pay interest until conversion. Triton's seventeen year $314 million debt issue (face value) with 8.25% interest sold at $253.01 per bond and could be converted into 15.6 shares. With the stock selling at $14.50 at time of issue, the $16.25 conversion price was well within range (Triton's high for 1989 was $16 5/8). A straight debt offering would have carried a coupon of 12.5%.

Maxus's LYONS retained some added options for the firm. While the holder could convert the notes into equity, the firm could elect to convert it into cash based on 8.5% interest after five years, or after ten years it could issue new notes at the then prevailing interest rate. The issue was oversubscribed at a conversion price of $8.05 with the stock selling at $7. The stock's high for 1988 was 9 5/8. Vice President and Treasurer of Maxus, Glen Brown, explained why LYONS were the financing of choice: "We chose LYONS because they were zero coupon, meaning no interest is paid out in the first five years. That allows us to reduce our cash outflow. And the dollars saved from not having to pay cash interest should, over the life of this issue, add a lot of value to Maxus."

Presidio Oil found a cash rich seam with its $100 million, 13.25% interest offering of gas indexed notes. Each one cent increase in the price of gas above $1.75 per mmbtu will push up the bond's interest rate by 2 1/2 basis points. Presidio won't balk at paying that extra interest. If the rate on the note increases by 1%, resulting in an additional $1 million in debt payments, the company would realize more than $7.5 million in added revenues from the hike in the price of gas.

Mr. Olson's suggested possible changes in the tax laws will not end the creativity of investment bankers demonstrated above. However, it may direct their endeavors toward capital structures he would find more efficacious. Any change in the tax law would cause a revision in a firm's optimal capital structure to whatever fits newly created economic constraints. If dividends were made tax deductible, as proposed by Mr. Olson, they would produce a tax shield similar to that of interest on debt. Limiting the amount of interest a firm could deduct according to some debt/equity ratio ceiling would also change the valuation and consequently the optimal capital structure, much as the minimum tax has changed investment decisions.

Mr. Olson can take comfort in knowing that all tides eventually turn, and the rising wave of debt financing is already ebbing as a function of a slowing economy and perhaps the absence of Michael Milken. One of the first signs of the beginning of a new trend was in August 1989, when investors turned their backs on Ohio Mattress's (Sealy) 15% junk bond issue. Many debt-laden companies are now selling divisions at 10% to 30% less than they had planned when they borrowed all those billions, adding a dose of reality to new would-be LBOs. The savings and loan bailout bill has raised another specter over the debt market. The bill gives S&Ls five years to sell off their junk bonds. Those bonds represent 17% of the junk bond market. After growing at 34% per annum since 1981, junk bonds are about to come back down to earth.

Regardless of whether or not Congress tinkers with the tax law, efficient capital markets will vote with dollars on the acceptability of corporate capital structures. While it is true that higher amounts of debt in cyclical industries may lead to severe financial constraints and/or bankruptcies, it is also true that rational investors will reject deals that lower firm values. Of course there will be excesses, bankruptcies and unhappy management. In equilibrium the efficient market shakes out the bad deals and maximizes value. Markets are always getting back to equilibrium, which implies some bumps along the way such as experienced in the October 1989 stock market dive precipitated by the collapse of the United Airlines deal. In the long-term, rough spots, while painful, create far fewer inefficiencies than constant tinkering with the tax laws.

POSTSCRIPT

Are Leveraged Buyouts Bad for the Bottom Line?

Do leveraged buyouts simply reflect business as usual, in which some people (raiders, bankers, knowledgeable inside executives, lawyers) get rich while others (employees, bondholders, long-range shareholders of the company) suffer? Or is this an unethical practice, from which businesspeople should abstain?

Until recently, most businesspeople would have abstained from participating in a leveraged buyout. In a sense, the leveraged buyout is made possible by massive changes in American society, which include the dissolution of old guard bonds of faithfulness to class and structure and the legitimization of the pursuit of self-interest across the social levels of society.

For much of America's economic history, people have relied on the banks to keep restraints on the pursuit of gain and the indulgence of greed. The banker was the embodiment of prudence and long-term thinking, the chief conservative of the community, financially and usually in all other respects, too.

Furthermore, the chief executive officers and boards of directors of the major corporations were builders rather than speculators, responsible to a small group of shareholders who believed that economic safety lay in building up the corporations. The destruction of a company for the sake of instant cash would not have occurred to any of them; a single discontented shareholder could always sell out his shares without disturbing the structure of the whole. And between them, the major corporations and the major banks controlled all the cash in the country; the money to make a multibillion-dollar offer for a huge company simply was not available.

Two major changes in the financial world upset this order. First, individual shareholders were replaced by institutional funds. Second, and possibly more important, the whole social order of friendship and class loyalty that bound major banks to major corporations has been toppled by the newly democratic mergers-and-acquisitions divisions of banking houses. While some will see a healthy opening of opportunities, appropriate to a democracy committed to the dream of success for everyone, others will be alarmed by the collapse of the institutions and social practices that succeeded in maintaining a degree of ethical restraint on a runaway economy.

Are LBOs a threat to American enterprise as a whole? Should we call for legislation to prohibit the practice? This seems to be Olson's view when he says, "For these times, we need builders more than we need master jugglers of corporate assets." The jugglers and the liquidators, the people who brought us the LBOs, also brought us the savings and loan debacle and the trillion-dollar deficit. It may be time to try a little building again.

SUGGESTED READINGS

Robert Almeder and David Carey, "In Defense of Sharks: Moral Issues in Hostile Liquidating Takeovers," *Journal of Business Ethics* (vol. 10, 1991).

Douglas Bandow, "Curbing Raiders is Bad for Business," *The New York Times* (February 7, 1988).

Carl C. Icahn, "The Case for Takeovers," *The New York Times Magazine* (January 29, 1989).

Laura Jereski, "Ill Will," *Forbes* (January 23, 1989).

Frank R. Lichtenberg, "Takeovers Slash Corporate Overhead," *The Wall Street Journal* (February 7, 1989).

Martin Lipton, "Paying the Price of Takeover Money," *Manhattan, Inc.* (May 1989).

Michael Lubatkin, "Value-Creating Mergers: Fact or Folklore?" *The Academy of Management Executive* (November 1988).

Lisa H. Newton, "Charting Shark-Infested Waters: Ethical Dimensions of the Hostile Takeover," *Journal of Business Ethics* (January–February 1988).

Robert B. Reich, "America Pays the Price," *The New York Times Magazine* (January 29, 1989).

ISSUE 6

Is Junk Bond Financing Advisable?

YES: Glenn Yago, from *Junk Bonds: How High Yield Securities Restructured Corporate America* (Oxford University Press, 1991)

NO: Ford S. Worthy, from "The Coming Defaults in Junk Bonds," *Fortune* (March 16, 1987)

ISSUE SUMMARY

YES: Glenn Yago, a faculty fellow of the Rockefeller Institute of Government at the State University of New York at Stony Brook, argues that high-yield securities, or "junk bonds," have aided the growth of small and forward-looking companies and have led to increases in jobs, productivity, and competitiveness in American industry.

NO: Ford S. Worthy, an associate editor for *Fortune* magazine, maintains that the promotion and sale of junk bonds reflect a dangerous exploitation of public ignorance and lack of foresight, and he predicts an unacceptably high level of default on these bonds.

The power that comes from having access to very large amounts of money has historically been confined to a very few persons. Before the modern age, only kings and their ministers had access to cash in amounts sufficient to bring about change—build roads and castles, establish factories, or go to war. After the Renaissance, commercial trade increased tremendously, and reservoirs of cash and capital could be found in successful merchant houses and the ascendant merchant banks. By the nineteenth century, capital sufficient to bring about change could be assembled by any of a large number of wealthy individuals and even more easily by groups of wealthy individuals. These groups of investors founded most of the great manufacturing corporations of the United States, either by purchasing shares of ownership in businesses or by lending large amounts of money to get businesses started. A central market in which to buy and sell those stocks and loans (bonds) was soon established. Once that central market was established, it was only a matter of time before access to that reservoir of cash became democratized.

The twentieth century produced new cash reservoirs. American laborers organized themselves into unions in the first quarter of the century, and they constantly bargained for generous pension plans—into which worker and employer would both contribute on a weekly basis—to supplement the recently established social security plan. The accumulated pension money was invested to increase its value over the course of the laborers' working lives. The fund managers were very conservative—they bought only bonds (stocks tended to go up and down) and only very safe ("investment-grade") bonds at that. The funds grew a few percent per year; the fund managers never thought to be more daring, and no one asked them to be.

In the 1970s and 1980s, interest rates went through the roof. Pressure suddenly fell on the fund managers to raise the average interest collected on the bonds in their portfolios. Raising that rate was difficult to do: the old, low-interest bonds were difficult or impossible to sell, so "raising the average" had to be accomplished by buying new bonds with astronomically high interest rates to offset the old ones. Clearly, if the market is doing its job, those bonds will always be the riskiest around—high interest if you can collect, but the company may not be in a position to repay. Swollen pension funds (and other institutional funds) were invested in such bonds in the 1980s. This meant that the "common laborer," willingly or not, had joined the once-small number of powerful investors.

Michael Milken, former junk bond manager for the investment banking firm Drexel Burnham Lambert Incorporated, saw early on that there were many corporations and other enterprises that wanted loans to accomplish some worthwhile cause but that could not afford a standard bank loan and that were too unsound to issue investment-grade bonds. He also found that there was a huge pool of cash desperately seeking high-yield (high-interest) bonds to buy (loans to make). The primary issue for the fund managers was not necessarily whether or not those loans would ever be paid back; the point was to get these high-yield instruments into the portfolios to raise the average yields. So the "junk bond" was born, and it was bought in huge quantities.

In the following selections, Glenn Yago defends the use of junk bonds, particularly as a method of raising quick capital for corporate restructuring. He argues that corporations restructured with the aid of junk bonds yield more money to the shareholders—proof positive that the restructured corporation runs more efficiently than it did before. Ford S. Worthy, in contrast, worries about the shortsightedness of those who use these bonds and those who buy them. He maintains that default looms for unwary investors and for their clients.

As you read these selections, consider what measures we should use to judge financial institutions. Worthy focuses on the dependability of investments; Yago focuses on the investors' return. Are they both aiming at too narrow a target? Who really benefits from the junk bond phenomenon: shareholders? employees? managers? investors? raiders? investment bankers? lawyers? Who is getting hurt, if anyone?

YES
Glenn Yago

PUBLIC POLICY RESPONSES TO HIGH YIELD BONDS

"Policy," according to former Federal Reserve Governor Henry Wallich, "is the name we give to our future mistakes." In light of what we have learned about high yield bonds and leveraged buyouts [LBOs], these words may prove to be a profound understatement.

The evidence shows that high yield companies outperform their industries in employment, sales, productivity, capital investment, and capital spending. Leveraged buyouts show dramatic improvements in a wide range of performance measures, and tend to outperform other companies in productivity, employment, and R & D [research and development] intensity. With all these benefits flowing out of the use of junk bonds, you would naturally expect public policy to favor them. Instead, Congressional leaders and state legislators have rushed to regulate, restrict, or reject high yield bonds and the transactions they make possible.

"We don't want to necessarily stop junk bonds or LBOs," one senator told me. "Things are just moving too fast, and we need to slow them down." Other, less moderate voices have been heard on Capitol Hill, using words like "scourge," "plague," and "greedmongers" to describe the practitioners in this new wave of corporate finance and business strategy. Borrowing language and arguments from a lobbying organization backed by the Business Roundtable, the *Congressional Record* has periodically been filled with long speeches about stopping the "raid on America." And despite the growing empirical evidence ... that leveraged buyouts create value for shareholders, corporations, and the economy, legislators continue to view them as "paper shuffling" and "shell games."

What could result from political resistance to high yield bonds? The efficient access to capital that funded the current wave of corporate restructuring could simply disappear, making it increasingly difficult for small and medium-sized companies to build new plants, develop new products, or respond to changing markets and technologies. Without access to high yield debt, companies would inevitably face the restrictive covenants associated with bank debt and private placements, or be forced to rely on expensive equity offerings in markets that are at best unpredictable.

Corporations would not be the only ones affected. Fixed income investors would lose an important way to increase their risk-adjusted returns, and equity investors would find acquisition premiums, that is, higher returns resulting from ownership change or the threat of ownership change, considerably harder to obtain. Political resistance to junk bonds and restructurings could reverse decades of credit liberalization that has provided attractive investment outlets for institutions and a cost-efficient source of funds for capital formation.

In the early days of the junk bond market, skepticism was more prevalent than resistance. In fact, opposition to structural changes through increased leverage didn't emerge until the fight against Big Oil, which was initially led by Boone Pickens and Mesa Petroleum in 1985. While many have tried to liken Pickens and other corporate raiders to the robber barons of the past, such comparisons miss the point. The more appropriate historical reference for Pickens is Huey Long, whose populist attacks against big oil companies and utilities defined a generation of economic reform legislation in state houses and Washington. Indeed, for forty years since the New Deal, efforts at business reform remained largely in the legislative arena. Over that period of time, however, corporate power continued to concentrate through waves of business combination and conglomeration unhindered by political regulation.

By the 1970s, the burgeoning consumer and environmental movements refocused attention on problems of industrial organization. Representative of those concerns were extensive deliberations by the Anti-Trust Subcommittee of the U.S. Senate led by the late Senator Phillip Hart (D-Michigan). Senator Hart's hearings for an Industrial Reorganization Act focused upon problems of "shared monopolies" in large automobile and oil companies that engaged in administered pricing and other anticompetitive market practices. Proposed solutions focused on government intervention and regulation leading to divestiture of various operations.

Beyond additional symbolic regulations, however, the legislated divestitures recommended in the Industrial Reorganization Act never occurred. Later antitrust regulations (e.g., Hart-Scott-Rodino), which required review of acquisitions in similar industries, had the unanticipated consequence of encouraging the types of unproductive horizontal diversifications and conglomeration that were negatively affecting corporate performance by the late 1970s. In short, public policy initiatives identified inappropriate solutions (government intervention) to a correctly perceived problem (conglomeration and concentrated corporate power leading to economic inefficiencies).

Instead of government intervention, competitive market pressures began to restructure American corporations. By the 1980s, concern over the power of large oil companies shifted from the public forum to individual firms, when Texaco, Phillips, and Unocal took turns in the spotlight as the focus of economic and political attention.

Ironically, these market pressures, which culminated in the intensive merger and acquisition activity of the mid- to late 1980s, accomplished the reforms that Congress had been unable even to conceive correctly, much less implement.

Pickens recalls learning how large corporations had begun to organize to stop contests for corporate control.

> First, they put pressure on our banks. Either directly, through the board positions they held, and later by inserting provisions requiring immediate debt repayment in case of change of control. If you lay down the membership of the Conference Board, the Business Roundtable, the American Petroleum Institute, and the National Petroleum Council, you will find big oil companies prominent in each one. In 1985, the Roundtable called a meeting and one of the CEOs who refused to participate called and told me about it. I think it was Roger Smith that asked for $50,000 from each member. I understand they raised $9 million for a PR and lobbying campaign to get Boone Pickens to stop takeovers. (Interview with T. Boone Pickens, Jr., May 14, 1989)

As Drexel Burnham's vice chairman and CEO, Frederick Joseph recounts about that time,

> I tend to be nonparanoid, but a lot of people whose judgment I respect have told me that there really are significant elements of social revolution vendetta in some of the legislative proposals, press coverage, responses by Wall Street competitors, and maybe in the enthusiasm of the prosecutors because we are a politically attractive target. (Interview with Mr. Frederick Joseph, November 1988)

According to Joseph, the first real rash of antitakeover, antijunk rhetoric and legislation came in 1985, and was led by Nicholas Brady and Howard Baker, men Joseph says he likes. Both of these advocates were hired by Unocal in the private sector and worked overtly to assist the company in its fight against Boone Pickens.

As Pickens recalls:

> In the Unocal deal, we got a call from the Bank of Montreal indicating that Volker (of the Federal Reserve) had called them and not approved of the bank making loans to guys like Boone Pickens. They dropped us.... Brady got up in front of the Senate and told about all the abuses that were going to go on if our takeover succeeded. He was being paid $5–20 million by Unocal and that was not revealed. I though this was unusual and so I followed him on the next panel and I said, "I think we need to get this record straight, that Nick Brady is working for Unocal." (May 14, 1989 interview)

At the time, raiders were going after companies that were sitting on vast assets that could have been better utilized, either for internal growth or to increase investor returns. The resulting takeover battles focused the public's attention on capital laws. As Frederick Joseph recalls:

> That caused thirty-one bills to be introduced in a single year, including the Junk Bond Control Act of 1985 by Pete Dominici. I went to see him and said, "Do you know what a junk bond is?" He said, "Nope, but I bet you I am going to learn now." (Author and interview, November 1988)

Legislative bills were promoted not only by well-connected oil companies, but also by financial firms that faced increasing competition as a result of massive restructuring caused by deregulation. Older, established financial institutions sought new protective legislation to insulate themselves from the threat of more competitive firms that were making full use of the junk bond market. According to Joseph,

> At the same time, some of the legislation introduced into the thrift industry

against junk bonds was the direct result of the big, old thrifts at the core of the political power in the industry finding it very difficult to compete with some more aggressive thrifts that were buying high yield bonds and getting very high returns, which put them in a position to pay higher rates or roll faster and expand aggressively. (November 1988)

Big thrifts were not the only financial institutions affected by the junk bond revolution. As we noted earlier, junk bonds provided a flexible, fixed-rate alternative to bank loans, causing corporate bonds to gain market share at the expense of bank financing. Insurance companies were also under pressure to earn competitive returns. Those who were unwilling or unable to invest in junk bonds suddenly found themselves at a competitive disadvantage, and attempted to artificially alter the rules to suit their investment policies. As Joseph notes,

Equitable led the fight in New York to restrict high yield bonds. Their problems were directly related to competing with insurance companies that were getting 300 to 400 basis points or more in their portfolio by buying high yield bonds. The political reaction was a response by people who either didn't want to or couldn't compete on the investment side with the high yield bond investors. (Interview, Frederick Joseph, November 1988)

During the hostile takeover battle between Mesa Petroleum and Unocal, Unocal petitioned the Federal Reserve Board in May 1985, requesting that margin requirements in Regulation G be applied to debt securities issued by a shell corporation involved in a tender offer. The Fed did apply Regulation G to certain types of transactions, and a Senate bill was later introduced to further amend margin requirements used in acquisitions. The net effect of the legislation was to restrict the amount of junk bonds that could be used to finance acquisitions by shell corporations.

As a person active in the junk bond market recalls looking over the landscape of Corporate America in the mid-1980s and noting,

Everywhere you looked, entrenched managers were pursuing negative present value projects. Gulf Oil was continuing to drill wells as the barrel price fell off a cliff, because that's what they'd always done. Thrifts kept putting out thirty-year fixed-rate mortgages, even though deregulation had made other mortgage products more popular.

As [junk bond manager Michael] Milken pointed out, these managers insisted on resisting change and defining their business by the past until somebody stopped them. "Not surprisingly," he said, "competitive forces started to stop them through new strategies and takeovers."

Boone Pickens recollects the following about that period:

If you go back to the late 70s and early 80s where the oil industry was clearly overcapitalized, you will find they were doing unusual things because there was no accountability to stop them. Nobody really paid any attention to these things other than a few academics examining the cash flow of the large oil companies who discovered they were opening the window and throwing money out.

Whatever the economic impact of high yield securities, the public policy response has been an overwhelming reaction to regulate the market's success.

NO

Ford S. Worthy

THE COMING DEFAULTS IN JUNK BONDS

Levine. Boesky. Siegel. Wall Street's gallery of rogues keeps growing, with every indication of more to come. But while the financial community waits nervously for the next insider trading scandal to break, another kind of shocker is brewing. Not as dramatic, perhaps—no one is likely to be led off in handcuffs —but with effects that ultimately could prove more far-reaching. The threat: an unprecedented level of defaults by the companies issuing junk bonds.

The fallout might rain down even on people who have never heard of these risky high-yield securities. Hundreds of institutions that have loaded up on the bonds could lose money, ranging from insurance companies to savings and loans. So could thousands of small-time investors who have bought shares in junk bond mutual funds. Undermine investors' confidence in junk bonds and you strike at the heart of Drexel Burnham Lambert, whose senior executive vice president, Michael Milken, pioneered their use and revolutionized corporate dealmaking in the process. Put a crimp in the ability of takeover artists to raise financing by selling junk bonds through Drexel or other investment banking firms, and the acquisition game slows down. Fewer companies will be menaced into restructuring, including some that still need to.

True, critics of junk bonds have been prophesying an imminent, cataclysmic wave of defaults for years (the sky is falling, the sky is falling). And true, despite the predictions, this high-yield corporate bond market has merely steamed ahead, proving amazingly resilient when bumps did occur. It bounced back after two jolts in 1986. In July LTV, the giant steelmaker, went into Chapter 11 and stopped payment on bonds with a face value of $2.1 billion, the biggest junk default ever. Then came the revelations last November that Ivan Boesky, a big Drexel customer, had connived in illegal insider trading and was now cooperating with government investigators in search of other malefactors. Prices of junk plummeted after each debacle, but rebounded impressively, enabling the overall market, as measured by a Drexel Burnham index, to sport a healthy 19% total return for the year.

This time around it may be different. *Fortune* has made one of the first comprehensive attempts to find out how shaky the junk bond market really is. The answer: not as bad as some Chicken Littles have been saying, but much more worrisome than the defenders of junk would have us believe. The market for junk bonds won't collapse, but it could be rocked to its foundations.

In an effort to gauge the potential problem, *Fortune* enlisted the help of Houlihan Lokey Howard & Zukin, a Los Angeles consulting firm nationally known for its work in analyzing the solvency of companies. The firm scrutinized a universe of about 500 companies that altogether had junk bonds with a face value of $72.5 billion outstanding at the end of 1986. Studying these, it identified 36 companies whose bonds, with a face value of $4 billion, seem particularly vulnerable. Looked at another way, some 5.5% of the junk bonds in our sample appear to be vulnerable. At first glance, 5.5% might not appear that threatening. Look again: It's over three times the historical rate of default for publicly traded junk bonds, around 1.5% a year, which Drexel and others have harped on in touting the securities.

These atomic bonds, as Houlihan Lokey calls the riskiest of them, are not necessarily destined to blow up or melt down. Many of the companies that issued them will undoubtedly find ways to survive: by bringing in new management, selling assets to repay debt, winning concessions from lenders, or selling out to stronger companies. Indeed, Drexel officials, who have expressed disdain for *Fortune's* project, say that the prospects for many of the companies listed here are so good that savvy investors would do well to view them as buying—not selling —opportunities. *Caveat emptor.*

To understand the danger that junk bonds present now, you have to understand the nature and history of the beast.

The two major bond-rating agencies refer to junk securities—those rated BB+ or below by Standard & Poor's, or Ba1 or less by Moody's Investors Service—as "speculative grade." Drexel prefers the appellation "high yield." By any name this is the riskiest of all marketable corporate debt. But the spectrum of risk within the junk market is incredibly broad. For example, B.F. Goodrich Corp. junk bonds currently yield about 9% a year, an indication that investors regard them as much less risky than certain Bethlehem Steel bonds, which if bought today and held to maturity would, God willing, yield nearly 17%.

Junk bonds represent about $145 billion of the $550-billion totality of all corporate bonds. Approximately $125 billion of junk is what's called straight debt, bonds whose holders receive regular fixed-interest payments, typically every six months, until maturity, when the principal is repaid. Holders of convertible debt (about $20 billion outstanding) have the option to exchange the bonds for other securities—usually common stock. About a third of all junk bonds are "fallen angels" that began life with investment-grade status and grew riskier as the issuer's fortunes declined. The other two-thirds were junk from day one.

The market for junk has grown wildly —from about $1.5 billion worth of lesser-quality bonds issued in 1978 to $7.4 billion in 1983 to $48 billion last year—largely because of the super-salesmanship of Drexel's Milken, the preeminent figure in corporate finance today. From his offices in Beverly Hills, Milken convinced investors that the expected yield on a diversified portfolio of junk bonds *over*compensated them for the risks entailed. Such bonds are bought and sold mostly on the basis of the spread between their yield and the yield on risk-free government bonds. A typical junk bond portfolio yielding, say, 11%, currently enjoys a spread of about four percentage points over the 7% yield investors can earn on government bonds of similar maturity. In theory the spread owes to the likelihood that the junk portfolio will suffer losses over time, for instance as individual bonds default.

* * *

Milken's genius was to recognize that in any year only a tiny percentage of companies issuing such bonds had failed to make an interest or principal payment on time. Moreover, bonds that do default lose only a portion of their value. As long as history repeated itself, an investor with a diversified portfolio of junk could expect his total return to be reduced by default losses of just one percentage point a year. Junk bonds seemed to promise free money, Milken and his fellow Drexel salesmen told their clients, because even after subtracting expected default losses, total returns from junk would be far higher than risk-free Treasury bonds.

Portfolio managers for insurance companies, pension funds, and mutual funds quickly caught on and poured money into the high-yield sector as never before. Everything else being equal, the flood of new money should have caused the interest rate spread between junk bonds and government bonds to narrow. Instead—and ominously—when interest rates on Treasuries and high-grade corporates began to fall a couple of years ago, yields on junk held steady. The wider spread was the market's way of saying that junk was getting trashier.

In their rush to invest, some institutional money managers skipped the exhaustive research that they customarily perform before buying risky issues, relying instead on the strength of the underwriter's endorsement. Many simply didn't have a sufficient number of qualified analysts to thoroughly screen the hundreds of new issues coming onto the market or to closely moinitor the scores of issues already in their portfolios. In addition, junk issuers and their bonds proved to be complex creatures that sometimes didn't lend themselves to analysis with traditional financial models. An executive at one rating service says that more than a third of the money managers he advises don't do any independent research on the bonds they buy.

* * *

Had they done their homework, they might have been wary of that low historical default rate. To begin with, the default rate for publicly traded junk debt—which averaged 1.5% annually for the period 1974–86, according to New York University finance professor Edward Altman—is based in part on years when the total amount of junk was paltry by today's standards. Nearly two-thirds of all outstanding junk bonds were issued in just the last three years, roughly half in the last two years. As Altman notes, it generally takes a few years for even the worst junk to spoil, so the most recently issued stuff hasn't had a real chance to affect default rates. Nor has the junk of recent vintage had to weather a downturn in the economy.

More important, the nature of the bonds in the market appears to have changed significantly in the past few years. In 1986 an estimated $12 billion in new junk bonds—roughly 25% of all the junk issued—was sold in connection with leveraged buyouts [LBOs], those extra-risky transactions where new owners essentially hock a company to buy it. In previous years LBO-related bonds represented such a small portion of the market that nobody bothered to keep statistics on them. It's not uncommon for LBOs to have nine parts debt for every one part equity, a recipe that few companies can live with for long. The people who do LBOs count on being able to swiftly pay down that debt by selling off some of the company's assets. "Everybody in an LBO deal is going for a quick home run," says a New York banker. Lots of junk owners could go down swinging if a recession slows down that resale market.

Most default statistics also fail to take into account instances where issuers come within an eyelash of bankruptcy before some sort of rescue mission saves them. Among the most common rescue operations is the exchange offer: A company gives its bondholders new securities in exchange for the old bonds. A company out of cash and on the brink might ask its bondholders to accept new bonds that carry a lower interest rate, or permit interest to be paid in stock rather than cash. Says Ray Minella, who runs Merrill Lynch's high-yield operations: "Most such exchange offers are bankruptcies without the benefit of a judge."

James A. Schneider, a Drexel executive and an expert on exchange offers, says that the idea is to give the ailing company enough time to get to a "better doctor" —an outside investor, perhaps, who's willing to give the company a big infusion of equity. If the patient goes on to survive, the investors who hang on to the bonds can do quite well. But many investors choose to sell out, often at prices less than 50% of the face value of their bonds. That's so close to what bonds sell at just

after defaulting—typically around 40% of face value—that some analysts refer to emergency exchange offers as "soft defaults." But these soft defaults don't show up in the historical rate.

The historical rate of default nonetheless continues to be the centerpiece of the case that Drexel and others make for junk bonds as a safe investment. Says Larry Post, Drexel's co-head of high-yield bond research: "Unless you think the overall credit quality of the market has gone down, there is no reason to believe that default rates in the future won't be similar to those of the past."

But that larger spread between junk and high-grade bonds suggests that the overall credit quality *has* gone down. Other evidence points the same way. For instance, the proportion of new junk bond issues landing in Standard & Poor's or Moody's lowest-rated categories or going unrated has increased from 6.3% of new issues in 1980 to over 40% last year, according to IDD Information Services, a research firm.

No one has a perfect formula to measure the risk that a company will default on its debt. S&P and Moody's, in making their judgments, consider a broad range of financial data reflecting both the company's past performance and management's projections for the future. They also make more subjective assessments: How sound is management? How likely is potential litigation against the company?

* * *

While those judgments may be quite valuable, *Fortune* asked Houlihan Lokey to devise a more rigidly objective series of measures to spot especially vulnerable companies. The approach that resulted relies heavily on how the marketplace values a company's stock. Says Marko A. Budgyk, the Houlihan Lokey analyst who developed and managed the study: "We believe that by looking at a company's stock price, you can get a very accurate reading of how investors perceive the company's prospects. In effect, you've got a million different investors telling you what they think of management, of that potential strike on the horizon, of that new product the company intends to conquer the world with."

Houlihan Lokey combed through both Standard & Poor's and Moody's bond guides for January, identifying companies with at least one straight or convertible bond outstanding that either agency rated as junk. From that sample of 792 companies, representing $125 billion in junk, it eliminated firms whose $33 billion of junk bonds are publicly traded but whose common stock is not. The study also excluded electric utilities, representing $11 billion in bonds, and banks and other financial services companies, another $9 billion. Both have characteristics that make comparisons with industrial and nonfinancial service companies of little value. Finally, there was no way to assess junk bonds issued in private placements, a category that represented $23 billion in new issues over the past two years, according to Merrill Lynch.

Houlihan Lokey next evaluated the remaining junk bond issuers in terms of three market–based criteria: the total market value of the company's stock and equity equivalents, the volatility of its stock price, and its leverage. The analysts calculated each company's leverage, dividing total debt by the market value of the equity. Total debt figures were based on the most recent quarterly financial statements. For the equity part of the ratio, Houlihan Lokey used the market

value of each company's equity on January 30. *Fortune* subsequently asked each company to confirm its debt and equity figures; if a company reported significant changes on its balance sheet since its last financial statement, we used the fresher numbers.

* * *

As a company's leverage increases, its ability to service its debts usually declines and the risk of default rises. In the view of Houlihan Lokey and most other experts, big companies, with more equity outstanding, are able to tolerate higher leverage than their smaller counterparts. Small companies—those with equity of less than $100 million—were considered vulnerable if their debt-to-equity ratio exceeded 2.5 to 1. Companies with between $100 million and $250 million in equity were considered vulnerable if their leverage was more than 3 to 1. For companies with equity of $250 million to $500 million, the cutoff point was 4 to 1; for companies larger than that, 5 to 1.

To show up on the final lists, a company with that high leverage had to meet yet another test. Houlihan Lokey took a reading of the relative stability of each company by measuring the price volatility of its common stock over the preceding six months. The higher a company's volatility, the greater the daily changes in how investors expect it to perform in the future. In general, companies with high volatility are perceived to be riskier than companies with low volatility.

What emerged from this sifting and resifting were 24 "atomic" companies whose junk bonds are highly vulnerable to default. Twelve others, either not so highly leveraged or not so volatile, were judged by Houlihan Lokey as slightly less risky, but sufficiently dicey to qualify as "subatomic." Again, this does not necessarily mean that the companies are going to default. But they do appear to face substantially higher risks than their peers within the world of junk. Houlihan Lokey didn't estimate probabilities of default, nor did it predict when default might occur.

The main strengths of the Houlihan Lokey approach stem from its reliance on the information captured in a company's stock price. Larry Post of Drexel has used a similar approach, in fact, in analyzing junk bond issuers for almost ten years. But as Post and others point out, the method has its limitations. For example, debt is sometimes structured so that the issuer can make interest payments in the form of shares of stock during troubled times, thus conserving precious cash. And companies don't make any cash payments on zero-coupon bonds until the bonds actually come due. In such cases, companies may find extraordinarily high leverage quite tolerable.

Houlihan Lokey's method also fails to consider the amount of cash a company has in the bank—"Cash being one of the best ways I know of," Post observes, "to make the interest payment on a bond." The towering pile of cash currently on the books of Revlon Group, a company that narrowly missed the cutoff for subatomics, is a big reason that the bond research firm McCarthy Crisanti & Maffei rates the company as having a mere 2% chance of default in the next two years. But, says Philip Maffei, noting that Revlon is controlled by the acquisitive Ronald Perelman, "you can't assume that all that cash is just going to sit there for the benefit of bondholders." That's why his rating firm believes the possibility of a Revlon default in the next *five* years is closer to 10%.

These important caveats aside, the companies on *Fortune's* list include some real prizes. Even as Houlihan Lokey was doing its initial sorting, Chapman Energy, a Dallas oil and gas company, defaulted on junk bonds with a face value of $22 million. Spendthrift Farm, a Kentucky horse-breeding operation that's an atomic, and subatomic Kaneb Services, an oil services company, both announced that they expect not to make interest payments due later this year. Says Kaneb's vice president, Robert Pando: "That's why they call them high-risk bonds."

* * *

Not surprisingly, most of the companies listed as atomic or subatomic are working overtime to bolster their balance sheets. In the past year, several have exchanged some of their old bonds for new ones with terms more lenient to them. Others, including Westworld Community Healthcare, are planning exchange offers. Lear Petroleum paid off enough bank debt in early January to transform itself from an atomic company to a subatomic.

Many executives at the listed companies took strong issue with Houlihan Lokey's methodology. Others argued that in going purely by the numbers the study failed to consider important mitigating factors. For example, Valero Energy, a subatomic, plans to spin off its natural gas pipeline operations into a limited partnership, a transaction that the company says will raise $700 million—cash it will use to pay off enough debt to cut its borrowings by more than half. Texas International has agreed to sell $120 million of assets for cash it can use to pay down its debt. An executive at Quanex, an atomic, emphasized that, unlike most junk bonds, its bonds are secured by a lien on two of its steel plants. "At the first default," he says, "the bondholders get the plants."

Who owns the junk that's likely to show up on the next heap of defaults? High-yield mutual funds own about $26 billion in junk, according to Lipper Analytical Services. *Fortune* examined the portfolios of 35 of the 50 or so funds that invest mainly in junk bonds, using the most up-to-date quarterly reports available. Four were too old to consider. The remaining 31 dated from June to December of [1986]. If atomics and subatomics in a fund's portfolio represented the same proportion as they do of the entire junk universe—including bonds *Fortune* excluded from its sample —then each fund would have about 2.8% of its holdings allocated to these most vulnerable types. As a group, however, the funds appeared to have a slight predilection for the risky stuff. Twenty-four of the 31 funds had more than 2.8% of the total value of their bond holdings invested in atomics or subatomics. The percentage of risky junk varied considerably from fund to fund: In June, Bull and Bear High Yield Fund owned atomics and subatomics with a face value of $20 million, representing about 18% of its $111 million invested in bonds. At the other extreme, Vanguard's High Yield Bond Portfolio, with total bond holdings of $954 million last July, owned atomics and subatomics amounting to only 1.9% of its portfolio.

Besides junk bond mutual funds, few buyers of junk disclose much about what they own. Pension funds, which own an estimated $15 billion in junk, must report their holdings only once a year, and only to the Internal Revenue Service, which doesn't make the information public. Insurance companies ($40 billion)

open the kimonos on their portfolios only once a year, in publicly available statements they file with state insurance commissioners. While most statements currently available are too old to matter, *Fortune* checked the December 1985 portfolios of Executive Life of New York and Presidential Life, both well known for investing in junk. They seem to be particularly savvy junk collectors: Both had minuscule holdings of atomics and subatomics. "I don't like the small deals," sniffed an investment officer at one of the companies as he was read the names on *Fortune*'s lists.

While a few institutional investors may have portfolios overloaded with the junkiest junk, it seems likely that the riskiest stuff is fairly evenly distributed. If the rest of a money manager's junk bonds perform as well as they have in the recent past, a default rate as high as 6% would knock down the total return on his portfolio by approximately 3.65 percentage points, an estimate based on Professor Altman's studies of how much value bonds typically retain after defaulting. In other words, the return would be reduced to about what he could earn on government bonds.

But *will* the other 94% of junk bonds go on performing as well as always? A 6% default rate would probably shake investors' confidence in a far broader segment of the market. An exodus from junk to higher-quality investments—or from low-grade junk to high-grade junk —would send bond prices tumbling. Even investors perspicacious enough to have avoided the defaulted bonds could see the values of their portfolios shrink, at least until the market regained investors' faith.

BANKS, TOO, LIKE JUNKY COMPANIES

Where there are junk bonds, there are often junk bank loans. Bankers generally don't like to talk about how inextricably connected to the junk bond market they have become. But contrary to the popular perception that companies that issue junk bonds aren't solid enough to borrow from banks, many issuers have apparently had no trouble lining up ample supplies of bank debt. Of course, they also pay a higher rate of interest on their loans than the average corporate customer. In addition to their junk bond borrowings, the companies on our atomic and subatomic lists owe another $5 billion—much of it to banks. Houlihan Lokey estimates that all the junk bond issuers it evaluated in creating the lists together owe close to $200 billion in bank debt.

Bankers insist that *their* loans are "well protected," whatever other defaults may occur. While loans to junk issuers are not generally secured by specific collateral, banks almost always have first claim on a company's assets in the event it goes bankrupt and has to liquidate. The bankers also fill their loan agreements with myriad covenants that give them the right to step in if a borrower starts getting sickly. "I've done deals where I knew my loan could be repaid no matter what kind of trouble the company eventually got into," says a top executive at a major New York bank. As for the bondholders, he adds, "I wasn't so sure they'd see their money back in a bankruptcy situation." For taking that extra risk, of course, junk bond investors earn a higher rate of interest than the banks do on their loans.

There is little indication that banks will want out of the market any time soon. First Chicago, Drexel's lead bank, did catch the junk bond jitters shortly after the Boesky affair broke, telling Drexel that it would no longer accept junk securities as collateral for short-term loans to the same extent it once had. But most banks continue to look at high-risk companies with the same hungry eyes as investors who buy their bonds.

* * *

A recession could have far more drastic consequences. Most economists say that as long as the economy keeps chugging along they won't worry too much about the junk bond market. But they add that even a modest downturn later this year, a scenario that few economists are predicting, could jeopardize junk issuers in already weak industries such as steel, construction, and restaurants. "Massive failures of companies with junk bonds are a distinct possibility in a downturn," says Edward Yardeni, chief economist for Prudential-Bache Securities. A shakeout, he says, "could feed on itself. Because there are so many companies financed this way, there could be sort of a domino effect."

What seems more likely is the emergence of a two-tier market in junk bonds. Investors and rating agencies, more aware of the vastly different tiers of quality, probably will invent a new line to divide "investment grade" junk from the "speculative" stuff. Drexel's Post, for one, maintains that the amount of independent analysis performed by junk investors has increased "substantially" in the past year. Drexel's competitors, seeking to make a name in the business, are also committing more resources to credit analysis.

There's quality—of sorts—to be had. Over the past two years, as Morgan Stanley's Martin Fridson notes, an impressive number of large, highly liquid junk issues have come onto the market, issued by the likes of BCI (formerly Beatrice), Colt Industries, and Phillips Petroleum. Another encouraging sign: Some issuers are beginning to pay off their junk debt by selling stock. If the stock market stays strong, many companies will have an opportunity to convert some of their debt into equity.

The emergence of big issuers along with scores of midsize but equally solid companies stands to encourage more investors to participate in the junk market. In fact, 15 large insurance companies surveyed recently by Morgan Stanley suggested that they ultimately plan to invest an additional $20 billion in high-yield bonds. That will presumably mean still more credit analysts crunching the numbers.

As more investors join the chase for high yields, the market should grow more efficient. The interest-rate advantage that quality junk bonds have offered compared with high-grade corporates should narrow. Indeed, while more junk bonds than ever before are likely to live up to their name over the next few years, far more are apt to become known by a new, less pejorative label. Blue-chip junk, anyone?

POSTSCRIPT

Is Junk Bond Financing Advisable?

Michael Milken, who was sentenced to 10 years in prison in November 1990 for securities fraud and conspiracy, has been released from jail and is now teaching in the graduate school of business at the University of California, Los Angeles. Most of the others who were indicted in the financial misdealings surrounding junk bonds in the 1980s are free on parole or never saw the inside of a prison. Meanwhile, it may be years before the corporate damage is assessed.

The junk bond phenomenon may not be over, contrary to predictions. But critics are quick to point out the damage: The reservoirs of cash are almost drained; huge projects and office buildings accomplished with the help of junk bonds stand bankrupt and empty in many cities; the investors, bankers, and lawyers who made the deals got rich, put their money into safe places, and got out; and the towns, the laid-off employees, and the pension funds are left holding the remainders. Yet junk still has its defenders. It is difficult to deny that work that was accomplished through the democratization of wealth would not have been done otherwise. The mistake may have simply been letting a few opportunists grab the profits from the use of other people's money.

SUGGESTED READINGS

William P. Barrett, "Sucker Play?" *Forbes* (August 5, 1991).

Phyllis Berman and Roula Khalaf, "We're Doing Just Fine," *Forbes* (March 18, 1991).

Tad Friend, "Michael Milken: Free at Last!" *Esquire* (May 1991).

Holt Hackney, "Company Watch: Don't Take My (Kroger) Junk Away!" *Financial World* (March 19, 1991).

Laura Jereski and Jason Zweig, "Step Right Up, Folks," *Forbes* (March 4, 1991).

John Rothchild, *Going for Broke: How Robert Campeau Bankrupted the Retail Industry, Unleashed the Junk Bond Crisis, and Brought the Booming Eighties to a Crashing Halt* (Viking Penguin, 1992).

Benjamin J. Stein, "Junk Bunk," *Barron's* (July 1, 1991).

Matthew Winkler, "Gold in Garbage," *Forbes* (September 2, 1991).

Suzanne Woolley, "How to Get a Good Yield—And a Decent Night's Sleep," *Business Week* (October 28, 1991).

Andy Zipser, "Mutual Choice: Junk Bondage—A Reply" *Barron's* (July 8, 1991).

ISSUE 7

Are Financial Derivative Instruments Always a Gamble?

YES: J. Patrick Raines and Charles G. Leathers, from "Financial Derivative Instruments and Social Ethics," *Journal of Business Ethics* (vol. 13, 1994)

NO: Timothy Middleton, from "The 'D' Word: Derivatives Are Best Left to Qualified Professionals," *Nest Egg* (May/June 1995)

ISSUE SUMMARY

YES: Associate professor of economics J. Patrick Raines and professor of economics Charles G. Leathers argue that trading in financial derivatives amounts to speculation and gambling in financial markets and that an undesirable change in social ethics has reduced opposition to the practice.

NO: Timothy Middleton, a contributing editor for *Nest Egg,* asserts that financial derivatives are regularly used for a variety of risk-reducing purposes by responsible investment professionals.

Derivatives are financial instruments whose returns are linked to the performance of underlying assets such as mortgages, bonds, currencies, or commodities. Although the commodities market has been around a long time and has had its share of criticism, it operates under an agreed contract; derivatives operate without such an agreed contract. They are used to hedge, or to protect from loss, against changes in the marketplace. If you buy futures in eggs, for instance, speculating that the price will go up at some future date, but you forget to sell as the market moves, when your date arrives, so will your eggs. This might become a big problem if you are not in need of a truckload of eggs. This possibility tends to regulate the futures commodities market. That is, the possibility of the commodity being delivered takes buying futures out of the realm of "gambling": the intent of the contract at purchase time (to make a profit through an advantageous trade) is, according to the law, limited by the words of the contract and the existence of a real commodity (in this case, eggs).

While derivatives are linked to the performance of underlying assets, that linkage has nothing to do with the way they operate. Let us take the case of Orange County, California, which is discussed by Timothy Middleton. In 1994 Orange County's speculators bought billions of dollars' worth of derivative securities linked to movements in a multiple of the difference between Swiss and U.S. interest rates. As the Swiss and U.S. interest rates changed, so did the amount of difference between them; as U.S. interest rates moved toward or away from Swiss interest rates, Orange County won or lost money on (a multiple of) the amount of the change. If the interest rates moved in the right direction, the yield on the investment was very high. As it happened, U.S. interest rates were raised by the Federal Reserve to clamp down on inflation during most of 1994 and the first months of 1995. That was the wrong direction for Orange County; the rate hikes sent the value of Orange County's portfolio on a downward spiral (keep in mind that if the yield is high, so are the risks).

What should be done to prevent this type of disaster? Arthur Levitt, the chairman of the Securities and Exchange Commission, has addressed this concern by asking state and local governments to monitor those who manage and invest the taxpayers' money. It is unclear if that request will be sufficient to protect local governments from uninformed or unscrupulous investment advisors. Would it be more effective to restrict the states and counties regarding exactly what they can and cannot buy?

J. Patrick Raines and Charles G. Leathers call derivatives trading "speculation" and "gambling," and they decry society's apparent tolerance of it. Timothy Middleton suggests that in the hands of capable investors, financial derivative instruments perform a valuable function. What weight should be given the values of freedom and justice in investment activities? Should government curb, with careful regulation, the activities of investment experts who manage public monies (but not necessarily those who speculate for their own profit or for the profit of private clients)? What could or would government regulation of the financial markets do to the choices for investors and the ability to raise money for those who wish to expand or gain from these markets? Can government do a better job of protecting the public till than a well-trained professional who knows the local territory?

As you read the following selections, try to find solutions to these questions: Should pension fund managers, government officials, or financial advisors be allowed to put at risk, for profitable gains or losses, the millions of dollars that the public funds to which they are entrusted contain? The public trusts their investments will grow and be there for them at some future date. If the mandate is to hold such funds for future distributions (retirement or savings), should risk of any sort be allowed? If the government protects these funds, what happens to the ability to optimize profits and growth?

YES

J. Patrick Raines and Charles G. Leathers

FINANCIAL DERIVATIVE INSTRUMENTS AND SOCIAL ETHICS

ABSTRACT. Recent finance literature attributes the development of derivative instruments (interest rate futures, stock index futures) to (1) technological advances, and (2) improved mathematical models for predicting option prices. This paper explores the role of social ethics in the acceptance of financial derivatives. The relationship between utilitarian ethical principles and the demise of turn-of-the-century bucket shops is contrasted with modern tolerance of financial derivatives based upon libertarian ethical precepts. Our conclusion is that a change in social ethics also facilitated the growth in trading in modern financial derivatives.

INTRODUCTION

One of the most important recent developments in financial markets has been the rise of financial derivative instruments from a secondary role to a position of dominance (Konishi and Dattatreya, 1991). Financial derivatives are contracts whose values are dependent upon the values of the underlying financial assets which trade separately. Prominent examples include futures contracts on the 30-year Treasury bond and stock index futures and options. Often referred to as "synthetic securities," modern financial derivatives have taken increasingly sophisticated forms and carry such exotic labels as swaptions, collars, caps, and circuses.

In finance literature, the rapid growth of trading in derivative instruments is largely attributed to (1) technological advances in communications and data processing, and (2) the use of sophisticated mathematics in financial theory to determine prices for financial options (Torres, 1991). But from a behavioral perspective, the prominent role of modern financial derivatives reflects changes in social ethics. In the late 1800's and early 1900's, social reformers vigorously lobbied for legislation limiting or prohibiting the relatively unsophisticated derivative instruments of that era. By the ethical precepts then in

From J. Patrick Raines and Charles G. Leathers, "Financial Derivative Instruments and Social Ethics," *Journal of Business Ethics*, vol. 13 (1994), pp. 197–204. Copyright © 1994 by D. Reidel Publishing Co., Dordrecht, Holland, and Boston, U.S.A. Reprinted by permission of Kluwer Academic Publishers.

vogue, speculative trading in commodities futures and options and transactions at bucket shops (mock brokerage houses) were construed as forms of gambling. In this paper, we note that if those ethical precepts still prevailed today, modern financial derivatives would be subject to a similar indictment.

ETHICAL OPPOSITION TO EARLY FINANCIAL DERIVATIVES

Opposition to trading in the early forms of financial derivatives was driven in part by the economic interests of several parties involved, in particular, agricultural producers and processors and officials of organized stock and commodity exchanges. But the popular influence of social precepts relating to gambling and speculation in financial and commodity markets provided the opposition with a fundamental claim to a broader social legitimacy. Even those motivated by pecuniary self-interest recognized the political expediency of couching their arguments in terms of social ethics relating to gambling.

Given the militant anti-gambling sentiment prevailing in the late 19th and early 20th century, moralistic judgements against the early financial derivatives rested on the fundamental principle that contracts settled by simply paying the differences in cash were devices for betting on price changes. This principle was invoked, directly or indirectly, in both the agrarians' campaign against trading in commodity futures (which organized exchanges successfully resisted) and the social reformers' crusades against operation of bucket shops (which the organized exchanges successfully turned to their own advantage).

Opposition to Trading in Commodity Futures

In the late 1800's, the agrarian interests mounted strong organized support for Congressional action aimed at restricting speculation in commodities futures. On purely economic grounds, farmers and millers believed that speculative commodity futures trading created unfavorable market prices. But on social and legal grounds, the argument was advanced that speculative trading in commodity futures constituted gambling because the commodities specified were not actually delivered.

Since the quantities of commodities specified in futures contracts often exceeded the total quantities in storage and production, proponents of anti-futures legislation contended that settlement of the contracts by delivery of actual commodities was physically impossible. The alleged trade in fictitious commodities was captured by the contemptuous term "wind wheat." In 1892, Congress very nearly passed a bill which would have effectively banned speculation in commodities futures by levying prohibitive taxes on "wind wheat" contracts. Since futures contracts involving commodities actually owned would have been exempted from the taxes, opportunities for farmers and millers to hedge against market price fluctuations through the use of commodity futures would not have been affected (Cowing, 1965).

The principle that distinguished legitimate financial contracts from gambling contracts was clearly incorporated in the legal status of options contracts in commodities markets. Under prevailing legal theory, an option "was inescapably a wagering contract because the purchaser could offer no intent other than a desire to profit by a price change. The intent to profit, where no goods were exchanged, was held to be socially unjustifiable" (Cowing, 1965). On that basis, options (which in theory could always be settled in cash) were viewed by the courts as unenforceable contracts.

Ultimately, the efforts to ban speculative trade in commodity futures failed because legal representatives of the organized commodity exchanges were able to draw a crucial distinction between options as gambling contracts and futures contracts. Despite the fact that only about 3 percent of futures contracts were actually settled by delivery of the commodities, the purchaser of a futures contract could demand actual delivery. The *right* to require delivery established an *intent* that was legitimate. Whether that intent was actually carried out into action was deemed to be immaterial (Cowing).

Ethical Opposition to Bucket-Shops
The anti-gambling sentiment prevalent in the early 1900s also manifested in ethical criticism of the stock market. Writing in 1904, Conant quoted a passage from an unnamed source on the ethics of stock exchanges:

> If, instead of betting on something so small as falling dice, one bets on the rise and fall of stocks..., the law will pay not the slightest attention. A gambling house for these larger purposes may be built conspicuously in any city, the sign 'Stock Exchange' may be set over its door, influential men appointed its officers, and the law will protect it and them as it does the churches. How infamous to forbid gambling on a small scale and almost to encourage it on a large! (Conant, 1904).

Conant strongly denied that stock exchanges were gambling houses. While conceding that betting on the rise and fall of stocks is a form of gambling, he asserted that such betting occurred not in the stock market but in bucket shops. Bucket shops, declared Conant, were of no use to the community, destructive to the morals and pocketbooks of young men, and could not be too severely censured (Conant, 1904).

Although a prevalent institution from the late 1800's through the 1920's, bucket shops seem now to be largely forgotten. As Kindleberger (1978) observed: "The term bucket shop has practically disappeared from the language since the Securities and Exchange Commission stamped it out after 1933 as an illegal practice. Nor is it discussed in the economic literature." Consequently, it is not surprising that transactions at bucket shops have not been properly recognized as an early form of financial derivatives whose values derived from the market prices of the underlying securities.

In modern terminology, bucket shops might be described as "simulated" brokerage houses. Transactions at real brokerage houses resulted in the actual buying and selling of securities on organized exchanges which determined the market prices. Bucket shops allowed customers to speculate on changes in those prices without any actual buying and selling taking place. Essentially, both the bucket shop operator and the customers were only pretending to buy or sell stocks (or commodities), but the obligation to pay based on price changes was real. In choosing the shares to be "traded," customers could go "long" or "short". If prices rose, those who had gone "long" realized gains, and if prices fell, those who had gone "short" profited.

Bucket shops provided opportunities to speculate on movements in prices without any ownership of shares being involved. In technical terminology, the expression "to bucket an order" meant that the receiver (the "bucketeer") covered the order himself without entering into a contract with another party or clearing the transaction (Hieronymus, 1971). Most patrons went "long," optimistically expecting prices to rise. This put the bucket shops in chronic short positions, such that if prices did rise the operators would incur losses. Although the odds were naturally in favor of the operators, various types of fraudulent practices were allegedly used to bilk the customers.

The movement to force closure of the bucket shops involved a curious alliance between social reformers motivated by high moral principle and representatives of the organized exchanges. The latter viewed the bucket shops as both irritating competitors and sources of negative public perceptions of the nature of trading in stock and commodities markets. Fraudulent practices by bucket shop operators, e.g., false reporting of stock prices, were widely and sensationally exposed by newspapers and popular magazines, fueling public hostility toward the shops. But the efforts to outlaw bucket shops ultimately rested on the principle that bucket shop transactions were in the nature of gambling contracts since no actual purchase and delivery of stocks or commodities was involved. Under the New York Anti-Bucket Shop Law, for example, the purchase or sale of securities was a penal offence if it was intended that the contract would be settled upon the basis of quotations on any exchange and without intending a bona fide sale, or when such market quotations reached a certain figure without intending a bona fide purchase or sale, or based on the differences in such market quotations at which such securities were bought or sold.

Utilitarian ethical theory provides an explanation for the efforts to abolish the bucket shops. A utilitarian regulatory philosophy was evolving at this time which held that commerce could be regulated to promote social welfare by maximizing societal benefits and minimizing harms. Utilitarian moral theory was manifested in the Interstate Commerce Act (1887), the Sherman Antitrust Act (1890) and, later, in the Clayton Act (1914). Such social legislation was engineered to protect the public from unfair competitive practices, fraud, deception, and dishonesty. Since bucket shop opponents believed gambling losses caused more unhappiness and conflict in society than social good, legislation was necessary to protect the public from the harm of this financial chicanery.

In general, regulation based upon utilitarian principles was supported by the business community and, in this specific instance, by legal stock exchanges because regulation of anticompetitive practices increased investor, consumer and competitor confidence and worked to everyone's advantage.

Despite stringent opposition from social reform groups and officials of organized exchanges, bucket shops proved to be highly resilient until the Securities and Exchange Commission [SEC] was created. Their popularity is not difficult to explain. In some respects, the bucket shops were more democratic than the organized exchanges. Indeed, bucket shop operators responded to attacks from organized exchanges by arguing that their operations provided lower income people the same opportunities to speculate on stock and commodity prices that were available to the privileged few who enjoyed access to the organized exchanges. Bucket shop transactions were not only in small amounts that ordinary people could make but could be made on a very thin margin. And unlike the organized exchanges, bucket shops did not discriminate on basis of race, sex, or age (see Fabian, 1990).

Moreover, despite the alleged frequency of fraudulent practices, e.g., falsifying price quotes, a number of men who later became major figures on the organized exchanges learned to read the ticker tape and developed their investment strategies in bucket shops. Indeed, some of those individuals, e.g., Jesse Livermore, were able to consistently beat the bucket shops (Cowing, 1965; Thomas, 1989).

On the surface, the eventual suppression of bucket shops by the SEC reflected the ability of the organized exchanges to exploit public hostility against the shops. By making the bucket shops the symbol of gambling on stock and commodity prices, the exchanges successfully diverted charges that speculation in commodity futures and in various types of stock market practices also constituted gambling. Speculation on organized exchanges was defended as being necessary to the efficient functioning of the real economy of production and distribution.

But the key factors in the demise of bucket shops were the strong social disapproval of gambling and the identification of bucket shop transactions as a form of gambling because no actual sales of stocks took place. If the only moral objection to bucket shops had been their fraudulent practices, the shops could have simply been regulated and allowed to remain open. Such a policy would certainly have been appropriate under what appears to be the modern ethical perspective on financial derivatives.

MODERN SOCIAL ETHICS AND FINANCIAL DERIVATIVES

While futures trading in commodities has long existed, trading in financial futures began in 1972, when the Chicago Mercantile Exchange (CME) introduced futures contracts in currency through its International Monetary Market division. Subsequently, futures contracts were introduced on Treasury bills, large bank CDs, and Eurodollar deposits. The success of the new "interest rate futures" (so-called because the values of the underlying securities are highly sensitive to changes in the interest rate) led to the introduction of options on those futures (Konishi and Dattatreya, 1991). Equity derivative instruments appeared in 1982 when the CME introduced the S&P 500 stock index futures contract. In the following year, the CME established trading in options on those futures.

Competitive development of new derivative instruments has become a booming high-tech business. The creation of "synthetic securities" which artificially replicate portfolios of the underlying securities can involve highly complex transactions (Crawford and Sihler, 1991). Major securities firms are now using new high-powered computers capable of developing highly sophisticated mathematical programs to create a host of new "synthetics" that can "identify hundreds of never-before-imagined trades in stocks, bonds, and currencies" (Torres, 1991).

As an example, a derivative instrument produced from a combination of Nikkei stock-index futures and exchange-traded stock-index options created a synthetic option that "cost less than the real thing" (Torres, 1991). The incentive for producing and marketing such "synthetics" is indicated by a profit of $500,000 realized by an investment bank on a single trade in one of the newly created options.

Proponents of the growing use of financial derivatives contend that these instruments improve the efficiency of financial markets by providing hedging devices to insure against risk and by increasing the degree of liquidity in the markets. Malkiel (1990), for example, defends derivative instruments on grounds that they "provide important risk-reducing benefits" and "reduce transactions costs since brokerage costs are lower in the futures market than in the stock market." Modern trading strategies, e.g., portfolio insurance and index arbitrage, use index futures to quickly, efficiently, and cheaply trade the "entire market" as if it were a single commodity.

Those trading strategies have generated growing concern over the effects of financial derivatives on the stability of financial markets. Stock index arbitrage (program trading) and portfolio insurance have been blamed for increasing the volatility of stock prices and contributing to stock market crash of 1987. In index arbitrage, speculators seek risk free gains by quickly substituting stock index futures for the stocks represented in those indexes, or vice-versa, using computerized trading systems. When the gap between prices of the indexed stocks in cash markets and the prices of the index futures becomes abnormally large, the higher priced instruments are sold and the lower-price ones are bought. Portfolio insurance involves computerized programs which protect portfolios of stocks by triggering large sales of stock index futures when stock prices begin to fall.

According to Mayer (1988), there was overwhelming evidence that "back-and-forth transactions in derivative instruments and stocks helped drive the market too high and then pushed it down too quickly." Roll (1989), however, argued that "taken as a characteristic in isolation, computer directed trading such as portfolio insurance and index arbitrage, if it had any impact at all, actually helped mitigate the market decline" (p. 57). International financial regulators have recently expressed fears that the global market for financial derivatives "is growing too fast, has too little regulation and is being used by some traders as a speculative arena" (Lipin and Power, 1992; see also, *The Economist* 1992).

In contrast to the publicly expressed concern about the effects of modern financial derivatives on market stability, relatively little has been said about the ethical aspects of modern financial derivatives. The *nature* of financial derivatives as gambling contracts has largely escaped critical attention in the recent literature. Borna and Lowry (1987) only briefly noted the resemblance of futures trading to gambling in arguing that speculative business practices in general should be considered as public gambling. Ethical inquiries instead have focused more on the *use* of financial derivatives. Horrigan (1987), for example, observed that "the world of the New Finance," where investors can adjust immediately to any financial strategy chosen by corporate management with actions that include "clever option positions," is ethically "not a nice place." Similarly, Shriver (1989) briefly cited ethical concerns about the impact of stock index futures on the stability of financial markets.

Yet, the contracts involved in modern derivative trading are fundamentally similar in nature to the commodity futures and bucket shop transactions of a century ago. Certainly, the "wind wheat" case against speculation in commodity futures would apply to modern derivative markets since the volume of trade in derivative instruments often exceeds the underlying assets trading in cash markets. The dollar value of the S&P 500 stock index futures contract, for example, runs about 60 percent more than the value of the actual stocks in that index traded on the New York Stock Exchange (Merrick, 1990).

More importantly, the ethical/legal principle cited in the battle against bucket shops—that contracts settled in cash constituted gambling contracts—would lead to a similar charge against stock index futures. Traditional futures contracts, such as those for gold or Treasury bills, allow final settlement by delivery of the underlying assets. But in stock index futures trading, the underlying securities (the individual stocks themselves) are never actually involved. Instead, stock index futures contracts are settled through cash payments, a deliberate design feature intended to avoid the costs and inconvenience of final settlement through physical delivery. In the case of the S&P 500 contract, for example, actual delivery would require the purchase and delivery of the properly weighted basket of 500 stocks (Merrick, 1990). (While the contracts are often settled by reverse trading before expiration date, over one-third are settled by cash.)

One of the ethical arguments against bucket shops was that the transactions had no effect on the determination of stock prices. According to economic philosophy rooted in ethical considerations of the nature of market prices tracing back to Aristotle, prices play a socially legitimate role by reflecting true values and efficiently allocating resources. Thus, transactions between buyers and sellers of actual stocks on organized exchanges which produced those prices were deemed to be socially legitimate functions. A double indictment of bucket shops was raised on this point. Transactions by bucket shop patrons not only failed to enter the price determination process. They also interfered with the ability of organized exchanges to establish socially efficient stock prices by diverting funds from those exchanges.

The relationship between trading in modern stock index futures and the determination of stock prices in cash markets, although more complex, is fundamentally not that different. In applying for permission to trade the S&P 500 index future, the Chicago Mercantile Exchange argued that trading in this contract would have no effect on prices in the cash market: "Arbitrage would not be possible because of the difficulty of buying or selling 500 stocks at once" (Mayer, 1988). Thus, there was an explicit intent from the beginning that buying and selling stock index futures contracts would not perform the socially beneficial function of establishing efficient prices of the actual shares of stock being traded in the cash market.

Subsequently, it has been recognized that prices in the index futures markets indirectly influence prices of stocks in the cash market through index arbitrage. That influence has also been recognized as periodically disrupting the ability of the cash markets to establish socially efficient prices. The explicit cash-settlement design of the stock index futures creates a special problem on expiration days when arbitrageurs "unwind" their positions. Arbitrageurs hold offsetting positions in stocks and index futures. At expiration, the futures price equals the price of the actual stocks in the index. The buy or sell orders that arbitrageurs place with the stock specialists on the day of expiration tend to create imbalances between supply and demand which result in temporary price swings. These imbalances occur because stock index futures contracts are settled in cash rather than through actual delivery of stocks.

The indirect effect of the cash settlement feature of stock index futures contracts has drawn critical attention from the SEC's Division of Market Regulation, but only in regard to the effects on price volatility. A staff report of a study of the October 1987 stock market crash recommended requiring physical settlement of index products, i.e., actual delivery of the underlying securities. The cash settlement feature of stock index futures contracts "eliminates the risk that a market participant must liquidate its position prior to the termination of the future or accept delivery (and make payment for) a market basket of stocks" (SEC, 1988). The absence of that risk may encourage institutional investors to assume excessively large positions with "tighter triggers" for selling when prices decline.

Social Ethics and Public Policies

The contrast between the strong ethical concern about the nature of financial derivatives in the early 1900s and the relative lack of such concern today has interesting public policy implications. If the moral perspective had not drawn such an absolute judgement that transactions in the bucket shops constituted gambling, the shops could have been simply regulated to suppress the fraudulent activities. The outcome would have been somewhat similar in effect to the indirect relationship described above between stock index futures and the cash market. As Hieronymus (1971) noted,

operators of bucket shops could have hedged their positions by taking positions in the actual stocks. No record exists of the extent to which bucket shop operators actually laid off their net open positions by trades on the exchanges. While the large brokerage houses attempted to prevent such actions, some brokers apparently were willing to work with the bucket shop operators.

Conversely, if the same social ethics were applied today to stock index futures—the principle that an intent to take delivery of the underlying securities must be explicit to the contract if the gambling charge was to be avoided—social concerns about program trading would disappear as stock index futures would not be permitted. But such a policy would also eliminate opportunities to hedge portfolios and the other benefits attributed to trading in financial futures and options. It is noteworthy that all the reports on the effects of financial derivatives on modern stock markets call for regulations, not prohibitions on use of derivative instruments.

CONCLUDING STATEMENT

The more tolerant attitude toward financial derivatives reflects the extent of change in society's ethical perspective on the relationship between speculative financial trading and gambling. An indication of that change is found in the sensitivity on part of financial writers to terms and analogies that might link trading on organized exchanges to betting. Financial journalists and writers who spoke for the organized exchanges in the early 1900's, e.g., Conant (1904), carefully avoided gambling terminology in their discourses on financial markets. In contrast, modern financial writers frequently (and happily) draw analogies between speculative stock and commodities trading and gambling.

The authors of a leading capital markets textbook, for example, state that "Stock index options can be used to *bet* on the movement of stock prices (speculating)..." (Fabozzi and Modigilani, 1992, emphasis added). The following statement appears in *The Wall Street Journals' Guide to Understanding Money and Markets:* "Speculators may be the highest flying *gamblers* in the financial world" (Wurman *et al.*, 1990, emphasis added). Crawford and Sihler (1991) write about "the new casino of futures and options." Perhaps most revealing is the concession by the editor of *The Journal of Portfolio Management* that the question is no longer as to whether investing in the stock market is a form of gambling but rather what kind of gambling: "The stock market is a lot more like poker and black jack than it is like roulette and craps" (Bernstein, 1990).

Critics of our thesis might argue that social ethics actually have not changed in a substantive fashion. Rather, the degree of ethical concern on part of society may simply vary with the types of participants involved. Social opposition to bucket shop transactions was particularly strong because most of the patrons were individuals who were perceived as being unsophisticated in their knowledge of financial markets and unable to afford the losses. Social indifference as to whether modern financial derivatives are gambling contracts stems from a recognition that the participants are large institutional investors with sufficient knowledge and ability to assume the risks involved. But if the opposition to bucket shops had rested primarily on a public perception that the

patrons needed protection, the more logical approach would have been to impose regulations on the shops to prohibit fraudulent activities. The strong public will to force closure of the shops arose from and was sustained by the perception that the social costs of gambling (economic losses, social disharmony) exceeded the gains to society from investment alternatives. During the 1980's, the prevalent philosophy of regulation was that financial markets were the most efficient method of meeting the needs of a dynamic economy. For example, in 1985 the Securities and Exchange Commission urged government-securities brokers to create a *self-regulating* national organization for the purpose of developing a code of ethics for the unregulated securities market. In hindsight, deregulation and the legendary fraud and abuses that occurred in the securities markets clearly reflects the dominance of ethical egoism and libertarian theories. Modern social reformers have advocated a maximum degree of individual freedom to allow economic agents to pursue their own self-interest in the belief that the public interest will be served. Thus, contemporary social indifference to the gambling characteristics of financial derivatives is rooted in the principle that maximum economic gain will result when self-interested investors have the freedom to assume financial risks and claim pecuniary rewards.

Ethical indifference to the booming trade in modern financial derivatives, which are similar in nature to bucket shop transactions, must therefore be seen as evincing a change in social ethics with regard to speculation and gambling in financial markets.

REFERENCES

Benson, G. C. S.: 1982, *Business Ethics in America* (Lexington Books, Lexington, MA).

Bernstein, P. L.: 1990, 'Of Crap, Black Jack, and Theories of Finance', *Journal of Portfolio Management* Fall, 1.

Borna, S. and J. Lowry: 1987 Apr, 'Gambling and Speculation', *Journal of Business Ethics*, 225–231.

Conant, C. A.: 1904, *Wall Street and the Country* (Greenword Press, New York).

Cowing, C. B.: 1965, *Populists, Plungers and Progressives* (Princeton University Press, Princeton).

Crawford, R. D. and W. W. Sihler: 1991), *The Troubled Money Business* (Harper Business).

Fabian, A.: 1990, *Card Sharps Dream Books and Bucket Shops* (Cornell University Press).

Fabozzi, F. J. and F. Modigliani: 1992, *Capital Markets* (Prentice Hall, Englewood Cliffs).

Gilman, S. P.: 1923, *Stock Exchange Law* (The Ronald Press Company, New York).

Hieronymus, T. A.: 1971, *Economics of Futures Trading* (Commodity Research Bureau, Inc., New York).

Horrigan, J. O.: 1987 Feb, 'The Ethics of the New Finance', *Journal of Business Ethics*, 97–110.

Kindleberger, C. P.: 1978, *Manias, Panics, and Crashes* (Basic Books, New York).

Konishi, A. and R. E. Dattatreya: 1991, *The Handbook of Derivative Instruments* (Probus Publishing Company, Chicago).

Lipin, S. and W. Power: 1992 Mar 24, "Derivatives' Draw Warnings From Speculators', *Wall Street Journal*, C1.

Malkiel, B. C.: 1990, *A Random Walk Down Wall Street* (New York).

Mayer, M.: 1988, *Markets* (W. W. Norton, New York).

Merrick, J.: 1990, 'Fact and Fantasy About Stock Index Futures Program Trading', in D. R. Fraser and P. S. Rose (eds.), *Readings on Financial Institutions and Markets* (Irwin, Homewood), pp. 365–377.

Roll, R. W.: 1989, 'The International Crash of 1987', *Black Monday and the Future of Financial Markets* (Irwin, Homewood).

Shriver, D. W.: 1989, 'Ethical Discipline and Religious Hope in the Investment Industry', in O. Williams *et al.* (eds.), *Ethics and the Investment Industry* (Rowman & Littlefield Publishers, Inc. Savage, MD), pp. 233–250.

The Economist: 1992 May 23, 'Taming the Derivatives Beast', 81–82.

Thomas, D. L.: 1989, *The Plungers and the Peacocks* (Morrow, New York).

Torris, C.: 1991 Oct 18, 'Mathematicians Race to Develop New Kinds of Trading Instruments', *Wall Street Journal*, C1.

U.S. Securities and Exchange Commission, Division of Market Regulation: 1988, *The October 1987 Break* (Commerce Clearing House, Inc., Chicago).

Wurman, R. S., A. Siegel, and K. M. Morris: 1990, *The Wall Street Journal Guide to Understanding Money and Markets* (Prentice Hall Press, New York).

NO

Timothy Middleton

THE "D" WORD: DERIVATIVES ARE BEST LEFT TO QUALIFIED PROFESSIONALS

When it was sold to a West Coast investor two years ago, it sounded too good to be true: a one-year government-guaranteed security paying 17% in interest. And indeed it was. This collateralized mortgage obligation, or CMO, is currently yielding 0.6%, because its maturity mushroomed to 25 years due to higher interest rates. When the investor, who had paid $8,700 for the CMO, tried to sell it recently, he was offered $1,500.

"This guy had no idea what his broker was selling him," says Kenneth R. Hyman, a trader at Associated Securities Corp. in Los Angeles, to whom the hapless investor turned for help. There was nothing Hyman could do. The customer was just another victim of derivatives.

Derivatives became the dirtiest word on Wall Street last year, after Orange County, California, and some income-oriented mutual funds offered by Piper Jaffray were devastated by rising interest rates. Early this year the venerable Barings, one of Britain's oldest banks, collapsed when one of its traders made colossal losing bets in the derivatives market on the direction of the Tokyo Stock Exchange.

While derivatives are centuries old and are used conservatively every day to hedge farmers' crops and investors' stocks, securities artificially carved out of other financial instruments lend themselves to speculation and thus to exploitation by commission-driven brokers.

Referring to the very kind of high-risk derivatives that plunged Orange County into bankruptcy, money manager James I. Midanek warns: "These things are being shown to retail investors by brokers. They say, 'After all, it's backed by an agency of the U.S. government—how wrong can you go?' Well, you can go very wrong."

The lessons of the past two years are clear: Don't touch derivatives unless you understand them thoroughly. As with any other financial product, if their yield is above average, so is their risk.

DECIPHERING DERIVATIVES

While derivatives can be as complicated as the financial objective they are created to carry out, conceptually there are only three kinds: forward-based contracts, such as futures; options; and securities based on assets or liabilities.

Forward contracts often involve interest rates, currencies, or commodities. In a rate agreement, the parties agree on an interest rate to be paid on a principal amount at some future date. The payoff is the difference between the contract rate and the prevailing rate at the time of settlement. The principal itself is never exchanged.

Currency contracts promise to exchange one currency for another at an agreed-upon rate on a future date. Commodities forward contracts are similar, except the underlying asset is a physical commodity, such as gold or pork bellies.

Another type of forward contract is the financial future. Usually tied to interest rates, currencies, or an equity index, such as the Standard & Poor's 500 Index, these contracts are standardized and trade on an organized exchange, whereas forward contracts are often individually negotiated.

Swap contracts are almost infinitely varied, but the basic concept is that the parties agree to exchange something in the future, such as an interest rate. Rate swaps are the commonest such contracts, although they can be pegged to commodity price indexes or currency exchange rates. In a simple interest-rate swap, one party locks in a fixed rate of interest on the principal amount, while the other agrees to pay a variable rate, which starts out lower than the fixed rate but is expected to rise over the period of the contract. The intended effect is for the parties to split the income, with the variable side getting the cash in the early years or months and the fixed side later on. If everything works as designed, the transaction is a wash; only risk has been shared.

Operations are a whole different animal. Here the holder has the right, but not the obligation, to take possession of the underlying security, which usually is a common stock. Call options give the purchaser the right to demand the underlying shares at the agreed price, and they increase in value if the share price exceeds the option amount on the settlement date. Otherwise they are worthless. Put options are the opposite. They increase in value if the share price declines. If it doesn't, they have no value.

Asset- or liability-based derivatives are linked to cash flows of the underlying securities. So-called strips consist of interest-only and principal-only shares in an income security, like a Treasury note. Collateralized mortgage obligations, or CMOs, are similar; a pool of mortgages is sliced into subsets, or tranches, with different risk characteristics. The least risky have low yields and are usually purchased by institutions, such as pension funds. High-yielding CMOs, which by definition are much riskier, are often sold to the public.

THE RISE OF EXOTICS

Money managers are constantly devising new variations on these themes, and these innovations are collectively called "exotic derivatives." There is almost nothing you can't do to a financial security to alter its risk profile, which is often the prime objective of a derivative. By the nature of their rapid evolution, exotics defy definition. Some of those currently operating in world markets include all or nothings (option contracts that only pay if a predetermined trigger point is reached) and inverse floaters (debt instruments whose interest moves the opposite of the underlying index).

"These are not anything that's really new," says Robert Herman, who traded derivatives for eight years before quitting to write about them for Knight-Ridder Financial, a news wire in New York City. "People have made fortunes and gone bust in the rice futures market for hundreds of years." Convertible bonds have a derivative—a stock option—embedded in them, on the same principle as structured notes. Stock warrants in essence are long-term call options. Says Herman, "These are products that have been around for generations and they are a very effective mechanism for transferring risk."

Investment professionals regularly use simple derivatives for a variety of risk-reducing purposes. KPMG Peat Marwick, the accounting firm, uses this example in a booklet, "Solving the Mystery of Derivatives," it published for its clients:

"A pension fund manager bought 100,000 shares of a large company when the price was $40 per share. Since that time the price has moved to $60. Because the fund requires certain cash dividend targets, the pension fund manager decides not to sell the shares despite concluding that the price is more likely to move down than up. In order to protect the existing profit of $20, the fund manager buys a put option on the stock at a strike price of $60, and pays a $2 premium for this right. The fund manager has thereby guaranteed that the combined stock and option value will not fall below $58 per share during the term of the put option, while continuing to receive the dividend on the stock."

To the extent a derivative reduces risk on one side of the transaction, it magnifies risk on the opposite side. Some investors —actually, speculators—happily assume such risk if they expect outsize rewards as compensation.

This is exactly the trap into which Orange County, California, fell. It purchased billions of dollars of structured notes that produced above-market yields when interest rates were declining. They were inverse floaters, yielding a variable rate that moved the opposite of real interest rates. When interest rates rose, Orange County was ruined.

DERIVATIVES AND MUTUAL FUNDS

"Those guys were gambling not investing," says Andrew M. Hudick, a financial planner in Roanoke, VA, and president of the National Association of Personal Financial Advisors.

When derivatives became Page One news, Hudick received frantic calls from his clients, who hold considerable assets in the form of mutual funds and were worried that their funds contained derivatives. Hudick explained that a great many funds use derivatives all the time to help protect their assets.

"When they're used the way they're supposed to be, in order to hedge a portfolio or protect some profits, then I think they're used appropriately," he says.

Midanek, chief investment officer of Solon Asset Management in Walnut Creek, CA, manages $500 million of fixed-income assets, mostly in the form of mortgage-backed securities. He uses a derivative called puts on U.S. Treasury notes to hedge bonds against possible increases in interest rates. Such a hike would depress the value of his bonds, because their value moves inversely with interest rates, but it would bolster the puts. If rates don't increase, the puts become worthless on their expiration date, and Midanek is out only the cost of the derivatives, which are measured in hundredths of a percentage point.

Midanek, who also manages the Solon Short-Duration Government Bond mutual funds, stresses that derivatives are so complex that trading them requires considerable expertise and numbers-crunching capacity on a computer. "We don't think this is a market for retail investors to use on their own," he says.

If you are confronted by a broker who wants to sell you anything other than straight debt or garden-variety equity, ask for a thorough explanation of ex-actly what the product is intended to accomplish for its issuer and how you're supposed to benefit from that. Collateralized mortgage obligations ultimately serve such government agencies as Fannie Mae and Freddie Mac as a lower-cost form of financing than straight bonds, because they shift risk from themselves to purchasers.

Also ask the salesperson to explain every single assumption underlying the sales pitch. CMOs require numerous assumptions about the outlook for mortgage prepayments as well as interest rates. Press the seller to explain, point by point, what happens if the opposite scenario unfolds.

And remember 1994, when many conservative bond investors saw the value of their capital erode 20%—and investors in many derivatives lost considerably more.

POSTSCRIPT

Are Financial Derivative Instruments Always a Gamble?

Consider the reasons for the stock and commodities markets in the first place, which is to help businesses and farmers to raise cash and also to help investors to make profits. Contrast these reasons with the objectives of public fund management, which tries to ensure security and liquidity. Also remember that investment houses, banks, and financial advisors are all in the business of giving professional advice and selling products to the public. The public in many cases has little or no understanding of the products and the risks involved and therefore depends on professionals to give them good advice.

Are derivatives in large portfolios a safe hedge that can reduce the risks of institutional investors? Is this true for the small investor in a mutual fund that buys derivatives to protect against loss? Or is Raines and Leathers's comparison of derivatives to poker or blackjack games a more accurate description?

Can the Securities and Exchange Commission or the government keep the stock and commodities markets from becoming "casinos" without eliminating the free-market system upon which they operate? Do social ethics change the basic ethical principals regarding financial dealings?

In a free-market economy, is self-regulation effective, or must the government work for the greater good?

SUGGESTED READINGS

Tim W. Ferguson, "The Dynamite and the Derivatives," *The Wall Street Journal* (February 28, 1995).

Roger Lowenstein, "Will Orange County Squeeze California?" *The Wall Steet Journal* (June 15, 1995).

Suzanne McGee, "Derivatives Could Hedge Career Growth," *The Wall Street Journal* (August 24, 1995).

Donald G. Simonson, "Vignettes from the Derivatives 'Crisis,'" *United States Banker* (September 1994).

Jeffrey Taylor, "Securities Firms Agree to Set Controls on Derivatives," *The Wall Street Journal* (March 9, 1995).

R. S. Wurman, A. Siegel, and K. M. Morris, *The Wall Street Journal Guide to Understanding Money and Markets* (Prentice Hall, 1990).

PART 3

Human Resources: The Corporation and the Employee

The workforce is changing. Employees in the United States and Canada, and to a lesser extent elsewhere in the world, are becoming very diverse: many ethnic groups are represented in the workplace, women and men are approaching equality in numbers in most fields, and an array of protected conditions —such as age, ethnicity, disability, and religious persuasion— are making corporate life complicated for employers. Employees are more aware of their rights and more willing to demand that their employers honor them than they've ever been. What can business do to protect the rights of this diverse group while protecting its own economic interests?

- Are Programs of Preferential Treatment Unjustifiable?

- Does Blowing the Whistle Violate Company Loyalty?

- Should Concern for Drug Abuse Overrule Concerns for Employee Privacy?

- Should Women Have the Same Right to Work as Men?

ISSUE 8

Are Programs of Preferential Treatment Unjustifiable?

YES: Lisa H. Newton, from "Reverse Discrimination as Unjustified," *Ethics* (July 1973)

NO: Richard Wasserstrom, from "A Defense of Programs of Preferential Treatment," *National Forum: The Phi Kappa Phi Journal* (Winter 1978)

ISSUE SUMMARY

YES: Professor of philosophy Lisa H. Newton argues that programs of preferential treatment represent reverse discrimination and are therefore antimerit and unjust. These programs replace fair procedures with political positioning and open preferential avenues to minorities.

NO: Professor of philosophy Richard Wasserstrom maintains that society is not fair and merit based to begin with, and he argues that there is no inconsistency in objecting to racist and sexist discrimination while favoring preferential treatment.

The civil rights movement in the United States began with the 1961 sit-ins at the lunch counters in Atlanta, Georgia, and the boycott of the buses in Montgomery, Alabama. At that time, racial discrimination meant that just because you were black, you would not get the good job, you would not get into the good school, you would not be served at the counter, and you would sit at the back of the bus. Leaders of the civil rights movement argued that such discrimination was devoid of sense, truth, or justice, and that all people should be treated equally, without attention to skin color. Ultimately, the Supreme Court ruled in favor of blacks, and racial discrimination in public places was forbidden.

A decade later, supporters of the women's liberation movement stressed many of the same points on behalf of women. Since the laws against discrimination were already in place, the goal of this second campaign was to change social policy. Society yielded for both movements and opened doors for African Americans and for women that had not been previously open to them.

Although society had taken some steps toward racial and gender equality, there remained an enormous gap between a society with a little less discrimination in it and the dream of a fully equal society. A fully equal society was unlikely to come about if the normal procedures, even scrupulously fair normal procedures, were allowed to work unaided. Only the lowest positions of society were open to the newly recognized power minorities, and because of their backgrounds, they would make very few gains in the foreseeable future.

Consider the possibilities of hiring a black vice president at a major corporation shortly after the antidiscrimination laws were passed. Vice presidential positions are open only to those with managerial experience, and because of a history of discrimination, no African Americans held positions in middle management. Entry-level managerial positions were open to African Americans, but they were also open to all MBAs on a basis of equal opportunity. And because of the same history of discrimination, there were almost no African American MBAs or graduates of good colleges to enter those MBA programs, or even ambitious graduates of good high schools, because most of them were from areas that had a history of legal racial segregation in their schools. Even in grammar school, histories of neighborhood discrimination resulted in lower scores and aspirations for African American children. Patterns of poverty, cultural deprivation, systematic extinction of hope and effort, and poor education rendered African Americans (and, for some fields, women) less prepared than their white male contemporaries to advance in the educational, professional, and business worlds. Laws were passed in the 1960s proclaiming equal opportunity across the land, but all racist and sexist attitudes did not magically disappear. With the change in laws, it still took generations for real equality to get a foothold; that was enough time for racist and sexist attitudes to be reinforced by the inferior performance of African Americans and women in tasks for which they had (deliberately) not been prepared.

Programs of preferential treatment were created to advance the pace of integration. No one has ever advocated putting anyone in a job he or she simply could not do, but some social critics believe that efforts to advance women and minority candidates up the corporate ladder as rapidly as possible could be justified in light of past injustices. Once there, the minorities could serve as excellent role models for others and could do a great deal to wipe out the negative stereotypes about the capabilities of certain races and genders. Other critics believe that such practices seem to invite the very abuses that brought about the civil rights movement to begin with.

As you read the following selections, ask yourself how you would choose to establish justice in our society. Lisa H. Newton argues that we are bound to follow strict merit-based procedures, come what may. Richard Wasserstrom counters with appeals to the social realities addressed by affirmative action programs. Note that both utilitarian and deontological arguments are employed by both sides. Both authors point to the social evils that will follow should the other's policy be implemented, and both cite justice as requiring their own policy.

YES

Lisa H. Newton

REVERSE DISCRIMINATION AS UNJUSTIFIED

I have heard it argued that "simple justice" requires that we favor women and blacks in employment and educational opportunities, since women and blacks were "unjustly" excluded from such opportunities for so many years in the not so distant past. It is a strange argument, an example of a possible implication of a true proposition advanced to dispute the proposition itself, like an octopus absent-mindedly slicing off his head with a stray tentacle. A fatal confusion underlies this argument, a confusion fundamentally relevant to our understanding of the notion of the rule of law.

Two senses of justice and equality are involved in this confusion. The root notion of justice, progenitor of the other, is the one that Aristotle (*Nichomachean Ethics* 5.6; *Politics* 1.2; 3.1) assumes to be the foundation and proper virtue of the political association. It is the condition which free men establish among themselves when they "share a common life in order that their association bring them self-sufficiency"—the regulation of their relationship by law, and the establishment, by law, of equality before the law. Rule of law is the name and pattern of this justice; its equality stands against the inequalities—of wealth, talent, etc.—otherwise obtaining among its participants, who by virtue of that equality are called "citizens." It is an achievement—complete, or, more frequently, partial—of certain people in certain concrete situations. It is fragile and easily disrupted by powerful individuals who discover that the blind equality of rule of law is inconvenient for their interests. Despite its obvious instability, Aristotle assumed that the establishment of justice in this sense, the creation of citizenship, was a permanent possibility for men and that the resultant association of citizens was the natural home of the species. At levels below the political association, this rule-governed equality is easily found; it is exemplified by any group of children agreeing together to play a game. At the level of political association, the attainment of this justice is more difficult, simply because the stakes are so much higher for each participant. The equality of citizenship is not something that happens of its own accord, and without the expenditure of a fair amount of effort it will collapse into the rule of a powerful few over an apathetic many. But at least it has been achieved, at some times in some

From Lisa H. Newton, "Reverse Discrimination as Unjustified," *Ethics*, vol. 83, no. 4 (July 1973). Copyright © 1973 by The University of Chicago. Reprinted by permission of University of Chicago Press.

places; it is always worth trying to achieve, and eminently worth trying to maintain, wherever and to whatever degree it has been brought into being.

Aristotle's parochialism is notorious; he really did not imagine that persons other than Greeks could associate freely in justice, and the only form of association he had in mind was the Greek *polis*. With the decline of the *polis* and the shift in the center of political thought, his notion of justice underwent a sea change. To be exact, it ceased to represent a political type and became a moral ideal: the ideal of equality as we know it. This ideal demands that all men be included in citizenship—that one Law govern all equally, that all men regard all other men as fellow citizens, with the same guarantees, rights, and protections. Briefly, it demands that the circle of citizenship achieved by any group be extended to include the entire human race. Properly understood, its effect on our associations can be excellent: it congratulates us on our achievement of rule of law as a process of government but refuses to let us remain complacent until we have expanded the associations to include others within the ambit of the rules, as often and as far as possible. While one man is a slave, none of us may feel truly free. We are constantly prodded by this ideal to look for possible unjustifiable discrimination, for inequalities not absolutely required for the functioning of the society and advantageous to all. And after twenty centuries of pressure, not at all constant, from this ideal, it might be said that some progress has been made. To take the cases in point for this problem, we are now prepared to assert, as Aristotle would never have been, the equality of sexes and of persons of different colors. The ambit of American citizenship, once restricted to white males

of property, has been extended to include all adult free men, then all adult males including ex-slaves, then all women. The process of acquisition of full citizenship was for these groups a sporadic trail of half-measures, even now not complete; the steps on the road to full equality are marked by legislation and judicial decisions which are only recently concluded and still often not enforced. But the fact that we can now discuss the possibility of favoring such groups in hiring shows that over the area that concerns us, at least, full equality is presupposed as a basis for discussion. To that extent, they are full citizens, fully protected by the law of the land.

It is important for my argument that the moral ideal of equality be recognized as logically distinct from the condition (or virtue) of justice in the political sense. Justice in this sense exists *among* a citizenry, irrespective of the number of the populace included in that citizenry. Further, the moral ideal is parasitic upon the political virtue, for "equality" is unspecified—it means nothing until we are told in what respect that equality is to be realized. In a political context, "equality" is specified as "equal rights"—equal access to the public realm, public goods and offices, equal treatment under the law—in brief, the equality of citizenship. If citizenship is not a possibility, political equality is unintelligible. The ideal emerges as a generalization of the real condition and refers back to that condition for its content.

Now, if justice (Aristotle's justice in the political sense) is equal treatment under law for all citizens, what is injustice? Clearly, injustice is the violation of that equality, discriminating for or against a group of citizens, favoring them with special immunities and privileges or depriving them of those guaranteed to the others. When the southern employer refuses to hire blacks in white-collar jobs, when Wall Street will only hire women as secretaries with new titles, when Mississippi high schools routinely flunk all black boys above ninth grade, we have examples of injustice, and we work to restore the equality of the public realm by ensuring that equal opportunity will be provided in such cases in the future. But of course, when the employers and the schools *favor* women and blacks, the same injustice is done. Just as the previous discrimination did, this reverse discrimination violates the public equality which defines citizenship and destroys the rule of law for the areas in which these favors are granted. To the extent that we adopt a program of discrimination, reverse or otherwise, justice in the political sense is destroyed, and none of us, specifically affected or not, is a citizen, a bearer of rights—we are all petitioners for favors. And to the same extent, the ideal of equality is undermined, for it has content only where justice obtains, and by destroying justice we render the ideal meaningless. It is, then, an ironic paradox, if not a contradiction in terms, to assert that the ideal of equality justifies the violation of justice; it is as if one should argue, with William Buckley, that an ideal of humanity can justify the destruction of the human race.

Logically, the conclusion is simple enough: all discrimination is wrong prima facie because it violates justice, and that goes for reverse discrimination too. No violation of justice among the citizens may be justified (may overcome the prima facie objection) by appeal to the ideal of equality, for that ideal is logically dependent upon the notion of justice. Reverse discrimination, then, which attempts no other justification than an appeal to equality, is wrong. But let us try to make the conclusion more plausible by suggesting some of the implications of the suggested practice of reverse discrimination in employment and education. My argument will be that the problems raised there are insoluble, not only in practice but in principle.

We may argue, if we like, about what "discrimination" consists of. Do I discriminate against blacks if I admit none to my school when none of the black applicants are qualified by the tests I always give? How far must I go to root out cultural bias from my application forms and tests before I can say that I have not discriminated against those of different cultures? Can I assume that women are not strong enough to be roughnecks on my oil rigs, or must I test them individually? But this controversy, the most popular and well-argued aspect of the issue, is not as fatal as two others which cannot be avoided: if we are regarding the blacks as a "minority" victimized by discrimination, what is a "minority"? And for any group—blacks, women, whatever—that has been discriminated against, what amount of reverse discrimination wipes out the initial discrimination? Let us grant as true that women and blacks were discriminated against, even where laws forbade such discrimination, and grant for the sake of argument that a history of discrimination must be wiped out by reverse discrimination. What follows?

First, are there other groups which have been discriminated against? For they should have the same right of restitution. What about American Indians, Chicanos, Appalachian Mountain whites, Puerto Ricans, Jews, Cajuns, and Orientals? And if these are to be included, the principle according to which we specify a "minority" is simply the criterion of "ethnic (sub) group," and we're stuck with every hyphenated American in the lower-middle class clamoring for special privileges for *his* group —and with equal justification. For be it noted, when we run down the Harvard roster, we find not only a scarcity of blacks (in comparison with the proportion in the population) but an even more striking scarcity of those second-, third-, and fourth-generation ethnics who make up the loudest voice of Middle America. Shouldn't they demand *their* share? And eventually, the WASPs will have to form their own lobby, for they too are a minority. The point is simply this: there is no "majority" in America who will not mind giving up just a bit of their rights to make room for a favored minority. There are only other minorities, each of which is discriminated against by the favoring. The initial injustice is then repeated dozens of times, and if each minority is granted the same right of restitution as the others, an entire area of rule governance is dissolved into a pushing and shoving match between self-interested groups. Each works to catch the public eye and political popularity by whatever means of advertising and power politics lend themselves to the effort, to capitalize as much as possible on temporary popularity until the restless mob picks another group to feel sorry for. Hardly an edifying spectacle, and in the long run no one can benefit: the pie is no larger—it's just that instead of setting up and enforcing rules for getting a piece, we've turned the contest into a free-for-all, requiring much more effort for no larger a reward. It would be in the interests of all the participants to reestablish an objective rule to govern the process, carefully enforced and the same for all.

Second, supposing that we do manage to agree in general that women and blacks (and all the others) have some right of restitution, some right to a privileged place in the structure of opportunities for a while, how will we know when that while is up? How much privilege is enough? When will the guilt be gone, the price paid, the balance restored? What recompense is right for centuries of exclusion? What criterion tells us when we are done? Our experience with the Civil Rights movement shows us that agreement on these terms cannot be presupposed: a process that appears to some to be going at a mad gallop into a black takeover appears to the rest of us to be at a standstill. Should a practice of reverse discrimination be adopted, we may safely predict that just as some of us begin to see "a satisfactory start toward righting the balance," others of us will see that we "have already gone too far in the other direction" and will suggest that the discrimination ought to be reversed again. And such disagreement is inevitable, for the point is that we could not *possibly* have any criteria for evaluating the kind of recompense we have in mind. The context presumed by any discussion of restitution is the context of rule of law: law sets the rights of men and simultaneously sets the method for remedying the violation of those rights. You may exact suffering from others and/or damage payments for yourself if and only if the others have violated your rights; the suffering you have endured is not sufficient reason for them to suffer. And remedial rights exist only where there is law: primary human rights are useful guides to legislation but cannot stand as reasons for awarding remedies for injuries sustained. But then, the context presupposed by any discussion of restitution is the context of preexistent full citizenship. No remedial rights could exist for the excluded; neither in law nor in logic does there exist a right to *sue* for a standing to sue.

From these two considerations, then, the difficulties with reverse discrimination become evident. Restitution for a disadvantaged group whose rights under the law have been violated is possible by legal means, but restitution for a disadvantaged group whose grievance is that there was no law to protect them simply is not. First, outside of the area of justice defined by the law, no sense can be made of "the group's rights," for no law recognizes that group or the individuals in it, qua members, as bearers of rights (hence *any* group can constitute itself as a disadvantaged minority in some sense and demand similar restitution). Second, outside of the area of protection of law, no sense can be made of the violation of rights (hence the amount of the recompense cannot be decided by any objective criterion). For both reasons, the practice of reverse discrimination undermines the foundation of the very ideal in whose name it is advocated; it destroys justice, law, equality, and citizenship itself, and replaces them with power struggles and popularity contests.

NOTES

1. A version of this paper was read at a meeting of the Society for Women in Philosophy in Amherst, Massachusetts, November 5, 1972.

NO

Richard Wasserstrom

A DEFENSE OF PROGRAMS OF PREFERENTIAL TREATMENT

Many justifications of programs of preferential treatment depend upon the claim that in one respect or another such programs have good consequences or that they are effective means by which to bring about some desirable end, e.g., an integrated, equalitarian society. I mean by "programs of preferential treatment" to refer to programs such as those at issue in the *Bakke* case—programs which set aside a certain number of places (for example, in a law school) as to which members of minority groups (for example, persons who are non-white or female) who possess certain minimum qualifications (in terms of grades and test scores) may be preferred for admission to those places over some members of the majority group who possess higher qualifications (in terms of grades and test scores).

Many criticisms of programs of preferential treatment claim that such programs, even if effective, are unjustifiable because they are in some important sense unfair or unjust. In this paper I present a limited defense of such programs by showing that two of the chief arguments offered for the unfairness or injustice of these programs do not work in the way or to the degree supposed by critics of these programs.

The first argument is this. Opponents of preferential treatment programs sometimes assert that proponents of these programs are guilty of intellectual inconsistency, if not racism or sexism. For, as is now readily acknowledged, at times past employers, universities, and many other social institutions did not have racial or sexual quotas (when they did not practice overt racial or sexual exclusion), and many of those who were most concerned to bring about the eradication of those racial quotas are now untroubled by the new programs which reinstitute them. And this, it is claimed, is inconsistent. If it was wrong to take race or sex into account when blacks and women were the objects of racial and sexual policies and practices of exclusion, then it is wrong to take race or sex into account when the objects of the policies have their race or sex reversed. Simple considerations of intellectual consistency—of what it means to give racism or sexism as a reason for condemning these social policies and practices—require that what was a good reason then is still a good reason now.

From Richard Wasserstrom, "A Defense of Programs of Preferential Treatment," *National Forum: The Phi Kappa Phi Journal*, vol. 58, no 1 (Winter 1978), pp. 15–18. Copyright © 1978 by *National Forum: The Phi Kappa Phi Journal*. Reprinted by permission.

The problem with this argument is that despite appearances, there is no inconsistency involved in holding both views. Even if contemporary preferential treatment programs which contain quotas are wrong, they are not wrong for the reasons that made quotas against blacks and women pernicious. The reason why is that the social realities do make an enormous difference. The fundamental evil of programs that discriminated against blacks or women was that these programs were a part of a larger social universe which systematically maintained a network of institutions that unjustifiably concentrated power, authority, and goods in the hands of white male individuals, and which systematically consigned blacks and women to subordinate positions in the society.

Whatever may be wrong with today's affirmative action programs and quota systems, it should be clear that the evil, if any, is just not the same. Racial and sexual minorities do not constitute the dominant social group. Nor is the conception of who is a fully developed member of the moral and social community one of an individual who is either female or black. Quotas that prefer women or blacks do not add to an already relatively overabundant supply of resources and opportunities at the disposal of members of these groups in the way in which the quotas of the past did maintain and argument the overabundant supply of resources and opportunities already available to white males.

The same point can be made in a somewhat different way. Sometimes people say that what was wrong, for example, with the system of racial discrimination in the South was that it took an irrelevant characteristic, namely race, and used it systematically to allocate social benefits and burdens of various sorts. The defect was the irrelevance of the characteristic used—race—for that meant that individuals ended up being treated in a manner that was arbitrary and capricious.

I do not think that was the central flaw at all. Take, for instance, the most hideous of the practices, human slavery. The primary thing that was wrong with the institution was not that the particular individuals who were assigned the place of slaves were assigned there arbitrarily because the assignment was made in virtue of an irrelevant characteristic, their race. Rather, it seems to me that the primary thing that was and is wrong with slavery is the practice itself—the fact of some individuals being able to own other individuals and all that goes with that practice. It would not matter by what criterion individuals were assigned; human slavery would still be wrong. And the same can be said for most if not all of the other discrete practices and institutions which comprised the system of racial discrimination even after human slavery was abolished. The practices were unjustifiable—they were oppressive— and they would have been so no matter how the assignment of victims had been made. What made it worse still, was that the institutions and the supporting ideology all interlocked to create a system of human oppression whose effects on those living under it were as devastating as they were unjustifiable.

Again, if there is anything wrong with the programs of preferential treatment that have begun to flourish within the past ten years, it should be evident that the social realities in respect to the distribution of resources and opportunities make the difference. Apart from everything else, there is simply no way in which all of these programs taken together could plausibly be viewed as capable of relegating white males to the kind of genuinely oppressive status characteristically bestowed upon women and blacks by the dominant social institutions and ideology.

The second objection is that preferential treatment programs are wrong because they take race or sex into account rather than the only thing that does matter—that is, an individual's qualifications. What all such programs have in common and what makes them all objectionable, so this argument goes, is that they ignore the persons who are more qualified by bestowing a preference on those who are less qualified in virtue of their being either black or female.

There are, I think, a number of things wrong with this objection based on qualifications, and not the least of them is that we do not live in a society in which there is even the serious pretense of a qualification requirement for many jobs of substantial power and authority. Would anyone claim, for example, that the persons who comprise the judiciary are there because they are the most qualified lawyers or the most qualified persons to be judges? Would anyone claim that Henry Ford II is the head of the Ford Motor Company because he is the most qualified person for the job? Part of what is wrong with even talking about qualifications and merit is that the argument derives some of its force from the erroneous notion that we would have a meritocracy were it not for programs of preferential treatment. In fact, the higher one goes in terms of prestige, power and the like, the less qualifications seem ever to be decisive. It is only for certain jobs and certain places that qualifications are used to do more

than establish the possession of certain minimum competencies.

But difficulties such as these to one side, there are theoretical difficulties as well which cut much more deeply into the argument about qualifications. To begin with, it is important to see that there is a serious inconsistency present if the person who favors "pure qualifications" does so on the ground that the most qualified ought to be selected because this promotes maximum efficiency. Let us suppose that the argument is that if we have the most qualified performing the relevant tasks we will get those tasks done in the most economical and efficient manner. There is nothing wrong in principle with arguments based upon the good consequences that will flow from maintaining a social practice in a certain way. But it is inconsistent for the opponent of preferential treatment to attach much weight to qualifications on this ground; because it was an analogous appeal to the good consequences that the opponent of preferential treatment thought was wrong in the first place. That is to say, if the chief thing to be said in favor of strict qualifications and preferring the most qualified is that it is the most efficient way of getting things done, then we are right back to an assessment of the different consequences that will flow from different programs, and we are far removed from the considerations of justice or fairness that were thought to weigh so heavily against these programs.

It is important to note, too, that qualifications—at least in the educational context—are often not connected at all closely with any plausible conception of social effectiveness. To admit the most qualified students to law school, for example—given the way qualifications are now determined—is primarily to admit those who have the greatest chance of scoring the highest grades at law school. This says little about efficiency except perhaps that these students are the easiest for the faculty to teach. However, since we know so little about what constitutes being a good, or even successful lawyer, and even less about the correlation between being a very good law student and being a very good lawyer, we can hardly claim very confidently that the legal system will operate most effectively if we admit only the most qualified students to law school.

To be at all decisive, the argument for qualifications must be that those who are the most qualified deserve to receive the benefits (the job, the place in law school, etc.) because they are the most qualified. The introduction of the concept of desert now makes it an objection as to justice or fairness of the sort promised by the original criticism of the programs. But now the problem is that there is no reason to think that there is any strong sense of "desert" in which it is correct that the most qualified deserve anything.

Let us consider more closely one case, that of preferential treatment in respect to admission to college or graduate school. There is a logical gap in the inference from the claim that a person is most qualified to perform a task, e.g., to be a good student, to the conclusion that he or she deserves to be admitted as a student. Of course, those who deserve to be admitted should be admitted. But why do the most qualified deserve anything? There is simply no necessary connection between academic merit (in the sense of being most qualified) and deserving to be a member of a student body. Suppose, for instance, that there is only one tennis court in the community. Is it clear that the

two best tennis players ought to be the ones permitted to use it? Why not those who were there first? Or those who will enjoy playing the most? Or those who are the worst and, therefore, need the greatest opportunity to practice? Or those who have the chance to play least frequently?

We might, of course, have a rule that says that the best tennis players get to use the court before the others. Under such a rule the best players would deserve the court more than the poorer ones. But that is just to push the inquiry back on stage. Is there any reason to think that we ought to have a rule giving good tennis players such a preference? Indeed, the arguments that might be given for or against such a rule are many and varied. And few if any of the arguments that might support the rule would depend upon a connection between ability and desert.

Someone might reply, however, that the most able students deserve to be admitted to the university because all of their earlier schooling was a kind of competition, with university admission being the prize awarded to the winners. They deserve to be admitted because that is what the rule of the competition provides. In addition, it might be argued, it would be unfair now to exclude them in favor of others, given the reasonable expectations they developed about the way in which their industry and performance would be rewarded. Minority-admission programs, which inevitably prefer some who are less qualified over some who are more qualified, all possess this flaw.

There are several problems with this argument. The most substantial of them is that it is an empirically implausible picture of our social world. Most of what are regarded as the decisive characteristics for higher education have a great deal to do with things over which the individual has neither control nor responsibility: such things as home environment, socioeconomic class of parents, and, of course, the quality of the primary and secondary schools attended. Since individuals do not deserve having had any of these things vis-á-vis other individuals, they do not, for the most part, deserve their qualifications. And since they do not deserve their abilities they do not in any strong sense deserve to be admitted because of their abilities.

To be sure, if there has been a rule which connects say, performance at high school with admission to college, then there is a weak sense in which those who do well at high school deserve, for that reason alone, to be admitted to college. In addition, if persons have built up or relied upon their reasonable expectations concerning performance and admission, they have a claim to be admitted on this ground as well. But it is certainly not obvious that these claims of desert are any stronger or more compelling than the competing claims based upon the needs of or advantages to women or blacks from programs of preferential treatment. And as I have indicated, all rule-based claims of desert are very weak unless and until the rule which creates the claim is itself shown to be a justified one. Unless one has a strong preference for the status quo, and unless one can defend that preference, the practice within a system of allocating places in a certain way does not go very far at all in showing that that is the right or the just way to allocate those places in the future.

A proponent of programs of preferential treatment is not at all committed to the view that qualifications ought to be wholly irrelevant. He or she can agree that, given the existing structure of any institution, there is probably some minimal set of qualifications without which one cannot participate meaningfully within the institution. In addition, it can be granted that the qualifications of those involved will affect the way the institution works and the way it affects others in the society. And the consequences will vary depending upon the particular institution. But all of this only establishes that qualifications, in this sense, are relevant, not that they are decisive. This is wholly consistent with the claim that race or sex should today also be relevant when it comes to matters such as admission to college or law school. And that is all that any preferential treatment program —even one with the kind of quota used in the *Bakke* case—has ever tried to do.

I have not attempted to establish that programs of preferential treatment are right and desirable. There are empirical issues concerning the consequences of these programs that I have not discussed, and certainly not settled. Nor, for that matter, have I considered the argument that justice may permit, if not require, these programs as a way to provide compensation or reparation for injuries suffered in the recent as well as distant past, or as a way to remove benefits that are undeservedly enjoyed by those of the dominant group. What I have tried to do is show that it is wrong to think that programs of preferential treatment are objectionable in the centrally important sense in which many past and present discriminatory features of our society have been and are racist and sexist. The social realities as to power and opportunity do make a fundamental difference. It is also wrong to think that programs of preferential treatment are in any strong sense either unjust or unprincipled. The case for programs of preferential treatment could, therefore, plausibly rest both on the view that such programs are not unfair to white males (except in the weak, rule-dependent sense described above) and on the view that it is unfair to continue the present set of unjust—often racist and sexist—institutions that comprise the social reality. And the case for these programs could rest as well on the proposition that, given the distribution of power and influence in the United States today, such programs may reasonably be viewed as potentially valuable, effective means by which to achieve admirable and significant social ideals of equality and integration.

POSTSCRIPT

Are Programs of Preferential Treatment Unjustifiable?

What kind of society do we want to live in? It is not enough to say that justice in society is important. We must also ask whether equality of opportunity is an adequate stand-in for equality of result. Is procedural justice enough for us when it does not yield substantial justice?

What values weigh in the balance in the attempt to come to terms with the issue of preferential treatment? Clearly, individual interest is going to be affected, and social patterns are going to change. Industries that were completely dominated by white males in the 1950s now employ African Americans and women in managerial positions.

Throughout the effort to create an equal society, it will be important to preserve the freedom to compete in America and to select the best product, service, or vendor on the free market. The tension between the values of the free society and the equal society is troubling, as is evident in the recent Supreme Court decisions on affirmative action, which show an unmistakable trend against affirmative action provisions.

Currently, programs of preferential treatment are losing favor in the United States. Moves to abolish all race-conscious preferment are under way in California and in many other states. For the first time in 30 years, more U.S. congresspeople are attacking affirmative action policies than are defending it. Businesses may be forced to reconsider their own practices of hiring and promoting minority candidates (some of which were legally mandated in the 1970s).

SUGGESTED READINGS

Robert K. Bobinson, Billie Morgan, and T. Yohannan, "Affirmative Action Plans in the 1990s: A Double-Edged Sword?" *Public Personnel Management* (Summer 1992).

Paula Dwyer and Tim Smart, "The Price of Discrimination May Well Go Up," *Business Week* (August 13, 1990).

James P. McCarty, "Eliminate Reverse Discrimination in Group LTD," *Life Association News* (August 1992).

Robert J. Nobile, "Can There Be Too Much Diversity?" *Personnel* (August 1991).

Peter Waldman, "Affirmative Action Faces Likely Setback," *The Wall Street Journal* (November 30, 1988).

ISSUE 9

Does Blowing the Whistle Violate Company Loyalty?

YES: Sissela Bok, from "Whistleblowing and Professional Responsibility," *New York University Education Quarterly* (Summer 1980)

NO: Robert A. Larmer, from "Whistleblowing and Employee Loyalty," *Journal of Business Ethics* (vol. 11, 1992)

ISSUE SUMMARY

YES: Philosopher Sissela Bok asserts that although blowing the whistle is often justified, it does involve dissent, accusation, and a breach of loyalty to the employer.

NO: Robert A. Larmer, an associate professor of philosophy, argues that attempting to stop illegal or unethical company activities may be the highest type of company loyalty an employee can display.

Whistle-blowing occurs when an employee discovers a wrong at his or her place of employment and exposes it, thereby saving lives or a great deal of money, but almost always at great expense to him- or herself. Since the readings that follow are theoretical, some specific cases might be useful. In "The Whistle Blowers' Morning After," *The New York Times* (November 9, 1986), N. R. Kleinfeld portrays five of the early whistle-blowers, some of whom have become famous as case studies in business schools across the country. Each one has an interesting story to tell; each claims that if he had it to do over again he would, for he likes living with a clear conscience. But each has also paid a price: great stress, sometimes ill health, career loss, financial ruin, and/or loss of friends and family.

Charles Atchinson blew the whistle on the Comanche Park nuclear plant in Glen Rose, Texas, a power station that was unsafe. It cost him his job, plunged him into debt, and left emotional scars on his family. Kermit Vandivier, who blew the whistle on the B. F. Goodrich Aircraft Brakes scandal, also lost his job. He has since begun a new career as a journalist. James Pope claimed that the Federal Aviation Administration (FAA) found in 1975 an effective device, known as an airborne collision avoidance system, that would prevent mid-air crashes; but it chose instead to pursue an inferior device it had had a hand in developing. Mr. Pope was "retired" early by the FAA. The most famous whistle-blower of all may be A. Ernest Fitzgerald (see *The High Priests of Waste*; *The Pentagonists*), the U.S. Air Force cost analyst who found huge cost overruns on Lockheed cargo planes that were being developed for the Air Force. After his revelations, he was discharged from the Air Force. He fought for 13 years to be reinstated, which he was, at full rank, in 1982. The common thread of these stories is that when someone detected a wrong and properly reported it, he was demoted, labeled a troublemaker, and disciplined or fired, even when the evidence was very much in his favor. All of them, incidentally, initially believed in their organizations, and not only were all of them sure that they were acting in an ethical manner, but they also believed that they would be thanked for their efforts and diligence.

Professors Myron Peretz Glazer and Penina Migdal Glazer, in *The Whistle Blowers: Exposing Corruption in Government and Industry* (Basic Books, 1989), tell the story of 55 whistle-blowers—why they did what they did, and what the consequences were for themselves and their families. The Glazers found that the dominant trait in these whistle-blowers was a strong belief in individual responsibility. As one of the spouses of a whistle-blower stated, "A corrupt system can happen only if the individuals who make up that system are corrupt. You are either going to be part of the corruption or part of the forces working against it. There isn't a third choice. Someone, someday, has to take a stand; if you don't, maybe no one will. And that is wrong."

The Glazers write that the strong belief in individual responsibility that drove these ethical resisters was often supported by professional ethics, religious values, or allegiance to a community. But the personal costs of public disclosure were high, and the results were less than satisfactory. In some cases the accused corporations made no changes. The whistle-blowers, however, had to recreate careers, relocate, and settle for less money in new jobs. For most resisters, the worst part was the devastating months or even years of dislocation, unemployment, and temporary jobs. In response to a question posed by the Glazers, 21 of the whistle-blowers advised other potential whistle-blowers to "forget it" or to "leak the information without your name attached." If blowing the whistle is unavoidable, however, then "be prepared to be ostracized, have your career come to a screeching halt, and perhaps even be driven into bankruptcy."

As you read the following selections, think about these cases and others you may have heard about. Consider the motivations involved in whistle-blowing and whether they reflect loyalty or disloyalty to the company. How would you view an instance of whistle-blowing if you or your company were the target? Who deserves the greatest consideration in potential whistle-blowing situations: the individual, the company, or the public?

YES

Sissela Bok

WHISTLEBLOWING AND PROFESSIONAL RESPONSIBILITY

"Whistleblowing" is a new label generated by our increased awareness of the ethical conflicts encountered at work. Whistleblowers sound an alarm from within the very organization in which they work, aiming to spotlight neglect or abuses that threaten the public interest.

The stakes in whistleblowing are high. Take the nurse who alleges that physicians enrich themselves in her hospital through unnecessary surgery; the engineer who discloses safety defects in the braking systems of a fleet of new rapid-transit vehicles; the Defense Department official who alerts Congress to military graft and overspending: all know that they pose a threat to those whom they denounce and that their own careers may be at risk.

MORAL CONFLICTS

Moral conflicts on several levels confront anyone who is wondering whether to speak out about abuses or risks or serious neglect. In the first place, he must try to decide whether, other things being equal, speaking out is in fact in the public interest. This choice is often made more complicated by factual uncertainties: Who is responsible for the abuse or neglect? How great is the threat? And how likely is it that speaking out will precipitate changes for the better?

In the second place, a would-be whistleblower must weigh his responsibility to serve the public interest against the responsibility he owes to his colleagues and the institution in which he works. While the professional ethic requires collegial loyalty, the codes of ethics often stress responsibility to the public over and above duties to colleagues and clients. Thus the United States Code of Ethics for Government Servants asks them to "expose corruption wherever uncovered" and to "put loyalty to the highest moral principles and to country above loyalty to persons, party, or government."[1] Similarly, the largest professional engineering association requires members to speak out against abuses threatening the safety, health, and welfare of the public.[2]

From Sissela Bok, "Whistleblowing and Professional Responsibility," *New York University Education Quarterly*, vol. 11 (Summer 1980), pp. 2–7. Copyright © 1980 by Sissela Bok. Reprinted by permission.

A third conflict for would-be whistle-blowers is personal in nature and cuts across the first two: even in cases where they have concluded that the facts warrant speaking out, and that their duty to do so overrides loyalties to colleagues and institutions, they often have reason to fear the results of carrying out such a duty. However strong this duty may seem in theory, they know that, in practice, retaliation is likely. As a result, their careers and their ability to support themselves and their families may be unjustly impaired.[3] A government handbook issued during the Nixon era recommends reassigning "undesirables" to places so remote that they would prefer to resign. Whistleblowers may also be downgraded or given work without responsibility or work for which they are not qualified; or else they may be given many more tasks than they can possibly perform. Another risk is that an outspoken civil servant may be ordered to undergo a psychiatric fitness-for-duty examination,[4] declared unfit for service, and "separated" as well as discredited from the point of view of any allegations he may be making. Outright firing, finally, is the most direct institutional response to whistleblowers.

Add to the conflicts confronting individual whistleblowers the claim to self-policing that many professions make, and professional responsibility is at issue in still another way. For an appeal to the public goes against everything that "self-policing" stands for. The question for the different professions, then, is how to resolve, insofar as it is possible, the conflict between professional loyalty and professional responsibility toward the outside world. The same conflicts arise to some extent in all groups, but professional groups often have special cohesion and claim special dignity and privileges.

The plight of whistleblowers has come to be documented by the press and described in a number of books. Evidence of the hardships imposed on those who chose to act in the public interest has combined with a heightened awareness of professional malfeasance and corruption to produce a shift toward greater public support of whistleblowers. Public service law firms and consumer groups have taken up their cause; institutional reforms and legislation have been proposed to combat illegitimate reprisals.[5]

Given the indispensable services performed by so many whistleblowers, strong public support is often merited. But the new climate of acceptance makes it easy to overlook the dangers of whistle-blowing: of uses in error or in malice; of work and reputations unjustly lost for those falsely accused; of privacy invaded and trust undermined. There comes a level of internal prying and mutual suspicion at which no institution can function. And it is a fact that the disappointed, the incompetent, the malicious, and the paranoid all too often leap to accusations in public. Worst of all, ideological persecution throughout the world traditionally relies on insiders willing to inform on their colleagues or even on their family members, often through staged public denunciations or press campaigns.

No society can count itself immune from such dangers. But neither can it risk silencing those with a legitimate reason to blow the whistle. How then can we distinguish between different instances of whistleblowing? A society that fails to protect the right to speak out even on the part of those whose warnings turn out to be spurious obviously opens the door to political repression. But from the moral point of view there are important differences between the aims, messages, and methods of dissenters from within.

NATURE OF WHISTLEBLOWING

Three elements, each jarring, and triply jarring when conjoined, lend acts of whistleblowing special urgency and bitterness: dissent, breach of loyalty, and accusation.

Like all dissent, whistleblowing makes public a disagreement with an authority or a majority view. But whereas dissent can concern all forms of disagreement with, for instance, religious dogma or government policy or court decisions, whistleblowing has the narrower aim of shedding light on negligence or abuse, or alerting to a risk, and of assigning responsibility for this risk.

Would-be whistleblowers confront the conflict inherent in all dissent: between conforming and sticking their necks out. The more repressive the authority they challenge, the greater the personal risk they take in speaking out. At exceptional times, as in times of war, even ordinarily tolerant authorities may come to regard dissent as unacceptable and even disloyal.[6]

Furthermore, the whistleblower hopes to stop the game; but since he is neither referee nor coach, and since he blows the whistle on his own team, his act is seen as a violation of loyalty. In holding his position, he has assumed certain obligations to his colleagues and clients. He may even have subscribed to a loyalty oath or a promise of confidentiality. Loyalty to colleagues and to clients comes to be pitted against loyalty to the public interest, to those who may be injured unless the revelation is made.

Not only is loyalty violated in whistleblowing, hierarchy as well is often opposed, since the whistleblower is not only a colleague but a subordinate. Though aware of the risks inherent in such disobedience, he often hopes to keep his job.[7] At times, however, he plans his alarm to coincide with leaving the institution. If he is highly placed, or joined by others, resigning in protest may effectively direct public attention to the wrongdoing at issue.[8] Still another alternative, often chosen by those who wish to be safe from retaliation, is to leave the institution quietly, to secure another post, and then to blow the whistle. In this way, it is possible to speak with the authority and knowledge of an insider without having the vulnerability of that position.

It is the element of accusation, of calling a "foul," that arouses the strongest reactions on the part of the hierarchy. The accusation may be of neglect, of willfully concealed dangers, or of outright abuse on the part of colleagues or superiors. It singles out specific persons or groups as responsible for threats to the public interest. If no one could be held responsible—as in the case of an impending avalanche—the warning would not constitute whistleblowing.

The accusation of the whistleblower, moreover, concerns a present or an imminent threat. Past errors or misdeeds occasion such an alarm only if they still affect current practices. And risks far in the future lack the immediacy needed to make the alarm a compelling one, as well as the close connection to particular individuals that would justify actual accusations. Thus an alarm can be sounded about safety defects in a rapid-transit system that threaten or will shortly threaten passengers, but the revelation of safety defects in a system no longer in use, while of historical interest, would not constitute whistleblowing. Nor would the revelation of potential problems in a system not yet fully designed and far from implemented.[9]

Not only immediacy, but also specificity, is needed for there to be an alarm capable of pinpointing responsibility. A concrete risk must be at issue rather than a vague foreboding or a somber prediction. The act of whistleblowing differs in this respect from the lamentation or the dire prophecy. An immediate and specific threat would normally be acted upon by those at risk. The whistleblower assumes that his message will alert listeners to something they do not know, or whose significance they have not grasped because it has been kept secret.

The desire for openness inheres in the temptation to reveal any secret, sometimes joined to an urge for self-aggrandizement and publicity and the hope for revenge for past slights or injustices. There can be pleasure, too—righteous or malicious—in laying bare the secrets of co-workers and in setting the record straight at last. Colleagues of the whistleblower often suspect his motives: they may regard him as a crank, as publicity-hungry, wrong about the facts, eager for scandal and discord, and driven to indiscretion by his personal biases and shortcomings.

For whistleblowing to be effective, it must arouse its audience. Inarticulate whistleblowers are likely to fail from the outset. When they are greeted by apathy, their message dissipates. When they are greeted by disbelief, they elicit no response at all. And when the audience is not free to receive or to act on the information—when censorship or fear of retribution stifles response—then the message rebounds to injure the whistle-blower. Whistleblowing also requires the possibility of concerted public response: the idea of whistleblowing in an anarchy is therefore merely quixotic.

Such characteristics of whistleblowing and strategic considerations for achieving an impact are common to the noblest warnings, the most vicious personal attacks, and the delusions of the paranoid. How can one distinguish the many acts of sounding an alarm that are genuinely in the public interest from all the petty, biased, or lurid revelations that pervade our querulous and gossip-ridden society? Can we draw distinctions between different whistleblowers, different messages, different methods?

We clearly can, in a number of cases. Whistleblowing may be starkly inappropriate when in malice or error, or when it lays bare legitimately private matters having to do, for instance, with political belief or sexual life. It can, just as clearly, be the only way to shed light on an ongoing unjust practice such as drugging political prisoners or subjecting them to electroshock treatment. It can be the last resort for alerting the public to an impending disaster. Taking such clear-cut cases as benchmarks, and reflecting on what it is about them that weighs so heavily for or against speaking out, we can work our way toward the admittedly more complex cases in which whistleblowing is not so clearly the right or wrong choice, or where different points of view exist regarding its legitimacy—cases where there are moral reasons both for concealment and for disclosure and where judgments conflict. . . .

INDIVIDUAL MORAL CHOICE

What questions might those who consider sounding an alarm in public ask themselves? How might they articulate the problem they see and weigh its injustice before deciding whether or not to reveal it? How can they best try to make sure their choice is the right one? In thinking about these questions it helps to keep in mind the three elements mentioned earlier: dissent, breach of loyalty, and accusation. They impose certain requirements—of accuracy and judgment in dissent; of exploring alternative ways to cope with improprieties that minimize the breach of loyalty; and of fairness in accusation. For each, careful articulation and testing of arguments are needed to limit error and bias.

Dissent by whistleblowers, first of all, is expressly claimed to be intended to benefit the public. It carries with it, as a result, an obligation to consider the nature of this benefit and to consider also the possible harm that may come from speaking out: harm to persons or institutions and, ultimately, to the public interest itself. Whistleblowers must, therefore, begin by making every effort to consider the effects of speaking out versus those of remaining silent. They must assure themselves of the accuracy of their reports, checking and rechecking the facts before speaking out; specify the degree to which there is genuine impropriety; consider how imminent is the threat they see, how serious, and how closely linked to those accused of neglect and abuse.

If the facts warrant whistleblowing, how can the second element—breach of loyalty—be minimized? The most important question here is whether the existing avenues for change within the organization have been explored. It is a waste of time for the public as well as harmful to the institution to sound the loudest alarm first. Whistleblowing has to remain a last alternative because of its destructive side effects: it must be chosen only when other alternatives have been considered and rejected. They may be rejected if they simply do not apply to the problem at hand, or when there is not time to go through routine channels or when the institution is so corrupt or coercive that steps will be taken to silence the whistleblower should he try the regular channels first.

What weight should an oath or a promise of silence have in the conflict of loyalties? One sworn to silence is doubtless under a stronger obligation because of the oath he has taken. He has bound himself, assumed specific obligations beyond those assumed in merely taking a new position. But even such promises can be overridden when the public interest at issue is strong enough. They can be overridden if they were obtained under duress or through deceit. They can be overridden, too, if they promise something that is in itself wrong or unlawful. The fact that one has promised silence is no excuse for complicity in covering up a crime or a violation of the public's trust.

The third element in whistleblowing—accusation—raises equally serious ethical concerns. They are concerns of fairness to the persons accused of impropriety. Is the message one to which the public is entitled in the first place? Or does it infringe on personal and private matters that one has no right to invade? Here, the very notion of what is in the public's best "interest" is at issue: "accusations" regarding an official's unusual sexual or religious experiences may well appeal to the public's interest without being information relevant to "the public interest."

Great conflicts arise here. We have witnessed excessive claims to executive privilege and to secrecy by government officials during the Watergate scandal in order to cover up for abuses the public had every right to discover. Conversely, those hoping to profit from prying into private matters have become adept at invoking "the public's right to know." Some even regard such private matters as threats to the public: they voice their own religious and political prejudices in the language of accusation. Such a danger is never stronger than when the accusation is delivered surreptitiously. The anonymous accusations made during the McCarthy period regarding political beliefs and associations often injured persons who did not even know their accusers or the exact nature of the accusations.

From the public's point of view, accusations that are openly made by identifiable individuals are more likely to be taken seriously. And in fairness to those criticized, openly accepted responsibility for blowing the whistle should be preferred to the denunciation or the leaked rumor. What is openly stated can more easily be checked, its source's motives challenged, and the underlying information examined. Those under attack may otherwise be hard put to defend themselves against nameless adversaries. Often they do not even know that they are threatened until it is too late to respond. The anonymous denunciation, moreover, common to so many regimes, places the burden of investigation on government agencies that may thereby gain the power of a secret police.

From the point of view of the whistleblower, on the other hand, the anonymous message is safer in situations where retaliation is likely. But it is also often less likely to be taken seriously. Unless the message is accompanied by indications of how the evidence can be checked, its anonymity, however safe for the source, speaks against it.

During the process of weighing the legitimacy of speaking out, the method used, and the degree of fairness needed, whistleblowers must try to compensate for the strong possibility of bias on their part. They should be scrupulously aware of any motive that might skew their message: a desire for self-defense in a difficult bureaucratic situation, perhaps, or the urge to seek revenge, or inflated expectations regarding the effect their message will have on the situation. (Needless to say, bias affects the silent as well as the outspoken. The motive for holding back important information about abuses and injustice ought to give similar cause for soul-searching.)

Likewise, the possibility of personal gain from sounding the alarm ought to give pause. Once again there is then greater risk of a biased message. Even if the whistleblower regards himself as incorruptible, his profiting from revelations of neglect or abuse will lead others to question his motives and to put less credence in his charges. If, for example, a government employee stands to make large profits from a book exposing the inequities in his agency, there is danger that he will, perhaps even unconsciously, slant his report in order to cause more of a sensation.

A special problem arises when there is a high risk that the civil servant who speaks out will have to go through costly litigation. Might he not justifiably try to make enough money on his public revelations—say, through books or public speaking—to offset his losses? In so doing he will not strictly speaking have *profited* from his revelations: he merely avoids being financially crushed by their sequels. He will nevertheless still be suspected at the time of revelation, and his message will therefore seem more questionable.

Reducing bias and error in moral choice often requires consultation, even open debate[10]: methods that force articulation of the moral arguments at stake and challenge privately held assumptions. But acts of whistleblowing present special problems when it comes to open consultation. On the one hand, once the whistleblower sounds his alarm publicly, his arguments will be subjected to open scrutiny; he will have to articulate his reasons for speaking out and substantiate his charges. On the other hand, it will then be too late to retract the alarm or to combat its harmful effects, should his choice to speak out have been ill-advised.

For this reason, the whistleblower owes it to all involved to make sure of two things: that he has sought as much and as objective advice regarding his choice as he can *before* going public; and that he is aware of the arguments for and against the practice of whistleblowing in general, so that he can see his own choice against as richly detailed and coherently structured a background as possible. Satisfying these two requirements once again has special problems because of the very nature of whistleblowing: the more corrupt the circumstances, the more dangerous it may be to seek consultation before speaking out. And yet, since the whistleblower himself may have a biased view of the state of affairs, he may choose not to consult others when in fact it would be not only safe but advantageous to do so; he may see corruption and conspiracy where none exists.

NOTES

1. Code of Ethics for Government Service passed by the U.S. House of Representatives in the 85th Congress (1958) and applying to all government employees and office holders.

2. Code of Ethics of the Institute of Electrical and Electronics Engineers, Article IV.

3. For case histories and descriptions of what befalls whistleblowers, see Rosemary Chalk and Frank von Hippel, "Due Process for Dissenting Whistle-Blowers," *Technology Review* 81 (June–July 1979); 48–55; Alan S. Westin and Stephen Salisbury, eds., *Individual Rights in the Corporation* (New York: Pantheon, 1980); Helen Dudar, "The Price of Blowing the Whistle," *New York Times Magazine*, 30 October 1979, pp. 41–54; John Edsall, *Scientific Freedom and Responsibility* (Washington, D.C.: American Association for the Advancement of Science, 1975), p. 5; David Ewing, *Freedom Inside the Organization* (New York: Dutton, 1977); Ralph Nader, Peter Petkas, and Kate Blackwell, *Whistle Blowing* (New York: Grossman, 1972); Charles Peter and Taylor Branch, *Blowing the Whistle* (New York: Praeger, 1972).

4. Congressional hearings uncovered a growing resort to mandatory psychiatric examinations.

5. For an account of strategies and proposals to support government whistleblowers, see Government Accountability Project, *A Whistleblower's Guide to the Federal Bureaucracy* (Washington, D.C.: Institute for Policy Studies, 1977).

6. See, e.g., Samuel Eliot Morison, Frederick Merk, and Frank Friedel, *Dissent in Three American Wars* (Cambridge: Harvard University Press, 1970).

7. In the scheme worked out by Albert Hirschman in *Exit, Voice and Loyalty* (Cambridge: Harvard University Press, 1970), whistleblowing represents "voice" accompanied by a preference not to "exit," though forced "exit" is clearly a possibility and "voice" after or during "exit" may be chosen for strategic reasons.

8. Edward Weisband and Thomas N. Franck, *Resignation in Protest* (New York: Grossman, 1975).

9. Future developments can, however, be the cause for whistleblowing if they are seen as resulting from steps being taken or about to be taken that render them inevitable.

10. I discuss these questions of consultation and publicity with respect to moral choice in chapter 7 of Sissela Bok, *Lying* (New York: Pantheon, 1978); and in *Secrets* (New York: Pantheon Books, 1982), Ch. IX and XV.

NO
Robert A. Larmer

WHISTLEBLOWING AND EMPLOYEE LOYALTY

Whistleblowing by an employee is the act of complaining, either within the corporation or publicly, about a corporation's unethical practices. Such an act raises important questions concerning the loyalties and duties of employees. Traditionally, the employee has been viewed as an agent who acts on behalf of a principal, i.e., the employer, and as possessing duties of loyalty and confidentiality. Whistleblowing, at least at first blush, seems a violation of these duties and it is scarcely surprising that in many instances employers and fellow employees argue that it is an act of disloyalty and hence morally wrong.[1]

It is this issue of the relation between whistleblowing and employee loyalty that I want to address. What I will call the standard view is that employees possess *prima facie* duties of loyalty and confidentiality to their employers and that whistleblowing cannot be justified except on the basis of a higher duty to the public good. Against this standard view, Ronald Duska has recently argued that employees do not have even a *prima facie* duty of loyalty to their employers and that whistleblowing needs, therefore, no moral justification.[2] I am going to criticize both views. My suggestion is that both misunderstand the relation between loyalty and whistleblowing. In their place I will propose a third more adequate view.

Duska's view is more radical in that it suggests that there can be no issue of whistleblowing and employee loyalty, since the employee has no duty to be loyal to his employer. His reason for suggesting that the employee owes the employer, at least the corporate employer, no loyalty is that companies are not the kinds of things which are proper objects of loyalty. His argument in support of this rests upon two key claims. The first is that loyalty, properly understood, implies a reciprocal relationship and is only appropriate in the context of a mutual surrendering of self-interest. He writes,

It is important to recognize that in any relationship which demands loyalty the relationship works both ways and involves mutual enrichment. Loyalty is

From Robert A. Larmer, "Whistleblowing and Employee Loyalty," *Journal of Business Ethics*, vol. 11 (1992), pp. 125–128. Copyright © 1992 by D. Reidel Publishing Co., Dordrecht, Holland, and Boston, U.S.A. Reprinted by permission of Kluwer Academic Publishers.

incompatible with self-interest, because it is something that necessarily requires we go beyond self-interest. My loyalty to my friend, for example, requires I put aside my interests some of the time.... Loyalty depends on ties that demand self-sacrifice with no expectation of reward, e.g., the ties of loyalty that bind a family together.[3]

The second is that the relation between a company and an employee does not involve any surrender of self-interest on the part of the company, since its primary goal is to maximize profit. Indeed, although it is convenient, it is misleading to talk of a company having interests. As Duska comments,

A company is not a person. A company is an instrument, and an instrument with a specific purpose, the making of profit. To treat an instrument as an end in itself, like a person, may not be as bad as treating an end as an instrument, but it does give the instrument a moral status it does not deserve...[4]

Since, then, the relation between a company and an employee does not fulfill the minimal requirement of being a relation between two individuals, much less two reciprocally self-sacrificing individuals, Duska feels it is a mistake to suggest the employee has any duties of loyalty to the company.

This view does not seem adequate, however. First, it is not true that loyalty must be quite so reciprocal as Duska demands. Ideally, of course, one expects that if one is loyal to another person that person will reciprocate in kind. There are, however, many cases where loyalty is not entirely reciprocated, but where we do not feel that it is misplaced. A parent, for example, may remain loyal to an erring teenager, even though the teenager demonstrates no loyalty to the parent. Indeed, part of being a proper parent is to demonstrate loyalty to your children whether or not that loyalty is reciprocated. This is not to suggest any kind of analogy between parents and employees, but rather that it is not nonsense to suppose that loyalty may be appropriate even though it is not reciprocated. Inasmuch as he ignores this possibility, Duska's account of loyalty is flawed.

Second, even if Duska is correct in holding that loyalty is only appropriate between moral agents and that a company is not genuinely a moral agent, the question may still be raised whether an employee owes loyalty to fellow employees or the shareholders of the company. Granted that reference to a company as an individual involves reification and should not be taken too literally, it may nevertheless constitute a legitimate shorthand way of describing relations between genuine moral agents.

Third, it seems wrong to suggest that simply because the primary motive of the employer is economic, considerations of loyalty are irrelevant. An employee's primary motive in working for an employer is generally economic, but no one on that account would argue that it is impossible for her to demonstrate loyalty to the employer, even if it turns out to be misplaced. All that is required is that her primary economic motive be in some degree qualified by considerations of the employer's welfare. Similarly, the fact that an employer's primary motive is economic does not imply that it is not qualified by considerations of the employee's welfare. Given the possibility of mutual qualification of admittedly primary economic motives, it is fallacious to argue that employee loyalty is never appropriate.

In contrast to Duska, the standard view is that loyalty to one's employer is appropriate. According to it, one has an obligation to be loyal to one's employer and, consequently, a *prima facie* duty to protect the employer's interests. Whistleblowing constitutes, therefore, a violation of duty to one's employer and needs strong justification if it is to be appropriate. Sissela Bok summarizes this view very well when she writes

> the whistleblower hopes to stop the game; but since he is neither referee nor coach, and since he blows the whistle on his own team, his act is seen as a violation of loyalty. In holding his position, he has assumed certain obligations to his colleagues and clients. He may even have subscribed to a loyalty oath or a promise of confidentiality. Loyalty to colleagues and to clients comes to be pitted against loyalty to the public interest, to those who may be injured unless the revelation is made.[5]

The strength of this view is that it recognizes that loyalty is due one's employer. Its weakness is that it tends to conceive of whistleblowing as involving a tragic moral choice, since blowing the whistle is seen not so much as a positive action, but rather the lesser of two evils. Bok again puts the essence of this view very clearly when she writes that "a would-be whistleblower must weigh his responsibility to serve the public interest *against* the responsibility he owes to his colleagues and the institution in which he works" and "that [when] their duty [to whistleblow]... *so overrides loyalties to colleagues and institutions,* they [whistleblowers] often have reason to fear the results of carrying out such a duty."[6] The employee, according to this

understanding of whistleblowing, must choose between two acts of betrayal, either her employer or the public interest, each in itself reprehensible.

Behind this view lies the assumption that to be loyal to someone is to act in a way that accords with what that person believes to be in her best interests. To be loyal to an employer, therefore, is to act in a way which the employer deems to be in his or her best interests. Since employers very rarely approve of whistleblowing and generally feel that it is not in their best interests, it follows that whistleblowing is an act of betrayal on the part of the employee, albeit a betrayal made in the interests of the public good.

Plausible though it initially seems, I think this view of whistleblowing is mistaken and that it embodies a mistaken conception of what constitutes employee loyalty. It ignores the fact that

> the great majority of corporate whistle-blowers... [consider] themselves to be very loyal employees who... [try] to use 'direct voice' (internal whistleblowing),... [are] rebuffed and punished for this, and then... [use] 'indirect voice' (external whistleblowing). They... [believe] initially that they... [are] behaving in a loyal manner, helping their employers by calling top management's attention to practices that could eventually get the firm in trouble.[7]

By ignoring the possibility that blowing the whistle may demonstrate greater loyalty than not blowing the whistle, it fails to do justice to the many instances where loyalty to someone constrains us to act in defiance of what that person believes to be in her best interests. I am not, for example, being disloyal to a friend if I refuse to loan her money for an investment I am sure will bring her financial ruin; even if she bitterly reproaches me for denying her what is so obviously a golden opportunity to make a fortune.

A more adequate definition of being loyal to someone is that loyalty involves acting in accordance with what one has good reason to believe to be in that person's best interests. A key question, of course, is what constitutes a good reason to think that something is in a person's best interests. Very often, but by no means invariably, we accept that a person thinking that something is in her best interests is a sufficiently good reason to think that it actually is. Other times, especially when we feel that she is being rash, foolish, or misinformed we are prepared, precisely by virtue of being loyal, to act contrary to the person's wishes. It is beyond the scope of this paper to investigate such cases in detail, but three general points can be made.

First, to the degree that an action is genuinely immoral, it is impossible that it is in the agent's best interests. We would not, for example, say that someone who sells child pornography was acting in his own best interests, even if he vigorously protested that there was nothing wrong with such activity. Loyalty does not imply that we have a duty to refrain from reporting the immoral actions of those to whom we are loyal. An employer who is acting immorally is not acting in her own best interests and an employee is not acting disloyally in blowing the whistle.[8] Indeed, the argument can be made that the employee who blows the whistle may be demonstrating greater loyalty than the employee who simply ignores the immoral conduct, inasmuch as she is attempting to prevent her employer from engaging in self-destructive behaviour.

Second, loyalty requires that, whenever possible, in trying to resolve a problem we deal directly with the person to whom we are loyal. If, for example, I am loyal to a friend I do not immediately involve a third party when I try to dissuade my friend from involvement in immoral actions. Rather, I approach my friend directly, listen to his perspective on the events in question, and provide an opportunity for him to address the problem in a morally satisfactory way. This implies that, whenever possible, a loyal employee blows the whistle internally. This provides the employer with the opportunity to either demonstrate to the employee that, contrary to first appearances, no genuine wrongdoing had occurred, or, if there is a genuine moral problem, the opportunity to resolve it.

This principle of dealing directly with the person to whom loyalty is due needs to be qualified, however. Loyalty to a person requires that one acts in that person's best interests. Generally, this cannot be done without directly involving the person to whom one is loyal in the decision-making process, but there may arise cases where acting in a person's best interests requires that one act independently and perhaps even against the wishes of the person to whom one is loyal. Such cases will be especially apt to arise when the person to whom one is loyal is either immoral or ignoring the moral consequences of his actions. Thus, for example, loyalty to a friend who deals in hard narcotics would not imply that I speak first to my friend about my decision to inform the police of his activities, if the only effect of my doing so would be to make him more careful in his criminal dealings. Similarly, a loyal employee is under no obligation to speak first to an employer about the employer's immoral actions, if the only response of the employer will be to take care to cover up wrongdoing.

Neither is a loyal employee under obligation to speak first to an employer if it is clear that by doing so she placed herself in jeopardy from an employer who will retaliate if given the opportunity. Loyalty amounts to acting in another's best interests and that may mean qualifying what seems to be in one's own interests, but it cannot imply that one take no steps to protect oneself from the immorality of those to whom one is loyal. The reason it cannot is that, as has already been argued, acting immorally can never really be in a person's best interests. It follows, therefore, that one is not acting in a person's best interests if one allows oneself to be treated immorally by that person. Thus, for example, a father might be loyal to a child even though the child is guilty of stealing from him, but this would not mean that the father should let the child continue to steal. Similarly, an employee may be loyal to an employer even though she takes steps to protect herself against unfair retaliation by the employer, e.g., by blowing the whistle externally.

Third, loyalty requires that one is concerned with more than considerations of justice. I have been arguing that loyalty cannot require one to ignore immoral or unjust behaviour on the part of those to whom one is loyal, since loyalty amounts to acting in a person's best interests and it can never be in a person's best interests to be allowed to act immorally. Loyalty, however, goes beyond considerations of justice in that, while it is possible to be disinterested and just, it is not possible to be disinterested and loyal. Loyalty implies a desire that the person to whom one is loyal take no moral stumbles, but that if moral stumbles have occurred that the person

be restored and not simply punished. A loyal friend is not only someone who sticks by you in times of trouble, but someone who tries to help you avoid trouble. This suggests that a loyal employee will have a desire to point out problems and potential problems long before the drastic measures associated with whistleblowing become necessary, but that if whistleblowing does become necessary there remains a desire to help the employer.

In conclusion, although much more could be said on the subject of loyalty, our brief discussion has enabled us to clarify considerably the relation between whistleblowing and employee loyalty. It permits us to steer a course between the Scylla of Duska's view that, since the primary link between employer and employee is economic, the ideal of employee loyalty is an oxymoron, and the Charybdis of the standard view that, since it forces an employee to weigh conflicting duties, whistleblowing inevitably involves some degree of moral tragedy. The solution lies in realizing that to whistleblow for reasons of morality is to act in one's employer's best interests and involves, therefore, no disloyalty.

NOTES

1. The definition I have proposed applies most directly to the relation between privately owned companies aiming to realize a profit and their employees. Obviously, issues of whistleblowing arise in other contexts, e.g., governmental organizations or charitable agencies, and deserve careful thought. I do not propose, in this paper, to discuss whistleblowing in these other contexts, but I think my development of the concept of whistleblowing as positive demonstration of loyalty can easily be applied and will prove useful.

2. Duska, R.: 1985, 'Whistleblowing and Employee Loyalty', in J. R. Desjardins and J. J. McCall, eds., *Contemporary Issues in Business Ethics* (Wadsworth, Belmont, California), pp. 295–300.

3. Duska, p. 297.

4. Duska, p. 298.

5. Bok, S.: 1983, 'Whistleblowing and Professional Responsibility', in T. L. Beauchamp and N. E. Bowie, eds., *Ethical Theory and Business*, 2nd ed. (Prentice-Hall Inc., Englewood Cliffs, New Jersey), pp. 261–269, p. 263.

6. Bok, pp. 261–2, emphasis added.

7. Near, J. P. and P. Miceli: 1985, 'Organizational Dissidence: The Case of Whistle-Blowing', *Journal of Business Ethics* 4, pp. 1–16, p. 10.

8. As Near and Miceli note 'The whistle-blower may provide valuable information helpful in improving organizational effectiveness... the prevalence of illegal activity in organizations is associated with declining organizational performance' (p. 1).

The general point is that the structure of the world is such that it is not in a company's long-term interests to act immorally. Sooner or later a company which flouts morality and legality will suffer.

POSTSCRIPT

Does Blowing the Whistle Violate Company Loyalty?

Whistle-blowing is a difficult choice. What would you do when faced with such a choice? The corporation is not the only setting for whistle-blowers. Would you report a friend for drug abuse, cheating on exams, or stealing? How do you weigh the possibility of damage being done to the community against the security of your own career (some damage done to many people versus much damage done to a few people)? If you see only painful consequences if you blow the whistle, does that settle the problem—or does simple justice and fidelity to law have a claim of its own?

Should we, as a society, protect the whistle-blower with legislation designed to discourage corporate retaliation? Richard T. DeGeorge and Alan F. Westin, two of the earliest business ethics writers to take whistle-blowing seriously, agree that companies should adopt policies that preclude the need for employees to blow the whistle. "The need for moral heroes," DeGeorge concludes in *Business Ethics*, 2d ed. (Macmillan, 1986), "shows a defective society and defective corporations. It is more important to change the legal and corporate structures that make whistle blowing necessary than to convince people to be moral heroes." In *Whistle Blowing: Loyalty and Dissent in the Corporation* (McGraw-Hill, 1981), Westin writes, "The single most important element in creating a meaningful internal system to deal with whistle blowing is to have top leadership accept this as a management priority. This means that the chief operating officer and his senior colleagues have to believe that a policy which encourages discussion and dissent, and deals fairly with whistle-blowing claims, is a good and important thing for their company to adopt.... They have to see it, in their own terms, as a moral duty of good private enterprise."

SUGGESTED READINGS

Rosemary Chalk, "Doing Right on Wrongdoing," *Technology Review* (February/March 1993).

Kenneth Kernaghan, "Whistle-Blowing in Canadian Governments: Ethical, Political and Managerial Considerations," *Optimum* (1991–1992).

Marcia P. Miceli, Janet P. Near, and Charles R. Schwenk, "Who Blows the Whistle and Why?" *Industrial and Labor Relations Review* (October 1991).

Kenneth Silverstein, "Proposed Whistle-Blowing Law Puts Corporations on Notice," *Corporate Cashflow* (December 1992).

ISSUE 10

Should Concern for Drug Abuse Overrule Concerns for Employee Privacy?

YES: Michael A. Verespej, from "Drug Users—Not Testing—Anger Workers," *Industry Week* (February 17, 1992)

NO: Jennifer Moore, from "Drug Testing and Corporate Responsibility: The 'Ought Implies Can' Argument," *Journal of Business Ethics* (vol. 8, 1989)

ISSUE SUMMARY

YES: Michael A. Verespej, a writer for *Industry Week,* argues that workers are the hardest hit when their co-workers use drugs, and he suggests that, for this reason, a majority of employees are tolerant of drug testing.

NO: Jennifer Moore, a researcher of business ethics and business law, asserts that a right is a right and that any utilitarian concerns that employers can cite to justify drug testing should not override the right of the employee to dignity and privacy on the job.

In 1928 U.S. Supreme Court justice Louis Brandeis defined the right of privacy as "the right to be let alone, the most comprehensive of rights and the right most valued by civilized men." The constitutional origins of that right are hazy, found variously in the Fourth Amendment (prohibiting illegal searches and seizures), the Fifth Amendment (prohibiting compulsory testimony), and parts of the Ninth Amendment. But the U.S. Constitution only limits *government* action, and worried Americans increasingly find that their employers can be a more dangerous threat to their privacy.

What right does an employee have to be "let alone" by his or her employer? Historically, none at all. Dictatorial employers had no qualms about making and enforcing rules governing not only job performance but dress and personal behavior on the job as well. Many also had rules for off-the-job behavior. School boards, for example, routinely enforced rules that required teachers to abstain from smoking and drinking, to attend church regularly, and to limit courting to one day a week. But with the advent of organized labor, the freedom of the employer to dictate the employee's lifestyle off the job almost disappeared. On-the-job requirements also ceased to be absolute. Although certain obvious safety rules could be enforced (such as prohibiting alcohol on the job and requiring that safety equipment be worn), the presumption was that rules should not be extended beyond necessity. Until very recently, we had seemed to be approaching an understanding that the employee's choices of amusements and associations off the job were sacrosanct and that his or her personal style of dress and grooming on the job could be regulated only to the extent that such appearances were reasonably job-related.

Then came drugs. Unlike alcohol, drugs can be easily concealed in one's clothing and cannot be detected on a person's breath after they are consumed. Seasoned foremen who would have no trouble spotting the slurred speech and wobbly walk caused by alcohol may not be able to detect drug use in their employees. The effect of drug use on judgment and behavior, especially for such people as pilots, bus drivers, and military personnel, can and does cause deaths.

While many may agree that this fact alone justifies testing for on-the-job drug use, there are many factors that complicate the issue. First, the only tests currently available to determine drug use are seriously invasive (unlike the Breathalyzer test for alcohol, for instance). In practice, the tester must take a blood sample from the worker or require the worker to give up a urine sample. The blood test requires a needle stick that some find painful and terrifying, and the urination must be observed to ensure that the test is valid—at an imaginable cost in embarrassment to the worker and to the observer. Second, the tests cannot distinguish between drug-use behavior on the job and off the job. Marijuana smoked on a Friday night may show up in urine that is expelled on the following Tuesday. So the worker subjected to testing at random may find his off-the-job activities severely restricted by the tests. To be sure, no one is interested in condoning off-the-job drug use, but the move from on-the-job regulation to 24-hour regulation is an unintended consequence that raises further legal and ethical issues.

Third, the tests are not always accurate. Most employers have a policy that if an employee fails one drug test, he or she can take another in order to ensure accuracy. If the employee fails twice, he or she is out. But the tests are only 90 to 95 percent accurate, at best. That means that 1 out of 10, or at best 1 out of 20, will yield a false positive (the employee will appear to have drugs in his or her system). One out of 100, or at best 1 out of 400, will yield a false positive upon retest of a false positive. But some firms have thousands of workers. Is it fair to impose a testing routine that commits gross injustice once in 100 cases—or even only once in 400 cases?

As you read the following selections, ask yourself how society ought to balance the conflicting demands of privacy for the worker and safety for society. Given the doubts surrounding the practice, is routine randomized drug testing justified? On the other hand, given the terrible dangers that attend drug use on the job, can society afford to do without it?

YES

Michael A. Verespej

DRUG USERS—NOT TESTING—
ANGER WORKERS

Drug testing by companies still elicits an emotional response from employees. But it's a far different one from four years ago.

Back then, readers responding to an IW [*Industry Week*] survey angrily protested workplace drug testing as an invasion of privacy and argued that drug testing should be reserved for occasions in which there was suspicion of drug use or in an accident investigation.

Today's prevailing view, based on a recent IW survey covering essentially the same questions, stands as a stark contrast. Not only do fewer employees see drug testing as an invasion of privacy, but a significantly higher percentage think that companies should extend the scope of drug testing to improve safety and productivity in the workplace.

Why aren't employees as leery of workplace drug testing as they were four years ago?

First, both the numbers and the comments suggest that employees and managers are less worried that inaccurate drug tests will brand them as drug users. Just 19.3% of those surveyed say that they consider drug testing an invasion of privacy, compared with 30% in the earlier survey.

Second, the tight job market appears to have made non-drug-users resent the presence of drug users in the workplace. Third, in contrast to four years ago, employees and managers are more concerned about the potential safety problems that drug users cause them than whatever invasion of privacy might result from a drug test. The net result: Unlike four years ago, employee thinking is now in sync with the viewpoints held for some time by top corporate management. "Job safety and performance are more important than the slight invasion of privacy caused by drug testing," asserts Lee Taylor, plant manager at U.S. Gypsum Co.'s Siguard, Utah, facility. "Freedom and privacy end when others are likely to be injured," adds the president of a high-tech business in Fort Collins, Colo.

G. A. Holland, chief estimator for a Bloomfield, Conn., construction firm, agrees: "Drug testing may be an invasion of privacy, but, because drug use puts others in danger, [drug testing] is an acceptable practice. The safety of employees overrides the right to privacy of another." Adds D. S. McRoberts, manager of a Green Giant food-processing plant in Buhl, Idaho: "The risks employees put themselves and their peers under when they use drugs justify testing."

Perhaps the most blunt response comes from Louis Krivanek, a consulting engineer with Omega Induction Services, Warren, Mich.: "I certainly wouldn't ride with a drinking alcoholic. Why should I work with a drug addict not under control?"

And the anti-drug-user attitude is not just a safety issue, either. "Drug users are also a financial risk to the employer," declares John Larkin, president of Overland Computer, Omaha, Nebr. "It's time to begin thinking about the health and welfare of the company," says William Pence, vice president and general manager of Kantronics Inc., Lawrence, Kans. "Drug testing is simply a preventive measure to ensure the future stability of a company."

The competitive factor also appears to be influencing workers' viewpoints. "A drug-free environment must exist if the quality of product and process is to be continuously improved," writes one employee.

"Productivity and company survival are too important to trust to an employee with a drug problem," says Jack Ver-Meulen, director of quality assurance at C-Line Products, Des Plaines, Ill. "Employees are a company's most valuable assets, and those assets must perform at the peak of their ability. Test them." One could argue that workers—and managers—have simply become conditioned to drug testing in the workplace because it is no longer the exception, but the rule. After all, 56% of the managers responding to the survey—twice as many

as four years ago—say their companies have drug-testing programs in place.

But the real reason for the change in opinion appears to be that four years of day-in, day-out experience with workplace drug problems have made managers and employees less tolerant of users. The attitude appears to be: Drug users are criminals and shouldn't be protected by the absence of a drug-testing program.

"Users are, by definition, criminals," declares Nick Benson, senior automation engineer at Babcock & Wilcox, Lynchburg, Va. "Drug users are breaking the law," states Naomi Walter, a data-processing specialist at Gemini Marketing Associates, Carthage, Mo. "So why let them get an advantage?"

Layoffs and plant and store closings are also behind the new lack of tolerance for the drug user. "I believe that if a company is paying a person to work for them," says one IW reader, "that person should be drug-free. A job is a privilege, not a right."

*   *   *

That lack of tolerance is reflected in significantly changed ideas of who in the workplace should be tested for drug use. A significantly higher percentage of respondents think that more workers should be tested at random or that all employees should be tested.

More than 45% of IW readers—compared with 29.6% four years ago—say that drug tests should be conducted at random. And 70.5% think all employees should be required to take drug tests. Only 60% felt that way in the last IW drug-testing survey. Not surprisingly, then, the percentage of readers who would take a drug test and who think that employers should be able to test employees for drug use is now 93%; it was 88% four years ago.

But several attitudes haven't changed. Workers and managers still think that when companies use drug testing, they should be required to offer rehabilitation through employee-assistance programs, that management should be tested as well as employees, and that alcohol problems are equally troublesome. "Employers should be prepared to help—not just fire someone if the drug or alcohol abuse is exposed," says H. A. Dellicker, programming manager at Siemens Nixdorf, Burlington, Mass. "You need a properly monitored rehabilitation program."

Readers are just as adamant that if the majority of employees is to be tested, then everyone should be included—all the way up to the CEO. "Drug testing should be conducted on all employees, from top management down to the lowest position," asserts Sharon Hyitt, a drafting technician at Varco Pruden Buildings, Van Wert, Ohio. And IW readers contend that any drug-testing program should test for alcohol abuse as well. "Drug testing stops short," argues a reader in Muncie, Ind. "Alcoholism is more widespread in our workplace and just as destructive."

A plant superintendent in Ohio agrees and laments, "Alcohol is the most abused drug in our workplace, but it is not covered under our testing program. While the 'heavy' drugs get the spotlight because of the violence associated with their distribution, alcohol does the most damage in the workplace."

A product-testing engineer agrees, "Alcohol should be included in the tests and then perhaps lunch-time drinking would decrease. Why is it O.K. for those who have three-martini lunches to come back to work and try to function?"

NO

Jennifer Moore

DRUG TESTING AND CORPORATE RESPONSIBILITY: THE "OUGHT IMPLIES CAN" ARGUMENT

In the past few years, testing for drug use in the workplace has become an important and controversial trend. Approximately 30% of Fortune 500 companies now engage in some sort of drug testing or screening, as do many smaller firms. The Reagan administration has called for mandatory testing of all federal employees. Several states have already passed drug testing laws; others will probably consider them in the future. While the Supreme Court has announced its intention to rule on the testing of federal employees within the next few months, its decision will not settle the permissibility of testing private employees. Discussion of the issue is likely to remain lively and heated for some time.

Most of the debate about drug testing in the workplace has focused on the issue of privacy rights. Three key questions have been: Do employees have privacy rights? If so, how far do these extend? What kinds of considerations outweigh these rights? I believe there are good reasons for supposing that employees do have moral privacy rights,[1] and that drug testing usually (though not always) violates these, but privacy is not my main concern in this paper. I wish to examine a different kind of argument, the claim that because corporations are responsible for harms committed by employees while under the influence of drugs, they are entitled to test for drug use.

This argument is rarely stated formally in the literature, but it can be found informally quite often.[2] One of its chief advantages is that it seems, at least at first glance, to bypass the issue of privacy rights altogether. There seems to be no need to determine the extent or weight of employees' privacy rights to make the argument work. It turns on a different set of principles altogether, that is, on the meaning and conditions of responsibility. This is an important asset, since arguments about rights are notoriously difficult to settle. Rights claims frequently function in ethical discourse as conversation-stoppers or non-negotiable demands.[3] Although it is widely recognized that rights are not absolute, there is little consensus on how far they extend, what kinds of considerations should be allowed to override them, or even how to go

From Jennifer Moore, "Drug Testing and Corporate Responsibility: The 'Ought Implies Can' Argument," *Journal of Business Ethics*, vol. 8 (1989), pp. 279–287. Copyright © 1989 by D. Reidel Publishing Co., Dordrecht, Holland, and Boston, U.S.A. Reprinted by permission of Kluwer Academic Publishers.

about settling these questions. But it is precisely these thorny problems that proponents of drug testing must tackle if they wish to address the issue on privacy grounds. Faced with the claim that drug testing violates the moral right to privacy of employees, proponents of testing must either (1) argue that drug testing does not really violate the privacy rights of employees;[4] (2) acknowledge that drug testing violates privacy rights, but argue that there are considerations that override those rights, such as public safety; or (3) argue that employees have no moral right to privacy at all.[5] It is not surprising that an argument that seems to move the debate out of the arena of privacy rights entirely appears attractive.

In spite of its initial appeal, however, I will maintain that the argument does not succeed in circumventing the claims of privacy rights. Even responsibility for the actions of others, I will argue, does not entitle us to do absolutely anything to control their behavior. We must look to rights, among other things, to determine what sorts of controls are morally permissible. Once this is acknowledged, the argument loses much of its force. In addition, it requires unjustified assumptions about the connection between drug testing and the prevention of drug-related harm.

AN "OUGHT IMPLIES CAN" ARGUMENT

Before we can assess the argument, it must be set out more fully. It seems to turn on the deep-rooted philosophical connection between responsibility and control. Generally, we believe that agents are not responsible[6] for acts or events that they could not have prevented. People are responsible for their actions only

if, it is often said, they "could have done otherwise". Responsibility implies some measure of control, freedom, or autonomy. It is for this reason that we do not hold the insane responsible for their actions. Showing that a person lacked the capacity to do otherwise blocks the normal moves of praise or blame and absolves the agent of responsibility for a given act.

For similar reasons, we believe that persons cannot be obligated to do things that they are incapable of doing, and that if they fail to do such things, no blame attaches to them. Obligation is empty, even senseless, without capability. If a person is obligated to perform an action, it must be within his or her power. This principle is sometimes summed up by the phrase "ought implies can". Kant used it as part of a metaphysical argument for free will, claiming that if persons are to have obligations at all, they must be autonomous, capable of acting freely.[7] The argument we examine here is narrower in scope, but similar in principle. If corporations are responsible for harms caused by employees under the influence of drugs, they must have the ability to prevent these harms. They must, therefore, have the freedom to test for drug use.

But the argument is still quite vague. What exactly does it mean to say that corporations are "responsible" for harms caused by employees? There are several possible meanings of "responsible". Not all of these are attributable to corporations, and not all of them exemplify the principle that "ought implies can". The question of how or whether corporations are "responsible" is highly complex, and we cannot begin to answer it in this paper.[8] There are, however, four distinct senses of "responsible" that appear with some regularity in the argument. They can be characterized, roughly, as follows: (a) legally liable; (b) culpable or guilty; (c) answerable or accountable; (d) bound by an obligation. The first is purely legal; the last three have a moral dimension.

Legal Liability

We do hold corporations legally liable for the negligent acts of employees under the doctrine of *respondeat superior* ("let the master respond"). If an employee harms a third party in the course of performing his or her duties for the firm, it is the corporation which must compensate the third party. *Respondeat superior* is an example of what is frequently called "vicarious liability". Since the employee was acting on behalf of the firm, and the firm was acting through the employee when the harmful act was committed, liability is said to "transfer" from the employee to the firm. But it is not clear that such liability on the part of the employer implies a capacity to have prevented the harm. Corporations are held liable for accidents caused by an employee's negligent driving, for example, even if they could not have foreseen or prevented the injury. While some employee accidents can be traced to corporate negligence,[9] there need be no fault on the part of the corporation for the doctrine of *respondeat superior* to apply. The doctrine of *respondeat superior* is grounded not in fault, but in concerns of public policy and utility. It is one of several applications of the notion of liability without fault in legal use today.

Because it does not imply fault, and its attendant ability to have done otherwise, legal liability or responsibility **a** cannot be used successfully as part of an "ought implies can" argument. Holding corporations legally liable for harms committed by intoxicated employees while at the same time forbidding drug-testing is not inconsistent. It could simply be viewed as yet another instance of liability without fault. Of course, one could argue that the notion of liability without fault is itself morally unacceptable, and that liability ought not to be detached from moral notions of punishment and blame. This is surely an extremely important claim, but it is beyond the scope of this paper. The main point to be made here is that we must be able to attribute more than legal liability to corporations if we are to invoke the principle of "ought implies can". Corporations must be responsible in sense **b, c,** or **d**—that is, *morally* responsible—if the argument is to work.

Moral Responsibility

Are corporations morally responsible for harms committed by intoxicated employees? Perhaps the most frequently used notion of moral responsibility is sense **b,** what I have called "guilt" or "culpability".[10] I have in mind here the strongest notion of moral responsibility, the sense that is prevalent in criminal law. An agent is responsible for an act in this sense if the act can be imputed to him or her. An essential condition of imputability is the presence in the agent of an intention to commit the act, or *mens rea*.[11] But does an employer whose workers use drugs satisfy the *mens rea* requirement? The requirement probably would be satisfied if it could be shown that the firm intended the resulting harms, ordered its employees to work under the influence of drugs, or even, perhaps (though this is less clear) turned a blind eye to blatant drug abuse in the workplace.[12] But these are all quite farfetched possibilities.

It is reasonable to assume that most corporations do not intend the harms caused by their employees, and that they do not order employees to use drugs on the job. Drug use is quite likely to be prohibited by company policy. If corporations are morally responsible for drug-related harms committed [by] employees, then, it is not in sense **b**.

Corporations might, however, be morally responsible for harms committed by employees in another sense. An organization acts through its employees. It empowers its employees to act in ways in which they otherwise would not act by providing them with money, power, equipment, and authority. Through a series of agreements, the corporation delegates its employees to act on its behalf. For these reasons, one could argue that corporations are responsible, in the sense of "answerable" or "accountable" (responsibility **c**), for the harmful acts of their employees. Indeed, it could be argued that if corporations are not morally responsible for these acts, they are not morally responsible for any acts at all, since corporations can only act through their employees.[13] To say that corporations are responsible for the harms of their employees in sense **c** is to say more than just that a corporation must "pay up" if an employee causes harm. It is to assign fault to the corporation by virtue of the ways in which organizational policies and structures facilitate and direct employees' actions.[14]

Moreover, corporations presumably have the same obligations as other agents to avoid harm in the conduct of their business. Since they conduct their business through their employees, it could plausibly be argued that corporations have an obligation to anticipate and prevent harms that employees might cause in the course of their employment. If this reasoning is correct, corporations are morally responsible for the drug-related harms of employees in sense **d**—that is, they are under an obligation to prevent those harms. The "ought implies can" argument, then, may be formulated as follows:

1. If corporations have obligations, they must be capable of carrying them out, on the principle of "ought implies can".
2. Corporations have an obligation to prevent harm from occurring in the course of conducting their business.
3. Drug use by employees is likely to lead to harm.
4. Corporations must be able to take steps to eliminate (or at least reduce) drug use by employees.
5. Drug testing is an effective way to eliminate/reduce employee drug use.
6. Therefore corporations must be permitted to test for drugs.[15]

THE LIMITS OF CORPORATE AUTONOMY

This is surely an important argument, one that deserves to be taken seriously. The premise that corporations have an obligation to prevent harm from occurring in the conduct of their business seems unexceptionable and consistent with the actual moral beliefs of society. There is not much question that drug use by employees, especially regular drug use or drug use on the job, leads to harms of various kinds. Some of these are less serious than others, but some are very serious indeed: physical injury to consumers, the public, and fellow employees—and sometimes even death.[16]

Moreover, our convictions about the connections between responsibility or obligation and capability seem unassailable. Like other agents, if corporations are to have obligations, they must have the ability to carry them out. The argument seems to tell us that corporations are only able to carry out their obligations to prevent harm if they can free themselves of drugs. To prevent corporations from drug testing, it implies, is to prevent them from discharging their obligations. It is to cripple corporate autonomy just as we would cripple the autonomy of an individual worker if we refused to allow him to "kick the habit" that prevented him from giving satisfactory job performance.

But this analogy between corporate and individual autonomy reveals the initial defect in the argument. Unlike human beings, corporations are never fully autonomous selves. On the contrary, their actions are always dependent upon individual selves who are autonomous. Human autonomy means self-determination, self-governance, self-control. Corporate autonomy, at least as it is understood here, means control over others. Corporate autonomy is essentially derivative. But this means that corporate acts are not the simple sorts of acts generated by individual persons. They are complex. Most importantly, the members of a corporation are frequently not the agents, but the objects, of "corporate" action. A good deal of corporate action, that is, necessitates doing something not only *through* corporate employees, but *to* those employees.[17] The act of eliminating drugs from the workplace is an act of this sort. A corporation's ridding itself of drugs is not like an individual person's "kicking the habit". Rather, it is one group of persons making another group of persons give up drug use.

This fact has important implications for the "ought implies can" argument. The argument is persuasive in situations in which carrying out one's obligations requires only *self*-control, and does not involve controlling the behavior of others. Presumably there are no restrictions on what one may do to oneself in order to carry out an obligation.[18] But a corporation is not a genuine "self", and there *are* moral limits on what one person may do to another. Because this is so, we cannot automatically assume that the obligation to prevent harm justifies employee drug testing. Of course this does not necessarily mean that drug testing is *unjustified*. But it does mean that before we can determine whether it is justified, we must ask what is permissible for one person or group of persons to do to another to prevent a harm for which they are responsible.

Are there any analogies available that might help to resolve this question? It is becoming increasingly common to hold a hostess responsible (both legally and morally) for harm caused by a drunken guest on the way home from her party. In part, this is because she contributes to the harm by serving her guest alcohol. It is also because she knows that drunk driving is risky, and has a general obligation to prevent harm. What must she be allowed to do to prevent harms of this kind? Persuade the guest to spend the night on the couch? Surely. Take her car keys away from her? Perhaps. Knock her out and lock her in the bathroom until morning? Surely not.

Universities are occasionally held legally and morally responsible for harms committed by members of fraternities —destruction of property, gang rapes, and injuries or death caused by hazing. What may they do to prevent such harms? They may certainly withdraw institutional recognition and support from the fraternity, refusing to let it operate on the campus. But may they expel students who live together off-campus in fraternity-like arrangements? Have university security guards police these houses, covertly or by force? These questions are more difficult to answer.

We sometimes hold landlords morally (though not legally) responsible for tenants who are slovenly, play loud music, or otherwise make nuisances of themselves. Landlords are surely permitted to cancel the leases of such tenants, and they are justified in asking for references from previous landlords to prevent future problems of this kind. But it is not clear that a landlord may delve into a tenant's private life, search his room, or tap his telephone in order to anticipate trouble before it begins.

Each of these situations is one in which one person or group of persons is responsible, to a greater or a lesser degree, for the prevention of harm by others, and needs some measure of control in order to carry out this responsibility.[19] In each case, there is a fairly wide range of actions which we would be willing to allow the first party, but there are some actions which we would rule out. Having an obligation to prevent the harms of others seems to permit us some forms of control, but not all. At least one important consideration in deciding what kinds of actions are permissible is the *rights* of the controlled parties.[20] If these claims are correct, we must examine the rights of employees in order to determine whether drug testing is justified. The relevant right in the case of drug testing is the right to privacy. The "ought implies can" argument, then, does not circumvent the claims of privacy rights as it originally seemed to do.

THE AGENCY ARGUMENT

A proponent of drug testing might argue, however, that the relation between employers and employees is significantly different from the relation between hosts and guests, universities and members of fraternities, or landlords and tenants. Employees have a special relation with the firm that employs them. They are *agents*, hired and empowered to act on behalf of the employer. While they act on the business of the firm, it might be argued, they "are" the corporation. The restrictions that apply to what one independent agent may do to another thus do not apply here.

But surely this argument is incorrect, for a number of reasons. First, if it were correct, it would justify anything a corporation might do to control the behavior of an employee—not merely drug testing, but polygraph testing, tapping of telephones, deception, psychological manipulation, whips and chains, etc.[21] There are undoubtedly some people who would argue that some of these procedures are permissible, but few would argue that all of them are. The fact that even some of them appear not to be suggests that we believe there are limits to what corporations may do to control employees, and that one consideration in determining these limits is the employees' rights.

Secondly, the argument implies that employees give up their own autonomy completely when they sign on as agents, and become an organ or piece of the corporation. But this cannot be true. Agency is a moral and contractual relationship of the kind that can only obtain between two independent, autonomous parties. This relationship could not be sustained if the employee ceased to be autonomous upon signing the contract. Employees are not slaves, but autonomous agents capable of upholding a contract. Moreover, we expect a certain amount of discretion in employees in the course of their agency. Employees are not expected to follow illegal or immoral commands of their employers, and we find them morally and legally blameworthy when they do so. That we expect such independent judgment of them suggests that they do not lose their autonomy entirely.[22]

Finally, if the employment contract were one in which employees gave up all right to be treated as autonomous human beings, then it would not be a legitimate or morally valid contract. Some rights are considered "inalienable"—people are forbidden from negotiating them away even if it seems advantageous to them to do so. The law grants recognition to this fact through anti-discrimination statutes, minimum wage legislation, workplace health and safety standards, etc. Even if I would like to, I may not trade away, for example, my right not to be sexually harassed or my right to know about workplace hazards.

Again, these arguments do not show that drug testing is unjustified. They do show, however, that if drug testing is justified, it is not because the "ought implies can" argument bypasses the issue of employee rights, but because drug testing does not impermissibly violate those rights.[23] To think that obligation, or responsibility for the acts of others, can circumvent rights claims is to misunderstand the import of the "ought implies can" principle. The principle tells us that there is a close connection between obligation or responsibility and capability.

But it does not license us to disregard the rights of others any more than it guarantees us the physical conditions that make carrying out our obligations possible. It may well prove that employees' right to privacy, assuming they have such a right, is secondary to some more weighty consideration. I take up this question briefly below. What has been shown here is that the issue of the permissibility of drug testing will not and cannot be settled *without* a close scrutiny of privacy rights. If we are to decide the issue, we must eventually determine whether employees have privacy rights, how far they extend, and what considerations outweigh them—precisely the difficult questions the "ought implies can" argument sought to avoid.

IS DRUG TESTING NECESSARY?

The "ought implies can" argument also has another serious flaw. The argument turns on the claim that forbidding drug testing prevents corporations from carrying out their obligation to prevent harm. But this is only true if drug testing is *necessary* for preventing drug-related harm. If it is merely one option among many, the forbidding drug testing still leaves a corporation free to prevent harm in other ways. For the argument to be sound, in other words, premise 5 would have to be altered to read, "drug testing is a necessary element in any plan to rid the workplace of drugs."

But it is not at all clear that drug testing *is* necessary to reduce drug use in the workplace. Its necessity has been challenged repeatedly. In a recent article in the *Harvard Business Review*, for example, James Wrich draws on his experience in dealing with alcoholism in the workplace and suggests the use of broadbrush educational and rehabilitative programs as alternatives to testing. Corporations using such programs to combat alcohol problems, Wrich reports, have achieved tremendous reductions in absenteeism, sick leave, and on-the-job accidents.[24] Others have argued that impaired performance likely to result in harm could be easily detected by various sorts of performance-oriented tests—mental and physical dexterity tests, alertness tests, flight simulation tests, and so on. These sorts of procedures have the advantage of not being controversial from a rights perspective.[25]

Indeed, many thinkers have argued that drug testing is not only unnecessary, but is not even an effective way to attack drug use in the workplace. The commonly used and affordable urinalysis tests are notoriously unreliable. They have a very high rate both of false negatives and of false positives. At best the tests reveal, not impaired performance or even the presence of a particular drug, but the presence of metabolites of various drugs that can remain in the system long after any effects of the drug have worn off.[26] Because they do not measure impairment, such tests do not seem well-tailored to the purpose of preventing harm—which, after all, is the ultimate goal. As Lewis Maltby, vice president of a small instrumentation company and an opponent of drug testing, puts it,

... [T]he fundamental flaw with drug testing is that it tests for the wrong thing. A realistic program to detect workers whose condition put the company or other people at risk would test for the condition that actually creates the danger.[27]

If these claims are true, there is no real connection between the obligation to prevent harm and the practice of drug testing, and the "ought implies can" argument provides no justification for drug testing at all.[28]

CONCLUSION

I have made no attempt here to determine whether drug testing does indeed violate employees' privacy rights. The analysis... above suggests that we have reason to believe that employees have some rights. Once we accept the notion of employee rights in general, it seems likely that a right to privacy would be among them, since it is an important civil right and central for the protection of individual autonomy. There are also reasons, I believe, to think that most drug testing violates the right to privacy. These claims need much more defense than they can be given here, and even if they are true, this does not necessarily mean that drug testing is unjustified. It does, however, create a *prima facie* case against drug testing. If drug testing violates the privacy rights of employees, it will be justified only under very strict conditions, if it is justified at all. It is worth taking a moment to see why this is so.

It is generally accepted in both the ethical and legal spheres that rights are not absolute. But we allow basic rights to be overridden only in special cases in which some urgent and fundamental good is at stake. In legal discourse, such goods are called "compelling interests".[29] While there is room for some debate about what counts as a "compelling interest", it is almost always understood to be more than a merely private interest, however weighty. Public safety might well fall into this category, but private monetary loss probably would not. While more needs to be done to determine what kinds of interests justify drug testing, it seems clear that if testing does violate the basic rights of employees, it is only justified in extreme cases— far less often than it is presently used. Moreover, we believe that overriding a right is to be avoided wherever possible, and is only justified when doing so is *necessary* to serve the "compelling interest" in question. If it violates rights, then drug testing is only permissible if it is necessary for the protection of an interest such as public safety and if there is no other, morally preferable, way of accomplishing the same goal. As we have seen above, however, it is by no means clear that drug testing meets these conditions. There may be better, less controversial ways to prevent the harm caused by drug use; if so, these must be used in preference to drug testing, and testing is unjustified. And if the attacks on the effectiveness of drug testing are correct, testing is not only unnecessary for the protection of public safety, but does not serve any "compelling interest" at all.

What do these conclusions tell us about the responsibility of employers for preventing harms caused by employees? If it is decided that drug testing is morally impermissible, then there can be no duty to use it to anticipate and prevent harms. Corporations who fail to use it cannot be blamed for doing so. They cannot have a moral obligation to do something morally impermissible. Moreover, if it turns out that there is no other effective way to prevent the harms caused by drug use, then it seems to me we may not hold employers morally responsible for those harms. This seems to me unlikely to be the case—there probably are other effective measures to control drug abuse in the workplace. But corporations can

be held responsible only to the extent that they are permitted to act. It would not be inconsistent, however, to hold corporations legally liable for the harms caused by intoxicated employees under the doctrine of *respondeat superior*, even if drug testing is forbidden, for this kind of liability does not imply an ability to have done otherwise.

NOTES

1. Employees do not, of course, have legal privacy rights, although the courts seem to be moving slowly in this direction. Opponents of testing usually claim that employees have *moral* rights to privacy, even if these have not been given legal recognition. See, for example, Joseph Des Jardins and Ronald Duska, "Drug Testing in Employment", in *Business Ethics: Readings and Cases in Corporate Morality*, 2nd edition, ed. W. M. Hoffman and J. M. Moore (McGraw-Hill, forthcoming).

2. See, for example, "Work-Place Privacy Issues and Employer Screening Policies," Richard Lehr and David Middlebrooks, *Employee Relations Law Journal* 11, 407. Lehr and Middlebrooks cite the argument as one of the chief justifications for drug testing used by employers. I have also encountered the argument frequently in discussion with students, colleagues, and managers.

3. Ronald Dworkin has referred to rights as moral "trumps". This kind of language tends to suggest that rights overwhelm all other considerations, so that when they are flourished, all that opponents can do is subside in silence. Rights are frequently asserted this way in everyday discourse, and in this sense rights claims tend to close, rather than open, the door to fruitful ethical dialogue.

4. In his article "Privacy, Polygraphs, and Work," *Business and Professional Ethics Journal* 1, Fall, 1981, 19, George Brenkert has developed the idea that my privacy is violated when some one acquires information about me that they are not entitled, by virtue of their relationship to me, to have. My mortgage company, for example, is entitled to know my credit history; a prospective sexual partner is entitled to know if I have any sexually transmitted diseases. Thus their knowledge of this information does not violate my privacy. One could argue that employers are similarly entitled to the information obtained by drug tests, and that drug testing does not violate privacy for this reason. A somewhat different move would be to argue that testing does not violate privacy because employees

give their "consent" to... drug testing as part of the employment contract. For a sustained attack on these and other Type 1 arguments, see Joseph Des Jardins and Ronald Duska, "Drug Testing in Employment".

5. One might defend this position on the ground that the employer "owns" the job and is therefore entitled to place any conditions he wishes on obtaining or keeping it. The problem with this argument is that it seems to rule out *all* employee rights, including such basic ones as the right to organize and bargain collectively, or the right not to be discriminated against, which have solid legal as well as ethical grounding. It also implies that ownership overrides all other considerations, and it is not at all clear that this is true. One might take the position that by accepting a job, an employee has agreed to give up all his rights save those actually specified in the employment contract. But this makes the employment contract look like an agreement in which employees sell themselves and accept the status of things without rights. And it overlooks the fact that we believe there are some things ("inalienable" rights) that persons ought not to be permitted to bargain away. Alex Michalos has discussed some of the limitations of the employment contract in "The Loyal Agent's Argument", in *Ethical Theory and Business*, 2nd edition, ed. Tom L. Beauchamp and Norman E. Bowie (Englewood Cliffs, NJ: Prentice-Hall, 1983), p. 247.

6. The term "responsibility" is deliberately left ambiguous here. Several different meanings of it are examined below.

7. See Immanuel Kant, *Critique of Practical Reason*, trans. Lewis White Beck (Indianapolis: Bobbs-Merril, 1956), p. 30.

8. In this paper I have tried to avoid getting embroiled in the question of whether or not corporations are themselves "moral agents", which has been the question to dominate the corporate responsibility debate. The argument I offer here does, I believe, have important implications for the problem of corporate agency, but does not require me to take a stand on it here. I am content to have those who reject the notion of corporations as moral agents read my references to corporate responsibility as shorthand for some complex form of individual or group responsibility.

9. One example would be negligent hiring, which is an increasingly frequent cause of action against an employer. Employers can also be held negligent if they give orders that lead to harms that they ought to have foreseen. Domino's Pizza is now under suit because it encouraged its drivers to deliver pizzas as fast as possible, a policy that accident victims claim should have been expected to cause accidents.

10. This understanding of moral responsibility often seems to overshadow other notions. In an article on corporate responsibility, for example, Manuel Velasquez concludes that because corporations are not responsible in this sense, they are "not responsible for anything they do". "Why Corporations Are Not Responsible For Anything They Do", *Business and Professional Ethics Journal* 2, Spring, 1983, 1.

11. There is also an *actus reus* requirement for this type of responsibility—that is, the act must be traceable to the voluntary bodily movements of the agent. Obviously, corporations do not have bodies, but the people who work for them do. The question, then, has become when may we call an act by one member of the corporation a "corporate act". If it is possible to do so at all, the decisive feature is probably the presence of some sort of corporate "intention." This is why I focus on intention here, and why intention has been central to the discussion of corporate responsibility.

12. There are some, like Velasquez, who hold that a corporation can never satisfy the *mens rea* requirement because this would require a collective mind. If this were true, the argument would collapse at the outset. Others believe that a *mens rea* can be attributed to corporations metaphorically, if it can be shown that company policy includes an "intention" to harm, and it is this model I follow here.

13. There are, of course, those who take precisely this position. See Velasquez, "Why Corporations Are Not Responsible For Anything They Do".

14. See, for example, Peter French, *Collective and Corporate Responsibility* (New York: Columbia University Press, 1984).

15. It is tempting to conclude from this argument that drug testing is not only permissible, but obligatory, but this is not the case. The reason why it is not provides a clue to one of the major weaknesses of the argument. Drug testing would be obligatory only if it were *necessary* for the prevention of harm due to drug use, but it is not clear that this is so. But [it] also means that it is not clear that corporations are deflected from their duty to prevent harm by a prohibition against drug testing. See below for a fuller discussion of this problem.

16. For example, it has been claimed that employees who use drugs cause four times as many work-related accidents as do other employees. The highly publicized Conrail crash in 1987 was determined to be drug-related. Of course there are harms to the company itself as well, in the form of higher absenteeism, lowered productivity, higher insurance costs, etc. But since these types of harm raise the question of what a company may do to preserve its self-interest, rather than what it may do to prevent harms to others for which they are responsible, I focus here on harm to employees, consumers, and the public.

17. In our eagerness to assign "corporate responsibility", this fact has frequently been overlooked. This in turn has led, I believe, to an oversimplified view of corporate action. I discuss this problem more fully in a paper in progress entitled "The Paradox of Corporate Autonomy".

18. It is an interesting question whether there are limitations on what individuals can do to themselves to control their own behavior. What about individuals who undergo hypnosis, or who have their jaws wired shut in order to lose weight? Are they violating their own rights? Undermining their own autonomy? It could be argued plausibly that these kinds of things are not permissible, on the Kantian ground that we have a duty not to treat ourselves as merely as means to an end. Of course, if there are such restrictions, it makes the "ought implies can" argument as applied to corporations even weaker.

19. None of these analogies is perfect. In the case of the hostess and guest, for example, the guest is clearly intoxicated. This is rarely true of employees who are tested for drugs; if the employee were visibly intoxicated, there would be no need to test. Moreover, in the hostess/guest case the hostess contributes directly to the intoxication. There are important parallels, however. In each case one party is held morally (and in two of the cases, legally) responsible for harms caused by others. Moreover, the first parties are responsible in close to the same way that employers are responsible for the acts of their employees: they in some sense "facilitate" the harmful acts, they have some capacity to prevent those acts, and they are thus viewed as having an obligation to prevent them. One main difference, of course, is that employees are "agents" of their employers....

20. There are other, utility-related considerations, as well—for example, harm to employees who are unjustly dismissed, a demoralized workforce, the costs of testing, etc. I concentrate here on rights because they have been the primary focal point in the drug testing debate.

21. The assumption here is that persons are entitled to do whatever they wish to themselves. See Note 18.

22. See Michalos, "The Loyal Agent's Argument".

23. Some violations of right, of course, are permissible....

24. James T. Wrich, "Beyond Testing: Coping with Drugs at Work", *Harvard Business Review* Jan.–Feb. 1988, 120.

25. See Des Jardins and Duska, "Drug Testing in Employment", and Lewis Maltby, "Why Drug Testing is a Bad Idea", *Inc.* June 1987. While other sorts of tests also have the potential to be abused, they are at least a direct measurement of something that an employer is entitled to know—performance capability. Des Jardins and Duska offer an extended defense of this sort of test.

26. See Edward J. Imwinkelreid, "False Positive", *The Sciences*, Sept.–Oct. 1987, 22. Also David Bearman, "The Medical Case Against Drug Testing", *Harvard Business Review* Jan.–Feb. 1988, 123.

27. Maltby, "Why Drug Testing is a Bad Idea", pp. 152–153.

28. It could still be argued that drug testing *deters* drug use, and thus has a connection with preventing harm, even though it doesn't directly provide any information that enables companies to prevent harm. This is an important point, but it is still subject to the restrictions discussed in the previous section. Not everything that has a deterrent value is permissible. It is possible that a penalty of capital punishment would provide a deterrent for rapists, or having one's hand removed deter shoplifting, but there are very few advocates for these penalties. Effectiveness is not the only issue here; rights and justice are also relevant.

29. The principle that fundamental rights may not be overridden by the state unless doing so is necessary to serve a "compelling state interest" is a principle of constitutional law, but it also reflects our moral intuitions about when it is appropriate to override rights. The legal principle would not apply to all cases of drug testing in the workplace because many of these involve private, rather than state, employees. But the principle does provide us with useful guidelines in the ethical sphere. Interestingly, Federal District Judge George Revercomb recently issued an injunction blocking the random drug testing of Justice Department employees on the ground that it did not serve a compelling state interest. Since there was no evidence of a drug problem among the Department's employees, the Judge concluded, there is no threat that would give rise to a compelling interest. See "Judge Blocks Drug Testing of Justice Department Employees", *New York Times* July 30, 1988, 7.

POSTSCRIPT

Should Concern for Drug Abuse Overrule Concerns for Employee Privacy?

In the controversy over drug testing, the two sides seem to be reasoning from different moral principles and to different consequences. The proponents of randomized drug testing cite the principle of Least Harm: left to themselves to take drugs, the workforce is likely to turn out terribly harmful results—damaged products, derailed trains, and the pervasive negligence that makes products unsafe and the workplace dangerous.

At least some professions—such as firefighter, peace officer, and airplane pilot—are not only incompatible with drug use but are also so important to the public's safety and vulnerable to public distrust that the public deserves assurances that such employees are demonstrably drug free. For the sake of those assurances alone there should be a policy of random drug testing for those occupations. Meanwhile, the threat of being tested should deter those workers from using drugs; this deterrence provides a separate consequentialist argument for the testing.

The opponents of drug testing, however, find more harm than good resulting from drug testing. Given the potential for error, good employees will be not only fired but stigmatized; the morale of the workforce will suffer as the invasions of privacy threaten the dignity and self-esteem of the worker; and the atmosphere of suspicion built up by the testing policy will result in worker resentment.

Both sides also cite nonconsequentialist arguments to their conclusions. Those in favor of drug testing cite the importance of subordinating individual freedom to community interest in times of emergency, and they find worker resentment of drug testing not only suspicious (what are they trying to hide?) but also antisocial and obstructionist. Those against drug testing cite the importance of individual privacy and dignity—especially against the kind of invasion that drug testing entails—and further cite the importance of maintaining trust between employer and employee, which is violated by drug testing policies.

Troubling for both sides is the scope of the principle. After all, why stop with drugs? Once the employer has a license to regulate personal habits for the greater good of the customer, the company, and society, why not put that license to work in other areas? Can the employer tell the employees not to smoke tobacco, on or off the job? It would be to an employer's advantage since health insurance costs are reduced for companies with smoke-free environments. What about alcohol? Alcohol is at least as dangerous as other recreational drugs, with far-reaching effects on areas as diverse as family happiness, general health, and safety on the roads. Can employers regulate dating habits among their employees similar to the old school boards' practices? And what about AIDS? What if any role should testing for HIV infection play in the workplace?

Finally, once testing for these dangers has begun, who will keep the records of those who fail, and who will have access to those records? Publicly revealing negative results of any test could constitute defamation of character. How could the confidentiality of employee records be ensured?

It is difficult to predict the future of drug testing in the workplace. If it is to be allowed—and, according to the surveys reported by Verespej, it should—more reliable tests are needed on the front line. There is now a very expensive test for which 99.9 percent accuracy is claimed, which is often used as a backup if an employee fails a drug test once. But generally, it is not used to screen candidates for employment, so there is still the risk of excluding good employees because of false positives or ruining credibility with too many false negatives. Primarily, drugs are not a company problem or an affliction of American business or capitalism. They are proliferating in the society at large, and until drugs are removed from the street, there is little hope of getting them out of the workplace. Under these circumstances, it seems that the certainty of invasion outweighs the possibility of preventing drug use. On the other hand, the corporations may be the perfect place to begin to confront drug abuse.

SUGGESTED READINGS

Richard L. Berke, "The Post-Arrest Drug Test Gets a Foothold," *The New York Times* (April 2, 1989).

Rob Brookler, "Industry Standards in Workplace Drug Testing," *Personnel Journal* (April 1992).

Bruce A. Campbell, "Alcohol and Drug Abuse in the Workplace: Major Problem or Myth?" *R. F. Goodell Business Quarterly* (Autumn 1990).

Jonathan S. Franklin, "Undercover in Corporate America," *The New York Times* (January 29, 1989).

Michael Janofsky, "Drug Use and Workers' Rights," *The New York Times* (December 28, 1993).

Charles L. Redel and Augustus Abbey, "The Arbitration of Drug Use and Testing in the Workplace," *Arbitration Journal* (March 1993).

J. K. Ross III and B. J. Middlebrook, "AIDS Policy in the Work Place, Will You Be Ready?" *Advanced Management Journal* (Winter 1990).

Barbara Steinburg, "Foolproofing Drug Tests Results," *Business and Health* (December 1990).

Kimberly A. Weber and Robin E. Shea, "Drug Testing: The Necessary Evil," *Bobbin* (August 1991).

ISSUE 11

Should Women Have the Same Right to Work as Men?

YES: George J. Annas, from "Fetal Protection and Employment Discrimination—The *Johnson Controls* Case," *The New England Journal of Medicine* (September 5, 1991)

NO: Hugh M. Finneran, from "Title VII and Restrictions on Employment of Fertile Women," *Labor Law Journal* (April 1980)

ISSUE SUMMARY

YES: George J. Annas, a professor of law and medicine, argues that women may not be legally excluded from traditionally male jobs without some real relation of gender to job performance. He maintains that health risks to children not yet conceived do not constitute such a relation and that, therefore, women's rights to equal employment cannot be abridged on that rationale.

NO: Hugh M. Finneran, former senior labor counsel for PPG Industries, Inc., holds that preventing women from coming into contact with substances that can deform or destroy a growing embryo is a legitimate excuse for excluding women from certain jobs.

Workplaces often abound with nasty and unpleasant substances, chemical and otherwise. Fortunately, very few of them are really hazardous to health, and of those that are, the worst (such as coal dust, which leads to black lung disease) are well known. Most worrisome are the "quiet hazards," substances that are associated with adverse physical reactions and suspected to be the cause of damage to various organ and physiological systems but that are not surely proven to do any real and lasting damage.

Among the most troubling of these quiet hazards are those that attack the reproductive system. Germ cells, the sperm for men and the ova for women, are both the most carefully segregated of the body's systems—they are almost immune from damage from germs coursing through our blood, for instance —and the most vulnerable to damage, for damage to those cells may pass on, in unpredictable ways, to the next generation.

Reproductive damage is divided into two categories: Some substances directly affect the sperm and ova and cause changes that can damage any child that is conceived by the union of those cells. Such substances are called *mutagens* because they cause mutations in the germ plasma. The second category, called *teratogens*, is even more frightening; they attack the developing embryo in the womb, interfering with the complex physiological reactions and anatomical development of the first several weeks of a human's life, causing deformities of limbs, organs, and the nervous system that are usually, but not always, incompatible with life.

With mutagens, men and women are on equal footing. Mutagens may affect the germ cells of both sexes, so it is equally possible for both sexes to pass adverse effects down to their children. Therefore, women may not be excluded from a work environment in which there is a risk of infection any more than men can. This was the first finding of the *Johnson Controls* case, which is discussed by George J. Annas in the following selection.

The second finding is more controversial: When it is believed that a substance in a workplace is a teratogen, the danger is not to the worker (male or female) but to the developing child in the womb of a female worker. There is no *prima facie* reason to object to a rule excluding children from a workplace that contains a substance that is demonstrably dangerous to children but not to adults. But teratogens do not affect young children, or babies, or (it is believed) even fetuses at the stage where the mother is visibly pregnant. They affect development most at its earliest stages, in the first few weeks after the embryo is implanted in the uterus. But at that stage, the woman herself (let alone her employer) usually does not know that she is pregnant. All the damage has been done by the time she knows that there is an embryo at risk.

It seems that the only practicable way to protect these children is to exclude from that workplace any woman who *might* become pregnant; that is, any woman of childbearing age not provably sterile. It could be argued that the exclusion is not sexist: both male and female embryos (the at-risk groups) are being excluded from the workplace by simply excluding all potential embryo carriers from the workplace. At the same time, it is sexist because although women must be excluded, there is no reason to exclude men. Is this legal? The arbiters of the *Johnson Controls* case say it is not.

Hugh M. Finneran wrote the selection that follows before *Johnson Controls*, but the issues he raises are still ethically significant. Whatever the law says, he suggests, in order to protect the new equality for women, we should make special efforts to protect the most vulnerable of workplace participants—especially since there is no way for an embryo to consent to the risk.

As you read these selections, ask yourself whether or not attempts to reach total equality between women and men have gone too far. Are there some aspects of life in which gender equality is impossible? Also ask yourself if society should attempt to maintain some wall of protection for the vulnerable (such as children) that does not exist for the not-so-vulnerable. Should compassion for and protection of weaker persons take precedence over individual rights?

YES

George J. Annas

FETAL PROTECTION AND EMPLOYMENT DISCRIMINATION—THE *JOHNSON CONTROLS* CASE

Employers have historically limited women's access to traditionally male, high-paying jobs.[1] In one famous case early in this century, the U.S. Supreme Court upheld an Oregon law that forbade hiring women for jobs that required more than 10 hours of work a day in factories. The Chief Justice explained that this restriction was reasonable because "healthy mothers are essential to vigorous offspring" and preserving the physical well-being of women helps "preserve the strength and vigor of the race."[2] This rationale was never particularly persuasive, and women's hours have not been limited in traditionally female, low-paid fields of employment, such as nursing. Although such blatant sex discrimination in employment is a thing of the past, the average man continues to earn "almost 50 percent more per hour than does the average woman of the same race, age, and education."[3]

The contemporary legal question has become whether employers can substitute concern for fetal health for concern for women's health as an argument for limiting job opportunities for women. The U.S. Supreme Court decided in March 1991 that the answer is no and that federal law prohibits employers from excluding women from job categories on the basis that they are or might become pregnant.[4] All nine justices agreed that the "fetal-protection policy" adopted by Johnson Controls, Inc., to restrict jobs in the manufacture of batteries to men and sterile women was a violation of law, and six of the nine agreed that federal law prohibits any discrimination solely on the basis of possible or actual pregnancy. The ruling in *International Union* v. *Johnson Controls* applies to all employers engaged in interstate commerce, including hospitals and clinics.

Title VII of the Civil Rights Act of 1964 forbids employers to discriminate on the basis of race, color, religion, sex, or national origin. Explicit discrimination on the basis of religion, sex, or national origin can be justified only

From George J. Annas, "Fetal Protection and Employment Discrimination—The *Johnson Controls* Case," *The New England Journal of Medicine*, vol. 325, no. 10 (September 5, 1991), pp. 740–743. Copyright © 1991 by The Massachusetts Medical Society. Reprinted by permission.

if the characteristic is a "bona fide occupational qualification." The federal Pregnancy Discrimination Act of 1978 made it clear that sex discrimination includes discrimination "on the basis of pregnancy, childbirth, or related conditions."[5]

THE FETAL-PROTECTION POLICY OF JOHNSON CONTROLS

Beginning in 1977, Johnson Controls advised women who expected to have children not to take jobs involving exposure to lead, warned women who took such jobs of the risks entailed in having a child while being exposed to lead, and recommended that workers consult their family doctors for advice. The risks were said to include a higher rate of spontaneous abortion as well as unspecified potential risks to the fetus. Between 1979 and 1983, eight employees became pregnant while their blood lead levels were above 30 μg per deciliter (1.45 μmol per liter) (a level the Centers for Disease Control had designated as excessive for children). Although there was no evidence of harm due to lead exposure in any of the children born to the employees, a medical consultant for the company said that he thought hyperactivity in one of the children "could very well be and probably was due to the lead he had."[6]

In 1982, apparently after consulting medical experts about the dangers to the fetus of exposure to lead, the company changed its policy from warning to exclusion:

... women who are pregnant or who are capable of bearing children will not be placed into jobs involving lead exposure or which could expose them to lead through the exercise of job bidding, bumping, transfer, or promotion rights.

The policy defined women capable of bearing children as all women except those who "have medical confirmation that they cannot bear children."

In 1984, a class-action suit was brought challenging the policy as a violation of Title VII of the Civil Rights Act of 1964. In 1988, a federal district court ruled in favor of Johnson Controls, primarily on the basis of depositions and affidavits from physicians and environmental toxicologists regarding the damage that exposure to lead could cause in developing fetuses, children, adults, and animals.[7] The U.S. Court of Appeals for the Seventh Circuit affirmed this decision in 1989 in a seven-to-four opinion.[6] The majority based its opinion primarily on the medical evidence of potential harm to the fetus and on their view that federal law permitted employers to take this potential harm into account in developing employment policies.

THE SUPREME COURT'S DECISION

The U.S. Supreme Court unanimously reversed the decision in an opinion written by Justice Harry Blackmun. The Court had no trouble finding that the bias in the policy was "obvious," since "fertile men, but not fertile women, are given a choice as to whether they wish to risk their reproductive health for a particular job."[4] The Court noted that the company did not seek to protect all unconceived children, only those of its female employees. The policy was based on the potential for pregnancy and, accordingly, directly in conflict with the Pregnancy Discrimination Act of 1978. The key to the case was determining whether the absence of pregnancy or the absence of the potential to become pregnant was a bona fide occupational qualification for a job in battery manufacturing.

Employment discrimination is permitted "in those certain instances where religion, sex, or national origin is a bona fide occupational qualification reasonably necessary to the normal operation of that particular business or enterprise."[4] The Court's approach was to determine whether Johnson Controls' fetal-protection policy came within the scope of those "certain instances." The statutory language requires that the occupational qualification affect "an employee's ability to do the job."[4] The Court determined that the defense was available only when it went to the "essence of the business" or was "the core of the employee's job performance."[4]

The Court had previously allowed a maximum-security prison for men to refuse to hire women guards because "the employment of a female guard would create real risks of safety to others if violence broke out because the guard was a woman." Thus, sex was seen as reasonably related to the essence of the guard's job: maintaining prison security. Similarly, other courts had permitted airlines to lay off pregnant flight attendants if it was considered necessary to protect the safety of passengers. The Court agreed that protecting the safety or security of customers was related to the essence of the business and was legitimate.

The welfare of unconceived fetuses, however, did not fit into either category of exception. In the Court's words, "No one can disregard the possibility of injury to future children; the BFOQ [bona fide occupational qualification], however, is not so broad that it transforms this deep social concern into an essential aspect of battery making." Limitations involving pregnancy or sex "must relate to ability to perform the duties of the job.... Women as capable of doing their jobs as their male counterparts may not be forced to choose between having a child and having a job." The Court concluded that Congress had left the welfare of the next generation to parents, not employers: "Decisions about the welfare of future children must be left to the parents who conceive, bear, support, and raise them rather than to the employers who hire those parents."[4]

The Court finally addressed potential tort liability should a fetus be injured by its mother's occupational exposure and later sue the company. The Court wrote that since the Occupational Safety and Health Administration (OSHA) had concluded that there was no basis for excluding women of childbearing age from exposure to lead at the minimal levels permitted under its guidelines, the likelihood of fetal injury was slight. And even if injury should occur, the injured child would have to prove that the employer had been negligent. If the employer followed OSHA guidelines and fully informed its workers of the risks involved, the Court concluded that liability seemed "remote at best." Thus, just as speculation about risks to children not yet conceived has nothing to do with job performance, speculation about future tort liability—at least one step further removed from harm to the fetus —is not job-related.

THE CONCURRING OPINIONS

Justice Byron White wrote the main concurring opinion for himself, Chief Justice William Rehnquist, and Justice Anthony Kennedy. Although they agreed with the outcome in this case, they dissented from the bona fide occupational-qualification analysis as it applied to tort liability, and warned that the case could be used to undercut certain privacy rights. These three justices believed that under some circumstances it should be permissible for employers to exclude women from employment on the grounds that their fetuses could be injured and sue the employers (the women themselves could not sue because they would be covered by workers' compensation as their exclusive remedy). Their rationale was that parents cannot waive the right of their children to sue, that the parents' negligence will not be imputed to the children, and that even in the absence of negligence, "it is possible that employers will be held strictly liable, if, for example, their manufacturing process is considered."[4] Avoiding such liability was, in the view of these justices, a safety issue relevant to the bona fide occupational-qualification standard.

The other point made by the three justices was relegated to a footnote, but it is of substantial interest. They argued that the Court's opinion could be read to outlaw considerations of privacy as a justification for employment discrimination on the basis of sex because considerations of privacy would not directly relate to the employees' ability to do the job or to customers' safety. They cited cases in which the privacy-related wishes of some patients to be cared for by nurses and nurses' aides of the same sex had been upheld as a bona fide occupational qualification, including an instance regarding the sex of nurses' aides in a retirement home[8] and a policy excluding male nurses from obstetrical practice in one hospital.[9] The justices in the majority responded to this issue by saying simply, "We have never addressed privacy-based sex discrimination and shall not do so here because the sex-based discrimination at issue today does not involve the privacy interests of Johnson Controls' customers."[4] This issue has been left for another day, but it should be noted that the obstetrical-nurse case rests on outmoded judicial stereotyping of obstetricians as men and nurses as women.[10]

IMPLICATIONS OF THE DECISION

The Court took the language of the Pregnancy Discrimination Act seriously, correctly observing that "concern for a woman's existing or potential offspring historically has been the excuse for denying women equal employment opportunities."[4] The purpose of the act was to end such employment discrimination, and the Court's opinion in *Johnson Controls* holds that recasting sex discrimination in the name of fetal protection is illegal. Johnson Controls had argued that its policy was ethical and socially responsible and that it was meant only to prevent exposing the fetus to avoidable risk. Judge Frank Easterbrook probably had the most articulate response to this concern in his dissent from the appeals-court decision:

> There is a strong correlation between the health of the infant and prenatal medical care; there is also a powerful link between the parents' income and infants' health, for higher income means better nutrition, among other things.... Removing women from well-paying jobs (and the attendant health insurance), or denying women access to these jobs, may reduce the risk from lead while also reducing levels of medical care and quality of nutrition.[6]

Judge Easterbrook argued that ultimately fetal-protection policies cannot require "zero risk" but must be based on reasonable risk. He correctly noted that it is good and reasonable to worry about the health of workers and their future children. But,

> to insist on *zero* risk... is to exclude women from industrial jobs that have been a male preserve. By all means let society lend its energies to improving the prospects of those who come after us. Demanding zero risk produces not progress but paralysis.[6]

The same zero-risk analysis can, of course, be applied to the possibility of tort liability as seen from the industry's perspective. The industry would like its risk to be zero. Six of the nine judges agreed that it is close to zero, or at least remote. As a factual matter, there has been only one recorded case of a child's bringing a lawsuit for injuries suffered while the mother was pregnant and continued to work. In this case, the jury found in favor of the employer, even though there was evidence that the employer had violated OSHA safety standards.[11] Two thirds of the justices on the U.S. Supreme Court think that state tort liability is preempted so long as the employer follows federal law, informs workers of the risks, and is not negligent. Added to this is the extraordinarily difficult issue of causation, even if the employer is negligent. Putting the two together may not eliminate all risk of liability, but the risk is as small as can reasonably be expected.

It has been persuasively suggested that fetal-protection policies that affect only women are based on the view that women are "primarily biologic actors" and not economic ones and that men are only economic actors who have no "biologic connections and responsibilities to their families."[12] The decision in *Johnson Controls* continues the legal and

social movement to provide equality of opportunity in the workplace. It does not eliminate the duty to minimize workplace exposure to toxic substances. Indeed, it would be a hollow victory for women to gain the right to be exposed to the same high levels of mutagens and other toxic substances that men are exposed to. The real challenge for public policy remains to turn industry's focus away from new methods of sex discrimination and toward new ways to reduce workplace hazards. In this area, physicians continue to have a prominent role.

Physicians specializing in occupational health should continue to work to reduce exposure to toxic substances in the workplace for all workers (by replacing such agents with other, less toxic substances, reducing their volume, and encouraging the use of protective gear). In addition, all workers should be warned about the health risks of all clinically important exposures that cannot be avoided, and encouraged to be monitored for the early signs of damage. Personal physicians should take a careful occupational history and be sufficiently informed to be able to tell their patients about the risks of exposure to various substances, including what is known about their mutagenicity and teratogenicity.* Armed with this information, workers—both men and women—will be able to make informed decisions about their jobs and the risks they are willing to run to keep them, as well as to pressure management intelligently to make the workplace safer.

Congress and the Court have made a strong statement about the use of fe-

*[Mutagenicity is the capacity to cause mutations; teratogenicity is the capacity to cause developmental malformations.—Eds.]

tal protection as a rationale to control or restrict the activities and decisions of women: the ultimate decision maker must be the worker herself. This policy is consistent with good medical practice as well—as is evident, for instance, in the policy of the American College of Obstetricians and Gynecologists on "maternal–fetal conflicts."[13] To paraphrase Justice Blackmun, it is no more appropriate for physicians to attempt to control women's opportunities and choices on the basis of their reproductive role than it is for the courts or individual employers to do so.

REFERENCES

1. Becker ME. From *Muller v. Oregon* to fetal vulnerability policies, 53 U. Chicago Law Rev. 1219 (1986).
2. Muller v. Oregon, 208 U.S. 412 (1908).
3. Fuchs VR. Sex differences in economic well-being. Science 1986; 232:459–64.
4. International Union v. Johnson Controls, 111 S.CT. 1196 (1991).
5. Pregnancy Discrimination Act of 1978, 92 Stat. 2076, 42 U.S.C. sec 2000e (k).
6. International Union v. Johnson Controls, 886 F.2d 871 (7th Cir. 1989) (en banc).
7. International Union v. Johnson controls, 680 F. Supp. 309 (E.D. Wis. 1988).
8. Fesel v. Masonic Home of Delaware, 447 F. Supp. 1346 (D.Del. 1978).
9. Buckus v. Baptist Medical Center, 510 F. Supp. 1191 (E.D.Ark. 1981).
10. Sex in the delivery room: is the nurse a boy or a girl? In: Annas GJ. Judging medicine. Clifton, N.J.: Humana Press, 1988:53–6.
11. Security National Bank v. Chloride Industrial Battery, 602 F. Supp. 294 (D.Kan. 1985).
12. Becker ME. Can employers exclude women to protect children? JAMA 1990; 264:2113–7.
13. American College of Obstetricians and Gynecologists Committee opinion no. 55, Committee on Ethics. Patient choice: maternal-fetal conflict. Washington, D.C.: American College of Obstetricians and Gynecologists, 1987.

NO

Hugh M. Finneran

TITLE VII AND RESTRICTIONS ON EMPLOYMENT OF FERTILE WOMEN

During the decade of the 1970s, there was a rapid expansion of the female work force accompanied by a simultaneous expansion of scientific knowledge concerning hazards of exposure to toxic substances in the workplace. Health hazards in industry present serious legal, medical, and sociological issues.

Recently, a dramatic awareness of the hazards to the employee's reproductive capacity, i.e., miscarriage, stillbirth, and birth defects, has materialized. The hazard to the reproductive capacity and fetal damage is not a unique problem for female workers. Rather, it is a problem which may impact upon all workers. This article, however, will restrict its analysis to factual situations where the employer considers the problems of exposure to chemicals as uniquely, or primarily, arising out of the female physiology and either restricts or refuses to hire females with childbearing ability. Physical conditions other than chemical substances may also be harmful to the fetus, i.e., radiation, heat stress, vibration, and noise, but will not be treated in this article....

Title VII of the Civil Rights Act of 1964 incorporates two theories of discrimination which must be considered in a legal analysis of restrictions (the term "restriction" includes a refusal to hire) placed on females because of health hazards. These are: disparate treatment and policies, practices, or procedures with disparate impact not justified by business necessity.

Two types of substances will be considered in this article: teratogens and mutagens. Teratogens are substances that can harm the fetus after conception by entering the placenta. Mutagens are substances that can cause a change in the genetic material in living cells.

DISPARATE TREATMENT

The Supreme Court in *International Brotherhood of Teamsters v. United States* stated: "Disparate treatment... is the most easily understood type of discrimination. The employer simply treats some people less favorably than others because of their race, color, religion, sex, or national origin. Proof of discriminatory motive is critical, although it can in some situations be inferred from the mere fact of differences in treatment...."

From Hugh M. Finneran, "Title VII and Restrictions on Employment of Fertile Women," *Labor Law Journal,* vol. 31, no. 4 (April 1980). Published and copyrighted © 1980 by Commerce Clearing House, Inc., 4025 W. Peterson Avenue, Chicago, IL 60646. Reprinted by permission.

The Equal Employment Opportunity Commission and the United States Department of Labor on February 1, 1980, issued, for comment, Interpretive Guidelines on Employment Discrimination and Reproductive Hazards. "An employer/contractor whose work environment involves employee exposure to reproductive hazards shall not discriminate on the basis of sex (including pregnancy or childbearing capacity) in hiring, work assignment, or other conditions of employment."

An employer's policy of protecting female employees from reproductive hazards by depriving them of employment opportunities without any scientific data is a per se violation of Title VII. The Guidelines' position, however, is that the exclusion of women with childbearing ability from the workplace is a per se violation. To arrive at such a conclusion without an analysis of the precise scientific and medical evidence is an erroneous and indefensible legal standard. Thus, an employer's exclusion of females on the basis of their susceptibility to the mutagenic effects of a toxic substance should not be a per se violation but should be analyzed under the rubric of disparate treatment or adverse impact.

One line of inquiry under the disparate treatment analysis would be whether the mutagenic substance has reproductive hazards for male and female employees. If the particular chemical substance has a mutagenic effect on male and female employees, the obvious question is why female workers are treated differently. The answer may be scientifically explained, but it raises the issue of disparate treatment. Indeed, the employer should consider whether there are any other substances in the workplace, other than the

substance relied on to exclude the female, which have mutagenic effects on males.

In essence, if the basis for the exclusion is the mutagenic characteristics of a substance, the employer would have to treat all employees, male and female, who are exposed to mutagenic effects in the same manner. The employer may face a serious possibility of a Title VII violation for disparate treatment unless the scientific justification for the differential treatment is very persuasive.

In establishing a prima facie case of sex discrimination, under the principles of *McDonnell Douglas Corp. v. Green* a female must show that: she belongs to a protected class; she applied or was qualified for a job for which the employer was seeking applicants; and despite her qualifications, she was rejected. She also must prove that, after her rejection, the employer continued to seek applicants with her qualifications.

Applying the *McDonnell Douglas* principles to a restriction on female employment, the female could establish a prima facie case of sex discrimination if a chemical substance has a mutagenic effect on the males but only females are excluded from exposure to the hazard by the employer's restrictive policy. In this assumed factual situation, the very basis for the restriction would be applicable to either of sex discrimination, the employer has the burden of proving the existence of a business necessity or a bona fide occupational qualification. Of course, proof of compelling scientific data that the degree or severity of risk was substantially greater might alter the existence of a prima facie case, but the court more likely would consider such evidence as an affirmative defense.

GENDER-BASED CLASSIFICATION

Varying the factual assumptions, let us consider the existence of a work environment in which the chemical substance is a teratogen and an employer restricts the employment of females with child-bearing ability. In these circumstances, the employer could argue that the exclusion is based on a neutral health factor rather than sex-based criteria. Since teratogens by definition harm a fetus after conception, the safety hazard is present only for females with childbearing ability and cannot affect males or females without childbearing ability. Thus, a strong argument could be presented that the exclusion of females based upon the teratogenic effect of a chemical substance is a health classification and is not gender based.

In *Geduldig v. Aiello,* the Supreme Court ruled that the exclusion of pregnancy-related disabilities from a state disability system was not sex discrimination but was a distinction based on physical condition "by dividing potential recipients into two groups—pregnant women and non-pregnant persons." Likewise, *General Electric Co. v. Gilbert* viewed pregnancy classifications as not being gender based.

At least one commentator has criticized the relevance of *Gilbert* and *Aiello* to the restriction of female employment in toxic workplaces, because the classification suffers from overinclusiveness since "many women in the excluded class delay or plan to avoid childbearing and thus face no additional risk at all." This contention is small comfort to an employer, however, since women have been known to change their plans and birth-control techniques are not universally effective.

Furthermore, some teratogens are cumulative and remain in the body long after the exposure has ceased. The legal issue is more complex where there is a restriction on the employment of a woman with childbearing ability where teratogens are present but mutagens with adverse reproductive effects present in the workplace affect males on whom no restrictions are placed.

The Pregnancy Disability Amendment to Title VII may have a bearing on the issue of whether the classification is gender based. "The terms 'because of sex' or 'on the basis of sex' include, but are not limited to, because of or on the basis of pregnancy, childbirth, or related medical conditions...."

The Pregnancy Amendment to Title VII does not state expressly that the terms "because of sex" or "on the basis of sex" includes a woman's childbearing ability or potential. The Guidelines, however, interpret "childbearing capacity" as prohibited by the Amendment. Such an interpretation is not without some doubt as to its validity. Nevertheless, if the Guidelines' construction is correct, a distinction based on childbearing ability would be considered gender-based disparate treatment. The practical consequences may be minimal since exclusions or restrictions on the employment of females with childbearing ability has a disparate impact and is best analyzed in this context.

DISPARATE IMPACT

The Supreme Court in *Griggs v. Duke Power Co.* held: "Under the Act, practices, procedures, or tests neutral on their face, and even neutral in terms of intent, cannot be maintained if they operate to 'freeze' the status quo of prior discriminatory employment practices." Thus, *Griggs* ruled that the employer's requirement of a high school diploma or passage of a test as a condition of employment was a prima facie race violation of Title VII, unless these requirements are a "business necessity." "The Act proscribes not only overt discrimination but also practices that are fair in form but discriminatory in operation. The touchstone is business necessity."

In *Dothard v. Rawlinson*, the Supreme Court held that the employer violated Title VII by requiring a minimum height of five feet two inches and a weight of 120 pounds for prison guards since the policy had a disparate impact on women. Likewise, *Nashville Gas Co. v. Satty* is relevant to the issue. In *Satty*, the employer denied accumulated seniority to female employees returning from pregnancy leaves of absence. The Court held that an employer may not "burden female employees in such a way as to deprive them of employment opportunities because of their different role." The conclusion appears inescapable that an employer's restriction on the employment of women with childbearing ability, and this includes restrictions limited to specific jobs, is a prima facie violation of Title VII's proscriptions against sex discrimination under *Griggs*, *Dothard*, and *Satty*.

BONA FIDE OCCUPATIONAL QUALIFICATION

Two affirmative defenses must be considered: bona fide occupational qualification [BFOQ] and business necessity. Title VII provides an affirmative defense to a charge of sex discrimination where sex "is a bona fide occupational qualification reasonably necessary to the normal operation of that particular business or enterprise...."

The Guidelines state: "narrow exception [for BFOQ] pertains only to situations where all or substantially all of the protected class is unable to perform the duties of the job in question. Such cannot be the case in the reproductive hazards setting, where exclusions are based on the premise of danger to the employee or fetus and not on the ability to perform." Under *Weeks v. Southern Bell Telephone & Telegraph Co.*, an employer relying on the bona fide occupational qualification exception "has the burden of proving that he had reasonable cause to believe, that is, a factual basis for believing, that all or substantially all women would be unable to perform safely and efficiently the duties of the job involved."

In the absence of medical evidence to the contrary, an employer's assumption is that all, or substantially all, females have the capacity of bearing children. Thus, the area of controversy will probably center on the issue of whether the safety of the fetus or future generations is reasonably necessary to the normal operation of the employer's business. However, plaintiffs may argue that all or substantially all females are not at risk since not all females plan to have a family.

Courts have sustained decisions by bus companies not to hire drivers over specified ages as being a BFOQ justified by increased safety hazards for third persons. In *Hodgson v. Greyhound Lines, Inc.*, the company refused to consider applications for intercity bus drivers from individuals thirty-five years of age or older. The Seventh Circuit held that the company was not guilty of age discrimination, since its hiring policy was a BFOQ justified by the increased hazards to third persons caused by hiring older drivers. "Greyhound must demonstrate that it has a rational basis in fact to believe that elimination of its maximum hiring age will increase the likelihood of risk of harm to its passengers. Greyhound need only demonstrate however a minimal increase in risk of harm for it is enough to show that elimination of the hiring policy might jeopardize the life of one more person than might otherwise occur under the present hiring practice."

The Fifth Circuit in *Usery v. Tamiami Trail Tours, Inc.*, in upholding the company's refusal to hire bus drivers over forty years of age, found that the policy was a BFOQ. The company had demonstrated "that the passenger-endangering characteristics of over-forty job applicants cannot practically be ascertained by some hiring test other than automatic exclusion on the basis of age."

The language of the BFOQ exception under the Age Discrimination Act is essentially the same as the language of the BFOQ exception under Title VII of the Civil Rights Act. Cases in the airline industry also have considered third-party safety as a sufficient BFOQ in situations involving involuntary pregnancy leaves of absence for flight attendants.

The concept of concern for third parties is sufficiently elastic to include the unborn. It is submitted that society, including employers, has an obligation to avoid action which will have an adverse effect on the health and well-being of future generations. With all the present concerns about the protection of our environment and endangered species, an enlightened judiciary should not callously turn its back on generations unborn. Indeed, on the more mundane and pragmatic basis, it is of the essence of a business venture to operate safely in a manner which avoids costly tort liability.

BUSINESS NECESSITY

The business necessity defense may also justify the exclusionary or restrictive practice. In order to prove this defense, the employer has the burden of establishing that: the practice is necessary to the safe and efficient operation of the business; the purpose must be sufficiently compelling to override the adverse impact; and the practice must carry out the business purpose. The employer also must establish that there are not acceptable alternative policies or practices which would better accomplish the business purpose or accomplish it with lesser adverse impact on the protected class.

PRENATAL INJURY

Since the safe and efficient operation is premised on the need to protect the fetus, tort law relating to prenatal injuries is pertinent. The potential tort liability bears on the necessity for the exclusion. The law of Texas will be reviewed in regard to prenatal injuries. Texas was selected because of its large petrochemical industry.

The parents of a child suffering prenatal injuries resulting in its death have cause of action under the Texas wrongful death statute, provided the child was born alive and was viable at the time the injury was inflicted. In so ruling, the court stated that the statutory requirement of the Texas wrongful death statute, that the deceased has suffered an injury for which he could have recovered damages had he survived, was met. This holding of necessity implied that the Texas Supreme Court recognized a cause of action for a surviving child who is born alive with a birth defect caused by prenatal injuries. For a child born with birth defects, the cause of action exists for prenatal injuries at any time during pregnancy.

The Texas courts apparently have not yet decided whether parents have a cause of action under the wrongful death statute in cases where a child is stillborn due to prenatal injuries. The inquiry in such a case would revolve around the issue of whether a fetus is a person within the meaning of the wrongful death statute. Other state courts interpreting their wrongful death statutes have split on the issue.

Assuming that liability is established, Texas courts allow surviving parents to recover damages under the wrongful death act to compensate them for the pecuniary value of the child's service that would have been rendered during minority, less the cost and expense of the child's support, education, and maintenance, as well as economic benefits reasonably expected to have been contributed after reaching majority.

While it is generally held that some evidence of pecuniary loss is necessary to support a wrongful death judgment, the Texas courts have recognized that such proof cannot be supplied with any certainty or accuracy in cases involving young infants. Therefore, they leave the damages question largely to the discretion of the jury. Of course, a prenatally injured infant who manages to survive would be able to sue for his own personal injuries, including pain and suffering, loss of earning capacity, and any other damages, if applicable. Recognizing the "deep pocket syndrome," employers have a reasonable basis for being concerned about large tort recoveries.

The female employee's willing and informed consent to the assumption of the risk is not binding to the unborn child. Hence, obtaining a waiver from the female employee is an act with no legal significance other than documenting the employer's awareness of the unavoidably unsafe condition of the workplace for the fetus for use against the employer in tort litigation.

The employer should not be required to assume the risk of significant tort liability which could threaten the very existence of the enterprise, depending on the financial assets of the employer and the severity of injuries. Courts have required employers in discrimination cases to assume additional expense to achieve compliance with Title VII (costs of validation studies, loss of customer patronage, and training costs), but it is submitted that the magnitude of the risks of exposure to prenatal injuries and reproduction hazards should result in a different decision. The financial impact on the employer is important but certainly not the most important factor. A lifetime of suffering by future generations is worthy of societal concern. The Civil Rights Act does not exist in a vacuum.

Whether the purpose of the restriction is sufficiently compelling to override the adverse impact on women and is necessary to accomplish the employer's business purpose of ensuring a safe workplace without reproductive hazards will be decided by the scientific and medical data relating to the severity of the health hazard of the particular substance.

LESS RESTRICTIVE ALTERNATIVES

Under the business necessity principles of *Robinson v. Lorillard*, the employer must demonstrate the absence of "less restrictive alternatives" before relying on the affirmative defense. The Guidelines indicate that four factors should be considered. These are: whether the employer is complying with applicable occupational federal, state, and local safety and health laws; respirators or other protective devices are used to minimize or eliminate the hazard; product substitution is used; and affected employees are transferred without loss of pay or other benefits to areas of the plant where the reproductive hazard is minimal or nonexistent.

The employer's obligation to comply with its safety obligations under the Occupational Safety and Health Act is eminently reasonable, provided that it is recognized that the employer's obligation under OSHA only requires the use of technologically and economically feasible engineering and administrative controls. If engineering and administrative controls are not feasible, the employer must protect his employees by the use of personal protective devices. It is fair and reasonable to require an employer to satisfy his legal obligations under safety and health laws before excluding females from the workplace.

To suggest, however, that the employers change their products or provide rate retention for employees restricted from hazardous exposure is extreme and without legislative support. If Congress had intended to require substitution of products and rate retention for employees under Title VII, it would have done so explicitly. When, as here, these matters are at best tangentially related to nondiscrimination, Title VII is silent on the subject, and wages and rates of pay and seniority of workers transferred to jobs other than their usual jobs are mandatory subjects of collective bargaining, then a reasonable interpretation of the legislation is that Title VII does not impose this obligation of management.

If an employer intends to sustain his business necessity defense, there must be evidence that the employer has explored the feasible alternatives to imposing restrictions on the employment of fertile females. One alternative which must be considered is a system for individual screening and evaluation with restrictions imposed on the female only if she becomes pregnant. Serious medical questions are posed by this alternative. Indeed, for some teratogenic substances the first weeks of pregnancy are the most critical. During this period, a woman may not know that she is pregnant, and sophisticated tests may not reveal the pregnancy. The administration of such a program might raise serious personnel problems since female employees might object to continuous monitoring to determine whether they are pregnant.

CONCLUSION

The decade of the 1970s was the era of the testing cases under Title VII. The decade of the 1980s will be the era of large class actions involving the exclusion of fertile females from exposure to reproductive hazards.

On the extreme of one side will be those arguing that Title VII rejects these protections as Victorian, romantic paternalism which deprives the individual woman of the power to decide whether the economic benefits justify the risks. On the other extreme, some employers will argue that any possible risk of harm to the female's offspring require her exclusion.

An informed judiciary should consider not only the economic interests of the female employee and the employer but the societal concern for the quality and happiness of future generations as well. The Supreme Court in *Roe v. Wade* recognized that a state may properly assert important interests in protecting potential life. After evaluating the level, duration, and manner of exposure in the specific employer's workplace, if there is reputable scientific evidence of a recognized reproductive hazard, either from a mutagen with significantly greater risk for female workers or a teratogen, the employer should be allowed to exclude females from that workplace if the business necessity criteria are satisfied. The employer should have the right and, indeed, the duty and obligation to operate his facility with due concern for the safety and health of future generations.

POSTSCRIPT

Should Women Have the Same Right to Work as Men?

The *Johnson Controls* decision holds that excluding women from workplaces, except on the genuine inability of a woman to do the job, is illegal. The fetal protection policy, designed to protect the fetus and not the woman, is therefore illegal. But is it wrong? The answer to this question turns on a commitment of values: values concerning equality, especially equality between the sexes; values concerning the family and reproduction; and, significantly, values concerning the bottom line and the conditions of labor. The problem at Johnson Controls, Inc., was that there was lead in the atmosphere, which is why the company had adopted the contested policy. Some argue that there was a simpler way out—that all gender issues, fetal protection issues, Occupational Safety and Health Administration (OSHA) issues, and others would be solved if the employers, Johnson Controls, had just eliminated the lead problem.

The issue of tort liability dominated the *Johnson Controls* case. Management argued, unsuccessfully, that leaving women in the workplace was a sure invitation to horrendous lawsuits. The Court found instead that the mother's right to compensation, should her fetus be damaged by the lead, was waived, since she was covered by workman's compensation. But, considering that the fetus was not covered by workman's compensation and had waived no rights whatsoever, do you agree with this argument?

SUGGESTED READINGS

"Comparable Worth in Industrialized Countries," *Monthly Labor Review* (November 1992).

Julia Flynn, "Julia Stasch Raises the Roof for Feminism," *Business Week* (January 25, 1993).

Val Hammond, "Opportunity 2000: A Culture Change Approach to Equal Opportunity," *Women in Management Review* (1992).

Harry A. Jessell, "Court Overturns FCC Gender Preference," *Broadcasting* (February 24, 1992).

Joanne D. Leck and David M. Saunders, "Hiring Women: The Effects of Canada's Employment Equity Act," *Canadian Public Policy* (June 1992).

Peter Lurie, "The Law as They Found It: Disentangling Gender-Based Affirmative Action Programs from Croson," *University of Chicago Law Review* (Fall 1992).

Charlene Marmer Solomon, "Are White Males Being Left Out?" *Personnel Journal* (November 1991).

John Southerst, "Public Policy: What Price Fairness?" *Canadian Business* (December 1991).

PART 4

Moving the Product: Marketing and Consumer Dilemmas

What right does a consumer have to expect that the product he or she buys will cause no harm? At the start of the twentieth century, the buyer tended to be stuck with a purchase, however reached, and responsible for her or his own safety in using the product. This is no longer the rule governing product liability. In this section, we look at five cases: advertising, in and of itself; the marketing of a product that is essentially harmful (tobacco); the production and marketing of a car that may or may not contain a dangerous design flaw (the Pinto); the marketing and pricing of pharmaceuticals; and an accusation of company misrepresentation. Questions of intent and effect are inextricably linked in all five cases.

- Are Pharmaceutical Price Controls Justifiable?

- Is Advertising Fundamentally Deceptive?

- Product Liability: Was Ford to Blame in the Pinto Case?

- Should Tobacco Advertising Be Banned?

- Does The Body Shop Misrepresent Itself and Its Products?

ISSUE 12

Are Pharmaceutical Price Controls Justifiable?

YES: Richard A. Spinello, from "Ethics, Pricing and the Pharmaceutical Industry," *Journal of Business Ethics* (August 1992)

NO: Pharmaceutical Manufacturers Association, from "Price Controls in the Economy and the Health Sector," *Backgrounder* (April 1993)

ISSUE SUMMARY

YES: Philosopher Richard A. Spinello argues that the pharmaceutical industry should regulate its prices in accordance with the principles of distributive justice, with special attention to the needs of the least advantaged.

NO: The Pharmaceutical Manufacturers Association, an association of 93 manufacturers of pharmaceutical and biological products who support high manufacturing standards and ethical business practices, argues that price controls are historically counterproductive in providing scarce goods for the consumer, especially in the health care sector.

How shall we distribute the scarce valuable products of our society? Current economic philosophies offer two alternatives: the free market and public provision. In a free market, tradable goods or money or services are exchanged between buyers and sellers at a rate that is acceptable to both. This system assumes that everyone can bring enough money or goods or services to the exchange to have their needs met. A public commodity, on the other hand, is available to all as needed; police protection is a good example of a public commodity. Where does health care and the products that are essential to health care fall in this division?

Before the 1900s, in the United States, physicians charged fees for visits, which the patient was expected to pay; all pharmaceuticals were sold at essentially what the market would bear; and the industry was profitable. The suffering of those who could not afford health care was occasionally relieved by private charities and by religious orders that set up hospitals for the poor. But on the whole, medical care and all that went with it was a marketable good.

In the twentieth century, several nations began to make health care available to all through public taxation, on the same basis as police and fire protection. The medical treatments available under socialized medicine, as it is called, included most of the treatments that were previously available only to those who could pay for them through the private sector.

The rationale for this extension of benefits was simple enough: we are all dependent for our prosperity on the productivity of the nation—that is, the productivity of its citizens—and that depends upon the national level of health. It makes sense to oppose disease and promote health with the same energy that is spent on opposing enemy armies and promoting sound fiscal policy. Early public health movements financed clean water and universal inoculations at public expense; medical treatments and drugs were a direct extension of this idea.

In nations that have socialized their health care provision, there have always been disputes over the acceptable boundaries of medical coverage: Should cosmetic surgery be covered? What about elaborate reconstructive surgery for the very old? Weight loss treatments? Psychiatric care, not including emergencies? However, treatment of disease—AIDS, for example—is always covered, and here is where the dispute begins.

The United States has never fully subscribed to socialized health care provision (or of socialized anything, for that matter), and there is no tax money allocated to underwrite the cost of manufacturing drugs. As part of its federal police power, the United States does have the legal apparatus to control prices of essential commodities if the lawmakers feel that these prices are unconscionably high. But are price controls to equalize access to essential medications justified?

The dispute centers on two points: First, do pharmaceutical companies have an obligation to take into account the needs of the poorest customers in setting their prices (in accordance with the principles of justice), or may they restrict sales to only those who can pay full price? Second, if price controls were established, would they work in practice to achieve the ends of justice, or would they bring about negative consequences such as the shutting down of drug research?

In the following selections, Richard A. Spinello argues that the principles of distributive justice justify the implementation of price controls. On the opposing side, the Pharmaceutical Manufacturers Association, in a paper prepared by Van Dyk Associates, Inc., a public policy consulting firm in Washington, D.C., reports that past attempts to administer price controls have all failed. As you read these selections, ask yourself what kind of arguments are being deployed by the disputants. Do the moral arguments advanced by Spinello carry enough weight to warrant a practical response? Do the empirical arguments advanced by the Pharmaceutical Manufacturers Association that price controls are ineffective in practice render the theoretical arguments irrelevant?

YES

Richard A. Spinello

ETHICS, PRICING AND THE PHARMACEUTICAL INDUSTRY

INTRODUCTION

A perennial ethical question for the pharmaceutical industry has been the aggressive pricing policies pursued by most large drug companies. Criticism has intensified in recent years over the high cost of new conventional ethical drugs and the steep rise in prices for many drugs already on the market. One result of this public clamor is that the pricing structure of this industry has once again come under intense scrutiny by government agencies, Congress, and the media.

The claim is often advanced that these high prices and the resultant profits are unethical and unreasonable. It is alleged that pharmaceutical companies could easily deliver less expensive products without sacrificing research and development. It is quite difficult to assess, however, what constitutes an unethical price or an unreasonable profit. Where does one draw the line in these nebulous areas? We will consider these questions as they relate to the pharmaceutical industry with the understanding that the normative conclusions reached in this analysis might be applicable to other industries which market *essential* consumer products. Our primary axis of discussion, however, will be the pharmaceutical industry where the issue of pricing is especially complex and controversial.

THE PROBLEM

Beyond any doubt, instances of questionable and excessive drug prices abound. Azidothymide or AZT is one of the most prominent and widely cited examples. This effective medicine is used for treating complications from AIDS. The Burroughs-Wellcome Company has been at the center of a spirited controversy over this drug for establishing such a high price—AZT treatment often costs as much as $6500 a year, which is prohibitively expensive for many AIDS patients, particularly those with inadequate insurance

From Richard A. Spinello, "Ethics, Pricing and the Pharmaceutical Industry," *Journal of Business Ethics*, vol. 11 (August 1992), pp. 617–626. Copyright © 1992 by D. Reidel Publishing Co., Dordrecht, Holland, and Boston, U.S.A. Reprinted by permission of Kluwer Academic Publishers.

coverage. The company has steadfastly refused to explicate how it arrived at this premium pricing level, but industry observers suggest that this important drug was priced to be about the same as expensive cancer therapy.[1] ...

ETHICAL QUESTIONS

The behavior of Burroughs and the tendency of most drug companies to charge premium prices for breakthrough medicines raises serious moral issues which defy easy answers and simple solutions. As Clarence Walton observed, "no other area of managerial activity is more difficult to depict accurately, assess fairly, and prescribe realistically in terms of morality than the domain of price" (1969, p. 209). This difficulty is compounded in the pharmaceutical industry due to the complications involved in ascertaining the true cost of production.

To be sure, every business is certainly entitled to a *reasonable profit* as a reward to its investors and a guarantee of long-term stability. But the difficulty is judging a reasonable profit level. When, if ever, do profits become "unreasonable?" It is even more problematic to determine if that profit is "unethical," especially if it is the result of premium prices.

Obviously, the issue of ethical or fair pricing assumes much greater significance when the product or service in question is not a luxury item but an essential one such as medicine. Few are concerned about the ethics of pricing a BMW or a waterfront condo in Florida. But the matter is quite different when dealing with vital commodities like food, medicine, clothing, housing, and education. Each of these goods has a major impact on our basic well-being and

our ability to achieve any genuine self-fulfillment. Given the importance of these products in the lives of all human beings, one must consider how equitably they are priced since pricing will determine their general availability. Along these lines several key questions must be raised. Should free market, competitive forces determine the price of "essential" goods such as pharmaceuticals? Is it morally wrong to charge exceptionally high prices even if the market is willing to pay that price? Is it ethical to profit excessively at the expense of human suffering? Finally, how can we even begin to define what constitutes reasonable profits?

Also, the issue of pricing must be considered in the context of the pharmaceutical industry's lofty performance guidelines for return on assets, return on common equity, and so forth. On what authority are such targets chosen over other goals such as the widest possible distribution of some breakthrough pharmaceutical that can save lives or improve the quality of life? Pharmaceutical companies would undoubtedly contend that this authority emanates from the expectations of shareholders and other key stakeholders such as members of the financial community. In addition, these targets are a result of careful strategic planning that focuses on long-term goals.

But a key question persistently intrudes here. Should *other* viewpoints be considered? Should the concerns and needs of the sick be taken into account, especially in light of the fact that they have such an enormous stake in these issues? In other words, as with many business decisions, there appear to be stark trade-offs between superior financial performance versus humane empathy and fairness. Should corporations consider the "human cost" of their objectives for excellent performance? And what role, if any, should fairness or justice play in pricing decisions? It is only by probing these difficult and complex questions that we can make progress in establishing reasonable norms for the pricing of pharmaceuticals. ... The strategic decisions of large organizations "inevitably involve social as well as economic consequences, inextricably intertwined" (Mintzberg, 1989, p. 173). Thus such firms are social agents whether they like it or not. It is virtually impossible to maintain neutrality on these issues and aspire to some sort of apolitical status. The point for the pharmaceutical industry and the matter of pricing seems clear enough. The refusal to take "non-economic" criteria into account when setting prices is itself a moral and social decision which inevitably affects society. Companies have a choice —either they can explicitly consider the social consequences of their decisions or they can be blind to those consequences, deliberately ignoring them until the damage is perceived and an angry public raises its voice in protest.

If companies do choose, however, to be attentive and *responsible* social agents they must begin to cultivate a broader view of their environment and their obligations. To begin with, they must treat those affected by their decisions as people with an important stake in those decisions. This stakeholder model, which has become quite popular with many executives, allows corporations to link strategic decisions such as pricing with social and ethical concerns. By recognizing the legitimacy of its stakeholders such as consumers and employees, managers will better appreciate all the negative as well as positive consequences of their decisions. Moreover, an honest stakeholder analysis will compel them to explore the financial and human implications of those decisions. This will enable corporations to become more responsible social agents, since explicit attention will be given to the social dimension of their various strategic decisions.

... According to Goodpaster and Matthews, the most effective solution to this and most other moral dilemmas is one "that permits or encourages corporations to exercise independent, non-economic judgment over matters that face them in their short- and long-term plans and operations" (1989, p. 161). In other words, the burden of morality and social responsibility does not lie in the marketplace or in the hand of government regulation but falls directly on the corporation and its managers.

Companies that do aspire to such moral and social responsibility will adopt *the moral point of view*, which commits one to view positively the interest of others, including various stakeholder groups. Moreover, the moral point of view assigns primacy to virtues such as justice, integrity, and respect. Thus, the virtuous corporation is analogous to the virtuous person: each exhibits these moral qualities and acts according to the principle that the single-minded pursuit of one's own selfish interests is a violation of moral standards and an offense to the community. The moral point of view also assumes that both the corporation and the individual thrive in an environment of cooperative interaction which can only be realized when one turns from a narrow self-interest to a wider interest in others.

PRICING POLICIES AND JUSTICE

This brings us back to the specific moral question of fair pricing policies for the pharmaceutical industry. The moral issue at stake here concerns justice and more precisely distributive justice. As we have remarked, justice has always been considered a primary virtue and thus it is an indispensable component of the moral point of view. According to Aristotle, justice "is not a part of virtue but the whole of excellence or virtue" (1962, p. 114). Thus, there can be no virtue without justice. This implies that if corporations are serious about assimilating the moral point of view and exercising their capacity for responsible behavior, they must strive to be just in their dealings with both their internal and external constituencies. Moreover, traditional discussions on justice in the works of philosophers such as Aristotle, Hume, Mill, and Rawls have emphasized distributive justice, which is concerned with the fair distribution of society's benefits and burdens. This seems especially relevant to the matter of ethical pricing policies.

Corporations which control the distribution of essential products such as ethical drugs like AZT can be just or unjust in the way they distribute these products. When premium prices are charged for such goods an artificial scarcity is created, and this gives rise to the question of how equitably this scarce resource is being allocated. The consequence of a premium pricing strategy whose objective is to garner high profits would appear to be an inequitable distribution pattern. As we have seen, due to the expensiveness of AZT and similar drugs they are often not available to the poor and lower middle class unless their insurance plans cover this expense or they can somehow secure government assistance which has not been readily forthcoming. However, if this distribution pattern can be considered unjust, what determines a just distribution policy?

There are, of course, many conceptions of distributive justice which would enable us to answer this question. Some stress individual merit (each according to his ability) while others are more egalitarian and stress an equal distribution of society's goods and services. Given a wide array of different theories on justice, where does the manager turn for some guidance and straightforward insights?

One of the most popular and plausible conceptions of justice is advanced by John Rawls in his well known work, *A Theory of Justice*. A thorough treatment of this complex and prolix work is beyond the scope of this essay. However, a concise summary of Rawls' work should reveal its applicability to the problem of fair pricing. Rawls' conception of justice, which is predicated on the Kantian idea of personhood, properly emphasizes the equal worth and universal dignity of all persons. All rational persons have a dual capacity: they possess the ability to develop a rational plan to pursue their own conception of the good life along with the ability to respect this same capacity of self-determination in others. This Kantian ideal underlies the choice of the two principles of justice in the original position. Furthermore, this choice is based on the assumption that the "protection of Kantian self-determination for all persons depends on certain formal guarantees—the equal rights and liberties of democratic citizenship—plus guaranteed access to certain material resources" (Doppelt, p. 278). In short, the essence of justice as fairness means that persons are entitled to an extensive system of liberties *and* basic material goods.

Unlike pure egalitarian theories, however, Rawls stipulates that inequities are consistent with his conception of justice so long as they are compatible with universal respect for Kantian personhood. This implies that such inequities should not be tolerated if they interfere with the basic rights, liberties, and material benefits all deserve as Kantian persons capable of rational self-determination. In other words, Rawls espouses the detachment of the distribution of primary social goods from one's merit and ability because these goods are absolutely essential for our self-determination and self-fulfillment as rational persons. These primary goods include "rights and liberties, opportunities and power, income and wealth" (Rawls, 1971, p. 92). Whatever one's plan or conception of the good life, these goods are the necessary means to realize that plan, and hence everyone would prefer more rather than less primary goods. Their unequal distribution in a just society should only be allowed if such a distribution would benefit directly the least advantaged of that society (the difference principle).

The key element in Rawls' theory for our purposes is the notion that there are material benefits everyone deserves as Kantian persons. The exercise of one's capacity for free self-determination requires a certain level of material well-being and not just the guarantee of abstract and formal rights such as freedom of expression and equal opportunity. Thus the primary social goods involve some material goods, like income and wealth. To a certain extent health care (including medicine) should be considered as one of the primary social goods since it is obviously necessary for the pursuit of one's rational life plan. Therefore, the distribution of health care should not be contingent upon ability and merit. Also it would

be untenable to justify an inequitable distribution of this good by means of Rawls' difference principle. It is difficult to imagine a scenario in which the unequal distribution of health care in our society would be more beneficial to the least advantaged than a more equal distribution which would assure all consumers access to hospital care, medical treatment, medicines, and so forth. If we assume that the least advantaged (a group which Rawls never clearly defines) are the indigent who are also suffering from certain ailments, there is no advantage to any inequity in the distribution of health care. Unlike other primary goods such as income and wealth it cannot be distributed in such a way that a greater share for certain groups will benefit the least advantaged. In short, this is a zero sum game—if a person is deprived of medical treatment or pharmaceutical products due to premium pricing policies that person has lost a critical opportunity to save his life, cure a disease, reduce suffering, and so on.

Thus, at least according to this Rawlsian view of justice with its Kantian underpinnings, there seems to be little room for the unequal distribution of a vital commodity such as health care in a just society. It follows, then, that the just pharmaceutical corporation must be far more diligent and consider very carefully the implications of pricing policies for an equitable distribution of its products. The alternative is government intervention in this process, and as we have seen, this has the potential to yield gross inefficiencies and ultimately be self-defeating. If these corporations charge premium prices and garner excessive profits from their pharmaceutical products, the end result will be the deprivation of these goods for certain classes of people. Such a pricing pattern systematically worsens the situation of the least advantaged in society, violates the respect due them as Kantian persons, and seriously impairs their capacity for free self-determination.

It should be emphasized, however, that this concern for justice does not imply that pharmaceutical companies should become charities by distributing these drugs free of charge or at prices so low they must sustain meager profits or even losses. To be sure, their survival, long-term stability, and ongoing research are also vital to society and can only be guaranteed through substantial profits. Thus, the demand for justice which we have articulated must be balanced with the need to realize key economic objectives which guarantee the long-term stability of this industry. As Kenneth Goodpaster notes, "the responsible organization aims at congruence between its moral and non-moral aspirations" (1984, p. 309). In other words, it does not see goals of justice and economic viability as mutually exclusive, but will attempt to manage the joint achievement of both objectives.

We are arguing, then, that pharmaceutical companies should seek to balance their legitimate concern for profit and return on investment with an equal consideration of the crucial importance of distributive justice. There must be an explicit recognition that for the afflicted certain pharmaceutical products are critical for one's well-being; hence they are as important as any primary social good and are deserved by every member of society. As a result these products should be distributed on the widest possible basis, but in a way that permits companies to realize a realistic and reasonable level of profitability.

It is, of course, quite difficult to define a "reasonable level of profitability." In many respects the definition of "reasonable" is the crux of the matter here. Unfortunately, as outsiders to the operations of drug companies we are ill prepared to judge whether development costs for certain drugs are inflated or truly necessary. As a result, these corporations must be trusted to arrive at their own definition of a reasonable profit, given the level of legitimate costs involved in researching and developing the drug in question. But we can look to some case histories for meaningful examples that would serve as a guide to a more general definition. One of the most famous controversies over drug prices concerned the Hoffman-LaRoche corporation and the United Kingdom in which the government's Monopoly Commission alleged that Hoffman-LaRoche was charging excessive prices for valium and librium in order to subsidize its research and preserve its monopoly position. In the course of the prolonged deliberations between the British government and the company reasonable profits were defined as "profits no higher than is necessary to obtain the 'desired' performance of industry from the point of view of the economy as a whole."[2] In general, then, under normal circumstances reasonable profits for a particular product should be consistent with the average return for the industry. Exceptions might be made to this rule of average returns if the risks and costs of development are inordinately and unavoidably high.

Thus, based on this Rawlsian ideal of justice I propose the following thesis regarding ethical pricing for pharmaceutical companies: for those drugs which are truly essential the just corporation will aim to charge prices that will assure the widest possible distribution of these products consistent with a reasonable level of profitability. In other words, these companies will seek to minimize the deprivation of material benefits which are needed by all persons for their self-realization by imposing restraints on their egocentric interests in premium prices and excessive profits.... Moreover, we must present some sort of methodology for reaching this determination.

... The more critical the product and the less likely it will be affordable to certain segments of society, the more prominent should be the consideration given to distributive justice in pricing policy deliberations. Justice cannot be the exclusive concern in these deliberations, but must be given its proportionate weight depending upon the way in which the questions in this framework are addressed. Thus, as pricing decisions duly consider factors such as production and promotion costs, etc., they should also take into account the element of distributive justice. Clearly, however, drugs that are less important for society because they deal with less serious ailments should not be subject to the same demands of justice as those for diseases which are truly life threatening or debilitating. Hence drug companies should have much more flexibility in pricing medicines for these less critical ailments....

This analysis does not by any means eliminate the frustrations regarding ethical pricing which were cited earlier by Walton. We can offer no definitive, quantitative formulae or comprehensive criteria to assure that pricing in this industry will always be fair and just. As with most moral decisions, much will depend on the individual judgment and moral sensitivity of the managers making those decisions.... It seems beyond doubt that responsible and fair pricing in the pharmaceutical industry is a serious moral imperative, since for so many consumers it is a matter of well-being or infirmity and perhaps even life or death.

We might consider once again the wisdom of Aristotle on this topic of justice. In the *Nicomachean Ethics* he writes that "we call those things 'just' which produce and preserve happiness for the social and political community" (1962, p. 113). If corporations respond to the demands of justice for the sake of the common good, it will help promote the elusive goal of a just community and a greater harmony between the corporation and its many concerned stakeholders.

NOTES

1. Holzman, D.: 1988, 'New Wonder Drugs at What Price?', *Insight* (March 21), pp. 54–55. For more recent data on drug prices see 'Maker of Schizophrenia Drug Bows to Pressure to Cut Costs', *The New York Times* (Dec. 6, 1990), pp. A1 and D3.

2. 'F. Hoffman-LaRoche and Company A.G.', Harvard Business School Case Study in Matthews, Goodpaster, Nash (eds.), *Policies and Persons* (McGraw Hill Book Company: N.Y., 1985).

REFERENCES

Aristotle: 1962, *Nicomachean Ethics*, trans. by M. Oswald (Library of Liberal Arts, Bobbs Merrill Company, Inc., Indianapolis).

Doppelt, G.: 1989, 'Beyond Liberalism and Communitarianism: Towards a Critical Theory of Social Justice', *Philosophy and Social Criticism* **14** (No. 3/4).

Goodpaster, K.: 1984, 'The Concept of Corporate Responsibility', in T. Regan (ed.), *Just Business: New Introductory Essays in Business Ethics* (Random House, New York).

Goodpaster, K. and Matthews, J.: 1989, 'Can a Corporation Have a Conscience', in K. Andrews (ed.), *Ethics in Practice* (Harvard Business School Press, Boston).

Mintzberg, H.: 1989, 'The Case for Corporate Social Responsibility', in A. Iannone (ed.), *Contemporary Moral Controversies in Business* (Oxford University Press, New York).

Rawls, J.: 1971, *A Theory of Justice* (Harvard University Press, Cambridge).

Walton, C.: 1969, *Ethos and the Executive* (Prentice Hall, Inc., Englewood Cliffs, N.J.).

NO

Pharmaceutical Manufacturers Association

PRICE CONTROLS IN THE ECONOMY AND THE HEALTH SECTOR

EXECUTIVE SUMMARY

The current national focus on health care reform has revived discussion of price controls as a possible policy instrument.

Such discussion is predictable because health-sector costs consistently have risen faster than the general rate of price inflation and—in part because of unintended inflationary consequences created by health-reform programs of the 1960s—have tended to be resistant to government efforts to date to contain them. If, as anticipated, current contemplated reform includes dramatic expansion of health system access, additional pressures for cost containment will be created.

This brief paper examines experience with price controls historically and, then, since World War II in the U.S. health sector. Major points:

1. Price controls have been attempted in many times and places dating back 40 centuries. Except in those times and places where national unity and consensus made controls easily enforceable—for instance, in World War II Great Britain where the country quite literally was fighting for its survival —they generally have failed. Moreover, when controls have been ended, inflation typically has equalled or exceeded the rate which would have been reached without controls. In the meantime, economic growth has been inhibited.

2. Controls, when applied, quickly create artificial scarcities, resource misallocations, and black markets. Large bureaucratic structures are required for administration. Problems of enforcement and equity arise. Since controls interfere with normal market mechanisms, issues of fairness (both to consumers and producers) quickly present themselves. Public support for controls quickly erodes.

3. In the United States, those government officials who have administered price controls universally counsel against their further use. These judgments are made, typically, on practical as well as theoretical bases.

From Pharmaceutical Manufacturers Association, "Price Controls in the Economy and the Health Sector," *Backgrounder* (April 1993). Copyright © 1993 by The Pharmaceutical Manufacturers Association. Reprinted by permission. Prepared independently for the Pharmaceutical Manufacturers Association by Van Dyk Associates, Inc., Washington, D.C.

4. In the health sector, the federal government has made numerous attempts since World War II to freeze or selectively control costs. None of these efforts has slowed a steady rise in health sector inflation.
5. The experience with overall drug-price controls has been limited in this country to Nixon-era controls. Their effect, however, was the same as with controls generally. Prices rose sharply after their relaxation.
6. Internationally, drug price controls also have proved ineffective. Additionally, they have reduced research into breakthrough drugs in countries where they have been adopted.
7. New health-sector price controls could be expected to create the same effects that prior controls have done. Alternative means of health-sector cost containment are available and already have been applied on a limited basis. All would be felt only over a longer period.

Summary: When faced with near-term general or sectoral inflation, national leaders often have turned to price controls. Such controls create enormous distortions and in the end do not quell inflation. Imperfect but applicable means of cost containment suggest themselves in the current effort toward health care reform....

CLEAR LESSONS FROM THE EXPERIENCE OF THE UNITED STATES AND OTHER NATIONS WITH PRICE CONTROLS

From Hammurabi, Babylonia, and the Roman Empire to the 1970s experiences of the United States, Japan, Canada, and Australia, price controls have been tried. And in every single instance, with the possible exception of wartime Britain, they have been found wanting. They basically did not work. Their only certain result in any country has been to reduce production. And such losses in production usually mean a profit squeeze, less investment in plant and equipment and in R&D [research and development], and less growth in the future.

Another lesson learned: All the great monetary stabilizers of this century have been classical economists who insisted upon balanced budgets and government living within its means at home and abroad, without borrowing from the central bank or printing more paper money of its own.

Not one resorted to price controls because all knew from previous history that price controls, freezes and "rollbacks" simply produced scarcities and artificial distortions.

Treasury Secretary Lloyd Bentsen, while Vice Chairman of the Congressional Joint Economic Committee in 1978, chaired a hearing in which he noted that one of the problems he had seen with wage and price controls was that there were so many ways that they could be evaded. His assessment:

"Mandatory wage and price controls don't stop inflation any more than the Maginot line stopped the defeat of the French Army. And they are not going to protect the American consumer from all of the hurt and the damage of inflation.... The Joint Economic Committee... found that the mere prospect of controls... resulted in a substantial increase to the consumers of this country and additional inflation because of manufacturers increasing prices in anticipation of the wage demands that resulted...."

PRICE CONTROLS IN THE U.S. HEALTH SECTOR

Since World War II the federal government has made several attempts to control health care costs, either by freezing prices across the board or by imposing selective controls on individual sectors such as hospitals or physicians. None of these initiatives has slowed the steady rise in what Americans are paying for health care through taxes, through private insurance, or out of their own pockets.

Throughout this period, any savings achieved by controls in one sector have been offset by increased spending in others. Economies achieved by shorter patient stays in hospitals have been erased by higher payments for nursing home and home health care. Hospitals barred from adding new beds have poured the money into new outpatient facilities and expensive diagnostic equipment. Placing a ceiling on prices that doctors could charge for treatments or office visits simply has produced a larger number of treatments or office visits. Indeed, Medicare administrators drawing up a new "resource-based" schedule of allowable physician fees have factored into their calculations the assumption that doctors automatically would offset half the reduction in their rates of payment by an increase in billings.

No scheme yet tried has produced actual dollars-and-cents savings. No scheme could—short of central government control of all health care costs and spending. And were that attempted, it would produce... shortages, dislocations, and other problems....

This section will examine... health care price controls initiated at the federal level in the last 50 years, and show how and why they failed. (The wage-price stabilization program during the Korean War is not discussed because professional fees, such as doctor bills and hospital charges, were excluded from controls.) It will then sketch alternative cost control initiatives mounted in the private sector, often with government support, that offer more hope for moderating health care inflation than does price regulation....

The Steady Expansion of Federally-Funded Health Services

... [I]n the U.S. experience, price controls have not stemmed the growth of health care spending. As a government program, price controls necessarily exist in a political environment where other pressures are operating in the direction of greater spending. Each year, Congressional budgetmakers make significant cuts in Administration Medicare and Medicaid requests—almost always through cuts to providers. Yet each year, actual payments increase.

Why is it that, despite the "success" of PPS [Prospective Payment System] in halving the growth of inpatient hospital costs (the single largest segment of the Medicare program), total spending for hospital care by Medicare and Medicaid has doubled in the seven years after PPS over the seven years before—from $230 billion to $460 billion?

Why has total federal spending for Medicaid increased by 73 percent in just the last two years while Medicare spending was rising far less rapidly?

The answer: At the same time the government was administering its price controls, it was taking other actions that raised its health care costs. Example:

- In the same legislation in which Congress froze physician fees, it required Medicaid to cover more children and more low income pregnant women and extended Medicare to mammographies.
- At the same time it reduced provider fees for Medicare, it was mandating states to cover expensive and medically-questionable treatments under Medicaid, for which it provides half the funds.
- At the same time it was implementing the RVS fee schedule [a revised payment system for Medicare physicians, begun in 1992], Congress significantly extended Medicare benefits for nursing homes, home health and hospice care.

The same political thinking that makes price controls attractive to them makes it hard for policymakers to restrain themselves from sweetening government health benefits packages to enlist Congressional and interest-group support. This bit of history is instructive in view of the declared objective of the Clinton Administration to extend health insurance to the 37 million uninsured while at the same time reducing health care costs.

PRICE CONTROLS ON PHARMACEUTICALS

Conclusions about the wisdom of price controls in the pharmaceutical sector must be drawn primarily from the experience of other countries. The United States has had only one experience with such controls—during the wage-price freeze of the Nixon Administration. Most other industrialized countries have long tried to regulate drug prices and

outlays as part of their broader programs of national health insurance. Only the United States and Denmark leave pricing to the competitive marketplace.

The U.S. Experience

The Nixon Administration Wage and Price Stabilization programs tried to control drug prices, with these results:

- In the three years prior to the program, the drug component of the Consumer Price Index had risen only 3 percent, considerably less than health care cost inflation generally.
- During the period of controls (April, 1971 through October, 1974) the Index increased by only 1.5 percent.
- As soon as controls were lifted, however, the typical "catch-up" effect was seen. Between 1975 and 1977, drug prices rose almost 12 percent. When the last impacts of price controls had faded from the economy, prices were probably higher than they would have been without controls.

Controls also were ineffective in curbing spending on drugs.

In the three years before they were instituted, patient drug costs rose by an average of $378 million a year. During the three control years, they rose $515 million a year. In the three years after, they rose $600 million a year....

Effects of Drug Price Controls Beyond Prices

... [I]t is clear that price controls on drugs in other countries have uniformly failed to accomplish their goal. It also is clear why controls, which are supposed to hold down spending, have had the opposite effect. If government decides for a pharmaceutical company how much it can charge for its products, the company has little incentive to conduct the extremely expensive search for truly innovative and breakthrough therapies. The odds against a drug in development making it to market are 5,000 to 1. Even when a drug advances to where it is actually tested in clinical trials on patients, the odds against its being marketed are 10 to 1. Unless there is pricing freedom, the financial reward is just not worth the risk.

Many firms in nations with strict price controls largely have abandoned the search for breakthrough drugs. Funds that might have been used for research have been shifted to increased promotion and marketing of existing drugs, seeking increased demand as a way of maintaining revenues in the face of controlled prices. Foreign firms also engage in low-risk research and development to come up [with] "new" drugs that are not innovative, and only marginally better than existing therapies, but are nonetheless eligible for higher controlled prices than the older drugs in their inventory.

A study of the French pharmaceutical industry, which was responsible for only 3 world class drugs between 1975 and 1989, concluded that "the calibre of research [has] deteriorated because severe price control has encouraged French companies to give priority to small therapeutic improvements which are useful in price negotiations." Of Japan, Dr. Heinz Redwood, a British researcher and policy analyst, says "There is a pronounced tendency to develop 'Japanese drugs for Japan' rather than for world health care. This is largely the result of the Japanese system of price regulation... which grants very high prices for new drugs, whilst putting heavy pricing pressure on older drugs."

In Italy, the Ruoppolo Commission, created to revamp the price control system to give greater encouragement to innovative activity, reported that:

> "The virtual freezing of the price of old products... has acted as a decisive incentive in the search by companies for new registrations in order to obtain more up-to-date prices; and then, by means of appropriate promotion, induce a prescription shift from the old to the new [drug]."

Were price controls to touch off the same syndrome here, it could have a profound effect not only on the nature of this country's pharmaceutical industry but on world health. The international community depends on innovative U.S. industry to provide it with new medicines. Almost 50 percent of the new drugs effective enough to be marketed globally in the past 20 years have been developed in the U.S. In biotechnology and immunology, it is 70 percent.

What Will Happen If New Price Controls Are Placed on Health Care?

Given previous experience with price controls generally, and on what has happened when they have been imposed in different forms upon the U.S. health care system, it is not difficult to speculate what will happen if federal policymakers impose what have been called "interim cost containment measures" to hold the line on prices for the period—probably several years—that will pass before a new national health insurance system can be passed into law, implemented by regulations, survive the inevitable court challenges, and actually begin to operate throughout the country.

1. Investment funds that would have flowed into the development of new

medical technology, new cures for disease and other advances will be diverted to other, more economically attractive channels.

2. The economic incentive to enter the health care field will decline, eventually leading to a shortage of physicians and other trained personnel.

3. Providers will continue to find ways to "game" the system, reducing hoped-for savings. To counter this, government will impose increasing supervision, restrictions, and paperwork on the activities of health care professionals.

4. The quality of health care will suffer. Physicians will spend less time with patients and there will be fewer drugs in hospital formularies. Shortages and waiting lists will develop as they have in other countries. Those who can afford it will try to preserve their current quality of care by creating a separate, privately-funded privileged system of health care as exists in Britain. This alternative system in turn will draw the best professionals and force the quality of care given the rest of us lower.

5. The inherent contradiction between universal system access and simultaneous cost containment inevitably will lead to de facto rationing of care. The Medicaid experience is instructive here. As Medicaid has become the largest item in their budgets, many states have severely restricted reimbursement under the program. Many doctors have responded by refusing to take Medicaid patients. To expand eligibility for Medicaid, the state of Oregon has had to adopt a rationing system, barring payment for whole categories of treatments. Sim-

ilarly, Great Britain denies expensive surgery to patients over a certain age.

Alternative to Controls Which Could Contain Costs

Health care costs can be contained without the distortions created by controls.

Most of the measures listed below now are being practiced in the health care system—many with the support and encouragement of government. Others are readily available. Strong incentives to use these measures would occur under "managed competition" schemes for health care reform.

- Expansion of Health Maintenance Organizations, group practice associations, and other organizations under which health care practitioners have no incentives to perform unneeded services.

- Expansion of Preferred Provider Organizations and other arrangements in which physicians give up higher fees for an assured caseload.

- Greater emphasis on prevention, early intervention, wellness, and lifestyle changes to lower the incidence of disease and the necessity for surgery.

- Requiring second opinions before surgery and other expensive services.

- Living wills, which give terminal patients the right to appoint someone to decide when to stop the use of high-cost technology whose only purpose is to prolong life according to its clinical definition.

- Drug utilization review systems, that are consistent with the principles developed by the American Medical Association, the American Pharmaceutical Association, and the Pharmaceutical Manufacturers Association. Such systems detect and correct inappropriate prescribing practices as well as fraud and abuse.

- Encouraging medical innovation, including the development of cost-effective therapies such as drugs as a cure for major diseases and a substitute for surgery.
- Greater research on the "outcomes" of alternative treatments, to spread knowledge among physicians about the most effective treatments and therapies.
- Education of patients so they can work more knowledgeably with their doctors. Patient information should be more widely available on computer networks.
- Tort reform to reduce the practice of "defensive" medicine to avoid malpractice suits which, according to the American Medical Association, costs the health care system $15 billion a year.
- Measures to reduce redundancy of expensive technologies and equipment in the same markets—i.e., where several hospitals and clinics in the same area invest in the same costly technologies whereas demand might justify only one such facility.
- The imposition of substantial deductibles and/or co-payments on the insured so as to require patients to make prudent choices about health expenditures. (A Rand Corporation study has shown that patients, when required to write a check on each physician visit, make visits with less frequency.)
- Voluntary industry measures to limit drug-price increases, with or without antitrust waivers, with provision for monitoring by credible third-party agency.

None of the above measures, of course, can be expected to produce immediate and dramatic reductions in health-sector inflation—particularly if implemented while health-sector access simultaneously is being dramatically expanded. Nor can they counteract and overcome those factors which plague the U.S. health system more greatly than those of other Western countries: High rates of poverty, violent crime, homelessness, aging, AIDS and drug abuse.

The aforementioned measures are appropriate ways of maintaining quality while reducing costs. Any government involvement should be designed to increase incentives to adopt such measures.

But the government cannot have it both ways by adopting incentives for the marketplace to manage care *and* government price controls on the components of care. To manage care, providers and insurers must invest significant fiscal and human resources into restructuring, expanding and monitoring health care delivery. Why invest when price controls will likely reward those providers who were most inefficient in the old fragmented system? Attempts to solve the data needs equity issues and enforcement rules would further slow enactment of proper incentives.

At the same time, however, it can be predicted with relative certainty that, given past international and U.S. experience, health-sector as well as other price controls—even when applied short-term—lead to distortions and, over time, do not result in net cost reductions.

POSTSCRIPT

Are Pharmaceutical Price Controls Justifiable?

The United States is more committed to the free market than any other developed nation. Consequently, the arguments advanced by the Pharmaceutical Manufacturers Association against pharmaceutical price controls tend to be accepted for all cases: attempts to regulate the market must fail. According to the laws of the market, if we try to support prices (as with the products of American farms), we will drive buyers from the market and tempt inefficient suppliers to stay in, both of which tend to drive prices *down*. Without price supports, prices would likely recover on their own as enthusiastic buyers outbid each other for the reduced amount of product. On the other hand, as in the case of pharmaceuticals, if we try to control prices, we will drive suppliers from the market and truncate the healthy process of competition that would have brought prices down naturally. Meanwhile, the company's reward for, and means for, pursuing research into better drugs would be destroyed.

But the principles of justice, which govern us as surely as the laws of supply and demand, require that we make our economic arrangements keeping in mind the fate of the least advantaged among us. Does the market do that? Which do we hold more dear, the liberty of the market or justice in distribution? As Spinello notes, people who have AIDS are dying. Is it likely that this fact will eventually persuade pharmaceutical manufacturers to accept price controls?

SUGGESTED READINGS

Judy Chaconas, "Providers Offer Prescription for Medicaid Drug-Pricing Law," *Trustee* (December 1991).

Joseph A. DiMasi et al., "The Cost of Innovation in the Pharmaceutical Industry," *Journal of Health Economics* (vol. 10, 1991).

David Hanson, "Report on Drug R & D Fuels Attack on Prices," *Chemical and Engineering News* (March 8, 1993).

Office of Technology Assessment, *Pharmaceutical R & D: Costs, Risks and Rewards* (Government Printing Office, 1993).

David Pryor, "Drugs *Must* Be Made Affordable," *The New York Times* (March 7, 1993).

Pamela Zurer, "NIH Weighs Role in Drug Pricing," *Chemical and Engineering News* (December 21, 1992).

ISSUE 13

Is Advertising Fundamentally Deceptive?

YES: Roger Crisp, from "Persuasive Advertising, Autonomy, and the Creation of Desire," *Journal of Business Ethics* (vol. 6, 1987)

NO: John O'Toole, from *The Trouble With Advertising* (Chelsea House, 1981)

ISSUE SUMMARY

YES: Philosopher Roger Crisp argues that persuasive advertising removes the possibility of real decision making by manipulating consumers without their knowledge, for no good reason, and thus destroys personal autonomy.

NO: John O'Toole, president of the American Association of Advertising Agencies, argues that advertising is only salesmanship functioning in the paid space and time of mass media and that it is no more coercive than an ordinary salesperson.

Advertisers do one thing—they persuade us to buy products that otherwise we would not buy. If we would buy the products anyway, there would be no point in producers spending the money to purchase magazine space or television time to display ads. That advertising seems necessary in today's market and is used to sell everything from cars to movies raises the question of whether the art of promotion aids the consumer or cons consumers into throwing money away on products they neither need nor desire.

Where, in pure capitalism, is there room for salesmanship? According to Scottish economist Adam Smith (1723–1790), the decision to buy is based solely on need, price, and (perceived) quality. The customer desires the exchange and wants to maximize the value obtained by it. But human psychology does not necessarily work as Smith's theory postulates. When some people shop, they are often tired and in a hurry, and they will buy the first thing they see that satisfies a need and that falls within an acceptable range of price and quality. As a matter of fact, they may buy the first thing that grabs their attention and looks attractive—and therein is the sales pitch. Attention and attractiveness are the keys to sales, and the customer's hypothesized needs, plans, and comparisons may have very little to do with the actual decision to buy.

Salesmanship, then, works in defiance of and at variance with the rational satisfaction of need in the free market. The salesman will not succeed in inducing people to buy things they never thought of or conceived a use for because he does not have the time to plant the idea of some new need and help it to grow. But when a willing buyer wanders into the market, the aggressive salesman can certainly accelerate the decision to buy and influence the buyer to choose one vendor rather than another.

If the salesman has more time, however, can he produce new needs? Suppose the national widget maker makes twice too many widgets one year, and there is no real need for the excess. Could he hire a salesman to persuade people that widgets make fine lawn ornaments (a use no one had thought of), that lawn ornaments are essential to the good life (also unthought), and that, therefore, they truly need his widgets? According to Smith's theory, consumers should see through such a ploy, and no sale would ever take place. But here is where advertising enters the consumer's life as a picture or a fantasy of a life more valuable than his or her own. By associating this beautiful life with a product, not really an object of need but beginning to seem so, the advertiser can build up an inclination to buy, well away from the point of sale, and predispose a consumer first to pay attention to, and then to *need*, the manufacturer's product. Sales, in that case, are not need driven, proceeding from the customer's life and needs, but are product driven, proceeding from the producer's desire to sell and the advertiser's skill.

In the following selections, Roger Crisp is primarily interested in the effect of advertising on the individual and the problems of preserving any notion of autonomy in a world overrun with persuasive messages. John O'Toole does not try to present advertising as an objective exercise in consumer education. But if salesmanship in the marketplace is acceptable, and it surely seems to be, then what possible objection can there be to extending salesmanship to the print and broadcast media?

As you read these selections, ask yourself how *you* react to advertising. Do you think about it? Talk back to it? Absorb it? Can you think of an advertisement that really changed your idea of what was good and valuable and worth buying? Should there be limits on pitches beyond the federal prohibition of outright deception? Why? Is advertising just clean fun that fools no one, entertains us, and in a thoroughly harmless way persuades us to try something we might like?

YES
Roger Crisp

PERSUASIVE ADVERTISING, AUTONOMY, AND THE CREATION OF DESIRE

In this paper, I shall argue that all forms of a certain common type of advertising are morally wrong, on the ground that they override the autonomy of consumers.

One effect of an advertisement might be the creation of a desire for the advertised product. How such desires are caused is highly relevant as to whether we would describe the case as one in which the autonomy of the subject has been overridden. If I read an advertisement for a sale of clothes, I may rush down to my local clothes store and purchase a jacket I like. Here, my desire for the jacket has arisen partly out of my reading the advertisement. Yet, in an ordinary sense, it is based on or answers to certain properties of the jacket —its colour, style, material. Although I could not explain to you why my tastes are as they are, we still describe such cases as examples of autonomous action, in that all the decisions are being made by me: What kind of jacket do I like? Can I afford one? And so on. In certain other cases, however, the causal history of a desire may be different. Desires can be caused, for instance, by subliminal suggestion. In New Jersey, a cinema flashed sub-threshold advertisements for ice cream onto the screen during movies, and reported a dramatic increase in sales during intermissions. In such cases, choice is being deliberately ruled out by the method of advertising in question. These customers for ice cream were acting 'automatonously', rather than autonomously. They did not buy the ice cream because they happened to like it and decided they would buy some, but rather because they had been subjected to subliminal suggestion. Subliminal suggestion is the most extreme form of what I shall call, adhering to a popular dichotomy, persuasive, as opposed to informative, advertising. Other techniques include puffery, which involves the linking of the product, through suggestive language and images, with the unconscious desires of consumers for power, wealth, status, sex, and so on; and repetition, which is self-explanatory, the name of the product being 'drummed into' the mind of the consumer.

The obvious objection to persuasive advertising is that it somehow violates the autonomy of consumers. I believe that this objection is correct, and that, if one adopts certain common-sensical standards for autonomy, non-persuasive forms of advertising are not open to such an objection. Very high standards for autonomy are set by Kant, who requires that an agent be entirely external to the causal nexus found in the ordinary empirical world, if his or her actions are to be autonomous. These standards are too high, in that it is doubtful whether they allow *any* autonomous action. Standards for autonomy more congenial to common sense will allow that my buying the jacket is autonomous, although continuing to deny that the people in New Jersey were acting autonomously. In the former case, we have what has come to be known in recent discussions of freedom of the will as *both* free will *and* free action. I both decide what to do, and am not obstructed in carrying through my decision into action. In the latter case, there is free action, but not free will. No one prevents the customers buying their ice cream, but they have not themselves made any genuine decision whether or not to do so. In a very real sense, decisions are made for consumers by persuasive advertisers, who occupy the motivational territory properly belonging to the agent. If what we mean by autonomy, in the ordinary sense, is to be present, the possibility of decision must exist alongside.

Arrington (1981) discusses, in a challenging paper, the techniques of persuasive advertising I have mentioned, and argues that such advertising does not override the autonomy of consumers. He examines four notions central to autonomous action, and claims that, on each count, persuasive advertising is exonerated on the charge we have made against it. I shall now follow in the footsteps of Arrington, but argue that he sets the standards for autonomy too low for them to

be acceptable to common sense, and that the charge therefore still sticks.

(a) *Autonomous desire:* Arrington argues that an autonomous desire is a first-order desire (a desire for some object, say, Pongo Peach cosmetics) accepted by the agent because it fulfils a second-order desire (a desire about a desire, say, a desire that my first-order desire for Pongo Peach be fulfilled), and that most of the first-order desires engendered in us by advertising are desires that we do accept. His example is an advertisement for Grecian Formula 16, which engenders in him a desire to be younger. He desires that both his desire to be younger and his desire for Grecian Formula 16 be fulfilled.

Unfortunately, this example is not obviously one of persuasive advertising. It may be the case that he just has this desire to look young again rather as I had certain sartorial tastes before I saw the ad about the clothes sale, and then decides to buy Grecian Formula 16 on the basis of these tastes. Imagine this form of advertisement: a person is depicted using Grecian Formula 16, and is then shown in a position of authority, surrounded by admiring members of the opposite sex. This would be a case of puffery. The advertisement implies that having hair coloured by the product will lead to positions of power, and to one's becoming more attractive to the opposite sex. It links, by suggestion, the product with my unconscious desires for power and sex. I may still claim that I am buying the product because I want to look young again. But the real reasons for my purchase are my unconscious desires for power and sex, and the link made between the product and the fulfillment of those desires by the advertisement. These reasons are not reasons I could avow to myself as good reasons for buying the product, and, again, the possibility of decision is absent.

Arrington's claim is that an autonomous desire is a first-order desire which we accept. Even if we allow that it is possible for the agent to consider whether to accept or to repudiate first-order desires induced by persuasive advertising, it seems that all first-order desires induced purely by persuasive advertising will be non-autonomous in Arrington's sense. Many of us have a strong second-order desire not to be manipulated by others without our knowledge, and for no good reason. Often, we are manipulated by others without our knowledge, but for a good reason, and one that we can accept. Take an accomplished actor: much of the skill of an actor is to be found in unconscious body-language. This manipulation we see as essential to our being entertained, and thus acquiesce in it. What is important about this case is that there seems to be no diminution of autonomy. We can still judge the quality of the acting, in that the manipulation is part of its quality. In other cases, however, manipulation ought not to be present, and these are cases where the ability to decide is importantly diminished by the manipulation. Decision is central to the theory of the market-process: I should be able to decide whether to buy product *A* or product *B*, by judging them on their merits. Any manipulation here I shall repudiate as being for no good reason. This is not to say, incidentally, that once the fact that my desires are being manipulated by others has been made transparent to me, my desire will lapse. The people in New Jersey would have been unlikely to cease their craving for ice cream, if we had told them that their desire had been subliminally induced. But they would no longer have voiced acceptance of this desire, and, one assumes, would have resented the manipulation of their desires by the management of the cinema.

Pace Arrington, it is no evidence for the claim that most of our desires are autonomous in this sense that we often return to purchase the same product over and over again. For this might well show that persuasive advertising has been supremely efficient in inducing non-autonomous desires in us, which we are unable even to attempt not to act on, being unaware of their origin. Nor is it an argument in Arrington's favour that certain members of our society will claim not to have the second-order desire we have postulated. For it may be that this is a desire which we can see is one that human beings *ought* to have, a desire which it would be in their interests to have, and the lack of which is itself evidence of profound manipulation.

(b) *Rational desire and choice:* One might argue that the desires induced by advertising are often irrational, in the sense that they are not present in an agent in full possession of the facts about the product. This argument fails, says Arrington, because if we require *all* the facts about a thing before we can desire that thing, then all our desires will be irrational; and if we require only the *relevant* information, then prior desires determine the relevance of information. Advertising may be said to enable us to fulfil these prior desires, through the transfer of information, and the supplying of means to ends is surely a paradigm example of rationality.

But, what about persuasive, as opposed to informative, advertising? Take puffery. Is it not true that a person may buy Pongo Peach cosmetics, hoping for an adventure in paradise, and that the product will not fulfil these hopes? Are they really in possession of even the relevant facts? Yes, says Arrington. We wish to purchase *subjective* effects, and these are genuine enough. When I use Pongo Peach, I will experience a genuine feeling of adventure.

Once again, however, our analysis can help us to see the strength of the objection. For a desire to be rational, in any plausible sense, that desire must at least not be induced by the interference of other persons with my system of tastes, against my will and without my knowledge. Can we imagine a person, asked for a reason justifying their purchase of Pongo Peach, replying: "I have an unconscious desire to experience adventure, and the product has been linked with this desire through advertising'? If a desire is to be rational, it is not necessary that all the facts about the object be known to the agent, but one of the facts about that desire must be that it has not been induced in the agent through techniques which the agent cannot accept. Thus, applying the schema of Arrington's earlier argument, such a desire will be repudiated by the agent as non-autonomous and irrational.

Arrington's claim concerning the subjective effects of the products we purchase fails to deflect the charge of overriding autonomy we have made against persuasive advertising. Of course, very often the subjective effects will be lacking. If I use Grecian Formula 16, I am unlikely to find myself being promoted at work, or surrounded by admiring members of the opposite sex. This is just straight deception. But even when the effects do manifest themselves, such advertisements have still overridden my autonomy. They have activated desires which lie beyond my awareness, and over behaviour flowing from which I therefore have no control. If these claims appear

doubtful, consider whether this advertisement is likely to be successful: 'Do you have a feeling of adventure? Then use this brand of cosmetics'. Such an advertisement will fail, in that it appeals to a *conscious* desire, either which we do not have, or which we realise will not be fulfilled by purchasing a certain brand of cosmetics. If the advertisement were for a course in mountain-climbing, it might meet with more success. Our conscious self is not so easily duped by advertising, and this is why advertisers make such frequent use of the techniques of persuasive advertising.

(c) *Free choice:* One might object to persuasive advertising that it creates desires so covert that an agent cannot resist them, and that acting on them is therefore neither free nor voluntary. Arrington claims that a person acts or chooses *freely* if they can adduce considerations which justify their act in their mind; and *voluntarily* if, had they been aware of a reason for acting otherwise, they could have done so. Only occasionally, he says, does advertising prevent us making free and voluntary choices.

Regarding free action, it is sufficient to note that, according to Arrington, if I were to be converted into a human robot, activated by an Evil Genius who has implanted electrodes in my brain, my actions would be free as long as I could cook up some justification for my behaviour. I want to dance this jig because I enjoy dancing. (Compare: I want to buy this ice cream because I like ice cream.) If my argument is right, we are placed in an analogous position by persuasive advertising. If we no longer mean by freedom of action the mere non-obstruction of behaviour, are we still ready to accept that we are engaged in free action? As for whether the actions of consumers subjected to persuasive advertising are voluntary in Arrington's sense, I am less optimistic than he is. It is likely, as we have suggested, that the purchasers of ice cream or Pongo Peach would have gone ahead with their purchase even if they had been made aware that their desires had been induced in them by persuasive advertising. But they would now claim that they themselves had not made the decision, that they were acting on a desire engendered in them which they did not accept, and that there was, therefore, a good reason for them not to make the purchase. The unconscious is not obedient to the commands of the conscious, although it may be forced to listen.

In fact, it is odd to suggest that persuasive advertising does give consumers a choice. A choice is usually taken to require the weighing-up of reasons. What persuasive advertising does is to remove the very conditions of choice.

(d) *Control or manipulation:* Arrington offers the following criteria for control:

A person C controls the behaviour of another person P if (1) C intends P to act in a certain way A, (2) C's intention is causally effective in bringing about A, and (3) C intends to ensure that all of the necessary conditions of A are satisfied. He argues that advertisements tend to induce a desire for X, given a more basic desire for Y. Given my desire for adventure, I desire Pongo Peach cosmetics. Thus, advertisers do not control consumers, since they do not intend to produce all of the necessary conditions for our purchases.

Arrington's analysis appears to lead to some highly counter-intuitive consequences. Consider, again, my position as

human robot. Imagine that the Evil Genius relies on the fact that I have certain basic unconscious desires in order to effect his plan. Thus, when he wants me to dance a jig, it is necessary that I have a more basic desire, say, ironically, for power. What the electrodes do is to jumble up my practical reasoning processes, so that I believe that I am dancing the jig because I like dancing, while, in reality, the desire to dance stems from a link between the dance and the fulfilment of my desire for power, forged by the electrodes. Are we still happy to say that I am not controlled? And does not persuasive advertising bring about a similar jumbling-up of the practical reasoning processes of consumers? When I buy Pongo Peach, I may be unable to offer a reason for my purchase, or I may claim that I want to look good. In reality, I buy it owing to the link made by persuasive advertising between my unconscious desire for adventure and the cosmetic in question.

A more convincing account of behaviour control would be to claim that it occurs when a person causes another person to act for reasons which the other person could not accept as good or justifiable reasons for the action. This is how brainwashing is to be distinguished from liberal education, rather than on Arrington's ground that the brainwasher arranges all the necessary conditions for belief. The student can both accept that she has the beliefs she has because of her education and continue to hold those beliefs as true, whereas the victim of brainwashing could not accept the explanation of the origin of her beliefs, while continuing to hold those beliefs. It is worth recalling the two cases we mentioned at the beginning of this paper. I can accept my tastes in dress, and do not think that the fact that their origin is unknown to me detracts from my autonomy, when I choose to buy the jacket. The desire for ice cream, however, will be repudiated, in that it is the result of manipulation by others, without good reason.

It seems, then, that persuasive advertising does override the autonomy of consumers, and that, if the overriding of autonomy, other things being equal, is immoral, then persuasive advertising is immoral.

An argument has recently surfaced which suggests that, in fact, other things are not equal, and that persuasive advertising, although it overrides autonomy, is morally acceptable. This argument was first developed by Nelson (1978), and claims that persuasive advertising is a form of informative advertising, albeit an indirect form. The argument runs at two levels: first, the consumer can judge from the mere fact that a product is heavily advertised, regardless of the form or content of the advertisements, that that product is likely to be a market-winner. The reason for this is that it would not pay to advertise market-losers. Second, even if the consumer is taken in by the content of the advertisement, and buys the product for that reason, he is not being irrational. For he would have bought the product *anyway*, since the very fact that it is advertised means that it is a good product. As Nelson says:

It does not pay consumers to make very thoughtful decisions about advertising. They can respond to advertising for the most ridiculous, explicit reasons and still do what they would have done if they had made the most careful judgements about their behaviour. 'Irrationality' is rational if it is cost-free.

Our conclusions concerning the mode of operation of persuasive advertising, however, suggest that Nelson's argument cannot succeed. For the first level to work, it would have to be true that a purchaser of a product can evaluate that product on its own merits, and then decide whether to purchase it again. But, as we have seen, consumers induced to purchase products by persuasive advertising are not buying those products on the basis of a decision founded upon any merit the products happen to have. Thus, if the product turns out to be less good than less heavily advertised alternatives, they will not be disappointed, and will continue to purchase, if subjected to the heavy advertising which induced them to buy in the first place. For this reason, heavy persuasive advertising is not a sign of quality, and the fact that a product is advertised does not suggest that it is good. In fact, if the advertising has little or no informative content, it might suggest just the opposite. If the product has genuine merits, it should be possible to mention them. Persuasive advertising, as the executives on Madison Avenue know, can be used to sell anything, regardless of its nature or quality.

For the second level of Nelson's argument to succeed, and for it to be in the consumer's interest to react even unthinkingly to persuasive advertising, it must be true that the first level is valid. As the first level fails, there is not even a *prima facie* reason for the belief that it is in the interest of the consumer to be subjected to persuasive advertising. In fact, there are two weighty reasons for doubting this belief. The first has already been hinted at: products promoted through persuasive advertising may well not be being sold on their merits, and may, therefore, be bad products, or products that the consumer would not desire on being confronted with unembellished facts about the product. The second is that this form of 'rational irrationality' is anything but cost-free. We consider it a great cost to lose our autonomy. If I were to demonstrate to you conclusively that if I were to take over your life, and make your decisions for you, you would have a life containing far more of whatever you think makes life worth living, apart from autonomy, than if you were to retain control, you would not surrender your autonomy to me even for these great gains in other values. As we mentioned above in our discussion of autonomous desire, we have a strong second-order desire not to act on first-order desires induced in us unawares by others, for no good reason, and now we can see that that desire applies even to cases in which we would *appear* to be better off in acting on such first-order desires.

Thus, we may conclude that Nelson's argument in favour of persuasive advertising is not convincing. I should note, perhaps, that my conclusion concerning persuasive advertising echoes that of Santilli (1983). My argument differs from his, however, in centering upon the notions of autonomy and causes of desires acceptable to the agent, rather than upon the distinction between needs and desires. Santilli claims that the arousal of a desire is not a rational process, unless it is preceded by a knowledge of actual needs. This, I believe, is too strong. I may well have no need of a new tennis-racket, but my desire for one, aroused by informative advertisements in the newspaper, seems rational enough. I would prefer to claim that a desire is autonomous and at least *prima facie* rational if it is not induced in the agent without his knowledge and for no good reason, and allows

ordinary processes of decisionmaking to occur.

Finally, I should point out that, in arguing against all persuasive advertising, unlike Santilli, I am not to be interpreted as bestowing moral respectability upon all informative advertising. Advertisers of any variety ought to consider whether the ideological objections often made to their conduct have any weight. Are they, for instance, imposing a distorted system of values upon consumers, in which the goal of our lives is to consume, and in which success is measured by one's level of consumption? Or are they entrenching attitudes which prolong the position of certain groups subject to discrimination, such as women or homosexuals? Advertisers should also carefully consider whether their product will be of genuine value to any consumers, and, if so, attempt to restrict their campaigns to the groups in society which will benefit (see Durham, 1984). I would claim, for instance, that all advertising of tobacco-based products, even of the informative variety, is wrong, and that some advertisements for alcohol are wrong, in that they are directed at the wrong audience. Imagine, for instance, a liquor-store manager erecting an informative bill-board opposite an alcoholics' rehabilitation centre. But these are secondary questions for prospective advertisers. The primary questions must be whether they are intending to employ the techniques of persuasive advertising, and, if so, how those techniques can be avoided.

ACKNOWLEDGEMENT

I should like to thank Dr. James Griffin for helpful discussion of an earlier draft of this paper.

REFERENCES

Arrington, R.: 1982, 'Advertising and Behaviour Control,' *Journal of Business Ethics* I, 1

Durham, T.: 1984, 'Information, Persuasion, and Control in Moral Appraisal of Advertising Strategy,' *Journal of Business Ethics* III, 3

Nelson, P.: 1978, 'Advertising and Ethics,' in *Ethics, Free Enterprise, and Public Policy,* (eds.) R. De George and J. Pichler, New York: Oxford University Press

Santilli, P.: 1983, 'The Informative and Persuasive Functions of Advertising: A Moral Appraisal,' *Journal of Business Ethics* II, 1.

NO   John O'Toole

THE TROUBLE WITH ADVERTISING

Advertising is an inescapable part of almost everyone's life in America. Thus, almost everyone has an attitude about the subject. And the attitudes, as expressed, seem extremely negative, in terms of both the product and those who produce it.

Back in 1975, Dr. Margaret Mead was quoted in one of our too-numerous trade journals as saying. "The only reason many people are in advertising is because no other business would pay them so much money." She added, "Most advertising people don't believe in the products they advertise or the words they are writing about their clients' products." In *The Lonely Crowd*, sociologist David Riesman writes, "Why, I ask, isn't it possible that advertising as a whole is a fantastic fraud, presenting an image of America taken seriously by no one, least of all by the advertising men who create it?"

According to a survey done in 1978 by Market Facts, Inc. for *Advertising Age* magazine, 43 percent of respondents not involved in advertising chose my craft as the one with "the lowest ethical standards." In 1977, a Gallup poll revealed the relative ranking of 20 occupational groups in terms of honesty and ethical standards. The public rated advertising practitioners 19th, just after labor union leaders and state officeholders. We did, however, beat car salesmen. The same year, a Harris survey asked respondents how much confidence they had in the people who ran various institutions. Ad agencies ranked last. Humorist Kin Hubbard once characterized us this way: "It used to be that a fellow went on the police force when all else failed, but today he goes into the advertising game."

Now, I am no more insensitive to boors, scam artists, dolts and loudmouths than the next person. And over something more than a quarter of a century in advertising, though I've encountered a few of each, I've not noticed a disproportionate representation in my craft—certainly no more than among the lawyers, doctors, journalists, accountants, academicians, clergymen, clerks, civil servants and businessmen I've met.

* * *

Why do people feel that way about us? Was it something we said? Where do these staunchly held and mainly negative impressions come from? Well, a book entitled *The Hucksters* made a mighty contribution. It was published in 1946 by Frederick Wakeman, who, I'm grieved to admit, worked for the same agency I work for now (but so did Alan Jay Lerner, whose lyrics for *Camelot* provided a cheerier type of fantasy).

The Hucksters depicted ad people as fast-talking, double-dealing, hard-drinking scoundrels who yielded every ethical point to unscrupulous clients. It would probably have faded away on the remainder shelves had it not been made into a movie starring Clark Gable. The film was a hit and reappears to this day, like a spirit that cannot find eternal rest, on late-night television. Subsequent movies developed the stereotype into a character as morally impoverished as those in *The Hucksters* but far less acute. The adman became an exploitable hustler who was usually played by Jack Lemmon. With a few refinements, this persona surfaced as second banana in the television series *Bewitched*, in which Dick York added the further dimension of ineptitude.

Then, of course, self-destructive and self-serving advertising people contributed their share to what they perceived as an increasingly popular myth. Autobiographical books detailing the zany goings-on inside advertising agencies "where anything can happen and usually does" began to proliferate. Most bore the same relationship to advertising as *Dr. Doolittle* does to zoology, but the public loved them because they amused and didn't challenge the mind by questioning the stereotype. Foremost among these was *From Those Wonderful Folks Who Brought You Pearl Harbor* by Jerry della Femina. Jerry works hard at being an enfant terrible and masking the fact that he's a serious advertising practitioner. He succeeded at both in his book.

All of this has shaped the impressions people have of those of us in advertising. But it's not the whole story. There have been novels and TV programs and films aplenty about corrupt congressmen, venal businessmen and crooked lawyers, yet members of those occupations can attend cocktail parties relatively unassailed. The reason is that their activities affect most people indirectly or through third parties. At least the products of their efforts are less proximate, less numerous and less ubiquitous than is advertising.

Attitudes about advertising, which color attitudes about those who practice it, are obviously a concern to me. Because of the importance of advertising to a system that produces a lot of good living and good jobs for a lot of good people, it's worth looking into what those attitudes are, what has caused them, who is at fault, and what can be done about it.

In the first instance, it's important to separate public attitudes—those measured by polling a sample of citizens representing all of us—from the attitudes of specialized publics: educators, journalists, consumer advocates and government. Each of the latter influence public opinion to some extent and should be looked at in terms of how and how much.

Whatever the influences, public attitudes toward advertising do not bring cheer to the heart of one who makes his living at it. A 1980 study by Yankelovich, Skelly & White reported that 70 percent of the American population was concerned with truth, distortion and exaggeration in advertising. A 1979 Louis Harris poll showed 81 percent feeling that "the claims for most products advertised on TV are exaggerated," and 52 percent saying that most or all TV advertising is "seriously misleading."

A survey conducted by my own company in 1977 found 36 percent of the national sample objecting to most TV advertising; the adjectives chosen most frequently were "dumb" and "juvenile." A 1974 study done by our industry association indicated that 59 percent of the respondents believed "most advertising insults the intelligence of the average consumer." It's interesting to note, however, that in the same study 88 percent said that advertising is essential and 57 percent that advertising results in better products.

The professional critics come at us from a somewhat different direction. Since there are few more professional or critical than John Kenneth Galbraith, let us begin with him. In *The New Industrial State*, Galbraith says, "In everyday parlance, this great machine, and the demanding and varied talents that it employs are said to be engaged in selling goods. In less ambiguous language, it means that it is engaged in the management of those who buy goods." Similarly, in his book *The Sponsor: Notes on a Modern Potentate*, Columbia University professor Erik Barnouw defines television advertising as "selling the unnecessary."

Philip Slater writes, in *The Pursuit of Loneliness*, "If we define pornography as any message from any communication medium that is intended to arouse sexual excitement, then it is clear that most advertisements are covertly pornographic." Novelist Mary McCarthy attacks us thusly in *On the Contrary*: "The thing, however, that repels us in these advertisements is their naive falsity to life. Who are these advertising men kidding? . . . Between the tired, sad, gentle faces of the subway riders and the grin-

ning Holy Families of the Ad-Mass, there exists no possibility of even a wishful identification." I could go on and on were it not for a narrow threshold for self-inflicted pain. I'll conclude with a definition of advertising by Fred Allen: "85 percent confusion and 15 percent commission."

The criticisms leveled against advertising by the general public are clearly of a different nature from those of the specialized groups. The people are faulting advertising on what it's doing wrong or what it's not doing well enough or what it's doing too much of. The specialists are criticizing advertising on the basis of a totally different set of standards. The distinction is important because it explains why the advertising industry often responds so ineptly to its professional critics. It's hard to come up with answers when you not only don't understand the question but can't conceive why anyone would ask it.

The fact is that academicians, journalists, consumer advocates and government regulators criticize—and dislike—advertising because it isn't something else.

It accomplishes little to carry on about automobiles because they weren't made to fly or to reproach dogs because they don't climb trees. It is not in the nature of dogs to do what cats do, nor were the evolutionary forces that produced them guided by any imperative to develop that capacity. By the same token, it accomplishes little to condemn advertising because it isn't journalism or education or entertainment. It is fruitless to hold that advertising should be hidden, since it is not advertising if it's not seen. And it is witless to excoriate advertising for having arcane powers to brainwash or to make people act against their will when it clearly wouldn't and couldn't function as advertising if it did.

Yet such charges form the case made against advertising by many professional critics. Before I answer them, it's important for all of us to understand what advertising actually *is*. Only then can we put aside criticism based on what it isn't and get down to the positive challenge of making it better.

Archeologists have discovered evidence of some kind of advertising among the artifacts of every civilization that communicated by writing. The moment one man began growing or raising more than he needed and saw the opportunity to have what someone else was producing, the concept of bartering was born. Now, the only way to extend bartering beyond the chance encounter of two individuals with corresponding needs and surpluses was for each to post what he had and what he wanted in a public place where many could learn about it. The introduction of currency simplified the process by allowing people to post only what they were offering.

This "poster" concept dominated advertising for millennia. Its elements were the item or service offered, the name and location of the offerer, and sometimes the price. Often the most gifted artists of the era were employed to visualize for the prospect what he would receive for his money. Toulouse-Lautrec was one, and the graphics he created to lure customers into the Moulin Rouge now hang in the great art museums of the world.

Such embellishments brought a new dimension of creativity to the simple exposition of product, seller and price but did not change the basic approach; the poster remained the principal form of advertising until relatively recent years. As newspapers and magazines appeared,

the poster concept was transferred to paid space in their pages. Early advertising agencies did little to advance the craft and develop its potential, for they had been formed essentially as brokers of space. They bought advertising space in quantity from newspapers and magazines at a 15 percent discount, then sold it to advertisers at full price. To justify this "commission," they counseled their clients on what to put in that space. But such advice was a relatively simple sideline to the space-brokering function since the poster concept more or less limited the information to product, seller and price.

In fact, in the early 1900s, the generally accepted definition of advertising was the one coined by the leading agency of the time (still in business today), N. W. Ayer. Ayer said advertising was "keeping your name before the public." But all that was to change with the new century. As a result of two men meeting in Chicago, the real energy of advertising was unlocked, its enormous potential tapped, and its true nature revealed.

One spring afternoon in 1904, in an office building at Wabash and Randolph Streets that was eventually replaced by Marshall Field's department store, two men were chatting. One was Ambrose Thomas, one of the founders of the Lord & Thomas advertising agency. The other was a bright young man named Albert Lasker, who, it was already apparent, would soon be running the agency.

Following a polite knock, an office boy came in with a note and handed it to Thomas. Upon reading it, Thomas snorted and gave it to Lasker. The note said: "I am downstairs in the saloon, and I can tell you what advertising is. I know that you don't know. It will mean much to me to have you know what it is and it will mean much to you. If you wish to know what advertising is, send the word 'yes' down by messenger." It was signed by a John E. Kennedy.

Thomas asked Lasker if he had ever heard of the man, and when Lasker said he hadn't, Thomas decided Kennedy was probably mad and wasn't worth wasting time on. But Lasker, who was dissatisfied with the concept of "keeping your name before the public," was willing to take a chance. He sent down for Kennedy, and the two spent an hour in Lasker's office. Then they headed for the saloon downstairs, not to emerge until midnight.

Kennedy was a former Royal Canadian Mounted Policeman, a dashing, mustachioed chap who in 1904 was employed as a copywriter for an elixir known as Dr. Shoop's Restorative. What he said to Lasker that day resulted in his being hired on the spot for the unheard-of salary of $28,000 a year. Within 24 months, he was making $75,000.

What did he say to Lasker? Simply this: "Advertising is salesmanship in print."

It seems so simple and obvious today. But what this definition did in 1904 was to change the course of advertising completely and make possible the enormous role it now plays in our economy. For, by equating the function of an advertisement with the function of a salesman who calls on a prospect personally, it revealed the true nature of advertising.

For the first time, the concept of persuasion, which is the prime role of a salesman, was applied to the creation of advertising. Information was considered in a new light, since information is what a salesman must be equipped with and what he uses to persuade. An ad was seen as a means of conveying the personality of the advertiser, just as a good salesman reflects the standards of his company. Reason and logic became part of advertising planning. And so, for the first time, did the consumer.

With its possibilities revealed, advertising exploded. Now it could be refined, made more effective and applied to new tasks. Agencies proliferated, and those that understood the new definition flourished. None flourished more than Lord & Thomas, the birthplace of the revolution. Under Albert Lasker's leadership it became the biggest, most successful agency of its time.

* * *

Advertising, then, is salesmanship functioning in the paid space and time of mass media. To criticize it for being that, for being true to its nature, is to question whether it should be permitted—a position taken by only the most rabid, none of whom have come up with a reasonable substitute for its role in the economy. And to criticize it for not being something else—something it might resemble but by definition can never be—is equally fruitless. Yet much of the professional criticism I spoke of has its feet planted solidly on those two pieces of shaky ground.

As a format of conveying information, advertising shares certain characteristics with journalism, education, entertainment and other modes of communication. But it cannot be judged by the same standards because it is essentially something else. This point is missed by many in government, both the regulators and the elected representatives who oversee the regulators.

The Federal Trade Commission was pushing not too long ago for one of those quasi-laws they call a Trade Regulation Ruling (when they were empowered to write the law of the land, I don't know; but that's another argument). This particular TRR would have required an ad or commercial for any product claiming to be nutritious to list all its nutritive elements. For two reasons advertising cannot comply with such a requirement and still end up as advertising.

One, advertising is salesmanship, and good salesmanship does not countenance boring the prospect into glassy-eyed semiconsciousness. Yet I am sure—and consumers on whom sample ads and commercials were tested agreed—that a lengthy litany of niacin, riboflavin, ascorbic acid and so on is as interesting as watching paint dry.

Less subjective is the fact that such a listing can't be given for many good, wholesome products within the confines of a 30-second commercial. Since that's the standard length today, the end result of the proposed TRR would have been to ban those products from television advertising. The FTC staff did not consider that advertising necessarily functions in the paid space and time of mass media. Adding 20 or more seconds of Latin makes that impossible.

This example illustrates the problems that can arise when regulators try to dictate what must go into advertising. An FTC attorney named Donald F. Turner was quoted by Professor Raymond Bauer in a piece for the *Harvard Business Review* as saying, "There are three steps to informed choice. (1) The consumer must know the product exists. (2) The consumer must know how the product performs. (3) He must know how it performs compared to other products. If advertising only performs step one and appeals on other than a performance basis, informed choice cannot be made."

This is probably true in an ad for a new floor wax from S. C. Johnson or an antiperspirant from Bristol-Myers. But what about a new fragrance from Max Factor? How do you describe how Halston performs compared with other products? Is it important for anyone to know? Is it salesmanship to make the attempt? Or suppose you're advertising Coca-Cola. There can't be many people left in the world who don't know Coke exists or how it performs. Granted, there may be a few monks or aborigines who don't know how it performs in relation to other products, but you can't reach them through advertising. So why waste the time or space?

The reason Coca-Cola advertises is to maintain or increase a level of awareness about itself among people who know full well it exists and what it tastes like, people whom other beverage makers are contacting with similar messages about their products. Simple information about its existence and its popularity—information that triggers residual knowledge in the recipient about its taste and other characteristics—is legitimate and sufficient. It does what a salesman would do.

On the other hand, advertising for a big-ticket item—an automobile, for instance—would seemingly have to include a lot of information in order to achieve its end. But the advertising is not attempting to sell the car. It is an advance salesman trying to persuade the prospect to visit a showroom. Only there can the principal salesman do the complete job. Turner's definition is neither pertinent nor possible in the case of automobiles. In such cases mass communications media cannot convey the kind of information one needs in order to "know how the product performs" or to "know how it performs compared to other products." You have to see it, kick the tires, ask the salesman questions about it, let the kids try out the windshield wipers. And surely you have to drive it.

In the paid space and time of mass media, the purpose of automobile advertising is to select the prospect for a particular car and, on the basis of its appeal to his income, life-style or basic attitudes, to persuade him he's the person the designers and engineers had in mind when they created this model. If the information is properly chosen and skillfully presented, it will point out the relevance of the car to his needs and self-image sufficiently to get him into the showroom. Then it's up to the salesman to sell him the car—but with a different package of information, including the tactile and experiential, than could be provided in the ad.

From time to time some government regulator will suggest that advertising information should be limited to price and function. But consider how paleolithic that kind of thinking is. Restricting advertising to a discussion of price and function would eliminate, among other things, an equally essential piece of information: what kind of people make and market this product or provide this service.

The reputation, quality standards, taste and responsibility of the people who put out a product is information that's not only important to the consumer but is increasingly demanded by the consumer. It's information that can often outweigh price and function as these differences narrow among products within the same category. It's information that is critical to the advertising my agency prepares for clients like Johnson's Wax, Sunkist Growers, Hallmark, Sears and many others. Advertising would not be salesmanship without it. Put it this way: if surgeons advertised and you had

a hot appendix, would you want the ads to be limited to price and function information?

The government regulators, and the consumer advocates dedicated to influencing them, do not understand what advertising is and how it is perceived by the consumer. And their overwhelming fear that one is always trying to deceive the other leads them to demand from advertising the kind of product information that characterizes *Consumer Reports*. They expect advertising to be journalism, and they evaluate it by journalistic standards. Since it is not, advertising, like the ugly duckling, is found wanting.

* * *

It is not in the nature of advertising to be journalistic, to present both sides, to include information that shows the product negatively in comparison with other entries in the category (unless, of course, the exclusion of such information would make the ad misleading or product usage hazardous). For example, advertising for Sunkist lemons, which might point out the flavor advantages of fresh lemons over bottled juice, should not be expected to remind people that fresh lemons can't be kept as long as a bottle of concentrate. Information is selected for journalism—or should be—to provide the recipient with as complete and objective an account as possible. Information is selected for advertising to persuade the recipient to go to a showroom or make a mental pledge to find the product on a store shelf.

Advertising, like the personal salesman, unabashedly presents products in their most favorable light. I doubt that there's a consumer around who doesn't understand that. For instance, would you, in a classified ad offering your house for sale, mention the toilet on the second floor that doesn't flush? I doubt that even a conscience as rigorous as Ralph Nader's would insist, in an ad to sell his own used car, on information about that worn fan belt or leaky gasket. No reader would expect it. Nor does anyone expect it from our clients.

Information, as far as advertising is concerned, is anything that helps a genuine prospect to perceive the applicability of a product to his or her individual life, to understand how the product will solve a problem, make life easier or better, or in some way provide a benefit. When the knowledge can't safely be assumed, it also explains how to get the product. In other words, it's salesmanship.

It is not witchcraft, another craft government regulators and otherwise responsible writers are forever confusing with mine. For the same reasons people like to believe that someone is poisoning our water supply or, as in the Joseph McCarthy era, that pinkos proliferate in our government and are trying to bring it down, someone is always rejuvenating the idea of subliminal advertising.

Subliminal advertising is defined as advertising that employs stimuli operating below the threshold of consciousness. It is supposed to influence the recipient's behavior without his being aware of any communication taking place. The most frequently cited example, never fully verified, involved a movie theater where the words "Drink Coke" were flashed on the screen so briefly that while the mind recorded the message, it was not conscious of receiving it. The result was said to be greatly increased sales of Coca-Cola at the vending counter.

I don't like to destroy cherished illusions, but I must state unequivocally that there is no such thing as subliminal advertising. I have never seen an example of it, nor have I ever heard it seriously discussed as a technique by advertising people. Salesmanship is persuasion involving rational and emotional tools that must be employed on a conscious level in order to effect a conscious decision in favor of one product over its competitive counterparts, and in order to have that decision remembered and acted upon at a later time. Furthermore, it's demeaning to assume that the human mind is so easily controlled that anyone can be made to act against his will or better judgment by peremptory commands he doesn't realize are present.

Even more absurd is the theory proposed by Wilson Bryan Key in a sleazy book entitled *Subliminal Seduction*. From whatever dark motivations, Key finds sexual symbolism in every ad and commercial. He points it out to his readers with no little relish, explaining how, after reducing the prospect to a pliant mass of sexual arousal, advertising can get him to buy anything. There are some who might envy Mr. Key his ability to get turned on by a photograph of a Sunkist orange.

Most professional critics are much less bizarre in their condemnations. Uninformed about the real nature of advertising, perhaps, but not mad. For instance, they often ascribe recondite powers to advertising—powers that it does not have and that they cannot adequately define—because it is not solely verbal. Being for the most part lawyers and academics, they are uncomfortable with information conveyed by means other than words. They want things spelled out, even in television commercials, despite the fact that television is primarily a visual medium. They do not trust graphic and musical information because they aren't sure that the meaning they receive is the same one the consumer is receiving. And since they consider the consumer much more gullible and much less astute than they, they sound the alarm and then charge to the rescue. Sorcery is afoot.

Well, from time immemorial, graphics and music have been with us. I suspect each has been part of the salesman's tool kit for as long as they have been salesmen. The songs of medieval street vendors and Toulouse-Lautrec's Jane Avril attest.

A mouth-watering cake presented photographically as the end benefit of Betty Crocker Cake Mix is just as legitimate as and more effective than a verbal description. The mysteriously exuberant musical communication "I Love New York" honestly conveys the variety of experiences offered by New York State; it is not witchcraft. It is not to be feared unless you fear yourself. But perhaps that is the cradle that spawns consumer advocates and government regulators. There is something murky in that psyche, some kink in the mentality of those who feel others are incapable of making mundane decisions for themselves, something Kafka-like in the need to take over the personal lives of Americans in order to protect them from themselves.

I read with growing disquiet a document put out by the Federal Trade Commission in 1979 entitled *Consumer Information Remedies*. In discussing how to evaluate consumer information, they wrote, "The Task Force members struggled long and hard to come up with a universally satisfactory definition of the *value* of consumer information. Should the Commission consider a mandatory disclosure to be a valuable piece of information, for instance, if it were later shown that although consumers understood the information, they did not use it when making purchase decisions? Is there a value in improving the *quality* of market decisions through the provision of relevant information, or is it necessary for the information to change behavior to have value?" The ensuing "remedies" make it clear that the staff really judges the value of a mandatory disclaimer by the degree to which it changes consumer behavior in the direction they are seeking.

But wait a minute. I'm a consumer, too. Who are they to be wondering what to do with me next if I understand but choose to ignore some dumb disclaimer they've forced an advertiser to put in his ad? It's my God-given right to ignore any information any salesman presents me with—and an ad, remember, is a salesman. And what's this about changing behavior? Well, mine is going to change if the employees of a government I'm paying for start talking like that out loud. It's going to get violent.

Later in the same document, the staff addresses "Sub-Optional Purchases." While I have no quarrel with their intent, I find my hackles rising as they define the problem in terms of people "misallocating resources," consumers wasting their dollars on "products that do not best satisfy their needs." Listen, fellows, those are *my* resources you're talking about. Those are *my* dollars, what there is of them after you guys in Washington have had your way with my paycheck. I'm going to allocate them as I damn well please. And if I want to waste a few on products that do not best satisfy my needs—an unnutritious but thoroughly delicious hot dog at the ball park, for example—try to stop me.

Perhaps I, in return, am seeking evidence of conspiracy. Perhaps I'm looking under beds. But I think I understand the true nature of government bureaucrats. They, on the other hand, do not understand that of advertising. They and other professional critics—the journalists, consumerists, academicians—don't understand that it's not journalism or education and cannot be judged on the basis of objectivity and exhaustive, in-depth treatment. Thorough knowledge of a subject cannot be derived from an advertisement but only from a synthesis of all relevant sources: the advertising of competitors, the opinions of others, the more impartial reports in newspapers, magazines and, increasingly, television.

The critics also don't understand that advertising isn't witchcraft, that it cannot wash the brain or coerce someone to buy what he doesn't want. It shouldn't be castigated for what it cannot and does not purport to do. And it isn't entertainment, either. A commercial should offer some reward to the viewer in return for his time, but that reward need not always take the form of entertainment. Sometimes the tone should be serious, even about seemingly frivolous subjects. Hemorrhoids are not funny to those who have them.

Advertising sometimes resembles other fields, just as an elephant resembles a snake to the blind man who feels its trunk, and a tree to another who feels its leg. But advertising is really salesmanship functioning in the paid space and time of mass media.

POSTSCRIPT

Is Advertising Fundamentally Deceptive?

The issue in advertising comes down to social expectation. If advertising is a gentle put-on that is expected and appreciated by all, a way of displaying a product for sale that might persuade a customer to try it once, and no more than that, then surely it is a harmless addition to the pages and airwaves of our experience. Advertising can be uplifting, appealing, funny, and even beautiful. If advertising remains only in the inessential margins of our lives, it can do no real harm. The manufacturer of the advertised product obtains value from having people try his product just once, and from that value comes the justification to hire the advertising firm and to place the messages in print or on the air. This placement in turn funds the magazines and the entertainment of radio and television, and it therefore brings otherwise unobtainable value to our lives. There seems to be no moral percentage in insisting on the strict theoretical line, that if advertising in any way influences you to spend a penny on anything that you would not have bought if not for the advertising, then it is manipulative and wrong.

But what if it is *not* at the margins of our lives? Those who take advertising more seriously hold that the practice is wrong because it distorts our perception of what is socially valuable and of what is personally redeeming.

The first line of attack on the advertising industry was developed originally by economist John Kenneth Galbraith in *The Affluent Society*. Galbraith was interested not so much in the decision to buy one good rather than another in the market but the decision to allot funds to the private rather than to the public sector. The decision to vote for or against taxes to buy public goods, after all, is an economic decision. Galbraith argued that since only private firms purchase advertising space and time, advertising distorts the normal decision-making process of a society in favor of the purchase of private goods (cars, swimming pools, and video games, for example) and against the selection of public goods (such as clean air, better roads, and pleasant parks), thus systematically starving the public sector in favor of the private. For Galbraith, then, advertising is not only a nuisance but a seriously unethical strategy to funnel the national wealth into the hands of the industrialists and away from public needs.

The second line of reasoning notes the psychological targets of typical advertising. People are weak, vulnerable, and plagued, on occasion, by feelings of inadequacy and social inferiority. These feelings are not at all marginal but go to the core of the social creatures that we are. They are painful, and we are grateful for relief. Advertising learns to ask questions that expose our vulnerabilities and then answers the questions with products that explicitly promise to strengthen us at those weak points. The deception of advertising is not in the lies that the advertisers tell but in the implication that there are products that can remedy the fear and imperfections of the human condition itself. As such, advertising is doubly harmful: it leads us to believe falsehoods about what will and will not make us smarter, more popular, thinner, more attractive to the opposite sex, and in all other ways the better social person many of us would like to be. More important, it portrays the weakness of human nature only as a deplorable and shameful condition, not to be acknowledged or faced in company with others who share it but to be quickly remedied before others notice. Fortunately, the advertising says, the remedy for human inadequacies, in the form of the advertised product, is at hand. If you cannot or do not purchase it, you have only yourself to blame for your continuing social failures.

In this manner, critics argue, humans are stripped of the real means to help them cope with their weaknesses—the support of other humans with similar weaknesses. Instead, they are isolated in their feelings of inadequacy and left with a false remedy that can never do what it so glowingly promises to do. When the false remedy is only a perfume that promises to make you fantastically attractive, one may still argue that no *real* harm is done, and that you really do enjoy the fantasy. But when the false remedy is a cigarette that purports to turn you into a strong and self-sufficient cowboy, then the purveyance of images and the law and practices that condone it begin to appear harmful.

Is advertising a fraud and a deception, the more fraudulent advertising being the more successful, or is advertising a harmless practice of American business, helping the economy by keeping goods, especially new goods, flowing?

SUGGESTED READINGS

Robert L. Arrington, "Advertising and Behavior Control," *Journal of Business Ethics* (1981).

Sissela Bok, *Lying: Moral Choice in Public and Private Life* (Pantheon Books, 1978).

William A. Cook, "Truth, in the Eye of the Beholder?" *Journal of Advertising Research* (December 1991).

John Fraedrich, O. C. Ferrell, and William Pride, "An Empirical Examination of Three Machiavellian Concepts: Advertisers vs. The General Public," *Journal of Business Ethics* (September 1989).

John Kenneth Galbraith, *The Affluent Society*, 3rd ed. (Houghton Mifflin, 1976).

Jonathan Karl, "Lotto Baloney," *The New Republic* (March 4, 1991).

Peter Nelson, "Advertising and Ethics," in Richard T. DeGeorge and Joseph A. Pichler, eds., *Ethics, Free Enterprise, and Public Policy: Original Essays on Moral Issues in Business* (Oxford University Press, 1978).

ISSUE 14

Product Liability: Was Ford to Blame in the Pinto Case?

YES: Mark Dowie, from "Pinto Madness," *Mother Jones* (September/October 1977)

NO: Ford Motor Company, from "Closing Argument by Mr. James Neal," Brief for the Defense, *State of Indiana v. Ford Motor Company*, U.S. District Court, South Bend, Indiana (January 15, 1980)

ISSUE SUMMARY

YES: Award-winning investigative journalist Mark Dowie alleges that Ford Motor Company deliberately put an unsafe car—the Pinto—on the road, causing hundreds of people to suffer burn deaths and horrible disfigurement. He argues that the related activities of Ford's executives, both within the company and in dealing with the public and the government, were criminal.

NO: James Neal, chief attorney for Ford Motor Company during the Pinto litigation, argues to the jury that Ford cannot be held responsible for deaths that were caused by others—such as the driver of the van that struck the victims—and that there is no proof of criminal intent or negligence on the part of Ford.

On August 10, 1978, three girls had stopped their car, a 1973 Ford Pinto, on U.S. Highway 22 near Goshen, Indiana, and were about to get under way again when they were struck from the rear at high speed by a van. The car immediately burst into flames, and the girls had no chance to escape before the flames reached them.

The blame for these girls' deaths fell not on the driver of the van but on the manufacturer of the Pinto. Questions that were asked were: What was wrong with the car? Why did it burst into flames so quickly? Mark Dowie, then–general manager of business operations of the magazine *Mother Jones*, had argued a year earlier that there was a great deal wrong with the Pinto. Dowie's argument, which is reprinted here, is based on data obtained for him by some disaffected Ford engineers. In it, he suggests that the Pinto had been rushed into production without adequate testing; that it had a vulnerable fuel system that would rupture with any rear-end collision; that even though the vulnerability was discovered before production, Ford had hurried the Pinto to the market anyway; and that successful lobbying thereafter had prevented government regulators from instituting a requirement for a safer gas tank. Most suggestive to the public was a document supplied by one of the engineers, an estimate of the probable costs of refitting valves to prevent fire in a rollover accident. It was a cost-benefit analysis that placed a dollar value on human life—among the estimates were the probability of a fatal accident, the amount of money needed to settle a lawsuit for the loss of a life, and the amount of money needed to do the refitting so that there would be less chance for that loss of life—and concluded that it was more economical to accept the higher probability of death occurring and then settle the suits as they come. The document caused serious damage to Ford Motor Company's reputation.

Ford endured two sets of court appearances as a result of Dowie's article. More common, and successful, were the civil suits, alleging culpable negligence that damaged the rights of other individuals. But the state of Indiana also brought a public prosecution for *criminal* negligence, and James Neal's brief, which also follows, was prepared for that trial.

The 1916 case *McPherson v. Buick* helps set the stage for this debate. In this case, McPherson successfully sued the Buick Motor Company for injury sustained as a direct result of a poorly manufactured product. This was the first instance of a consumer's suing a manufacturer (as opposed to the seller), and it marked the transfer of product liability cases from the form of action known as "contract" to the form of action known as "tort" (in this case, negligence). The logic is that not only is an individual agreement breached when a shoddy product injures a consumer but a general obligation on the part of a manufacturer (an implied "warrant of merchantability") to avoid putting an unsafe product on the market is not met. Given the myriad ways that people can injure themselves, that obligation seems to be very broad indeed.

With regard to the Pinto case, was Ford guilty of deliberate malfeasance? Was it a series of unlucky decisions made in good faith? Or was this just a very unfortunate accident? As you read these selections, ask yourself what conditions need to be satisifed in order to attribute "responsibility" to any person or company. Also, what kinds of risks do people assume when buying a car, a motorcycle, or a can of tuna fish? For what is the manufacturer responsible? Should we be willing to assume more risks in the enormously competitive market that prevails among small automobiles? Does the product liability suit unjustly cripple American efforts to compete in highly competitive industries? Is this something that we should be concerned about?

YES

Mark Dowie

PINTO MADNESS

One evening in the mid-1960s, Arjay Miller was driving home from his office in Dearborn, Michigan, in the four-door Lincoln Continental that went with his job as president of the Ford Motor Company. On a crowded highway, another car struck his from the rear. The Continental spun around and burst into flames. Because he was wearing a shoulder-strap seat belt, Miller was unharmed by the crash, and because his doors didn't jam he escaped the gasoline-drenched, flaming wreck. But the accident made a vivid impression on him. Several months later, on July 15, 1965, he recounted it to a U.S. Senate subcommittee that was hearing testimony on auto safety legislation. "I still have burning in my mind the image of that gas tank on fire," Miller said. He went on to express an almost passionate interest in controlling fuel-fed fires in cars that crash or roll over. He spoke with excitement about the fabric gas tank Ford was testing at that very moment. "If it proves out," he promised the senators, "it will be a feature you will see in our standard cars."

Almost seven years after Miller's testimony, a woman, whom for legal reasons we will call Sandra Gillespie, pulled onto a Minneapolis highway in her new Ford Pinto. Riding with her was a young boy, whom we'll call Robbie Carlton. As she entered a merge lane, Sandra Gillespie's car stalled. Another car rear-ended hers at an impact speed of 28 miles per hour. The Pinto's gas tank ruptured. Vapors from it mixed quickly with the air in the passenger compartment. A spark ignited the mixture and the car exploded in a ball of fire. Sandra died in agony a few hours later in an emergency hospital. Her passenger, 13-year-old Robbie Carlton, is still alive; he has just come home from another futile operation aimed at grafting a new ear and nose from skin on the few unscarred portions of his badly burned body. (This accident is real; the details are from police reports.)

Why did Sandra Gillespie's Ford Pinto catch fire so easily, seven years after Ford's Arjay Miller made his apparently sincere pronouncements—the same seven years that brought more safety improvements to cars than any other period in automotive history? An extensive investigation by *Mother Jones* over the past six months has found these answers:

• Fighting strong competition from Volkswagen for the lucrative small-car market, the Ford Motor Company rushed the Pinto into production in much less than the usual time.

• Ford engineers discovered in preproduction crash tests that rear-end collisions would rupture the Pinto's fuel system extremely easily.

• Because assembly-line machinery was already tooled when engineers found this defect, top Ford officials decided to manufacture the car anyway —exploding gas tank and all—*even though Ford owned the patent on a much safer gas tank.*

• For more than eight years afterwards, Ford successfully lobbied, with extraordinary vigor and some blatant lies, against a key government safety standard that would have forced the company to change the Pinto's fire-prone gas tank.

By conservative estimates Pinto crashes have caused 500 burn deaths to people who would not have been seriously injured if the car had not burst into flames. The figure could be as high as 900. Burning Pintos have become such an embarrassment to Ford that its advertising agency, J. Walter Thompson, dropped a line from the end of a radio spot that read "Pinto leaves you with that warm feeling."

Ford knows the Pinto is a firetrap, yet it has paid out millions to settle damage suits out of court, and it is prepared to spend millions more lobbying against safety standards. With a half million cars rolling off the assembly lines each year, Pinto is the biggest-selling subcompact in America, and the company's operating profit on the car is fantastic. Finally, in 1977, new Pinto models have incorporated a few minor alterations necessary to meet that federal standard Ford managed to hold off for eight years. Why did the company delay so long in making these minimal, inexpensive improvements?

• Ford waited eight years because its internal "cost-benefit analysis," *which places a dollar value on human life,* said it wasn't profitable to make the changes sooner.

Before we get to the question of how much Ford thinks your life is worth, let's trace the history of the death trap itself. Although this particular story is about the Pinto, the way in which Ford made its decision is typical of the U.S. auto industry generally. There are plenty of similar stories about other cars made by other companies. But this case is the worst of them all.

* * *

The next time you drive behind a Pinto (with over two million of them on the road, you shouldn't have much trouble finding one), take a look at the rear end. That long silvery object hanging down under the bumper is the gas tank. The tank begins about six inches forward of the bumper. In late models the bumper is designed to withstand a collision of only about five miles per hour. Earlier bumpers may as well not have been on the car for all the protection they offered the gas tank.

Mother Jones has studied hundreds of reports and documents on rear-end collisions involving Pintos. These reports conclusively reveal that if you ran into that Pinto you were following at over 30 miles per hour, the rear end of the car would buckle like an accordion, right up to the back seat. The tube leading to the gas-tank cap would be ripped away from the tank itself, and gas would immediately begin sloshing onto the road around the car. The buckled gas tank would be jammed up against the differential housing (that big bulge in the middle of your rear axle), which contains four sharp, protruding bolts likely to gash holes in the tank and spill still more gas. Now all you need is a spark from a cigarette, ignition, or scraping metal, and both cars would be engulfed in flames. If you gave that Pinto a really good whack —say, at 40 mph—chances are excellent that its doors would jam and you would have to stand by and watch its trapped passengers burn to death.

This scenario is no news to Ford. Internal company documents in our possession show that Ford has crash-tested the Pinto at a top-secret site more than 40 times and that *every* test made at over 25 mph without special structural alteration of the car has resulted in a ruptured fuel tank. Despite this, Ford officials denied under oath having crash-tested the Pinto.

Eleven of these tests, averaging a 31-mph impact speed, came before Pintos started rolling out of the factories. Only three cars passed the test with unbroken fuel tanks. In one of them an inexpensive light-weight plastic baffle was placed between the front of the gas tank and the differential housing, so those four bolts would not perforate the tank. (Don't forget about that little piece of plastic, which costs one dollar and weighs one pound. It plays an important role in our story later on.) In another successful test, a piece of steel was placed between the tank and the bumper. In the third test car the gas tank was lined with a rubber bladder. But none of these protective alterations was used in the mass-produced Pinto.

In pre-production planning, engineers seriously considered using in the Pinto the same kind of gas tank Ford uses in the Capri. The Capri tank rides over the rear axle and differential housing. It has been so successful in over 50 crash tests that Ford used it in its Experimental Safety Vehicle, which withstood rear-end impacts of 60 mph. So why wasn't the Capri tank used in the Pinto? Or, why wasn't that plastic baffle placed between the tank and the axle—something that would have saved the life of Sandra Gillespie and hundreds like her? Why was a car known to be a serious fire hazard deliberately released to production in August of 1970?

* * *

Whether Ford should manufacture subcompacts at all was the subject of a bitter two-year debate at the company's Dearborn headquarters. The principals in this corporate struggle were the then-president Semon "Bunky" Knudsen, whom Henry Ford II had hired away from General Motors, and Lee Iacocca, a spunky Young Turk who had risen fast within the company on the enormous success of the Mustang. Iacocca argued forcefully that Volkswagen and the Japanese were going to capture the entire American subcompact market unless Ford put out its own alternative to the VW Beetle. Bunky Knudsen said, in effect: let them have the small-car market; Ford makes good money on medium and large models. But he lost the battle and later resigned. Iacocca became president and almost immediately began a rush program to produce the Pinto.

Like the Mustang, the Pinto became known in the company as "Lee's car." Lee

Iacocca wanted that little car in the showrooms of America with the 1971 models. So he ordered his engineering vice president, Bob Alexander, to oversee what was probably the shortest production planning period in modern automotive history. The normal time span from conception to production of a new car model is about 43 months. The Pinto schedule was set at just under 25.

... Design, styling, product planning, advance engineering and quality assurance all have flexible time frames, and engineers can pretty much carry these on simultaneously. Tooling, on the other hand, has a fixed time frame of about 18 months. Normally, an auto company doesn't begin tooling until the other processes are almost over: you don't want to make the machines that stamp and press and grind metal into the shape of car parts until you know all those parts will work well together. *But Iacocca's speed-up meant Pinto tooling went on at the same time as product development.* So when crash tests revealed a serious defect in the gas tank, it was too late. The tooling was well under way.

When it was discovered the gas tank was unsafe, did anyone go to Iacocca and tell him? "Hell no," replied an engineer who worked on the Pinto, a high company official for many years, who, unlike several others at Ford, maintains a necessarily clandestine concern for safety. "That person would have been fired. Safety wasn't a popular subject around Ford in those days. With Lee it was taboo. Whenever a problem was raised that meant a delay on the Pinto, Lee would chomp on his cigar, look out the window and say 'Read the product objectives and get back to work.'"

The product objectives are clearly stated in the Pinto "green book." This is a thick, top-secret manual in green covers containing a step-by-step production plan for the model, detailing the metallurgy, weight, strength and quality of every part in the car. The product objectives for the Pinto are repeated in an article by Ford executive F. G. Olsen published by the Society of Automotive Engineers. He lists these product objectives as follows:

1. TRUE SUBCOMPACT
   - Size
   - Weight
2. LOW COST OF OWNERSHIP
   - Initial price
   - Fuel consumption
   - Reliability
   - Serviceability
3. CLEAR PRODUCT SUPERIORITY
   - Appearance
   - Comfort
   - Features
   - Ride and Handling
   - Performance

Safety, you will notice, is not there. It is not mentioned in the entire article. As Lee Iacocca was fond of saying, "Safety doesn't sell."

Heightening the anti-safety pressure on Pinto engineers was an important goal set by Iacocca known as "the limits of 2,000." The Pinto was not to weigh an ounce over 2,000 pounds and not to cost a cent over $2,000. "Iacocca enforced these limits with an iron hand," recalls the engineer quoted earlier. So, even when a crash test showed that that one-pound, one-dollar piece of plastic stopped the puncture of the gas tank, it was thrown out as extra cost and extra weight.

People shopping for subcompacts are watching every dollar. "You have to keep in mind," the engineer explained, "that the price elasticity on these subcompacts is extremely tight. You can price yourself right out of the market by adding $25 to the production cost of the model. And nobody understands that better than Iacocca."

Dr. Leslie Ball, the retired safety chief for the NASA manned space program and a founder of the International Society of Reliability Engineers, recently made a careful study of the Pinto. "The release to production of the Pinto was the most reprehensible decision in the history of American engineering," he said. Ball can name more than 40 European and Japanese models in the Pinto price and weight range with safer gas-tank positioning. Ironically, many of them, like the Ford Capri, contain a "saddle-type" gas tank riding over the back axle. *The patent on the saddle-type tank is owned by the Ford Motor Co.*

Los Angeles auto safety expert Byron Bloch has made an in-depth study of the Pinto fuel system. "It's a catastrophic blunder," he says. "Ford made an extremely irresponsible decision when they placed such a weak tank in such a ridiculous location in such a soft rear end. It's almost designed to blow up—premeditated."

A Ford engineer, who doesn't want his name used, comments: "This company is run by salesmen, not engineers; so the priority is styling, not safety." He goes on to tell a story about gas-tank safety at Ford.

Lou Tubben is one of the most popular engineers at Ford. He's a friendly, outgoing guy with a genuine concern for safety. By 1971 he had grown so concerned about gas-tank integrity that he asked his boss if he could prepare a presentation on safer tank design.

Tubben and his boss had both worked on the Pinto and shared a concern for its safety. His boss gave him the go-ahead, scheduled a date for the presentation and invited all company engineers and key production planning personnel. When time came for the meeting, a grand total of two people showed up—Lou Tubben and his boss.

"So you see," continued the anonymous Ford engineer ironically, "there *are* a few of us here at Ford who are concerned about fire safety." He adds: "They are mostly engineers who have to study a lot of accident reports and look at pictures of burned people. But we don't talk about it much. It isn't a popular subject. I've never seen safety on the agenda of a product meeting and, except for a brief period in 1956, I can't remember seeing the word safety in an advertisement. I really don't think the company wants American consumers to start thinking too much about safety—for fear they might demand it, I suppose."

Asked about the Pinto gas tank, another Ford engineer admitted: "That's all true. But you miss the point entirely. You see, safety isn't the issue, trunk space is. You have no idea how stiff the competition is over trunk space. Do you realize that if we put a Capri-type tank in the Pinto you could only get one set of golf clubs in the trunk?"

* * *

Blame for Sandra Gillespie's death, Robbie Carlton's unrecognizable face and all the other injuries and deaths in Pintos since 1970 does not rest on the shoulders of Lee Iacocca alone. For, while he and his associates fought their battle against a safer Pinto in Dearborn, a larger war against safer cars raged in Washington. One skirmish in that war involved Ford's successful eight-year lobbying effort against Federal Motor Vehicle Safety Standard 301, the rear-end provisions of which would have forced Ford to redesign the Pinto.

But first some background:

During the early '60s, auto safety legislation became the *bête-noire* of American big business. The auto industry was the last great unregulated business, and if *it* couldn't reverse the tide of government regulation, the reasoning went, no one could.

People who know him cannot remember Henry Ford II taking a stronger stand than the one he took against the regulation of safety design. He spent weeks in Washington calling on members of Congress, holding press conferences and recruiting business cronies like W. B. Murphy of Campbell's Soup to join the anti-regulation battle. Displaying the sophistication for which today's American corporate leaders will be remembered, Murphy publicly called auto safety "a hula hoop, a fad that will pass." He was speaking to a special luncheon of the Business Council, an organization of 100 chief executives who gather periodically in Washington to provide "advice" and "counsel" to government. The target of their wrath in this instance was the Motor Vehicle Safety Bills introduced in both houses of Congress, largely in response to Ralph Nader's *Unsafe at Any Speed*.

By 1965, most pundits and lobbyists saw the handwriting on the wall and prepared to accept government "meddling" in the last bastion of free enterprise. Not Henry. With bulldog tenacity, he held out for defeat of the legislation to the very end, loyal to his grandfather's invention and to the company that makes it. But the Safety Act passed the House and Senate unanimously, and was signed into law by Lyndon Johnson in 1966.

While lobbying for and against legislation is pretty much a process of high-level back-slapping, press-conferencing and speech-making, fighting a regulatory agency is a much subtler matter. Henry headed home to lick his wounds in Grosse Pointe, Michigan, and a planeload of the Ford Motor Company's best brains flew to Washington to start the "education" of the new federal auto safety bureaucrats.

Their job was to implant the official industry ideology in the minds of the new officials regulating auto safety. Briefly summarized, that ideology states that auto accidents are caused not by *cars*, but by 1) people and 2) highway conditions.

This philosophy is rather like blaming a robbery on the victim. Well, what did you expect? You were carrying money, weren't you? It is an extraordinary experience to hear automotive "safety engineers" talk for hours without ever mentioning cars. They will advocate spending billions educating youngsters, punishing drunks and redesigning street signs. Listening to them, you can momentarily begin to think that it is easier to control 100 million drivers than a handful of manufacturers. They show movies about guardrail design and advocate the clear-cutting of trees 100 feet back from every highway in the nation. If a car is unsafe, they argue, it is because its owner doesn't properly drive it. Or, perhaps, maintain it.

In light of an annual death rate approaching 50,000, they are forced to admit that driving is hazardous. But the car is, in the words of Arjay Miller, "the safest link in the safety chain."

Before the Ford experts left Washington to return to drafting tables in Dearborn they did one other thing. They managed to informally reach an agreement with the major public servants who would be making auto safety decisions. This agreement was that "cost-benefit" would be an acceptable mode of analysis by Detroit and its new regulators. And as we shall see, cost-benefit analysis quickly became the basis of Ford's argument against safer car design.

* * *

Cost-benefit analysis was used only occasionally in government until President Kennedy appointed Ford Motor Company President Robert McNamara to be Secretary of Defense. McNamara, originally an accountant, preached cost benefit with all the force of a Biblical zealot. Stated in its simplest terms, cost-benefit analysis says that if the cost is greater than the benefit, the project is not worth it—no matter what the benefit. Examine the cost of every action, decision, contract, part, or change, the doctrine says, then carefully evaluate the benefits (in dollars) to be certain that they exceed the cost before you begin a program or—and this is the crucial part for our story—pass a regulation.

As a management tool in a business in which profits matter over everything else, cost-benefit analysis makes a certain amount of sense. Serious problems come, however, when public officials who ought to have more than corporate profits at heart apply cost-benefit analysis to every conceivable decision. The inevitable result is that they must place a dollar value on human life.

Ever wonder what your life is worth in dollars? Perhaps $10 million? Ford has a better idea: $200,000.

Remember, Ford had gotten the federal regulators to agree to talk auto safety in terms of cost-benefit analysis. But in order to be able to argue that various safety costs were greater than their benefits, Ford needed to have a dollar value figure for the "benefit." Rather than be so uncouth as to come up with such a price tag itself, the auto industry pressured the National Highway Traffic Safety Administration to do so. And in a 1972 report the agency decided a human life was worth $200,725. (For its reasoning, see [Table 1].) Inflationary forces have recently pushed the figure up to $278,000.

Furnished with this useful tool, Ford immediately went to work using it to prove why various safety improvements were too expensive to make.

Nowhere did the company argue harder that it should make no changes than in the area of rupture-prone fuel tanks. Not long after the government arrived at the $200,725-per-life figure, it surfaced, rounded off to a cleaner $200,000, in an internal Ford memorandum. This cost-benefit analysis argued that Ford should not make an $11-per-car improvement that would prevent 180 fiery deaths a year. (This minor change would have prevented gas tanks from breaking so easily both in rear-end collisions, like Sandra Gillespie's, and in rollover accidents, where the same thing tends to happen.)

Ford's cost-benefit table [Table 2] is buried in a seven-page company memorandum entitled "Fatalities Associated with Crash-Induced Fuel Leakage and Fires." The memo argues that there is no financial benefit in complying with proposed safety standards that would admittedly result in fewer auto fires, fewer burn deaths and fewer burn injuries. Naturally, memoranda that speak so casually of "burn deaths" and "burn injuries" are not released to the public. They are very effective, however, with Department of

Table 1

What's Your Life Worth? Societal Cost Components for Fatalities, 1972 NHTSA Study

Component	1971 Costs
Future productivity losses	
Direct	$132,000
Indirect	41,300
Medical costs	
Hospital	700
Other	425
Property damage	1,500
Insurance administration	4,700
Legal and court	3,000
Employer losses	1,000
Victim's pain and suffering	10,000
Funeral	900
Assets (lost consumption)	5,000
Miscellaneous accident cost	200

Total per fatality: $200,725

Here is a chart from a federal study showing how the National Highway Traffic Safety Administration has calculated the value of a human life. The estimate was arrived at under pressure from the auto industry. The Ford Motor Company has used it in cost-benefit analyses arguing why certain safety measures are not "worth" the savings in human lives. The calculation above is a breakdown of the estimated cost to society every time someone is killed in a car accident. We were not able to find anyone, either in the government or at Ford, who could explain how the $10,000 figure for "pain and suffering" had been arrived at.

Transportation officials indoctrinated in McNamarian cost-benefit analysis.

All Ford had to do was convince men like John Volpe, Claude Brinegar and William Coleman (successive Secretaries of Transportation during the Nixon-Ford years) that certain safety standards would add so much to the price of cars that fewer people would buy them. This could damage the auto industry, which was still believed to be the bulwark of the American economy. "Compliance to these standards," Henry Ford II prophesied at more than one press conference, "will shut down the industry."

The Nixon Transportation Secretaries were the kind of regulatory officials big business dreams of. They understood and loved capitalism and thought like businessmen. Yet, best of all, they came into office uninformed on technical automotive matters. And you could talk "burn injuries" and "burn deaths" with these guys, and they didn't seem to envision children crying at funerals and people hiding in their homes with melted faces. Their minds appeared to have leapt right to the bottom line—more safety meant higher prices, higher prices meant lower sales and lower sales meant lower profits.

So when J. C. Echold, Director of Automotive Safety (which means chief anti-safety lobbyist) for Ford wrote to the Department of Transportation—which he still does frequently, at great length—he felt secure attaching a memorandum that in effect says it is acceptable to kill 180 people and burn another 180 every

Table 2

$11 vs. a Burn Death: Benefits and Costs Relating to Fuel Leakage Associated With the Static Rollover Test Portion of FMVSS 208

Benefits

Savings: 180 burn deaths, 180 serious burn injuries, 2,100 burned vehicles.
Unit cost: $200,000 per death, $67,000 per injury, $700 per vehicle.
Total benefit: 180 × ($200,000) + 180 × ($67,000) + 2,100 × ($700) = $49.5 million.

Costs

Sales: 11 million cars, 1.5 million light trucks.
Unit cost: $11 per car, $11 per truck.
Total cost: 11,000,000 × ($11) + 1,500,000 × ($11) = $137 million.

From Ford Motor Company internal memorandum: "Fatalities Associated with Crash-Induced Fuel Leakage and Fires."

---

year, *even though we have the technology that could save their lives for $11 a car.*

Furthermore, Echold attached this memo, confident, evidently, that the Secretary would question neither his low death/injury statistics nor his high cost estimates. But it turns out, on closer examination, that both these findings were misleading.

First, note that Ford's table shows an equal number of burn deaths and burn injuries. This is false. All independent experts estimate that for each person who dies by an auto fire, many more are left with charred hands, faces and limbs. Andrew McGuire of the Northern California Burn Center estimates the ratio of burn injuries to deaths at ten to one instead of the one to one Ford shows here. Even though Ford values a burn at only a piddling $67,000 instead of the $200,000 price of life, the true ratio obviously throws the company's calculations way off.

The other side of the equation, the alleged $11 cost of a fire-prevention device, is also a misleading estimation. One document that was *not* sent to Washington by Ford was a "Confidential" cost analysis *Mother Jones* has managed to obtain, showing that crash fires could be largely prevented for considerably *less* than $11 a car. The cheapest method involves placing a heavy rubber bladder inside the gas tank to keep the fuel from spilling if the tank ruptures. Goodyear had developed the bladder and had demonstrated it to the automotive industry. We have in our possession crash-test reports showing that the Goodyear bladder worked well. On December 2, 1970 (*two years before* Echold sent his cost-benefit memo to Washington), Ford Motor Company ran a rear-end crash test on a car with the rubber bladder in the gas tank. The tank ruptured, but no fuel leaked. On January 15, 1971, Ford again tested the bladder and again it worked. The total purchase and installation cost of the bladder would have been $5.08 per car. That $5.08 could have saved the lives of Sandra Gillespie and several hundred others.

* * *

When a federal regulatory agency like the National Highway Traffic Safety Administration (NHTSA) decides to issue a new standard, the law usually requires it to invite all interested parties to respond before the standard is enforced—a reasonable enough custom on the surface. However, the auto industry has taken advantage of this process and has used it to delay lifesaving emission and safety standards for years. In the case of the standard that would have corrected that fragile Pinto fuel tank, the delay was for an incredible eight years.

The particular regulation involved here was Federal Motor Vehicle Safety Standard 301. Ford picked portions of Standard 301 for strong opposition back in 1968 when the Pinto was still in the blueprint stage. The intent of 301, and the 300 series that followed it, was to protect drivers and passengers *after* a crash occurs. Without question the worst postcrash hazard is fire. So Standard 301 originally proposed that all cars should be able to withstand a fixed barrier impact of 20 mph (that is, running into a wall at that speed) without losing fuel.

When the standard was proposed, Ford engineers pulled their crash-test results out of their files. The front ends of most cars were no problem—with minor alterations they could stand the impact without losing fuel. "We were already working on the front end," Ford engineer Dick Kimble admitted. "We knew we could meet the test on the front end." But with the Pinto particularly, a 20-mph rear-end standard meant redesigning the entire rear end of the car. With the Pinto scheduled for production in August of 1970, and with $200 million worth of tools in place, adoption of this standard would have created a minor financial disaster. So Standard 301 was targeted for delay, and, with some assistance from its industry associates, Ford succeeded beyond its

wildest expectations: the standard was not adopted until the 1977 model year. Here is how it happened:

There are several main techniques in the art of combating a government safety standard: a) make your arguments in succession, so the feds can be working on disproving only one at a time; b) claim that the real problem is not X but Y (we already saw one instance of this in "the problem is not cars but people"); c) no matter how ridiculous each argument is, accompany it with thousands of pages of highly technical assertions it will take the government months or, preferably, years to test. Ford's large and active Washington office brought these techniques to new heights and became the envy of the lobbyists' trade.

The Ford people started arguing against Standard 301 way back in 1968 with a strong attack of technique b). Fire, they said, was not the real problem. Sure, cars catch fire and people burn occasionally. But statistically auto fires are such a minor problem that NHTSA should really concern itself with other matters.

Strange as it may seem, the Department of Transportation (NHTSA's parent agency) didn't know whether or not this was true. So it contracted with several independent research groups to study auto fires. The studies took months which was just what Ford wanted.

The completed studies, however, showed auto fires to be more of a problem than Transportation officials ever dreamed of. Robert Nathan and Associates, a Washington research firm, found that 400,000 cars were burning up every year, burning more than 3,000 people to death. Furthermore, auto fires were increasing five times as fast as building fires. Another study showed that 35 per cent of all fire deaths in the U.S. occurred in automobiles. Forty per cent of all fire department calls in the 1960s were to vehicle fires—a public cost of $350 million a year, a figure that, incidentally, never shows up in cost-benefit analyses.

Another study was done by the Highway Traffic Research Institute in Ann Arbor, Michigan, a safety think-tank funded primarily by the auto industry (the giveaway there is the words "highway traffic" rather than "automobile" in the group's name). It concluded that 40 per cent of the lives lost in fuel-fed fires could be saved if the manufacturers complied with proposed Standard 301. Finally, a third report was prepared for NHTSA by consultant Eugene Trisko entitled "A National Survey of Motor Vehicle Fires." His report indicates that the Ford Motor Company makes 24 per cent of the cars on the American road, yet these cars account for 42 per cent of the collision-ruptured fuel tanks.

Ford lobbyists then used technique a) —bringing up a new argument. Their line then became: yes, perhaps burn accidents do happen, but rear-end collisions are relatively rare (note the echo of technique b) here as well). Thus Standard 301 was not needed. This set the NHTSA off on a new round of analyzing accident reports. The government's findings finally were that rear-end collisions were seven and a half times more likely to result in fuel spills than were front-end collisions. So much for that argument.

By now it was 1972; NHTSA had been researching and analyzing for four years to answer Ford's objections. During that time, nearly 9,000 people burned to death in flaming wrecks. Tens of thousands more were badly burned and scarred for life. And the four-year delay meant that well over 10 million new unsafe vehicles went on the road, vehicles that will be crashing, leaking fuel and incinerating people well into the 1980s.

Ford now had to enter its third round of battling the new regulations. On the "the problem is not X but Y" principle, the company had to look around for something new to get itself off the hook. One might have thought that, faced with all the latest statistics on the horrifying number of deaths in flaming accidents, Ford would find the task difficult. But the company's rhetoric was brilliant. The problem was not burns, but... impact! Most of the people killed in these fiery accidents, claimed Ford, would have died whether the car burned or not. They were killed by the kinetic force of the impact, not the fire.

And so once again, as in some giant underwater tennis game, the ball bounced into the government's court and the absurdly pro-industry NHTSA began another slow-motion response. Once again it began a time-consuming round of test crashes and embarked on a study of accidents. The latter, however, revealed that a large and growing number of corpses taken from burned cars involved in rear-end crashes contained no cuts, bruises or broken bones. They clearly would have survived the accident unharmed if the cars had not caught fire. This pattern was confirmed in careful rear-end crash tests performed by the Insurance Institute for Highway Safety. A University of Miami study found an inordinate number of Pintos burning on rear-end impact and concluded that this demonstrated "a clear and present hazard to all Pinto owners."

Pressure on NHTSA from Ralph Nader and consumer groups began mounting. The industry-agency collusion was so obvious that Senator Joseph Montoya (D-N.M.) introduced legislation about Standard 301. NHTSA waffled some more and again announced its intentions to promulgate a rear-end collision standard.

Waiting, as it normally does, until the last day allowed for response, Ford filed with NHTSA a gargantuan batch of letters, studies and charts now arguing that the federal testing criteria were unfair. Ford also argued that design changes required to meet the standard would take 43 months, which seemed like a rather long time in light of the fact that the entire Pinto was designed in about two years. Specifically, new complaints about the standard involved the weight of the test vehicle, whether or not the brakes should be engaged at the moment of impact and the claim that the standard should only apply to cars, not trucks or buses. Perhaps the most amusing argument was that the engine should not be idling during crash tests, the rationale being that an idling engine meant that the gas tank had to contain gasoline and that the hot lights needed to film the crash might ignite the gasoline and cause a fire.

Some of these complaints were accepted, others rejected. But they all required examination and testing by a weak-kneed NHTSA, meaning more of those 18-month studies the industry loves so much. So the complaints served their real purpose—delay; all told, an eight-year delay, while Ford manufactured more than three million profitable, dangerously incendiary Pintos. To justify this delay, Henry Ford II called more press conferences to predict the demise of American civilization. "If we can't meet the standards when they are published," he warned, "we will have to close down. And if we have to close down some production because we don't meet standards we're in for real trouble in this country."

* * *

While government bureaucrats dragged their feet on lifesaving Standard 301, a different kind of expert was taking a close look at the Pinto—the "recon man." "Recon" stands for reconstruction; recon men reconstruct accidents for police departments, insurance companies and lawyers who want to know exactly who or what caused an accident. It didn't take many rear-end Pinto accidents to demonstrate the weakness of the car. Recon men began encouraging lawyers to look beyond one driver or another to the manufacturer in their search for fault, particularly in the growing number of accidents where passengers were uninjured by collision but were badly burned by fire.

Pinto lawuits began mounting fast against Ford. Says John Versace, executive safety engineer at Ford's Safety Research Center, "Ulcers are running pretty high among the engineers who worked on the Pinto. Every lawyer in the country seems to want to take their depositions." (The Safety Research Center is an impressive glass and concrete building standing by itself about a mile from Ford World Headquarters in Dearborn. Looking at it, one imagines its large staff protects consumers from burned and broken limbs. Not so. The Center is the technical support arm of Jack Echold's 14-person anti-regulatory lobbying team in World Headquarters.)

When the Pinto liability suits began, Ford strategy was to go to a jury. Confident it could hide the Pinto crash tests, Ford thought that juries of solid American registered voters would buy the industry doctrine that drivers, not cars, cause accidents. It didn't work. It seems that juries are much quicker to see the truth than bureaucracies, a fact that gives one confidence in democracy. Juries began ruling against the company, granting million-dollar awards to plaintiffs.

"We'll never go to a jury again," says Al Slechter in Ford's Washington office. "Not in a fire case. Juries are just too sentimental. They see those charred remains and forget the evidence. No sir, we'll settle."

Settlement involves less cash, smaller legal fees and less publicity, but it is an indication of the weakness of their case. Nevertheless, Ford has been settling when it is clear that the company can't pin the blame on the driver of the other car. But, since the company carries $2 million deductible product-liability insurance, these settlements have a direct impact on the bottom line. They must therefore be considered a factor in determining the net operating profit on the Pinto. It's impossible to get a straight answer from Ford on the profitability of the Pinto and the impact of lawsuit settlements on it —even when you have a curious and mildly irate shareholder call to inquire, as we did. However, financial officer Charles Matthews did admit that the company establishes a reserve for large dollar settlements. He would not divulge the amount of the reserve and had no explanation for its absence from the annual report.

Until recently, it was clear that, whatever the cost of these settlements, it was not enough to seriously cut into the Pinto's enormous profits. The cost of retooling Pinto assembly lines and of equipping each car with a safety gadget like that $5.08 Goodyear bladder was, company accountants calculated, greater than that of paying out millions to survivors like Robbie Carlton or to wid-

ows and widowers of victims like Sandra Gillespie. The bottom line ruled, and inflammable Pintos kept rolling out of the factories.

In 1977, however, an incredibly sluggish government has at last instituted Standard 301. Now Pintos will have to have rupture-proof gas tanks. Or will they?

* * *

To everyone's surprise, the 1977 Pinto recently passed a rear-end crash test in Phoenix, Arizona, for NHTSA. The agency was so convinced the Pinto would fail that it was the first car tested. Amazingly, it did not burst into flame.

"We have had so many Ford failures in the past," explained agency engineer Tom Grubbs, "I felt sure the Pinto would fail."

How did it pass?

Remember that one-dollar, one-pound plastic baffle that was on one of the three modified Pintos that passed the pre-production crash tests nearly ten years ago? Well, it is a standard feature on the 1977 Pinto. In the Phoenix test it protected the gas tank from being perforated by those four bolts on the differential housing.

We asked Grubbs if he noticed any other substantial alterations in the rear-end structure of the car. "No," he replied, "the [plastic baffle] seems to be the only noticeable change over the 1976 model."

But was it? What Tom Grubbs and the Department of Transportation didn't know when they tested the car was that it was manufactured in St. Thomas, Ontario. Ontario? The significance of that becomes clear when you learn that Canada has for years had extremely strict rear-end collision standards.

Tom Irwin is the business manager of Charlie Rossi Ford, the Scottsdale, Arizona, dealership that sold the Pinto to Tom Grubbs. He refused to explain why he was selling Fords made in Canada when there is a huge Pinto assembly plant much closer by in California. "I know why you're asking that question, and I'm not going to answer it," he blurted out. "You'll have to ask the company."

But Ford's regional office in Phoenix has "no explanation" for the presence of Canadian cars in their local dealerships. Farther up the line in Dearborn, Ford people claim there is absolutely no difference between American and Canadian Pintos. They say cars are shipped back and forth across the border as a matter of course. But they were hard pressed to explain why some Canadian Pintos were shipped all the way to Scottsdale, Arizona. Significantly, one engineer at the St. Thomas plant did admit that the existence of strict rear-end collision standards in Canada "might encourage us to pay a little more attention to quality control on that part of the car."

The Department of Transportation is considering buying an American Pinto and running the test again. For now, it will only say that the situation is under investigation.

* * *

Whether the new American Pinto fails or passes the test, Standard 301 will never force the company to test or recall the more than two million pre-1977 Pintos still on the highway. Seventy or more people will burn to death in those cars every year for many years to come. If the past is any indication, Ford will continue to accept the deaths.

According to safety expert Byron Bloch, the older cars could quite easily be retrofitted with gas tanks containing fuel cells. "These improved tanks would add at least 10 mph improved safety performance to the rear end," he estimated, "but it would cost Ford $20 to $30 a car, so they won't do it unless they are forced to." Dr. Kenneth Saczalski, safety engineer with the Office of Naval Research in Washington, agrees. "The Defense Department has developed virtually fail-safe fuel systems and retrofitted them into existing vehicles. We have shown them to the auto industry and they have ignored them."

Unfortunately, the Pinto is not an isolated case of corporate malpractice in the auto industry. Neither is Ford a lone sinner. There probably isn't a car on the road without a safety hazard known to its manufacturer. And though Ford may have the best auto lobbyists in Washington, it is not alone. The anti-emission control lobby and the anti-safety lobby usually work in chorus form, presenting a well-harmonized message from the country's richest industry, spoken through the voices of individual companies—the Motor Vehicle Manufacturers Association, the Business Council and the U.S. Chamber of Commerce.

Furthermore, cost-valuing human life is not used by Ford alone. Ford was just the only company careless enough to let such an embarrassing calculation slip into the public records. The process of willfully trading lives for profits is built into corporate capitalism. Commodore Vanderbilt publicly scorned George Westinghouse and his "foolish" air brakes while people died by the hundreds in accidents on Vanderbilt's railroads.

The original draft of the Motor Vehicle Safety Act provided for criminal sanction against a manufacturer who willfully placed an unsafe car on the market. Early in the proceedings the auto industry lobbied the provision out of the bill. Since then, there have been those damage settlements, of course, but the only government punishment meted out to auto companies for non-compliance to standards has been a minuscule fine, usually $5,000 to $10,000. One wonders how long the Ford Motor Company would continue to market lethal cars were Henry Ford II and Lee Iacocca serving 20-year terms in Leavenworth for consumer homicide.

NO

Ford Motor Company

CLOSING ARGUMENT BY MR. NEAL

If it please the Court, Counsel, ladies and gentlemen:

Not too many years ago our broad American Industry straddled the world like a giant.

It provided us with the highest standards of living ever known to man.

It was ended, eliminated, no more. Now it is an Industry weakened by deteriorating plants and equipment, weakened by lack of products, weakened by lack of manpower, weakened by inadequate capital, weakened by massive Government controls, weakened by demands on foreign oil and reeling from competition from foreign manufacturers.

I stand here today to defend a segment of that tattered Industry.

One company that saw the influx of foreign, small-made cars in 1967 and '68 and tried to do something about it, tried to build a small car with American labor that would compete with foreign imports, that would keep Americans employed, that would keep American money in America.

As State's witness, Mr. Copp, admitted, Ford Motor Company would have made more profit sticking to the bigger cars where the profit is.

That would have been the easiest way.

It was not the way Ford Motor Company took.

It made the Ford to compete. And this is no easy effort, members of the jury.

As even Mr. Copp admitted, the Automobile Industry is extremely regulated.

It has to comply with the Clean Air Act, the Safety Act, the Emissions Control Act, the Corporate Average Fuel Economy Act, the Safety Act, and OSHA as well as a myriad of Statutes and Regulations applicable to large and small businesses generally, and, again, as Mr. Copp admitted, it now takes twice as many Engineers to make a car as it did before all the massive Government controls.

Nevertheless, Ford Motor Company undertook the effort to build a sub-compact, to take on the imports, to save jobs for Americans and to make a profit for its stockholders.

This rather admirable effort has a sad ending.

From U.S. District Court, South Bend, Indiana, *State of Indiana v. Ford Motor Company* (January 15, 1980).

On August 10, 1978, a young man gets into a van weighing over 4,000 pounds and heads towards Elkhart, Indiana, on a bad highway called "U.S. 33."

He has a couple of open beer bottles in his van, together with his marijuana which he may or may not have been smoking. . . .

As he was cruising along on an open stretch of highway in broad daylight at at least 50 to 55 miles per hour, he drops his "smoke," ignores his driving and the road, and fails to see a little Pinto with its emergency flashers on stopped on the highway ahead.

He plows into the rear of the Pinto with enormous force and three young girls are killed.

Not the young man, but Ford Motor Company is charged with reckless homicide and arraigned before you.

I stand here to defend Ford Motor Company, and to tell you that we are not killers. . . .

Mr. Cosentino gave you the definition of "reckless homicide" as "plain, conscious and unjustifiable disregard of harm, which conduct involves substantial deviation from acceptable standards of conduct."

This case and the elements of this case, strictly speaking, involve 40 days, July 1, 1978 to August 10, 1978, and the issue is whether, during that period of time, Ford Motor Company recklessly, as that term is defined, omitted to warn of a danger and repair, and that reckless omission caused the deaths involved. . . .

[I]n my opening statement, I asked you to remember nine points, and I asked you to judge me, my client, by how well or how poorly we supported those nine points.

Let me run through briefly and just tick them off, the nine points, with you, and then let me get down to discussing the evidence and record with respect to those nine points.

One, I said this was a badly-designed highway, with curbs so high the girls couldn't get off when they had to stop their car in an emergency.

Two, I said that the girls stopped there with their emergency flashers on, and this boy in a van weighing more than 4,000 pounds, with his eyes off the road, looking down trying to find the "smoke," rammed into the rear of that Pinto at at least 50 miles an hour, closing speed.

And by "closing speed," I mean the differential speed.

That is Points 1 and 2.

Point 3, I said the 1973 Pinto met every fuel-system integrity standard of any Federal, State or Local Government.

Point No. 4, I said, Ford Motor Company adopted a mandatory standard dealing with fuel-system integrity on rear-impact of 20 miles per hour moving-barrier, 4,000 pound moving-barrier, and I said that no other manufacturer in the world had adopted any standard, only Ford Motor Company.

Five, I said that the Pinto, it is not comparable to a Lincoln Continental, a Cadillac, a Mercedes Benz or that Ascona, or whatever that exotic car was that Mr. Bloch called—but I did say No. 5, it is comparable to other 1973 subcompacts.

No. 6, I said that . . . we would bring in the Engineers who designed and manufactured the Pinto, and I brought them from the stand, and they would tell you that they thought the Pinto was a good, safe car, and they bought it for themselves, their wives and their children to drive.

No. 7, I told you that we would bring in the statistics that indicated to us as to our state of mind that the Pinto performed as well or better than other subcompacts.

And, No. 8, I said we would nevertheless tell you that we decided to recall the Pinto in June of 1978, and having made that decision for the reasons that I—that I told you I would explain, we did everything in our power to recall that Pinto as quickly as possible, that there was nothing we could have done between July 1, 1978 and 8-10-1978, to recall the Pinto any faster.

And finally, No. 9, I said we would demonstrate that any car, any subcompact, any small car, and even some larger cars, sitting out there on Highway 33 in the late afternoon of August 10, 1978 and watching that van roar down that highway with the boy looking for his "smoke" —any car would have suffered the same consequences.

Those are the nine points I ask you to judge me by, and let me touch on the evidence, now, with respect to those nine points....

The van driver, Duggar, took his eyes off the road and off driving to look around the floor of the van for a "smoke."

Duggar had two open beer bottles in the car and a quantity of marijuana.

Duggar was not prosecuted for reckless homicide or for possession of marijuana, even though his prior record of conviction was:

November, '73, failure to yield right-of-way;

April, '76, speeding 65 miles an hour in a 45 mile an hour zone;

July, '76, running stop sign;

June, '77, speeding 45 in a 25 zone;

August, '77, driver's license suspended;

September, '77, driving with suspended license;

December, '77, license suspended again.

Mr. Cosentino, you got up in front of this jury and you cried.

Well, I cry, too, because Mr. Duggar is driving, and you didn't do anything about him with a record like that except say, "Come in and help me convict Ford Motor Company, and I will help you get probation."

We all cry.

But crying doesn't do any good, and it doesn't help this jury.

The big disputed fact in this case regarding the accident, ladies and gentlemen, is the closing speed. The differential speed, the difference between the speed the Pinto was going, if any, and the speed the van was going.

That is the big disputed fact in regard to this accident.

And whether the Pinto was stopped or not is relevant only as it affects closing speed....

Mr. Duggar testified—I guess he is great about speed, because while he's looking down there for his "smoke," he knows he is going 50 miles per hour in the van.

But he said he was going 50 miles per hour at the time of impact, and he said the Pinto was going 15.

But here is the same man who admits he was going at least 50 miles per hour and looking around down "on a clear day," trying to find the "smoke" and looked up only to see the Pinto ten feet ahead of him.

Here is a witness willing to say under oath that the Pinto was going 15 miles per hour, even though he had one-sixth of a second—one-sixth of a second to make the judgment on the speed.

Here is a witness who says he had the time to calculate the speed of the Pinto but had no time even to try to apply brakes because there were no skid marks.

And here is a witness who told Dr. Galen Miller, who testified here, that—told him right after the accident that in fact the Pinto was stopped.

And here was a witness who made a deal with the State.

And here was a witness who's not prosecuted for recklessness.

And here is a witness who is not prosecuted for possession of marijuana.

So the State's proof from Mr. Alfred Clark through Mr. Duggar is kind of a smorgasbord or a buffet—you can go in and take your choice.

You can pick 15—5 miles per hour, if you want to as to differential speed, or you can take 35 miles per hour.

And the State, with the burden of proof says, "Here," "Here," "Here. I will give you a lot of choice."

"You want choices? I will give you choices. Here. Take 5. Take 15. 10, 15, 20, 25, 30, 35."

Because, ladies and gentlemen of the jury,—and I'm sure you are—the alternatives the State offers you are closing speeds of anywhere from 5 miles —on the low side—to 35 miles on the high side as a differential speed in this accident....

Mr. Toms, the former National Highway Traffic Safety Administrator, told you that in his opinion the 20 mile per hour rear-impact moving-barrier was a reasonable and acceptable standard of conduct for 1973 vehicles.

Why didn't Ford adopt a higher standard?

Mr. MacDonald, a man even Mr. Copp —do you remember this? Mr. MacDonald sitting on the stand, the father of the Pinto, as Mr. Cosentino called him—and he didn't deny it.

He says, "Yes, it is my car."

Mr. MacDonald, a man even Mr. Copp —on cross examination I asked him, I said:

"Q Mr. Copp, isn't it a fact that you consider Harold MacDonald an extremely safety-conscious Engineer?"

And he said:

"A Yes, sir."

Mr. MacDonald, that extremely safety-conscious Engineer, told you he did not believe a higher standard could be met for 1973 cars without greater problems, such as handling, where more accidents and death occur.

Mr. Copp, let's take the State's witness, Copp.

Mr. Copp admitted that even today, seven years later, the Federal Government Standard is only 30 miles per hour, 10 miles higher than what Ford adopted —voluntarily adopted for itself for 1973.

And Mr. Copp further testified that a 30 mile an hour would be equivalent only to a 31.5 or 32 mile car-to-car.

So, ladies and gentlemen of the jury, Mr. Cosentino tells you about, "Oh, isn't it terrible to put these cars out there, wasn't it awful—did you know?"

Well, do you know that today, the—today, 1980 model cars are required to meet only a 30 mile an hour rear-impact moving-barrier standard? 1980 cars.

And that that is equivalent to a 32 mile an hour car-to-car, and yet Ford Motor Company, the only company in the world, imposed upon itself a standard and made a car in 1973, seven years ago, that would meet 26 to 28 miles an hour, within 5, 6 or 7 miles of what the cars are required by law to meet today.

Mr. Cosentino will tell you, frankly, the cars today, in his judgment, are defective and he will prosecute.

What a chaos would evolve if the Government set the standard for automobiles and says, "That is reasonable," and then Local Prosecutors in the fifty states around the country start saying, "I am not satisfied, and I am going to prosecute the manufacturer."

Well, Mr. Cosentino may say that the standard should be 40.

The Prosecutor in Alabama may say, "No, it should be 50."

The Prosecutor in Alaska may say, "No, it should be 60."

And the Prosecutor in Tennessee—they say—you know, "I am satisifed—I am satisfied with 30," or, "I think it should be 70."

How can our companies survive?

Point 5, the 1973 Pinto was comparable in design and manufacture to other 1973 subcompacts.

I say again, ladies and gentlemen, we don't compare the Pinto with Lincolns, Cadillacs, Mercedes Benz—we ask you to compare the Pinto with the other three subcompacts.

Let's take the State's witnesses on this point first.

Mr. Bloch—Mr. Cosentino didn't mention Mr. Bloch, but I don't want him to be forgotten.

Mr. Bloch and Mr. Copp complain about the Pinto, and that is easy.

Let's descend to the particulars. Let's see what they really said.

Well, they complain about the metal, the gage of the metal in the fuel tank; you remember that?

And then on cross examination it was brought out that the general range of metal in fuel tanks ranged between twenty-three-thousandths of an inch and forty-thousandths of an inch.

That is the general range. Twenty-three-thousandths on the low to forty-thousandths on the high, and lo and behold, what is the gage of metal in the Pinto tank?

Thirty-five-thousandths.

And Mr. Bloch admits that it is in the upper third of the general range.

And they complain about the bumper on the Pinto.

And, remember, I said we would show that the Pinto was comparable to other '73 subcompacts.

They complain about the bumper, but then they admit on cross examination the Vega, the Gremlin, the Colt, the Pinto and the Toyota had about the same bumper.

And they complain of a lack of a protective shield between the tank and the axle, but they admitted on cross examination that no other 1973 car had such a shield, and Mr. Copp admits that there was no significant puncture in the 1973—in the Ulrich accident caused by the axle, and you remember I had him get up here and say, "Point out where this protective shield would have done something, where this puncture source we are talking about—" and you remember, it is so small—I can't find it now.

So much for the protective shield.

And then they complained about the insufficient rear structure in the Pinto, but they both admit that the Pinto had a left side rail hat section and that the Vega had none, nothing on either side, that the Pinto had shear plates, these plates in the trunk, and that neither the Vega, the Gremlin or the Colt or Toyota had any of these.

And the Vega used the coil-spring suspension, when the Pinto had a leaf-spring, and that was additional structure.

I am not going through all those—well, I will mention one more thing.

They talked about puncture sources, there is a puncture source there, puncture source here, but on cross examination, they end up by admitting that the puncture sources on all subcompacts have about the same—and in about the same space....

Mr. MacDonald testified, "Yes, I thought the Pinto was a reasonably safe car. I think the '73 Pinto is still a reasonably safe car, and I bought one, I drove it for years for myself."

Mr. Olsen—you remember little Mr. Frank Olsen?

He came in here, has his little eighteen-year-old daughter—he said, "I am an Engineer responsible for the Pinto. I think it is a safe car. I bought one for my little eighteen-year-old daughter, and she drove it for several years."

And Mr. Freers, the man who Mr. Cosentino objected to going over the fact that he was from Rose-Hullman, and on the Board of Trustees there—Mr. Freers said, "I like the Pinto. I am an Engineer responsible for the Pinto, and I bought a '73 Pinto for my young son and he drove it several years."

And then Mr. Feaheny says, "I am one of the Engineers responsible for the Pinto, and I bought one for my wife, the mother of my six children, and she drove it for several years."

Now, when Mr. Cosentino tried to say there was something phoney about that —he brought out their salaries.

And I—I don't know how to deal with the salary question.

It just seems to me to be so irrelevant, like some other things I am going to talk about in a minute that I am just going to simply say, "It is irrelevant," and go on.

But he said to these people—he suggested to you, suggested to these people, "Well, you make a lot of money, you can afford better than a Pinto."

Like, "You don't really mean you had a Pinto?"

And Mr. Feaheny says, "Yes, I could afford a more expensive car, but, you know, I—all of us, we have been fighting, we come out with something we thought would fight the imports, and we were proud of it, and our families were proud of it."

Do you think, ladies and gentlemen of the jury, that Mr. MacDonald was indifferent, reckless, when he bought and drove the Pinto?

He drives on the same roads, he has the —subject to the same reckless people that Mr. Cosentino didn't prosecute.

Do you think that Mr. Olsen was reckless and indifferent when he gave a Pinto to his eighteen-year-old daughter, a '73 Pinto?

Do you think that Mr. Freers was reckless when he gave one to his young son?...

Finally, ladies and gentlemen—not "finally," but Point No. 8: Notwithstanding all I have said, Ford Motor Company decided on June 8th, 1978, to recall the Pintos to improve fuel systems and did everything in its power to recall it as quickly as possible.

This is really what this case, I guess, is all about, because that period of time involved is July 1, 1978 until August 10, 1978.

And the Court will charge you, as I said, the elements are whether we recklessly failed to warn and repair during that period of time.

And whether that reckless omission, if any, caused the deaths.

And you may ask—and I think it is fair to ask—why recall the Pinto, the '73 Pinto, if it is comparable to other subcompacts, if statistics say it is performing as well as other '73 subcompacts?

And if Ford had a standard for '73 that no other manufacturer had?

And Feaheny and Mr. Misch told you why.

The Federal Government started an investigation. The publicity was hurting the Company.

They thought the Government was wrong, but they said, "You can't fight City Hall."

"We could fight and fight and we could go to Court and we could fight, but it's not going to get us anywhere. If we can improve it, let's do it and let's don't fight the Federal Government."

Maybe the Company should not have recalled the '73 Pinto.

Douglas Toms did not think, as he told you on the stand under oath, that the '73 Pinto should have been recalled.

He had information that the Pinto did as well as other cars;

That Pinto fire accidents equaled the total Pinto population or equaled the percentage of Pinto population to all car population.

And Mr. Bloch, on the other hand, says, "All of them should be recalled."

He said, "The Pinto should have been recalled."

He said, "The Vega should have been recalled."

He said, "The Gremlin should be recalled."

And he didn't know about the Dodge Colt.

Nevertheless, the Company did decide to recall the Pinto. And they issued widely-disseminated Press Releases on June 9, 1978.

It was in the newspapers, TV, radio, according to the proof in this case.

And thereafter the Government regulated what they did in the recall.

That is what Mr. Misch told you.

He said, "From the time we started —June 9, 1978—to August 10, Mr.—the Federal Government regulated what we did."

Now, Mr. Cosentino is prosecuting us.

And the Federal Government has regulated us.

Mr. Misch said, "The Federal Government reviewed what kind of Press Releases we should issue, what kind of Recall Letter we should issue, what kind of a Modification Kit that they would approve."

Even so—it is undisputed, absolutely undisputed that we did everything in our power to recall as fast as possible— nights, days, weekends.

And notwithstanding all of that, the first kit—the first complete kit was assembled August 1, 1978.

And on August 9, 1978, there were only 20,000 kits available for 1,600,000 cars.

And this was not Ford's fault. Ford was pushing the suppliers, the people who were outside the Company doing work for them.

And Mr. Vasher testified that he got the names of the current owners from R. L. Polk on July 17;

That the Ulrich name was not among them;

That he sent the Recall Letter in August to the original owner because he had no Ulrich name.

Now,—and he said he couldn't have gotten the Ulrich name by August 10.

Now, Mr. Cosentino said, "Well, the Ulrich Registration was on file with the State of Indiana and it is open to the public."

Well, Ford Motor Company doesn't know where these 1,600,000 cars are. It has to use R. L. Polk because they collect the information by the VIN Numbers.

If Ford Motor Company went to each state, they would go to fifty states and they would have each of the fifty states run through its files 1,600,000 VIN Numbers.

And Mr. Vasher, who is the expert in there, said it would take months and months to do that.

And, finally, ladies and gentlemen, the Government didn't approve the Modification Kit until August 15, 1978.

But the State says that we should have warned—we should have warned 1973 Pinto owners not to drive the car.

But the Government never suggested that.

Based on our information, and confirmed by the Toms testimony, our cars were performing as well—or better than—other '73 subcompacts.

As Mr. Misch so succinctly stated, "We would have been telling the Pinto owners to park their Pintos and get into another car no safer—and perhaps even less safe—than the Pinto."...

Well, we submit that the physical facts, the placement of the—the placement of the gasoline cap, where it is found, the testimony of Levi Woodard, and Nancy Fogo—demonstrate the closing speed in this case was at least 50 to 60 miles per hour.

Mr. Copp, the State's witness, testified that no small car made in America in 1973 would withstand 40 to 50 miles per hour—40 to 50 rear-impact. No small car made in America in 1973 would withstand a 40-plus mile per hour rear-impact.

The Dodge Colt would not have; the Vega could not have; the Gremlin would

not have; and certainly even the Toyota would not have.

Mr. Habberstad told you that no small car—and some big cars—would have withstood this crash.

And he established by the crash-tests you have seen that the Vega could not withstand 50;

That the Gremlin could not withstand 50;

That the Toyota Corolla with the tank over the axle could not withstand 50;

And that even a full-sized Chevrolet Impala cannot withstand 50 miles per hour.

If it made no difference what kind of car was out there, members of the jury, how can Ford Motor Company have caused the deaths? ...

I am not here to tell you that the 1973 Pinto was the strongest car ever built.

I'm not here to tell you it is equal to a Lincoln, a Cadillac, a Mercedes—that funny car that Mr. Bloch mentioned.

I'm not here to tell you a stronger car couldn't be built.

Most of us, however, learn early in life that there is "no Santa Claus," and, "There's no such thing as a free lunch."

If the public wanted it, and could pay for it, and we had the gasoline to drive it, Detroit could build a tank of a car—a car that would withstand practically anything, a car that would float if a careless driver drove it into the water.

A car that would be invulnerable even to the "Duggars" of the world.

But, members of the jury, only the rich could afford it and they would have to stop at every other gasoline station for a refill.

I am here to tell you that the 1973 Pinto is comparable to other '73 subcompacts, including that Toyota, that Corolla with the tank over the axle.

I am here to tell you it was not designed by some mysterious figure you have never seen.

It was designed and manufactured by Harold MacDonald, Frank Olsen and Howard Freers.

I am here to tell you these are the decent men doing an honorable job and trying to do a decent job.

I am here to tell you that Harold MacDonald, Frank Olsen, and Howard Freers are not reckless killers.

Harold MacDonald is the same man, State's witness, Copp, called an "extremely safety-conscious individual."

Frank Olsen is the same "Frank Olsen" Mr. Copp said was a "good Engineer."

And Howard Freers is the same "Howard Freers" Mr. Copp said was a "man of honesty and integrity."

I am here to tell you that these men honestly believe and honestly believed that the 1973 Pinto was—and is—a reasonably safe car—so safe they bought it for their daughters, sons and family.

Do you think that Frank Olsen believed he was acting in plain, conscious, unjustifiable disregard of harm?

When he bought a '73 Pinto for his eighteen-year-old daughter?

Or Howard Freers, when he bought one for his young son?

I am here to tell you that the design and manufacture of an automobile is not an easy task;

That it takes time to know whether a change in one part of the 14,000 parts of a car will or will not cause greater problems elsewhere in the car or its performance.

I am here to tell you that safety is a matter of degree;

That no one can say that a car that will meet a 26 to 28 mile per hour rear-impact is unsafe and one that will meet a 30 to 32 impact is safe.

I am here to tell you that if this country is to survive economically, it is really time to stop blaming Industry or Business, large or small, for our own sins.

I am here to tell you that no car is now or ever can be safe when reckless drivers are on the road.

I am here to tell you that Ford Motor Company may not be perfect, but it is not guilty of reckless homicide.

Thank you, members of the jury.

And God bless you in your deliberations.

POSTSCRIPT

Product Liability: Was Ford to Blame in the Pinto Case?

Was Ford guilty? The jury said no, but the larger issue remains: Who takes responsibility when many factors combine to bring about an injury?

Consider the following: Ford Motor Company obeyed the law, but the law may not have been all that it *should* have been. The reason for this is that the Ford Motor Company spent a great deal of money lobbying Congress to prevent the release of new and higher legal safety standards in order to be able to sell the Pinto for a lower price and thus increase its market share and its profits. Is the government, through its agencies, guilty for not fulfilling its role as protector of the consumer? What was the government's duty at this point? To protect those consumers of the automobile? To protect the workers in the Ford Motor Company factories? To protect the American manufacturers against encroachments from foreign competition? Does government have some absolute duty in these cases, or are legislators asked only to bring about the greatest good for the greatest number? How could they have done that in this case? Three girls are not very many. Could it be shown that all people who safely enjoyed their Pintos at the lower cost outweigh, in their happiness, the enormous unhappiness of the three dead girls and their families and friends?

Ford Motor Company found new structural allies when the criminal negligence case was brought against it. Under the U.S. Constitution, the legal system tends to protect the defendant in these cases. The tradition in the United States is to protect the rights of the individual against the interests of the community. In this case, the "individual" was one of the largest corporations in the world. However, legal traditions held true, and the rights of Ford were supported when the company was acquitted.

Manufacturers know how to make a safe car. They *could* build one like a tank and rig it to go no faster than 30 miles per hour, but very few people would buy it. So they make relatively unsafe cars that people will buy—lighter and faster, but more likely to crumple and burn in an accident. Is this trade-off acceptable to a nation that is used to making choices? Or should we be more diligent about eliminating threats to safety?

SUGGESTED READINGS

Lawrence A. Benningson and Arnold I. Benningson, "Product Liability: Manufacturers Beware!" *Harvard Business Review* (May–June 1974).

Richard T. DeGeorge, "Ethical Responsibilities of Engineers in Large Organizations: The Pinto Case," *Business and Professional Ethics Journal* (Fall 1981).

Richard A. Epstein, "Is Pinto a Criminal?" *Regulation* (March–April 1980).

Niles Howard and Susan Antilla, "What Price Safety? The 'Zero-Risk' Debate," *Dun's Review* (September 1979).

Alvin S. Weinstein et al., *Products Liability and the Reasonably Safe Product: A Guide for Management, Design and Marketing* (John Wiley, 1978).

ISSUE 15

Should Tobacco Advertising Be Banned?

YES: Mark Green, from "Luring Kids to Light Up," *Business and Society Review* (Spring 1990)

NO: John C. Luik, from "Tobacco Advertising Bans and the Dark Face of Government Paternalism," *International Journal of Advertising* (vol. 12, 1993)

ISSUE SUMMARY

YES: Mark Green, the commissioner of Consumer Affairs in New York City, attacks a popular cigarette advertising campaign that seems to be aimed directly at children and claims that such unconscionable methods of advertising should be prevented.

NO: Professor of philosophy John Luik argues that restricting the freedom of commercial speech cannot be justified unless it is shown to be absolutely necessary to avoid certain harm, which has not been done in the case of tobacco advertising.

The quarrel here is specifically about tobacco advertising. Some background on the product is necessary to understand the problem with marketing it.

First, there is a good amount of evidence that smoking tobacco is hazardous to one's health. Wherever tobacco is consumed, mortality and morbidity rates go up in direct proportion to the amount of tobacco consumed, especially when the tobacco is smoked. Smoking cigarettes is the most common form of tobacco use.

Second, curbing the tobacco industry is, economically, very serious business. It is a multibillion-dollar industry that employs tens of thousands. It builds and finances schools, churches, state governments, and regional economies. It was America's first export product, and it remains one of the best. The market for tobacco is still growing all over the world, and the export of tobacco might be one of the most hopeful ways to reduce the U.S. trade deficit.

Third, there is no compulsion to smoke cigarettes and lots of encouragement not to smoke them. Yet, people do choose to smoke all the same. Setting aside the claim that just being in the same room with a smoker can harm nonsmokers, people should have a right to make decisions about their own health. The issue, as John Luik sees it, is that banning tobacco advertising would represent an erosion of citizen autonomy, or the basic freedom of American people to make their own choices with respect to their own lives.

The dilemma here begins before the first ad hits the page: There is reason to believe that certain sorts of behavior are harmful to those who engage in them. In the normal exercise of the police power of the state, we could try to make sure that people do not indulge in that behavior, either by educating the people to avoid it, by quietly abolishing the purveyors of the means to engage in it, or both. But some people will not abstain, and the tobacco industry is too big and economically important to be shut down without a very clear consensus that it should be done.

In this situation, the proposal to ban the advertising of tobacco from all media (it has already been banned from radio and television) has certain attractions. First, to underscore Mark Green's point, it would end the exposure of young people to the traditional images of sophistication and worldliness that go with smoking. This would strengthen the claims of the tobacco industry that they are not trying to lure new smokers into the habit but are only trying to communicate product information to those who are already smokers. Since the major function of advertising is to persuade a nonuser to try the product once, there is no reason to advertise tobacco. If smokers wish to receive product information, they can sign up to receive it. It is not clear, however, that there is any sense in which smokers need such information.

On the positive side, banning advertising would leave the industry alone to make money abroad. There are signs that it will continue to do this well. At present, American cigarettes are being sold and promoted abroad; America is encouraging farmers in the Third World to grow tobacco and sending agronomists to teach them how to do it. There seems to be no problem with Third World receptivity: Farmers enjoy growing a high-income crop; governments enjoy the taxes collected both on cigarette sales and on the income from the tobacco crops; and the tobacco customers of the developing countries, a large and growing population, enjoy having available to them products of a higher quality than their indigenous industry could provide. Whether or not Americans have a right to take advantage of that receptivity for their own profit is another question—closely related to the question of taking advantage of that receptivity at home.

As you read the following selections, ask yourself what weight should be given to human freedom and what weight should be given to human welfare. In general, what is the responsibility of business in this dilemma? To serve customers what they want until the law tells it not to? Or to take a proactive stance and arrange business dealings so as to do the least harm and promote the most good for those affected by such dealings?

YES

Mark Green

LURING KIDS TO LIGHT UP

Earlier this year, Mark Green, the New York City Commissioner of Consumer Affairs, wrote the following letter to Louis V. Gerstner, Jr., the chairman and chief executive officer of RJR Nabisco. The letter appeals to the tobacco manufacturer to end its current Camel cigarette advertising campaign, which Green views as a thinly veiled attempt to lure children to start smoking.

As the father of two young children and the new Commissioner of Consumer Affairs, I am appalled at your "Smooth Character" Camel advertising campaign which risks addicting children to cigarettes.

I first noticed the prevalence and pitch of your ads in mid-January. On one day, I saw a Smooth Character poster when I bought a paper in the morning at the 86th Street and York Avenue newsstand, then another on the crosstown bus ("Un Tipo Suave," it read in Spanish), and yet another on the Lexington Avenue subway en route to work. Finally, later that day, I came across your huge, pull-out poster "suitable for framing" in *Rolling Stone*, along with language urging readers to send away for any of eight colorful posters. The posters involve cartoon characters such as your "Old Joe" camel and comely women, along with symbols one needn't be Freud to understand.

WHERE THERE'S SMOKE

However, it wasn't until I spotted the perforated fold at the bottom of the *Rolling Stone* poster, which allows readers to delete the congressionally mandated warning label, that I decided to write you to ask this question: Isn't this ad campaign an obvious attempt to lure children into smoking in violation of the tobacco industry's own 1964 code against advertising directed at children?

True, the *Rolling Stone* ad does say in extremely small print that a person sending in a coupon for posters is supposed to "certify that I am a smoker 21 years of age or older." On the other hand:

* Who puts posters up on their walls—kids or adults?

- Who watches and talks about cartoon characters—kids or adults?
- Who is impressionable enough to associate smoking with success and sex —kids or adults?
- Why do these advertisements run in magazines such as *Rolling Stone, National Lampoon,* and *Movies, U.S.A.,* which have so many teenage readers? (*Movies, U.S.A.* says its target is "a captive audience of one million moviegoers" who are, in its words, "youthful and image-conscious.")
- Was *Advertising Age* correct when it said on July 11, 1988, that "R. J. Reynolds is updating its Camel and Salem advertising to lure younger voters away from Marlboro country?"
- Why don't any of the posters one can order by mail have warning labels on them?

You know the adage that if something walks like a duck and quacks like a duck... it's a duck. Based on the most obvious circumstantial evidence, RJR's campaign is not a duck but a camel aimed directly at the health of our children. It was just such concerns that prompted the authors of *Barbarians at the Gate* to write of Theodore Forstmann, one of RJR's suitors, "Debating future demand in the teen market made him feel like a drug pusher."

Already, children in 1990 America live under multiple threats: One in five lives in poverty, the worst rate in the industrial West; more than a third in our city schools drop out before senior year; the United States has the highest rate of teenage pregnancy and one of the lowest investments in primary education among industrial nations; one-parent and no-parent families are on the rise, especially in minority areas. For those and other

reasons, New York City Mayor David Dinkins made the welfare of children his top priority in his Inaugural Address last month. And today, at my swearing-in, I followed suit and pledged to focus on children as consumers.

UNCONSCIONABLE CAMEL?

At the same time, tobacco is not just another product. It is the number-one preventable cause of death and disease in America and the only product that causes disease and death in its normal use. The Surgeon General estimates that smoking causes nearly 400,000 premature deaths annually—or fifty times more than those who die from drug abuse; the Federal Office on Smoking and Health concluded in 1987 that smoking contributed to 16 percent of all deaths (heart disease, lung cancer, emphysema, etc.), including more than 2,500 deaths of infants attributed to smoking by the mother. And, of course, smoking is a very powerful addiction, as much so as alcohol and drugs. Indeed, even after undergoing heart and lung surgery, half of all smokers still continue their habit.

Consequently, the goal of public officials concerned with already imperiled children must be to discourage them from smoking in the first place. Some 80 percent of all adults who smoke began before or during their teen years; 50 percent of all smokers first lit up by age 13, and 25 percent by 11. Smoking can also be a "gateway" to illegal drugs: "Virtually all children involved in hard drug use," concluded Sen. Edward Kennedy (D-Mass.), "began with cigarettes." So if we can keep our teenagers tobacco-free, they will live longer, healthier lives.

Which brings me back to your Smooth Character advertising campaign. I am writing you as my first official act because there are few if any marketplace abuses worse than inducing children to smoke, and RJR's ads appear to be inherently misleading, if not unconscionable.

They're potentially misleading because their images convey that smoking a Camel leads to social success and happiness, not to disease and death. And in our MTV era, many kids get more information from images than words. It is very hard to square your ads with the *Tobacco Industry's Principles Covering Cigarette Advertising and Sampling*'s provision that "Cigarette advertising shall not suggest that smoking is essential to social prominence, distinction, success, or sexual attraction."

The ads are potentially unconscionable because they appear to be targeted to unsophisticated minors who feel immortal and are uniquely subject to peer pressure—and who may, as a result, get addicted for life, a shortened life at that. For example, 35 percent of high school seniors don't think that smoking a pack a day causes serious harm. And while 95 percent of high school smokers believe they will later stop smoking, eight years later only 25 percent of them have.

INDUSTRY ARGUMENTS

In reviewing the literature in your industry, I find that tobacco spokespeople make at least four arguments to frustrate government actions designed to reduce these health hazards—namely, paternalism, censorship, preemption, and advertising.

Legislation to restrict or even ban cigarette advertising, for example, is attacked as "paternalism" and "censorship." Of course, the Latin origin of paternalism is "pater," meaning like a fa-

ther. But what's wrong with acting like a parent when government tries to protect children from harm?

As for censorship, there is no First Amendment right to sell or advertise a dangerous product, as four Supreme Court decisions over a half century make clear. Unlike political speech, commercial speech can be regulated, which is precisely what our consumer protection law does when it forbids false or misleading advertising. In any event, the worst censorship of all is a product that censors life itself.

Periodically, when local officials such as myself attempt to reduce this health hazard, industry holds up federal law as a bar. But the preemption clause that is cited applies to local attempts to add to the Federal Trade Commission's warning label, not to actions against, for example, misleading ads or unconscionable trade practices. Also, it's getting harder to maintain the fiction that warning labels on cigarette packs are sufficient disclosure when the FTC has twice described (in 1969 and 1981) the warning's "futility," when it doesn't even use provable words like "addiction," or "death," and when it is all but invisible on billboards, including your famous one in Times Square. Or, as satirist Calvin Trillin has written, "Anyone who wants to see that warning would have to have the sort of long-range vision usually associated with the pilot of an F-14."

Last, industry leaders argue that the $2.6–billion-plus spent on cigarette ads and other promotions—or $9 for every man, woman and child—doesn't persuade anyone to smoke. At best, it is said, these ads only influence a small percentage of existing smokers to switch among brands. Whether you personally believe this thesis or not, surely Madison Avenue doesn't.

Advertising experts agree that market expansion, especially for an industry that loses over 2 million consumers a year who die or quit, is an important objective of nearly all advertising. Emerson Foote, former chairman of McCann-Erickson, one of the world's largest advertising agencies, once remarked that "I am always amused by the suggestion that advertising, a function that has been shown to increase consumption of virtually every other product, somehow miraculously fails to work for tobacco products." Foote's view is seconded by advertising executive Charles Sharp, a former vice president of Ogilvy & Mather: "By depicting a product as an integral part of a highly desirable life-style and personal image, in addition to current users, an advertiser can attract individuals who do not currently use that product but who want to emulate that life-style [and] want to be like the people in the ads."

SIX QUESTIONS

Your industry finds itself in the ironic position of killing off your own consumers. A thousand times a day, or forty times an hour, there's a funeral and grieving because someone was addicted to smoking. If the public were told that a new product society could live without had killed forty people a year, there would be outrage and probably a legislative prohibition. Companies talking about their First Amendment right to sell such a product would be laughed out of court or Congress. Yet cigarettes kill not forty people a year but an hour.

A group of tobacco executives who have previously told us that smoking is not dangerous now tells us that

AD INDUSTRY FIDDLES WHILE AMERICA BURNS

There are nearly a dozen bills before Congress to restrict print advertising for tobacco products. As the pols in the smoke-free backrooms of Washington contemplate such legislation, not only the cigarette industry is worried.

The Leadership Council on Advertising, an advertising industry lobbying group, estimates that more than 4,000 jobs would be lost and 165 periodicals would fold if tobacco advertising were banned. This study, as reported in *Publishing News*, is "designed to diffuse some of the anti-tobacco din around the halls of Congress."

Of course, 4,000 jobs are about 1 percent of the number of people who die prematurely each year from diseases caused by smoking. And the study apparently does not account for the potential success of the legislation's goal: to reduce the number of smokers. If an ad ban were to work, people might live longer and, thus, buy and read more magazines. Up to 400,000 people is one heck of an untapped market.

$2.6 billion in advertising and promotion doesn't increase smoking and that cartoon posters that appeal to children weren't intended for children. Frankly, that insults our intelligence and injures the most vulnerable among us. And it makes my job as a parent that much harder.

Consequently, I'd like to solicit your responses to six questions, while preserving my options for possible future action. For if RJR now acts with the responsibility of, say, Johnson & Johnson during the Tylenol tragedy, it could yet find some common ground with concerned parents and avoid an outright ban on all advertising:

1. Since data proves that "the vast majority of new [smoking] recruits are children and teenagers," according to a health coalition including the American Cancer Society, do you still maintain that these Camel ads aren't intended for this very audience?
2. Isn't it inherently misleading to associate a disease-causing product such as smoking with attractive, healthy women?
3. Would you agree to immediately stop marketing all Smooth Character posters, especially since they lack federal warnings?
4. Would you agree to stop all Smooth Character ads on billboards within three months since viewers include children and since the warning label is essentially unreadable?
5. Would you agree to cease and desist your entire Smooth Character ad campaign by 1991, or before the 500th anniversary of Columbus' discovery of America *and* tobacco?
6. Would you consider supporting: (a) Rep. Henry Waxman's legislation allowing only informational cigarette ads without pictures (like securities ads); and (b) Sen. Edward Kennedy's bill, which encourages federally funded counteradvertising for undereducated cigarette consumers?

Mr. Gerstner, beyond any legal requirements, I am appealing to your demonstrated sense of civic obligation to avoid unnecessary disease and death. For prior to becoming chairman and CEO, you did serve on the National Cancer Advisory Board on Cancer Prevention and Early Detection, a body which urged America to evolve into a "tobacco-free" society by the year 2000. Given your personal sensitivity to this urgent topic, I hope RJR might now aspire to be a good corporate citizen and consider cooperative efforts to reduce the incidence of teenage smoking.

For kids' sake, I look forward to your prompt and favorable response.

NO
John C. Luik

TOBACCO ADVERTISING BANS AND THE DARK FACE OF GOVERNMENT PATERNALISM

The question is whether the State has the right through the elimination of all competing messages, to impose on its citizens its view and only its view of what is right in an attempt to mould their thoughts and behaviour?

—Justice Chabot

Liberty in a free and democratic society does not require the State to approve the personal decisions made by its citizens; it does, however, require the State to respect them.

—Justice Wilson

It is by now *de rigueur* amongst the right thinking to dismiss both the tobacco industry and its patrons as, at best moral myopics and at worst moral outlaws unworthy of consideration in civilized society. Thus the first reaction of many who read Canadian Judge Jean-Jude Chabot's decision affirming the right of tobacco companies to advertise their products will be to dismiss it as an idiosyncratic piece of dry legal argument emanating from a purely provincial court that completely fails to grasp the real dimension of the tobacco problem in contemporary society. However, to read Justice Chabot's judgement in such a fashion is to be profoundly unfair, for the decision deals with such crucial and central issues as the nature and value of freedom of expression, of autonomy, respect and rational public policy in a democratic society that go far beyond the question of the legitimacy of tobacco advertising bans. Though the Chabot decision is about such bans, it is equally about the State's right, both covertly and directly, to legislate not just a style of living but also a style of thinking.

The Chabot decision is admittedly complex and deals in part with issues that are relevant only to Canada. But the central part of the decision centres on two interrelated issues which, because they lie at the heart of what a democratic government and a democratic society are fundamentally about, are of

From John C. Luik, "Tobacco Advertising Bans and the Dark Face of Government Paternalism," *International Journal of Advertising*, vol. 12 (1993). Copyright © 1993 by *International Journal of Advertising*. Reprinted by permission of Cassell PLC, London. Notes omitted.

significance far beyond Canada. The first of these issues is the question of the legitimacy of government paternalism, of the State's attempts to suppress particular styles of living through legislating the 'truth'. The second issue is the question of the legitimacy of government restriction of fundamental rights such as freedom of expression, individual autonomy and respect, when such restrictions are undertaken without compelling evidence that they will produce a significant good that outweighs the harm arising from the restriction. We will examine each of these questions in turn.

If posed in a slightly different fashion, the answer to the question of what is wrong with bans on tobacco advertising is that such bans offend our democratic sensibilities in two respects. First, they are based on values fundamentally at odds with individual autonomy and respect; and second, they are based on shoddy, biased and unreliable evidence.

PATERNALISM AND HEALTH PATERNALISM

In order to understand how banning tobacco advertising constitutes an unacceptable instance of government paternalism, we need to understand first the general nature of paternalism; second, what paternalism means in the specific context of health and health-related measures undertaken by the government; and third, how such paternalism is fundamentally opposed to the two basic values of democratic society, personal autonomy, particularly freedom of expression and respect.

Paternalism comes in at least two varieties: a weaker version and a stronger version. What is common to both versions is a series of assumptions about rea-

son, autonomy and the nature of persons that include the following: (1) Autonomy is not the foundational democratic value inasmuch as considerations of happiness and welfare frequently take precedence over it; (2) Individuals are frequently irrational in that they a) often do not understand their interests, and b) even if they do understand their interests, they do not know the means best suited for the realization of those interests; (3) Individuals need the State's help in a) discovering and realizing their 'true' interests, and b) avoiding irrational courses of action that entail unhappy consequences, e.g., the permanent alienation of their capacity for voluntary action. What is common to both versions is the belief that the State is justified in protecting competent adult persons from the harmful consequences of their actions through restricting their autonomy by forcing them to act or not to act in certain ways. The weaker and less offensive version of paternalism argues that the State can protect persons from the harmful consequences of their actions by forcing them to act in certain ways when a person's actions are neither fully informed nor fully 'his own'. The stronger version of paternalism asserts that the State can protect persons from the harmful consequences of their actions by forcing them to act or not to act in certain ways, even when a person's actions are fully voluntary and informed. In this instance the State asserts that it has the right to substitute its values and judgements about risks and rewards, its philosophy of an acceptable course of action and its determination of what constitutes a good life for those of the individual. In effect, strong paternalism justifies the State's action to prevent a possible harm that a reasonable person understands but chooses to ignore, for instance, smoking.

We can understand the nature and scope of both versions of paternalism by examining them within the context of a specific and restricted type of paternalist claim: health paternalism. Health paternalism is the claim that: (1) Health is the pre-eminent value which outweights, in most instances, all other values such that a rational person would not normally put his health at risk in the interests of some other value; (2) There is but one healthy/rational way to live one's life and such a way does not include activities that carry with them significant risks to well-being or longevity; (3) Individuals have a moral obligation to order their lives in this healthy-rational way; and (4) The State is justified, indeed the State has a moral obligation, to ensure that its citizens conform to this healthy-rational paradigm, even if they wish not to or are unable to through their own efforts. Health paternalism is thus a subtle shift away from the rarely contested right of individuals to good health to the right of the State to manipulate and coerce its citizens into conforming to a socially sanctioned definition of good health. And one justifiable instance of such coercion is the suppression of any inducement to unhealthy living, e.g. tobacco advertising.

Despite its highly problematic character, health paternalism has been to some degree immune from the sorts of objections that are routinely brought against other forms of paternalism. For instance, arguments fashioned along similar lines that called for the State to protect individuals against themselves by establishing and enforcing a 'correct' political, religious or artistic lifestyle would be quickly denounced as totalitarian. Health paternalism's immunity from criticism stems in part from two factors. First, the practice of medicine has a long tradition, preached by physicians and usually casually accepted by patients, of turning one's health over to the experts. Second, health paternalism's policy recommendations— for instance, banning tobacco advertisements—are perceived as being based either on fact and thus being entirely objective and unquestionable, or on 'indubitable' values.

HEALTH PATERNALISM AND TOBACCO

The structure and substance of many of the arguments deployed against the use and promotion of tobacco products is based on paternalism in general and health paternalism in particular. For instance, weak paternalist opponents to the tobacco industry argue that inasmuch as the use of tobacco products is addictive, individuals who use them have not made genuinely voluntary and informed decisions and the State is thus justified in intervening in the lives of these persons to save them from themselves. Or, to take another example, the strong paternalist opponent of the tobacco industry frequently argues that even though the individual who uses tobacco products uses them voluntarily and in full knowledge of their possible consequences, his decision is none the less irrational and deserves to be altered by the State. Again, the health paternalist argues that those who use tobacco products fail to understand the meaning of such scientifically unquestionable concepts as health, rational and risk, or if they understand the meaning of these concepts they are unable or unwilling to accept their moral obligation to act upon them. From the health paternalist's perspective, those who use tobacco are either doing so because they cannot help themselves or because, despite everything they know, they choose to do so. In the former instance they are weak and in the latter instance they are foolish and immoral. In both instances they are unhealthy and in need of salvation. As for those who promote tobacco products, they are, from the perspective of health paternalism, either intellectually dishonest and morally despicable or intellectually ignorant and morally naïve. In either instance they deserve to be suppressed.

Put in this fashion the health paternalist appears to have all of the trump cards, whether moral, logical or scientific, in the debate about tobacco advertising and use. We wish to argue, however, that: (1) Health paternalism a) rests on an unexamined and dubious assumption about the value of health and the relationship between health and rationality, and b) it restricts individual autonomy and demeans the dignity and worth of individuals in ways that are inappropriate in a democratic society; and (2) Without the support of such an unacceptable health paternalism there is no place for tobacco advertising bans in the democratic tradition.

THE VIABILITY OF HEALTH PATERNALISM: THE PRIMACY OF HEALTH

Let us begin with the assumptions of the health paternalist. Health paternalism, as was noted above, appears to be intellectually compelling because it argues from what seems to be the high ground of scientific objectivity and finality. 'Health'— i.e. sound body and mind, the proper functioning of the organism—is apparently something about which we can in-

disputably be certain. But even assuming that we can arrive at a scientifically precise and unquestionable definition of what being healthy is, this fails to provide health paternalism with a scientific status for the reason that health paternalism gives a highly ideological, value-laden characterization to the concept of being healthy and the place of health in an individual's life. Being healthy for the health paternalist is the prime moral value and individuals have a duty to themselves and others to order their lives around this obligation and governments have the obligation to compel them to do so if they choose not to follow this path. The health paternalist builds into his model of a rational/good/ideal/normal person the primary value assumption that reducing health risks and increasing longevity is an unquestionable value and that all rational/moral people will do so. From this he concludes that departures and inducements to depart (e.g. tobacco advertisements) from this model are wrong.

But is this in fact the case? Is it self-evident that a rational/good person will order his life so as to maximize his health? Is it obvious that to trade off an increased health risk or shortened life span for some other value is wrong, and not simply wrong but so grossly wrong that it is justifiably suppressed by the State? Do we not make such trade-offs routinely? 'Consider an individual who wishes to travel to another town. The person could travel by car or by train. The risk of accident and injury is far less by train but the individual decides to go by car because of the increased convenience. Is the individual irrational?'... Is... a healthy, long and comparatively unexciting life to be preferred to a risky, short and exciting one?

As Joel Feinberg reminds us:

Imprudence may not pay off in the long run, and impulsive adventurers and gamblers may be losers in the end, but they do not always or necessarily have regrets. Hangovers are painful and set back one's efforts, but careful niggling prudence is dull and unappealing. Better the life of spontaneity, impulse, excitement, and risk, even if it be short, and even if the future self must bear the costs. We all know that there are people who have such attitudes and have them authentically.

... In short, health paternalism is flawed in the first instance because it mistakenly describes the place of health and longevity in the value schemes of many individuals by failing to allow for the trade-offs between health and other values that are routinely made and that we do not characterize as either irrational or immoral. An individual's life plan might include quite idiosyncratic readings of such things as health, risk, fulfilment and happiness, as well as quite idiosyncratic determinations of how to make trade-offs between them, and not, simply in virtue of its idiosyncratic character, be irrational.

In response to this line of argument the health paternalist can claim that while it is true that certain individuals may not acknowledge the primacy of health and may prefer the alleged rewards of risk-taking to either well-being or longevity, they should not act this way, and the State is justified, *for their own good*, in preventing them from adopting this course of action. Thus the health paternalist inevitably finds himself in the position of advocating as a matter of public policy significant restrictions on individual autonomy.

It is this belief in the moral necessity of protecting individuals from themselves that provides the foundation for restrictions on both the use and promotion of tobacco products. Since the smoker ... refuses to accept the 'fact' that health is the pre-eminent value, that there is one healthy/rational way to order his life, and that he has a moral obligation to live this way, then he opens himself up to the fourth claim, namely, that the State is justified, indeed has a moral obligation, to ensure that he conforms to the healthy/rational paradigm. Put in another fashion, since we cannot accept the values or the rationality of the smoker or the potential smoker we must protect these individuals from their wrong choices by eliminating the possibility of those wrong choices. And advertising bans are one extremely effective way of eliminating the possibility of wrong choices about smoking. ...

THE VIABILITY OF HEALTH PATERNALISM: TOBACCO ADVERTISING BANS AND THE PRIMACY OF AUTONOMY

Tobacco advertising bans infringe the right to individual autonomy in at least three senses. In the first sense they suppress the right to free expression in that they deprive not only speakers of their right to say certain things but also listeners of their right to hear certain things. As Justice Chabot observes:

The Act deprives a third of the adult population of Canada, consumers of the product, of information regarding existing products, new trademarks or products, changes to products in terms of tar, nicotine and CO, in short information which will allow them to make informed economic choices. As previously noted by the Court, freedom of commercial expression protects both the speaker and the listener and plays a significant role in allowing individuals to make informed choices, which represents an important aspect of self-fulfillment and personal autonomy.

... Indeed, in an even more specific sense the process of advertising is founded on the same sorts of freedom—freedom to enquire, create and advocate—that are to be found in political, religious and cultural life. As the political philosopher John Gray has argued,

Freedom of expression in the arts and freedom of expression in advertising are not two categorically different things, subject to different standards and having different justifications; they are the same freedom, exercised in different contexts, with the same justification.

The second problem with such a line of argument is that it could be urged against other forms of speech as well, forms that are considered legitimate. Political and religious speech, for instance, is rarely devoid of appeals to our emotions as well as to our intellects. Are we then through parity of reasoning to conclude that the 'manipulative' emotionalism of the fundamentalist preacher who seeks to 'control' our religious choices is speech that should be suppressed? Or what of the illogical rantings of the populist politician? The difficulty with much speech is that it is, when viewed from a certain perspective manipulative and uninformed, but when judged from another perspective persuasive and legitimate. In order to judge conclusively what kind of speech it is, we must secure some 'objective' vantage point from which the 'truth' of the matter becomes clear. When the argument is cast in this form, it becomes

obvious that advocates of restrictions on speech must of necessity justify those restrictions by claiming that the speech they wish to suppress is somehow in error and that they—the advocates of suppressing such speech—possess the truth about the matter in question. Suppressing speech is thus a form of legislating the truth.

Such a position is, however, open to at least two quite decisive objections. The first is that such restrictions on speech and such officially determined readings of truth are inherently undesirable because they necessarily destroy personal autonomy through fudging the environment in which individuals discover for themselves what is true and false and through imposing a state-enforced doctrine of what to think and how to live.

Indeed, this is precisely why the connection between freedom of speech, individual autonomy and democracy is so necessarily intimate and why government paternalism, however benign, is such a menace to the democratic ethos. Without freedom of speech and the intellectual, cultural, economic and political diversity that it represents, genuine individual autonomy becomes impossible, and without genuine individual autonomy the democratic process is in turn impossible. When the government, for whatever reasons, seeks to control freedom of speech, it inevitably attempts, generally in the most covert and hence most reprehensible fashion, to restrict individual autonomy. And in restricting individual autonomy it undermines democracy itself.

The second objection is that even if such restrictions on speech were desirable, they are in most instances impossible in practice given that they require that those who are suppressing a certain type of speech be indisputably in possession of the truth of the matter. But where is one to find such a vantage point of truth and objectivity and how are we to judge whether those who claim to have found it have really done so? Who, for instance, is really in possession of the truth: the fundamentalist preacher or his agnostic critic? Freedom of speech is considered valuable largely because of the assumption that no individual or group is likely to have the entire truth about anything, and truth is more likely to emerge through the vigorous clash of opposing points of view than through the incontestable edicts of some authority.

Given this crucial connection between commercial expression and individual autonomy, the Supreme Court of Canada, as Judge Chabot notes, rejected the argument that commercial expression is unworthy of constitutional protection.

The Supreme Court of Canada unanimously rejected this argument. It held to the contrary, that commercial speech not only has intrinsic social value as a means of expression, but, in addition, that it constitutes an important aspect of individual self-fulfillment and personal autonomy....

Over and above its intrinsic value as expression, commercial expression which, as has been pointed out, protects listeners as well as speakers plays a significant role in enabling individuals to make informed economic choices, an important aspect of individual self-fulfillment and personal autonomy. The Court accordingly rejects the view that commercial expression serves no individual or societal value in a free and democratic society and for this reason is undeserving of any constitutional protection. (Emphasis J. Chabot)

... Tobacco advertising bans... infringe the right to autonomy in a second and indeed far more serious sense in that they indirectly attempt to manipulate the social environment in such a fashion as to control the thoughts and choices of citizens. And such attempts to manipulate the thoughts and choices of citizens through suppressing competing points of view, in effect through eliminating certain kinds of information, have no place in a democratic society. As US Supreme Court Justice Blackmun observed with respect to attempts by the State to restrict information about a product, such attempts can never be justified since they represent a 'covert attempt by the State to manipulate the choices of its citizens, not by persuasion or direct regulation but by depriving the public of the information needed to make a free choice'. Indeed, as Justice Dickson... notes, 'coercion includes indirect forms of control which determine or limit alternative courses of conduct available to others'.

The State's purpose in banning speech about tobacco products is clearly to effect such an 'indirect form of control' in order to restrict both one's awareness of and beliefs about certain sorts of behaviours and lifestyles. It is not just that the State attempts to control what its citizens believe about a particular choice, but also that it attempts to eliminate the realization that the choice exists. This form of manipulation is in the end no less coercive than the 'direct commands to act or refrain from action on pain of sanction' cited by Justice Dickson since its purpose is to 'determine or limit alternative courses of conduct'....

CONCLUSION

The Chabot decision thus shows that the case for tobacco advertising bans is irremediably flawed in that upon close inspection it turns out to be both theoretically and empirically bankrupt. What it promises is the worst of all possible exchanges—a significant impairment of our democratic health through the erosion of the core values of autonomy and respect in return for no demonstrable improvement in our collective physical health.

'The spirit of the age', writes Lewis Lapham,

> favors the moralist and the busybody, and the instinct to censor and suppress shows itself not only in the protests for and against abortion or multiculturalism but also in the prohibitions against tobacco and pet birds. It seems that everybody is forever looking out for everybody else's spiritual or physical salvation. Doomsday is at hand, and the community of the blessed ... can be all too easily corrupted by the wrong diet, the wrong combination of chemicals, the wrong word.

The spirit of our age may well find its clearest voice in the neo-puritanism of a health paternalism that urges us to suppress, censor and ultimately manage the lives of others for their own good. But the values of autonomy and respect still remind us how deeply such urges trespass on the most crucial of democracy's rights: the right, for better or for worse, to be ourselves.

POSTSCRIPT

Should Tobacco Advertising Be Banned?

Green and Luik seem to argue past each other. In the name of autonomy, Luik wants to ensure a no-censorship policy for rational adults; in the name of harm prevention, Green wants to ensure protection of vulnerable adolescents from harmful messages. But since there is no practicable way of sending one set of messages to rational adults and another set to vulnerable adolescents, the question of advertising must remain as one question, and we may have to choose which of the two values is more important in this case.

When we cannot achieve agreement on the moral status of the endpoint or product of an inquiry—when we cannot decide which value is more important—we may simply have to agree that there is no just outcome and that each side has an equal right to prevail. But we may be able to agree on a just procedure, a way of reaching a decision that all can trust, and agree to accept whatever result the procedure yields, despite what our preference may have been to begin with. One just procedure would be to submit the proposal to ban advertising to the appropriate legislature and accept the results of the debate, the vote, and the acquiescence of the executive branch and the courts.

SUGGESTED READINGS

Michele Barry, "The Influence of the U.S. Tobacco Industry on the Health, Economy, and Environment of Developing Countries," *The New England Journal of Medicine* (March 28, 1991).

Rae Corelli, "Smokers Go to War," *Macleans* (January 17, 1991).

Kathleen Deveny, "With Help of Teens, Snuff Sales Revive," *The Wall Street Journal* (May 3, 1990).

Joseph R. DiFranza and John W. Richards, Jr., "RJR Nabisco's Cartoon Camel Promotes Camel Cigarettes to Children," *Journal of the American Medical Association* (December 11, 1991).

Michael McCarthy, "Tobacco Critics See a Subtle Sell to Kids," *The Wall Street Journal* (May 3, 1990).

Morton Mintz, "The Nicotine Pushers: Marketing Tobacco to Children," *The Nation* (May 6, 1991).

ISSUE 16

Does The Body Shop Misrepresent Itself and Its Products?

YES: Jon Entine, from "Shattered Image," *Business Ethics* (September/October 1994)

NO: Gordon Roddick, from "Rebuttal to 'Shattered Image,'" A Letter to Subscribers of *Business Ethics* (September 22, 1994)

ISSUE SUMMARY

YES: Investigative reporter Jon Entine argues that The Body Shop's claims to superior ethical standards in the conduct of business are hypocritical and false.

NO: Gordon Roddick, chairman and co-owner of The Body Shop, defends the integrity of the company and mounts a critique of Entine's reporting methods.

On the surface, this dispute is about whether or not The Body Shop exploits and mistreats its franchisees and whether or not the company misrepresents the percentage of natural ingredients that go into its products.

But this surface dispute is just the beginning. The following debate between Jon Entine and Gordon Roddick represents a scrabble for the moral high ground between a business and an investigative journalist. The business claims to be effective in doing good in the world; the journalist claims that its business practices are no better than those of the rest of the business world and that it therefore has no right to call itself "ethical." The dispute really represents a much deeper conflict in the corporate world: Can any profit-making corporation honestly claim a motive to do good? Or is the fact that any given company strives to make a profit and arranges its corporate life to make that profit proof that any claims to "ethical" behavior are just so much advertising copy? When a corporation tries to "do the right thing" by being socially conscious and environmentally correct but also tries to grow and make a profit, is it setting itself up as a target for attacks in the event that it fails in either of these areas?

No corporation tells us the whole truth about its products (or else why would we need organizations like the Consumers Union?). We expect that marketing strategies will include selective truth (but not lies) and puffery (without falsehood). That's the free-market way. Furthermore, we expect those in charge of marketing strategies to use their research to learn what sorts of appeals are most likely to make the public happy about their products and buy them consistently. That's their job. And we know that products like cosmetics (The Body Shop's specialty), whose appeal is based more on "image" than "performance," will require more puffery than those whose performance can be measured (diesel engines, for instance). That's in the nature of the product. The question is, must companies that make environmental or ethical claims be held to their professed standards more rigidly than companies that make other kinds of claims (fantastic or associational, for instance)?

In the following selections, Jon Entine accuses the owners of The Body Shop, a cosmetics company, of falsely portraying its products and business practices as socially responsible. Gordon Roddick directly responds to Entine's attack, maintaining that the company's standards are highly ethical and that its projected image is entirely accurate.

In a highly competitive business such as cosmetics, particularly when conducted on an international level, it takes a flexible management process to react to the marketplace. Can this be compatible with high ethical standards?

YES   Jon Entine

SHATTERED IMAGE

The two-year ordeal was finally over. After protracted negotiations with The Body Shop, Stacy and Larry Benes had sold back their franchise in Charlottesville, Virginia. When they had been granted a shop, the company had already selected the location and negotiated the mall lease. The Benes say The Body Shop gave them verbal projections of a healthy first-year profit, but they ended up losing $10,000 a month.

From the first day, they say they struggled with spoiled products and a wide gap between company promises and practices. The Benes have now come to believe that The Body Shop had never been the open, caring, family-oriented company that had fired their imagination. It was only later, as they talked with other franchisees, that they discovered their situation was not isolated.

Now, a year after barely escaping bankruptcy, the Benes count themselves among the lucky ones. Yet, their dreams of starting a new business and blending it with their Sixties idealism are irreparably destroyed. A year after "the great escape," as they call it, the Benes remain fearful that the British cosmetics giant will sue them for agreeing to speak to the Federal Trade Commission (FTC), now investigating The Body Shop's franchise practices. "I used to think Anita Roddick walked on water," Stacy says. "I am quite frankly, afraid of them. I felt like I was dealing with the Gambino crime family."

It's an astonishing tale, make even more so because it echoes similar concerns in more than one hundred on-the-record interviews with current and former franchisees, employees, trading partners, suppliers, cosmetics experts, and social researchers. They tell a remarkable story of a company riddled with contradictions.

Among the more notable findings in a year-long investigation by this reporter:

- Despite its reputation as an innovative natural cosmetics company, cosmetics experts say The Body Shop uses many outdated, off-the-shelf product formulas filled with nonrenewable petro-chemicals.

From Jon Entine, "Shattered Image," *Business Ethics* (September/October 1994). Copyright © 1994 by Jon Entine. Reprinted by permission.

- The company has a documented history of quality control problems, including selling products that are "contaminated" and contain formaldehyde, according to former Body Shop quality control managers and one of its own consulting scientists.

- The Body Shop sources a tiny amount of ingredients through its Trade Not Aid program, although it is a centerpiece of the company's image.

- Its charitable contributions and its progressive environmental standards fall short of company statements.

- The company invented stories about the exotic origins of some of its products, according to two of Anita Roddick's early co-workers.

- In March, the FTC launched an investigation of The Body Shop. It has subpoenaed at least one former franchisee, according to an FTC document, and has requested information from current franchisees.

- The company has a history of legal threats against journalists who have sought to publish the behind-the-gloss facts of The Body Shop myth.

This unflattering portrait contrasts sharply with Anita Roddick's pristine image. "Anita," said Ralph Nader a few years back, "is the most progressive business person I know." Management guru Peter Drucker called her one of his "all-time heroes."

How did The Body Shop, fraught with so many contradictions, come to be considered the unquestioned icon of socially responsible business? Is this the case of a company that somehow lost its moral compass, or the tale of a business that never had one?

THE MAKING OF THE MYTH

The Body Shop story began in 1976 when Anita Roddick opened a small cosmetics shop in Brighton, a faded resort town on England's south coast. Roddick pledged that she would run her business differently, selling cosmetics with no-frill promises in no-frill packages. She struck a responsive chord when she claimed that her fragrances, lotions, and shampoos were "natural" and "100 percent pure."

Over the years, this quirky and charismatic entrepreneur became a symbol of honesty in an industry built on false promises. She called cosmetics makers immoral frauds who "lie," "cheat" and "exploit women" for a quick buck. Investment bankers, who floated her stock in 1984 and made her a multi-millionaire, she condemned as "blood-sucking dinosaurs" and "monsters." She became a huge celebrity, and her company flourished.

Anita and her husband Gordon, who own a quarter of The Body Shop stock, today have an estimated net worth of over $200 million and yearly income of $1.3 million. Together they run a worldwide empire of 1,050 stores in forty-five countries with annual world-wide retail sales of $700 million. Yet, The Body Shop is not just about making money, they say: "We see ourselves not just as a creator of profits for our shareholders, but as a force for good, working for the future of the planet," Anita has said. "Enlightened capitalism is the best way of changing society for the better. I think you can trade ethically, be committed to social responsibility, global responsibility, empower your employees without being afraid of them. I think you can rewrite the book on business."

It's a remarkable and inspiring success story, but like most company histories it is a mixture of hyperbole and truth. In the case of The Body Shop, however, the gap between myth and reality is strikingly large. "Anita is a myth-o-maniac," says Mara Amats, a consultant who set up The Body Shop's paper-making project in Nepal. "She instinctively understands the facile nature of the press and plays to it."

The myth-building began with the founding of the company. There has been a long-running controversy about whether the Roddicks copied the name and the concept from an existing cosmetics company in Berkeley, California, called The Body Shop, founded in 1970. The British Body Shop has denied this, and in her autobiography, *Body and Soul,* Anita reports she got the idea for the name from auto body shops when she visited the Bay Area in 1971. "I found out later there were already other stores in the U.S.A. which had made the same connection," she writes.

But Roddick's first business partner, cosmetologist Mark Constantine (who is under a gag order prohibiting him from discussing it), and others suggest that Anita knew about the Berkeley company. Comparisons of their store design, typography, literature, products, and marketing reveal uncanny similarities.

In just one of many examples, the Berkeley Body Shop wrote in its one-page product sheet in 1971, "All of our products are biodegradable and made to our specifications in Berkeley." "Bottles 20 cents or bring your own." In her price sheet, issued seven years later, Anita wrote, "All our products are biologically soft and made to our specifications." "Bottles 12 p, or bring your own."

Many of Anita Roddick's early cosmetics were identical to the Berkeley Body Shop's, including such distinctive products as loofah sponges and glycerine and rosewater lotion with vitamin E. In a 1994 catalog, Roddick's Body Shop claims she came up with the idea for Japanese Washing Grains when "we were introduced during a trip to the Orient." In fact, according to a Berkeley Body Shop employee, the product was invented by that company in the early '70s and was based on a recipe from an employee's Korean grandmother.

* * *

The Body Shop's most basic myth is that it sells "natural" products. "Natural" has always had an elusive meaning, of course, and The Body Shop, like most cosmetics companies of the 1970s, used nonrenewable petrochemical ingredients. Constantine and Roddick didn't know any better at the time, and there were no government labeling requirements. They also liberally added synthetic dyes and artificial colors to create that "fun" look that is so much a part of The Body Shop image. Constantine, with Roddick's encouragement, added small amounts of "botanical" ingredients and The Body Shop myth was born.

"Anita knew almost nothing about cosmetics," Constantine says. "She and Gordon were entrepreneurs. It was just us, mixing cosmetics in my kitchen. It was great fun."

The Body Shop was still just a handful of hippie stores eager for attention. Constantine, Anita, and Janis Raven, a public-relations expert hired by the Roddicks in 1979, became the merry myth-makers, concocting elaborate fables about some of their best-selling natural-sounding cosmetics. Anita has traveled widely in her hippie days, and Raven used that history to craft the image of Anita-the-world-traveler, hobnobbing with bare-breasted native Indians spreading mysterious goop on their faces.

"What we were looking for was unusual ingredients," Raven recalls. The [pineapple] facial wash, you know, we talked about Anita going to Sri Lanka and seeing the women rubbing pineapples over them. You know, that kind of nonsense."

Why was it nonsense?

"Because it wasn't true. That was Mark's information, and we just decided to make it a bit more romantic," she says.

"Janis and I would provide the cosmetics and how to talk to the press," says Constantine. "We just stayed in the background, which was fine by me. We had a great time." The two say the company made up one fable after another: cocoa butter inspired by Hawaiian natives, peppermint foot lotion mixed on request of the London Marathon, eye gel developed for a computer firm concerned about worker eye strain. It seemed fun at the time. Who could have dreamt that the stories would eventually come under scrutiny?

The Body Shop's campaigning for progressive causes didn't begin until 1986. The company was facing its first serious challenge to its natural marketing niche from Revlon and the British retailer Marks & Spencer. Looking for a way to promote her best-selling range of products made with jojoba oil, a substitute for whale spermaceti, Roddick hooked up with Greenpeace in the U.K., printing up catchy, colorful fundraising posters for a "save the whale" campaign. It generated a blizzard of positive publicity. But Greenpeace chapters in some countries were critical of The Body Shop's use of petrochemical ingredients, and refused to extend the campaign. Roddick, who genuinely cared about whales, was upset. In her book, she blamed the falling out on bureaucratic bungling at Greenpeace.

Undeterred, she soon launched a second promotion, a tie-in with other natural cosmetics companies and animal rights groups which opposed the testing of cosmetic products on animals. Sales soared, and the high-decibel campaign was followed by a sharp curtailment of animal testing at many firms. In the next few years, Roddick heightened her image by enthusiastically campaigning for one popular cause after another: rescuing the rainforest, recycling, helping Romanian orphans, increasing AIDS awareness. By the late '80s, Anita Roddick had been transformed in the public's mind from a quirky, outspoken entrepreneur to a leading spokesperson for progressive capitalism.

The Roddicks had eyed expansion possibilities in the U.S., the world's most lucrative market, for years, but faced the Berkeley problem. In 1987, they paid $3.5 million to the original Body Shop store owners (who changed the company name to Body Time). The following year, they began opening stores in New York City and Washington, D.C. Anita's profile, and the company's profits, soared.

Questions were already simmering about the company's image and practices. But when the press started looking into issues that may have called into question the company's pristine image, Gordon often threatened libel action. And because U.K. libel laws favor the plaintiff (truth is not necessarily a defense), the company succeeded in stopping a number of stories.

Michael Johnson, the former editor of London-based *International Management* magazine and now a public relations executive at Burson-Marstellar, recalls his surprise in 1986 when he contacted the Roddicks about a story on the origins of the company. When he suggested the Roddicks may have lifted The Body Shop idea from the Berkeley entrepreneurs, Johnson says Gordon exploded. "It's a gangsterish operation beneath its kindly exterior," he says. Fearful of an expensive suit, Johnson toned down his story.

In 1991, the London *Daily Mail* killed an article detailing the controversy over the origins of The Body Shop after receiving threats of libel action. Two years later, The Body Shop won a $4,500 defamation suit against the British documentary program "Dispatches," for a critique of its animal testing policies. (Under U.K. law, though, the program was obligated to pay all court costs and lost profits as a result of the program, adding another $2.25 million.) This spring, the London *Daily Telegraph* spiked an exposé. Most recently, *Vanity Fair* decided not to run a story after it received a series of letters threatening a libel suit—not in the U.S., but in Britain, where the magazine publishes an edition.

Are the critical news stories warranted? Has the company misled a mostly adoring public? "I think we have had the intention every time to be perfectly honest," says Angela Bawtree, The Body Shop's head of investor relations. "We're still a young company," Bawtree says. "We're an enthusiastic company. Anita's personality is important in this."

Indeed it is. In her office, Anita posts a sign that reads: "The Body Shop is the world's most honest cosmetic company." It's certainly true that Roddick has helped popularize some innovative management concepts, but the com-

pany's performance leaves many disturbing questions. What follows is only a sampling.

NATURAL COSMETICS

The casual customer who reads one of The Body Shop's brochures, "What is Natural," might think she is getting a helping hand in deciphering the hieroglyphic-like claims of competing "natural" cosmetics companies. "We can't and shouldn't be grouped together with the myriad of other companies crying 'natural!'" it reads. "Because, as you probably know, we're not like other companies."

Many specialists in natural cosmetics call that claim into question. In a 1993 review of Body Shop products, under the heading "Products to Avoid," natural cosmetics expert Zia Wesley-Hosford noted the company's wide use of artificial colors, fragrances, synthetic preservatives, and other petrochemicals.

And in a comment typical of many cosmetics experts—including Body Shop suppliers—a highly regarded consultant, who requested anonymity for fear of legal action, says, "It is not a very innovative company. Roddick uses petrochemically sourced ingredients such as mineral oil, petrolatum, carbomers, and isopropyl myristate, which some natural cosmetics companies have phased out." Rishi Schweig, president of FeatherRiver, a major West Coast distributor of natural cosmetics and personal care products, sums it up this way: "If you take The Body Shop name off the products and put 'Payless Drug Store' on the label, you get an idea of the products' quality."

Bawtree says The Body Shop uses "naturally based" ingredients wherever possible, but adds the company's top priority is "energy conservation and minimal packaging," and that it is sometimes less efficient to use a natural ingredient. "When it makes sense, we do."

QUALITY CONTROL

The Body Shop claims all its raw materials are "micro-biologically tested and subjected to our latest analytical techniques." But reports from three unannounced Food and Drug Administration (FDA) inspections in 1992 and 1993 and interviews with top Body Shop scientists, four former quality control managers, and numerous franchisees indicate a history of quality control irregularities.

One dramatic example occurred during the summer of 1993. Faced with a Christmas backlog, The Body Shop periodically suspended its standard microbial testing for months, hoping to save time and money, according to former quality control managers. "We are under such demand right now that they take the product in right off the truck, fill it up into bottles, and it goes out the door." said Scott Takach in the late summer of 1993, when he was still the number two manager in quality control. The suspension of those tests were direct violations of Good Manufacturing Practice (GMP), the industry-wide standards to which The Body Shop subscribes.

The gamble backfired after a bulk shipment of banana shampoo came in from the U.K. in August 1993. According to Takach and internal company documents, The Body Shop first violated GMP standards by skipping the required test on the bulk containers. It then filled the shampoo, giving it batch number 239N, and sent one bottle to a lab for testing. But instead of waiting for the results to come back before distributing the remaining bottles, as GMP standards require, the company sent the bottled shampoo to regional distribution centers. Two centers sent them on to stores. When the tests came back a week later, they revealed *e coli* bacteria at levels 1,000 percent above acceptable industry standards. "You get that kind of reading from swabbing a toilet bowl," said one test lab manager.

Then, instead of notifying francisees and pulling the shampoo off store shelves, quality control managers sent out new samples twice more, hoping to get an acceptable reading. In the meantime, unknowing store owners continued to sell the contaminated shampoo. FDA documents indicate more than 140 bottles were sold.

Bawtree characterizes that incident as an isolated, albeit unfortunate, mistake that was the direct result of the company's move from New Jersey to North Carolina. "As a result of the move, we had increasing problems with low stock and were shipping things out as fast as we could," she explains. "We told our distributors to hold the product until test results came in. For whatever reason, one of the distributors let them out. That was an error. Under normal circumstances that practice would not occur."

Takach and other Body Shop employees, however, say the company also suspended GMP procedures at its former plant in New Jersey at other times when it faced a tight schedule.

And franchisees from around the world report a running battle to get The Body Shop to take back bad product. For instance, when former Asian head franchisee Anne Downer alerted The Body Shop in October 1990 that its Elderflower Eye Gel had mold growing around the lids and inside the jars, she was startled at the company's response:

"We... confirm that moulds are present," technical manager Patrick Love wrote in a November 1990 letter. "However, we have also tested the product and found that it has not been affected by the mould that is present on the cap. All we can say at this stage is that the product remains unaffected and is therefore safe for use."

"We were constantly trying to deal with product-related problems," Downer says. "Many were near the end of their shelf-life, many others were unstable or contaminated. But they never wanted to deal with it."

One of The Body Shop's consulting scientists, Dr. Dieter Wundram, with the German consumer magazine *Okö-Test*, says The Body Shop has had widespread microbial contamination problems for years—"bugs," he calls them. To control the bacterium, he says, they've added large amounts of synthetic preservatives. According to Dr. Wundram, that, in turn, has resulted in the formation of formaldehyde in three of the products evaluated by the magazine: the best-selling carrot moisture cream, self-tanning lotion, and its baby lotion. After a series of negative reviews in *Okö-Test*, The Body Shop pulled the formulations off the shelves— but only in Germany, according to a former top executive.

ANIMAL TESTING

Roddick is known for her high-profile opposition to animal testing. And Body Shop literature has declared the company is "Against Animal Testing." If consumers take this to mean the company never uses ingredients tested on animals,

they will be misled. The reality is far more complex.

The Body Shop's current policy is what's known as "the five-year rolling rule." The company says it won't purchase cosmetic ingredients tested on animals within the past five years, although it readily acknowledged that it is impossible to avoid all ingredients ever tested on animals.

Over the years, The Body Shop has used ingredients tested on animals by its suppliers within five years. In one example, in 1991, the company purchased Vitamin E acetate from Hoffman LaRoche for use in its sunscreen line. According to company documents, the supplier had tested the ingredient on animals in 1989 and 1991. The Body Shop characterized the ingredient as a pharmaceutical and, as such, not subject to its rule banning animal-tested *cosmetics* ingredients, says Dave Djerrasi, vice president of cosmetics specialities at Hoffman LaRoche.

More recently, The Body Shop has increased its use of ingredients that at some point have been tested on animals. In an internal memo dated May 19, 1992, the company's purchasing manager acknowledged that 46.5 percent of its ingredients had been tested on animals, up from 34 percent the year before.

ENVIRONMENTAL PROTECTION

The Body Shop portrays itself as an environmentally progressive company, claiming that it will "ensure that environmental laws are complied with at all times and, in the event of difficulties, they will be reported to regulatory authorities without delay." But, David Brook, who resigned in 1992 as head of The Body Shop's U.S. environmental department and is now a lawyer with the New Jersey

Attorney General's office, says The Body Shop's environmental story presented in its publications is "window dressing." He says the company had never recycled nearly as extensively as it implied, and noted several occasions when product from the company's facility leaked into the local sewerage system.

Public records document three cases of discharge of non-biodegradable product—though a sewerage authority official suspected more. "I don't think they could have discharged quantities that large by accident," says Michael Wynne, executive director of the Hanover Sewerage Authority in New Jersey. "And even if it was an accident, they were required by law to report it, which they didn't."

Bawtree contends there were only two product discharges, and no fines were levied or charges filed. "In both instances," she says, "we reported it to the head of the sewerage authority.

ETHICAL TRADE

The Body Shop's Trade Not Aid program—the ethical sourcing of cosmetics or sundries from the developing world—has been a centerpiece of the company's marketing strategy for years. But questions have been raised about its ethical trading projects. Last September at a meeting with fair trade organizations, Anita and Gordon estimated that the company's Trade Not Aid sourcing accounted for far less than one percent of its ingredients, according to Richard Adams, executive director of the U.K. research organization New Consumer.

And some of the Trade Not Aid products are not purchased from "fair trade" sources. For instance, over the years The Body Shop has sourced a substantial amount of babassu oil for its "Rainforest Bath Beads" from the British-based Croda Chemical Company (which makes the oil from nuts that do not grow in the rainforest) and from Cultural Survival Enterprises (CSE), a for-profit trade group in Massachusetts. CSE has said it has sourced most of its supply from the mainstream commercial markets.

According to fair trade representatives who work with the company, The Body Shop doesn't pay "first-world wages for third-world products," as it claims in its publicity. The company's partnership with the Nañhu people in Mexico is a case in point. Anita Roddick was feted when she came to film her American Express commercial there last year. "She had great charm and charisma," recalls Alison Rockett, a Body Shop consultant who helped organize the visit. "They love her." But the anthropologist with the Mexican nonprofit group that runs the project says the company pays less than other buyers, insisting on a "volume discount."

For the Nañhu's body scrub mitts, Peter Winkel of Xochipilli established a price of $2.20 each, which would leave the Indians about $.17 per item after expenses. Of all the buyers, only The Body Shop balked at the terms—insisting on $2.05 a mitt, which would have left the Indians even less. Xochipilli decided to reduce its own portion of the revenue instead.

Having spent many days with Anita during her several visits with the Nañhu, Winkel says he finds her "contradictory." Does she have a good heart? "I'm not sure," he says. "I've seen too many faces of Anita."

In another example, The Body Shop has sourced blue corn from the Pueblo Indians. But according to Geoffrey Brooks, president of Brooks Industries, which manufactures hydrolized protein from blue corn for use in a Body Shop product, "They use levels that have no efficacy at all. It's just a marketing gimmick."

Recently, the company recruited Jacqui MacDonald of Bridgehead Trading, an alternative trading group in Canada, to run its Trade Not Aid program, a move Bawtree says underscores The Body Shop's commitment to the program. But she adds that it's important to keep it in perspective. "By nature, these projects are small," she explains. "You're dealing with small communities. You obviously want to build a business model that is sustainable. It takes time. It is a growing part of our business, but it is a small part of the whole."

CORPORATE PHILANTHROPY

According to a company fact sheet, "The Body Shop donates an inordinately high percentage of pre-tax profits to often controversial charitable campaigns." However, a review of the public records shows that between 1986 and 1993, the company's charitable donations ranged from .36 percent to 1.24 percent of pre-tax profits. According to the Council on Economic Priorities, average annual pre-tax charitable donations for a U.S. company are 1.9 percent; Patagonia gives 10 percent. After being repeatedly questioned last year about the discrepancy, The Body Shop increased charitable contributions for fiscal 1994 to 2.97 percent.

CORPORATE GOVERNANCE

The Body Shop has never had an outside board member, and is currently in violation of seven provisions of the Code of Best Practices of the Corporate Governance reforms established two years ago by the London Stock Exchange to promote independent checks on companies. Bawtree says the company plans to add two independent board members in March.

FRANCHISING

Perhaps most troublesome of all is the unfolding news of The Body Shop's relations with its franchisees. About 95 percent of its stores are independently owned, and the company's profits come mostly from wholesaling goods to these shops. Total franchisee start-up costs, including a franchise fee of $40,000, plus inventory and renovation, range from $270,000 to $490,000. Body Shop franchisee problems have surfaced in England, Scotland, France, Canada, Asia, and elsewhere. In mid-June, The Body Shop paid a reported $3 million to its former head franchisee in Norway to settle a breach-of-contract suit. Its former head franchisee for Singapore and seven other countries recently filed a conspiracy and breach-of-contract suit seeking to recover an estimated $200 million.

The House Committee on Small Business—which has introduced franchise reform legislation—has been receiving calls from distressed Body Shop franchisees for more than a year now. "The Body Shop appears to use most of the abusive practices that are standard in the franchising industry," says Dean Sagar, an economist with the committee. Sagar and FTC officials identify a number of problems and practices:

- **Deceptive financial data.** In the past, the company appears to have provided prospective franchisees with misleading profit and cost estimates. For instance, one prospective franchisee was told to expect a return as high as 15–23 percent. The franchisee's banker was submitted different data projecting an 8 percent return. And even these projections were greatly overstated. In other instances, the company also arranged for potential buyers to review data from Body Shop-owned stores or head franchisees, which buy product at a lower markup, and operate with far different cost structures.

- **Unfair competition.** Other franchise chains, such as Radio Shack, send out information-only catalogues. The Body Shop appears to be the only major franchise operation in the U.S. which competes with its own franchisees by direct sales through mail-order catalogues.

- **Misleading company representation.** The Body Shop supplies prospective franchisees with videos and publications that paint a picture of the company which appears to contradict the facts.

FTC officials met with Body Shop executives in January. In March, the FTC subpoenaed at least one former franchisee, and since then, the agency has requested information from an unknown number of current franchisees. Sources at the agency say it utilitzes subpoenas to protect franchisees from retaliatory suits. FTC investigations typically take a year or more before charges are filed.

Bawtree characterizes the FTC action as an "inquiry," not an investigation, and she contends that the problems are overblown. Half of the fifty-eight U.S. franchisees have opened more than one shop, she says, which indicates they're doing well, and about three-fourths of U.S. franchisees are profitable. "Generally, we have very good relations with our franchisees," she says. "We're certainly not in the business of making it hard on them."

A MANAGEMENT PROBLEM OR A MORALITY TALE?

These issues raise a fundamental question: Are the problems at The Body Shop related to weak management at a time when the company was growing too quickly? Or is this a company that lacks a moral center?

To Bawtree's way of thinking, the problems are simply a matter of fine tuning. "There is a case for saying this company grew quickly and had a lot of enthusiasm," she says. "All young companies don't have the management structure from day one."

And there are indications that the company is responding to the criticisms. In recent months, The Body Shop has reviewed its management structure. Anita Roddick has moved from her former position as managing director (equivalent to the president of a U.S. corporation) to chief executive, where she will be responsible for the "future direction and style" of the business, rather than day-to-day operations, Bawtree says. Stuart Rose, a board member who has been managing day-to-day operations for years, was officially named managing director in late July.

The Body Shop also has established a new position, head of information audit, to look more closely at how the company presents itself. And three new executive directors from inside the company have been appointed to the board.

"I think probably it's good that the pressure's on us, in a way," Bawtree says. "It keeps us on our toes."

But Richard Adams of New Consumer, who The Body Shop has verbally threatened with libel action for publishing his concerns, is skeptical. "It's like plea bargaining," he says. "They're saying, 'We plead guilty to the minor charge of making small mistakes or being overenthusiastic or perhaps telling the odd fib or two, but in exchange we are asking you not to go into detail about fair trade, about how The Body Shop started, about our relations with Body Shop franchisees.' I think they're desperately hoping this trade-off will happen."

* * *

All companies have a moral obligation to live up to their ideals and the marketing claims they espouse. The Body Shop's product ingredients would not be news if the company hadn't chosen to market their purity. Its ethical trading contradictions would not merit much attention if Roddick hadn't made it the centerpiece of the company's marketing strategy.

"There are no perfect corporations," says Steve Schueth, vice president of socially responsible investing at the Calvert Group. "If we looked closely at a company like DuPont, we might find a story not dissimilar to The Body Shop story right now. The difference is that DuPont is not out there claiming to be a model of socially responsible business practices. The gap between image and reality at the Body Shop appears to be huge."

It's a gap other companies must also learn to bridge, says Jon Lickerman, Calvert's director of social research. "So many so-called progressive companies have noble corporate philosophies but mistreat their own employees, vendors, and customers," he says. "It's sad, but it's a pattern I see frequently."

As Anita herself might say, companies must walk their talk. Progressive programs, recklessly executed and misleadingly presented, do not further the cause of socially responsible business.

Individuals and organizations promoting that cause must also adjust their perspective. We have generally assumed that only the "bad guys" needed watching, and that companies who appeared to share our values, like The Body Shop, were beyond reproach. It's time to examine that assumption. "We can no longer dismiss the oil companies or other industries we used to think of as 'dirty businesses,'" says Gary Hirshberg, founder of Stonyfield Farm Yogurt and co-chair of the Social Venture Network's board of directors.

Joan Bavaria, founder of Franklin Research, and one of the drafters of the CERES Principles, calls for a new criteria of social responsibility—what researchers are now calling "transparency." Instead of screening companies solely on "environmentalism" or "affirmative action," she says the character of a company should be measured by its willingness to honestly disclose its problems and open itself to outside scrutiny. It's a principle the socially responsible business movement itself must have the courage to embrace. The disclosure of The Body Shop's inconsistencies will certainly bring added scrutiny to other companies that espouse a social mission—and to the movement itself. But as uncomfortable as the consequences might be, the story must be told. "I feel sorry for people who say this type of information shouldn't come out," says Peter Kinder, founder of the social investment firm Kinder, Lydenberg, and Domini. "Because if this movement cannot withstand a bad apple, then we don't have a movement."

NO

Gordon Roddick

REBUTTAL TO "SHATTERED IMAGE"

Dear fellow *Business Ethics* subscriber,

I sit down to write this letter with some anger and considerable sadness. It concerns the article "Shattered Image," which appeared in the September/October issue of *Business Ethics*. As you are probably aware, that article contained allegations that maligned and defamed our company, my wife and me. Although a representative of The Body Shop is quoted in the article, making it appear that we were given an opportunity to respond, in fact we were not informed of most of the charges prior to publication. Such treatment would be indefensible under any circumstances, but it is especially troubling when the right to a fair hearing is denied by a magazine with "ethics" in its title.

It has become clear that writing to you personally is the only way we can be sure you will have the chance to hear our side of the case. Hence, this letter.

Frankly, it is difficult to know where to begin rebutting an article filled with as many lies, distortions, and gross inaccuracies as this one. I suppose we have to give the author some credit for throwing together such an impressive volume of information. It is his attempt to confuse and misrepresent the reality of a company that has struggled hard for 18 years to be in the forefront of a movement seeking a different way of doing business.

Where the information comes from is another matter. Of the 22 sources named in the article, 10 are disgruntled former employees or franchisees, current competitors, or disappointed bidders for our business, all of whom obviously have personal reasons for wanting to make The Body Shop look bad. Four other sources have either strenuously denied their quotes or said their words have been used out of context in a way that entirely distorts their meaning. Yet another five sources are cited for opinions they expressed about social investment in general, opinions that have been turned around so as to make them appear to be highly critical of The Body Shop.

There is, in fact, almost no attempt to observe the normal standards of journalism. The article cites two people as "independent experts," for example, without mentioning that they are among our competitors. Elsewhere, a competitor's marketing newsletter is used to provide "expert analysis," again without noting the obvious conflict of interest. And another alleged "source," the Federal Trade Commission [FTC], has already issued a flat-out denial that it has commented on The Body Shop practices in any way, shape, or form. We understand from the FTC that *Business Ethics* have agreed to print a correction in the next issue.

But to see what is really going on here, it is necessary to look at some of the specific allegations in detail. Consider the opening snapshot of two former franchisees, Stacy and Larry Benes, who are portrayed as terrified, bankrupt people somehow done in by our malfeasance. The implication is that such stories are common throughout our organization. Nothing could be further from the truth.

To begin with, there is more to the Beneses' story than the author chose to report. Stacy and Larry Benes were like many other people who come to us for a franchise, whenever we begin trading in a country or a region. They bring us their hopes and dreams, which may or may not be achievable. We try to select franchisees with realistic expectations and the ability to fulfill them. It is very much in our interest as a franchisor to do so. Sometimes we make mistakes in our selection.

In the case of the Beneses, we were led to believe that Larry had a full-time job and Stacy would run the shop, which would thus have to provide income for just one person. Whatever they say now, they were clearly told at the time that a single shop in Charlottesville, Va., could not possibly do more, at least in the first few years. Whether it could do even that well depended to a great degree on what

the Beneses were prepared to put into it. Sadly, they turned out to be neither good franchisees nor good retailers. They so mismanaged the business that a group of their employees came to us to complain about their behavior and their values. Meanwhile, they were taking out more than $80,000 a year for themselves in their first year of operations—somewhat more than either Anita or I were paid annually during The Body Shop's first decade. Eventually, they wound up in financial difficulty, owing the company more than $200,000 for products they had bought from us on credit and then sold. Rather than sue them for payment, we agreed to repurchase the store.

As unfortunate as such episodes are, it is ridiculous to suggest they are typical of our relationships with franchisees. Within 24 hours of this article's publication, 95% of our U.S. franchisees signed a letter repudiating the accusations in it. The fact is that we operate on a worldwide basis trading either directly or through head franchisees in more than 40 countries with more than 1,100 stores, of which 1,000 are owned by approximately 650 franchisees. There are always some disputes between franchisor and franchisees. That's the nature of business. But our disputes have actually been far milder than is common. In 18 years of operation, we have terminated the contract of only one franchisee, and that was in England. (She had fired all her employees on grounds that could only be described as lunatic. We put them on our payroll, some 50 people in all, many of whom had mortgages and other financial obligations, and we kept paying them until the dispute was resolved.) In addition, we had litigation in Norway that was settled amicably. There is presently litigation in

Singapore, but we are hopeful it, too, can be settled.

Such conflicts are the daily bread of any business. The unusual part is that we have had so few of them, as *Business Ethics* would surely have discovered had it checked the facts of this article with independent franchising experts. Instead, it appears to have relied on the author's own biased sources, who naturally confirmed what they'd already said to him.

The same pattern repeats itself throughout the article. There is, for example, the assertion that we stole The Body Shop's name, concept, and products from Jane Saunders and Peggy Short, who have a natural cosmetics business of the same name based in Berkeley, Ca. The charge is pure rubbish. Jane and Peggy do not make such claims. They have stated that the company "didn't rip us off" and that there have always been "fundamental differences" between their stores and ours. (I am using their words here.) Had they thought otherwise, we would probably not have been able to develop the warm and cordial relationship we have with them and their companies, a relationship that continues to this day.

Indeed, the fundamental differences in our retail styles and appearance are instantly obvious to anyone who visits the two companies' shops. After the author of "Shattered Image" showed up at the Saunders', we heard from Jane Saunders' daughter Ann, who wrote us saying a man named Jon Entine (the author of the *Business Ethics* article) had "barged in" on her and started making claims about our supposed larceny. She told him she "had no knowledge of anything he was talking about." She said "his 'facts' are wrong." Entine has since alleged that there is a gag order

preventing Jane Saunders, Peggy Short, and others from commenting on the relationship. In her letter, Ann wrote that she specifically told him there was no such gag order.

Another person supposedly under a gag order is Mark Constantine, who was a major supplier to us for more than a decade and whom we worked with to develop many of our early products. He wrote me after reading the opinions ascribed to him in the article. Judge his remarks about Entine for yourself:

> It would appear that he has edited or, worse, twisted my comments.
>
> Taking a few of the points, "Roddick's first business partner, cosmetologist Mark Constantine (who is under a gag order prohibiting him from discussing it)," ... "suggest[s] that Anita knew about the Berkeley company."
>
> Oh how I wish I had been your business partner! ... "cosmetologist," I am not a cosmetologist.
>
> "Under a gag order," No gag order, See the interview in last Sunday's Mirror as an example. Anyway, how can I suggest something if I'm under a gag order?
>
> *He* suggested that Anita knew about the Berkeley company, and I was shocked when he asked me, I didn't deny it because I did not know. I was entertained to see the examples he chose for similarities: "loofah sponges and glycerin and rosewater lotion."
>
> I take offense at the next paragraph "The Body Shop's most basic myth." Anita was the first person to recognize that the products that I formulated had a greater amount of "naturals" than any others on the market, then or now. She gave me a much needed break at a time when no one was interested in natural ingredients as anything but label claims. I went to great pains to explain this, and the guy phoned me back and read this

paragraph to me. It was rubbish then, and I told him, and it's still rubbish now.

Mark's letter reflects the frustration we have all felt in trying to deal with this article. There are sensible questions that could be raised, and we would all learn from such a discussion. I make no appeal for The Body Shop to be exempt from criticism or scrutiny. We are happy to open up our hearts, our minds, and our company to those who wish to examine us, provided they accept their responsibility to be balanced and fair.

But I am at a loss to find *anything* balanced or fair in this article. In its zeal to impugn our commitment to our principles, it goes after our Trade Not Aid program, building its attack around an utterly irrelevant statistic—the percentage of our ingredients that come from Trade Not Aid projects. What is this number supposed to reveal? It certainly tells nothing about the effectiveness of our efforts. Or the amount of time and energy we have put into nurturing these projects. Or the obstacles we have had to overcome due to the lack of infrastructure in disenfranchised, Third World communities—transport difficulties, investment problems, absence of technological capabilities, cultural issues, the need to build trust and personal relationships, and so on. One single ingredient, such as Brazil nut oil or cocoa butter, may take two years or more to source and develop. Believe me, there are much easier ways to do business than by taking on the problems of such projects. We don't do it to "save the planet." In most cases, we do it because we are asked to help by the disenfranchised communities themselves. The only significant measure of our success is the number of people who are directly and beneficially affected by our activities.

That number, I am proud to say, runs into the thousands. It can best be verified by talking to the communities we have assisted—another thing *Business Ethics* neglected to do.

A letter was written to *Business Ethics* on 26th August 1994 from Jerry Kinsman, the program manager of Santa Ana Agricultural Enterprises (The Pueblo of Santa Ana is a federally recognized American Indian Tribe located in New Mexico). In this letter he says: "*I hope you will give some importance to what representatives of Body Shop's trading partners have to say about that company.*"

However, *Business Ethics* chose to ignore that request.

Kinsman writes:

"Be assured that the people of Santa Ana Pueblo are very pleased with and proud of the connection with Body Shop. Whereas the direct profit from sales to BSI [The Body Shop] has been very beneficial, it should be noted that the relationship has had an indirect multiplier effect on the Tribe's Blue Corn business. Public notice from the association, in and of itself has brought in more public notice—and more business. Santa Ana has become *The* place to find out about Blue Corn and *The* place to observe successful Native American development efforts. Has Body Shop been the singular cause of that accomplishment? Clearly not! More than any other factor, the Tribe's achievements are a function of some very savvy people knowing what they want *for themselves*. Has Body Shop been important? Clearly yes! . . . I must inform you that Santa Ana is not a victim of BSI. Rather, the Tribe is an ardent supporter of its approach to trade."

And let me tell you about a Trade Not Aid project that produces *no* ingredients for our products. It is called *The Big*

Issue and it is a newspaper sold by about 2,000 vendors, almost all of them homeless people, in London, Edinburgh, Glasgow, Manchester, and several other cities in our own backyard. Its average weekly circulation is 200,000. It has been going for three years now and has been financially self-sufficient on an operating basis for some time. Recently it moved into a new building with a print shop, meeting rooms, and a cafe.

I myself started this project after seeing the homeless newspaper called *Street News* being sold in New York. I persuaded an old friend of mine to be the editor. Together we launched *The Big Issue* despite a feasibility study warning against the idea. The Body Shop put in $450,000 over two years, and The Body Shop Foundation contributed another $350,000. As large as the investment was, the possibility of losing the money was not, in fact, the greatest risk we faced. Far more serious was the risk that the project might go wrong and wind up harming our reputation. That is always a danger when you work with disadvantaged people. In the case of the homeless, you are wide open to accusations of promoting drug abuse, violence, alcoholism, welfare fraud, and so on—all issues around which passions run high. The possibility of scandal is a given. You can't avoid it, especially in the early phases of a project, when you are feeling your way and haven't yet figured out the necessary controls. So far we have been lucky. We have also had an enormous amount of help— from the police authorities, commercial businesses, and non-profit foundations. We have thanked them all in the newspaper itself Still the fact remains that the risk was, and is, ours. If scandal comes, if the project fails, The Body Shop will take the heat.

We are not looking here for credit, or recognition. I would not have brought it up at all but for this unscrupulous attack in a magazine called *Business Ethics*. I mention *The Big Issue* only because it is one of several projects that we talk little about, but that have provided some small measure of hope or work for a lot of people. Those people are the entire reason for doing these things. Yet they are the ones who get lost when high-minded organizations quibble about the percentage of ingredients produced under our Trade Not Aid policy.

I could go on and on cataloguing the error and misrepresentation in this article, but it would take a small book to answer every one of Entine's allegations. We have, in fact, prepared such a document and would be happy to send it to you if you are interested. Meanwhile, there are a couple of other matters I must address, including the charge by Entine, and the editors of *Business Ethics*, and others that we have used thuggery and legal threats to suppress legitimate criticism of The Body Shop.

Let me say straight off that Anita and I are very protective of the business we have built, and we have probably been oversensitive and overdefensive to criticism at times. But look at the history. In 1992, representatives of a company called Fulcrum Productions approached us about a program on The Body Shop they wanted to make for Channel 4, a British television channel. They asked for our help, assuring us they would produce a fair and balanced piece. We let them film at our headquarters in England and our Soapworks factory in Glasgow. We gave them volumes of printed material as well as in-house videos, films, and stills that they wound up using in the program. They had full access to the company. We answered every question they raised. Both Anita and I made ourselves available for interviews on camera. Subsequently, the producer admitted, under oath, that we had been very cooperative.

The program Fulcrum produced was a shamefully biased piece that defamed The Body Shop, Anita, and me. In order to keep it from being sold into the 40-odd other countries where we trade, we decided after lengthy deliberation to sue Channel 4 and Fulcrum Productions.

We won the libel action after a grueling six-week trial in the British High Court. Thousands of documents, internal memos, position papers, and videos were paraded before the jury, along with every other scrap of information that might possibly be relevant. Anita and I and others in the company were cross-examined for days on end. I personally put in four days in the witness box. The intensity of the process made a social audit look like a day at the fairground.

Contrary to what you may have heard, truth *is* a defense against libel in the U.K. Had the charges in the program proved to be truthful, Fulcrum and Channel 4 would have won the case, and we would have had to pay their legal bills. Instead, we were completely vindicated. The jury found in favor of Anita, myself, and The Body Shop. The defendants had to pay damages of 276,000 pounds plus our court costs. Our total award required them to pay us in excess of one and a half (1.5) million dollars. In addition, they were served with an injunction forbidding them from repeating any of the defamatory statements they were found to have made, including those concerning

our public positions on environmental, human rights, and animal testing issues.

It would be difficult to imagine a more public airing of the issues surrounding The Body Shop. It would be equally unimaginable that rational human beings would willingly subject themselves twice to the level of stress involved in such a court action.

Four weeks after the end of the trial, Jon Entine showed up at our headquarters in England, saying he was working on a piece about The Body Shop for ABC's Prime Time Live. We gave him hundreds of pages of documents and offered to provide more. Within days, however, we began hearing from suppliers, franchisees, and independent organizations about his investigation of us. His technique was literally to harass people until he got something he could use. He called one of our suppliers more than seven times in two days. Whenever he got hold of somebody, he would misrepresent what another person had said in an aggressive attempt to elicit "on-the-record" responses from the person he was talking to. These remarks he would then repeat to his next subject, distorting them as necessary. In this manner, he created a maelstrom of misinformation and fear wherever he went.

We eventually got fed up with all this and contacted people at ABC to advise them of their producer's outrageous behavior. Entine left ABC with the program unfinished. He alleges, of course, that we intimidated the network. It is hard to believe that a major news organization with a reputation for hard-nosed investigative journalism would be intimidated by the likes of The Body Shop, especially if we are as supposedly evil and as despicable as he had said on many occasions. Then again, we do not know for sure what happened at ABC. Our best source is the deputy editor of *The Sunday Times*, England's leading weekend newspaper, who wrote me a letter on October 8, 1993, after we had questioned a story the newspaper had run on the proposed Prime Time Live piece following its cancellation: In his letter he said:

> "We [*The Sunday Times*] have now established what we did not know then: that ABC discovered Entine had made a number of mistakes in his methodology, so serious that they had in effect fired him some 10 days before. Entine, probably unknown to ABC, was however picking up his messages from a phone on his old desk in the ABC building. We now understand from ABC sources that Entine is regarded as out of control and has been running around saying some wild things."

So, whatever may have happened inside ABC, Entine was misrepresenting himself as part of ABC to a journalist at *The Sunday Times* after he had already left the network. Moreover, he was telling the journalist that the Prime Time Live segment would be shown when he knew it would not. As it turned out, he was playing much the same game with the Food and Drug Administration [FDA].

Unbeknownst to us, Entine, while still at ABC, had gone to the FDA with a number of untrue allegations, leading inspectors to make a surprise visit to our new headquarters in Wake Forest, N.C. They issued no citations or violation notices. Undeterred, Entine, now gone from ABC, but leaving the FDA inspector with the impression that he was still with them and headed our way with hidden cameras, got the FDA to make a second inspection. Again, no citations. Having failed twice, Entine did not give up—he obtained a copy of the internal FDA notes of their visits and leaked them to other journalists, trying to start a story that we had problems with the FDA.

There was one problem with his strategy, however, and he was well aware of it. The internal documents made it absolutely clear that the FDA inspections were initiated *"in response to allegations made by a Prime Time news reporter..."*. Entine found a simple solution to his problem. By his own admission, he falsified the FDA documents to blot out his name and all references to himself as the source of the "complaints"; he circulated the FDA documents that directly misled other reporters to believe he, Jon Entine, was not at the start, middle and end of this whole episode.

Let's face it: this is not the behavior of a responsible journalist. I dare say it is not the behavior of a journalist at all. I certainly cannot imagine a real journalist launching a campaign to drive down the share price of a company he was writing about. Yet Entine did just that, even calling up Peter Lynch's office to urge him to dump Fidelity's holdings of The Body Shop stock. Entine also showed up in Toronto at a meeting of the Social Investment Forum and harangued the assembly about The Body Shop until he was told to sit down. He then proceeded to hand out copies of a grossly defamatory article he had written about us for *Vanity Fair*, which had rejected it. This same article he circulated to social activists, fair trade organizations, animal rights advocates, and others on both sides of the Atlantic. Still others he called up and harangued about *"the most evil corporation* [he had] *encountered in twenty years of reporting,"* as he described us to Jay Harris, the publisher of *Mother Jones*, a magazine that has tangled with some pretty evil corporations in its day. Entine was quoted in one newspaper saying that his impending revelations would be *"the story of the century,* "putting us right up there with the moon landing, two world wars, the Holocaust, the war in Vietnam, the end of the Soviet Union, and countless human and ecological disasters. All of which would have been worth a good laugh had he not also taken to harassing Anita in public and in private. At that point, his obsession became both unnerving and a bit frightening.

In the face of such attacks, I make no apologies for anything we have done to protect ourselves. It is not "legal thuggery" to defend your family, your employees, your friends and associates, your principles, and your reputation from someone who is hell-bent on doing as much damage to them as he can. There is a difference between criticism and character assassination. Just as there are environmental laws to stop polluters, so there are libel laws to stop irresponsible and damaging reports. Yes, we protested vigorously to *Vanity Fair* for assigning an article on The Body Shop to Jon Entine. We told the magazine we would cooperate with any responsible journalist they cared to have write about us, but we would not deal with Entine under any circumstances. *Vanity Fair* dropped the article. *Business Ethics* picked it up.

I cannot tell you how disheartening it is to find the attack on us coming now from people with whom we had always supposed we shared common commitments and common values. That Entine succeeded in driving down our share price was thanks largely to Franklin Research and Development, whose President, Joan Bavaria, wrote a column for *Business Ethics* in the same issue. Franklin sold 50,000 shares of The Body Shop stock on the strength of Entine's rejected *Vanity Fair* article. This information was relayed to the *Financial Times* in London, which ran an article about it, setting off a firestorm in the British press. Only later did Franklin even make a pretense of investigating Entine's charges. How this qualifies as "ethical investing" is beyond me.

Which brings us to *Business Ethics.* When we learned of the magazine's intention to publish a version of Entine's article, we informed the editors of our history with him and asked for an opportunity to review the piece for factual inaccuracies. The editors declined. One of our staff, Angela Bawtree, then visited the *Business Ethics* offices, but very few of the allegations contained in the article were put to her. Editor Craig Cox later refused her offer of follow-up information.

The editors have since tried to portray themselves as crusading journalists standing up to a bullying corporation. They have boasted loudly about taking out libel insurance. They have made much of their fear of publishing in Britain and their insistence that distributors sign pledges not to sell the magazine in any Commonwealth country. But, as noted above, truth is a defense against libel under British law. They face no risk if their article is factual. If we did sue them (something we have not threatened to do), they could recover all their legal expenses—assuming, that is, they could prove the accuracy of Entine's charges. So why didn't they publish in the U.K.? And what were their motives in publishing the article at all?

Perhaps the answer lies in a letter that Marjorie Kelly, publisher and editor-in-chief of *Business Ethics* sent to her financial backers in August, just prior to publication of the Entine article.

"This piece will be talked about," she wrote. "It will create a stir.... *It's the best thing we've ever done. It could put us on the map.*"

The emphasis, I'm afraid, is hers.

Let me reiterate in closing that we have a detailed response to every single allegation Entine makes in his article and elsewhere. We will happily provide those responses to all who care to read them, but now we wish to get back to work. We have taken a severe kicking from the press on both sides of the Atlantic and elsewhere in the world. Perhaps there is some balance in that. We have also had a lot of good press over the years, some of it excessive in its enthusiasm. I suppose we should learn to live with excessive attacks as well.

In the future, I hope there will be objective and detailed reporting on our business. Some of the conclusions would no doubt be critical, but I am also certain a fair analysis would reveal a company that has tried very hard and has much to be proud of. We chose a difficult and thorny path. With the help of many others, we will continue to tread that path with pride and vigor.

In any event, the time for anger is past. We know the world is filled with businesses concerned with "putting something back." We hope they will not sit around too long in detailed analysis and therapy as a result of the hoopla created by this attack on us.

After the Channel 4 libel case, we ourselves began the process of producing a methodology for a definitive social audit of our company, following the lead of Ben & Jerry's and other companies. It is a mammoth undertaking, aimed at analyzing our social performance against the expectations created by ourselves and others. Along with our financial and environmental reports, it should provide a complete picture of the business, available to all. We expect to have a report by mid 1995. It will come as a great relief, most of all to us, who will use it to improve on the shortcomings it will undoubtedly highlight.

And what of *Business Ethics*? To date, two prominent members of its editorial advisory board have resigned, questioning the ethics of the magazine. We wonder if Marjorie Kelly has achieved the circulation boost she was counting on. The episode has certainly provided a reminder of the potential conflict between business needs and editorial principles. Perhaps Marjorie's words at the end of her "Musings" piece in the same issue of *Business Ethics* should now be read in a new light:

"What we may have neglected in our enthusiasm is ethics. Good, old-fashioned ethics. Also known as integrity. It's not something to shout about in our marketing packages, but if we can't live up to it, we won't have much to shout about for long."

We agree entirely. Enthusiasm in the pursuit of greater circulation is no substitute for ethics. I can only hope that the standards Marjorie articulates will be applied to *Business Ethics* magazine in the future.

POSTSCRIPT

Does The Body Shop Misrepresent Itself and Its Products?

Entine believes that The Body Shop made claims about their business practices that did not stand up to close scrutiny. Roddick rebuts Entine's claims based on his belief in the company and in the way his company has operated.

There are many ethical standards to take into consideration as you debate this issue. Is justice served by any of the claims made by either Entine or Roddick? Do you think that attempts by The Body Shop to do business with South American Indians are meant to be helpful to the Indians, or are they just a publicity stunt? Are true but incomplete claims about a product necessarily less ethical than full disclosure? What about trade secrets and company loyalty? Who has the most to gain or lose by spreading half-truths and making false claims about a product? What about Entine's responsibilities? Does a reporter who performs an investigation have the right to make judgments based on his work that could affect the reputation of a business? Both Entine and Roddick direct charges of misrepresentation toward each other in debating this issue. What ethical principle is ignored when this happens? Is it possible to effectively conduct business in a world full of competitors and still realize a profit while making a simultaneous effort to help clean up the environment, bring Third World countries into the twenty-first century, and provide aid to those who are less fortunate?

SUGGESTED READINGS

Joan Bavaria, Eric Becker, and Simon Billenness, "Body Shop Scrutinized—Faces Allegations of Social Performance," *Investing for a Better World* (September 15, 1994).

Matt Moffett, "Kayapo Indians Lose Their 'Green' Image—Former Heroes of Amazon Succumb to Lure of Profit," *The Wall Street Journal* (December 29, 1994).

Anita Roddick, *Body and Soul: Profits With Principles—The Amazing Success Story of Anita Roddick and The Body Shop* (Crown, 1991).

Anita Roddick, Jon Entine, and Richard Kirshenbaun, "Beyond The Body Shop Brouhaha," *Utne Reader* (January/February 1995).

PART 5

Environmental Policy and Corporate Responsibility

Mankind's attempts to protect the environment have involved many conflicts over fundamental values. We know that the environment must be protected, but the natural environment cannot participate in our political processes as an interest group nor can it buy itself protection on the open market. So we have to put aside the fundamental model of human action as rule-governed competition; nature cannot compete. In this section, we consider debates on property rights and the environment and on market incentives for businesses to clean up pollution.

- Should Property Rights Prevail Over Environmental Protection?

- Are Market Incentives Sufficient to Clean Up the Water?

ISSUE 17

Should Property Rights Prevail Over Environmental Protection?

YES: Richard Epstein, from "Property Rights and Environmental Protection," *Cato Policy Report* (May/June 1992)

NO: John Echeverria, from "Property Rights and Environmental Protection," *Cato Policy Report* (May/June 1992)

ISSUE SUMMARY

YES: Professor of law Richard Epstein notes that if the government takes a person's private property, it must pay that person the market value, or at least "fair compensation," for it. Epstein argues that if a law is passed that robs an individual's property of all value, that amounts to the same thing, and he or she should therefore be compensated.

NO: John Echeverria, a legal counsel to the National Audubon Society, argues that property rights have never included a right to do public harm and that environmental regulations, like other laws, do not violate a right to one's property.

The United States has always held the belief of liberty under law. However, the truth is that every law limits liberty in some way. Even though all American citizens have a right to liberty, every law infringes some possible rights, and every new law infringes some existing right. This is how it must be, for conditions change, needs evolve, and, above all, our knowledge base expands. It could be argued that all the major changes that have evolved in society during the twentieth century have come about because of the growth of knowledge. One of the largest areas of change-producing knowledge is the workings of the natural environment and environmental health.

As recently as two centuries ago, after 10,000 years of settled agricultural living, the connection between waterborne microorganisms and disease was not understood, the connection between airborne particulates and lung dysfunction was not understood, and the connection between sanitation in living habits—from latrine use to cleanliness of food and utensils—and general public health was a complete mystery. Infant and child mortality was extremely high in the most civilized societies as well as in the least, and epidemics raged through the cities periodically. People's lives were changed dramatically by knowledge (empirically grounded, if not scientifically grounded at the time) of connections between disease and unsanitary conditions and by government action following swiftly upon that knowledge. The government action inevitably limited liberty: the liberty to dispose of wastes indiscriminately as in the past, to use wells without controls as in the past, and to raise animals for food under the same unsanitary conditions as generations of farmers had in the past. The result of all that legislation is that we are currently alive in greater numbers and are far healthier than humans have been at any other time in history.

Knowledge continues to advance, including knowledge of the workings of the natural environment. On the downside, the success of the first wave of public health legislation has allowed a greater number of people than anticipated to occupy the fragile ecosystems of our salt- and fresh-water borders. The area under contention in *Lucas v. South Carolina Coastal Council*, the case that launches the debate that follows, would never have been inhabited by human beings a century or two ago; the mosquitoes from the swamps would have ensured that periodic epidemics of yellow fever and malaria swept the beaches clean of human inhabitants. Now we have the knowledge to protect ourselves from disease and other natural foes, and, consequently, nature cannot stop us from building on the barrier beaches and wetlands of our coasts.

As we have gained the technology to build on these fragile ecosystems, we have also learned why we should not: the marshes and the dunes should be left alone—unfilled, undug, undumped in—if we wish to preserve the larger life of the sea and the inland coastal areas. So where nature used to exercise its own rough zoning prerogatives through periodic disease and hurricanes, legislation now steps in to ensure public health and safety in the long run.

The debate that follows turns on two points: First, is there any wisdom in creating the environmental protection legislation under question? Or are the agencies of government, the legislature and the regulatory agency, carrying the desire for ecosystem preservation too far, into what Richard Epstein calls "institutional overclaiming"? Second, whatever the wisdom of the legislation, does it constitute a "taking" under the Constitution, requiring compensation for the property owner whose property falls under the regulations? After all, there may be excellent, even compelling, reasons for a superhighway, but if you knock down my house in order to build it, you have to pay me for my house.

As you read the following selections, ask yourself what is really meant by the right of private property. Is property an exclusive "right" held *against* the commonwealth? Or is it primarily a "stewardship" held *within* the commonwealth, utilized by private parties for public good as well as private?

YES
Richard Epstein

PROPERTY RIGHTS AND ENVIRONMENTAL PROTECTION

In December 1986 David H. Lucas purchased two undeveloped waterfront lots, which were zoned for single-family homes, on the Isle of Palms, South Carolina. Lucas's intention was to build one home to sell and a second as his own residence. In 1988, after Hurricane Hugo, South Carolina passed the Beachfront Management Act [BMA], which prohibited all new construction beyond certain setback lines and thereby rendered Lucas's property essentially useless for the purposes he had intended. The trial court found that the BMA constituted a "taking" and awarded Lucas compensation. The South Carolina Supreme Court reversed that decision, and Lucas appealed to the U.S. Supreme Court, which will soon decide whether government must compensate property owners under the Fifth Amendment's takings clause when it forbids them to develop their land. . . .

If you understand exactly what a comprehensive system of property rights entails, not only do you say that there is no opposition between property rights and environmentalism but you also say that property rights and environmental claims are mutually supportive when correctly understood.

Even though we recognize zones of autonomy, there have to be some limitations on what property owners can do with their own. It is in those limitations, I think, that one finds the effective reconciliation of property rights and environmental concerns.

The common law of nuisance, which developed over time to police disputes between property owners, is best understood as a mechanism designed to arbitrate and to reconcile disputes so as to maximize the value of each person's respective property holdings. The moment one starts to deviate from that understanding, there will be excesses in one direction or the other. If landowners, for example, are entitled to pollute more or less at will, then activities that are relatively small in value will be allowed to continue even though they cause enormous harms to other individuals. And if a system of land-use restrictions is imposed as a matter of positive law when there are no such externalities, relatively trivial gains will be exacted at the cost of enormous private losses. The system must maximize the value of inconsistent claims under general rules.

The eminent domain clause of the Fifth Amendment says, "Nor shall private property be taken for public use without just compensation." It says nothing of the justifications for governments' assuming control of property without compensating the owners—an activity that goes under the heading of police power. Therefore, to understand *Lucas* [*v. South Carolina Coastal Council*], we must first ask what kinds of activities engaged in by government *do* constitute a taking, that is, do move into the sphere of protected liberties. Then we must ask whether we can find some kind of public justification for the restrictions thus imposed.

On the first issue, it is quite clear that the common law did not draw a distinction that the constitutional lawyers insist on drawing: the modern claim that there is a vast distance between physical occupation by government and a mere regulation or restriction of use. That contemporary distinction is designed to say that we don't have to look closely at anything government does if it leaves a person in bare possession of his property.

In effect, the position of the environmentalists on this issue is, "We will allow you to keep the rind of the orange as long as we can suck out all of its juice for our own particular benefit." But exclusive possession of property is not an end in itself. The reason you want exclusive possession is to make some use of your property and if you can't make good use of it, you'd like to be able to sell or trade it to somebody else. The modern law essentially says that all those use and disposition decisions are subject to public veto.

What's wrong with that? Chiefly, it encourages a massive amount of irresponsible behavior on the part of government in its treatment of private endeavors. Essentially, a government now knows that it can attain 90 percent of its objectives and pay nothing. Why, then, would it ever bother to assume the enormous burden of occupying land for which it would then have to pay full market value? Thus, we see government regulations pushing further and further, regardless of private losses, which will never be reflected on the public ledgers —precisely the situation we find in *Lucas*.

We have in *Lucas* a change in value brought about, not because people don't want to live on the beach anymore, but because they are prohibited from using their land in the ordinary fashion. And the simplest question to ask is, what kinds of public benefits could justify that private loss?

Nobody on the Isle of Palms or anywhere else along the Carolina coast regards the restrictions in question as having been enacted for his benefit. We know that because before the regulation was imposed, land values were very high and appreciating rapidly; after the regulation was imposed, everybody who was subject to it was wiped out. When we see such a huge wipeout, we have to look for the explanation of the statute that caused it, not in the protection of the local community, but in external third-party interests who will gain something, although far less than the landowners have lost.

In the usual case, when we take property for public use, we want to make sure that there's no disproportionate burden on the affected parties, but that consideration is rightly discarded when we can say to a particular fellow that we're concentrating losses on him because he has done something of great danger to the public at large. So we now have to think about Mr. Lucas's one-family house sitting on the beach front and find in it the kind of terror that might be associated with heavy explosives or ongoing, menacing pollution.

Can we do it? I think the question almost answers itself. There is no way that we can get within a thousand miles of a common law nuisance on the facts of this particular case. There is no immediate threat of erosion. We're told we're really worried about the infliction of serious external harms. Can we get an injunction on the grounds that the roof might blow off a particular building and land in the hapless fields of a neighbor? The question again more or less answers itself.

The original statute made very little if any reference whatsoever to the problem of safety. It referred instead to promoting leisure among South Carolina citizens, promoting tourism, and promoting a general form of retreat. The moment we see safety introduced during litigation, we have to wonder whether it's a pretext for some other cause.

Another difficulty involves the breadth of the restriction. If the concern is hurricane damage, the appropriate solution is, not to limit the statute in question to just beach-front owners, but to pass a general order that says: after Hurricane Hugo, nobody is entitled to rebuild in South Carolina—in Charleston or anywhere else.

There's also the question of the relationship between means and ends. If there was $10 billion worth of damage attributable to the hurricane, at least $100 of that damage must have been attributable to flying debris and falling houses. That is a trivial problem, and even if it were serious, there are surely better ways of dealing with it. We might say, for example, that anybody whose house could be found littering the beach had to remove all debris.

We hear over and over again that the government's environmental programs will shrink in size if compensation is required in *Lucas*. Those programs *should* shrink, because when government is allowed to take without compensation, it claims too much for environmental causes relative to other kinds of causes that command equal attention. Unless we introduce a system that requires the government to take and pay when it restricts private use not associated with the prevention of harms, we'll face an institutional overclaiming problem. The expansion of government will become the major issue. The just compensation clause is designed to work a perfectly sensible and moderate accommodation, to force the government to make responsible choices.

... According to Mr. Echeverria, it would be within the state's power to order everybody who has a home on those islands to dismantle it immediately so that there would be no flying roofs to hurt anybody else. The state could order the demolition of old construction as well as enjoin new construction.

Moreover, the beach front is not the only area peculiarly exposed to the environmental and hurricane risks that we're talking about. What about Charleston? It's also exposed to those risks. Do we say, in effect, that in the name of environmental protection we must raze the entire city without compensation because somebody's house might fall on somebody else's?

This is not a question of environmental interaction. We now have a set of restrictions that promises to cause billions in private losses, and we've heard it said that we can stop houses from being knocked down by ordering them to be razed.

There is no sense of proportion or balance in Echeverria's position. An ounce of environmental angst is sufficient to allow draconian measures that forbid the very activities that enable people to use the environment constructively. This is a classic case of overclaiming, which occurs because the environmental lobby can go to the state legislature and say, "Let us have our way. You're not going to have to pay for this." And environmentalists can prove that the benefit is greater than the political cost. But that's the wrong test. From a social point of view, the *right* test is whether the benefit is greater than the cost inflicted on the property holders.

NO

John Echeverria

PROPERTY RIGHTS AND
ENVIRONMENTAL PROTECTION

As everybody in this room knows, our national politics is driven by sound bites. The same is true in a judicial context. The hard facts of a particular case can make bad law, and the sound bite in this case is that David Lucas purchased a piece of property for about $1 million and two years later the South Carolina legislature passed a law that left him with nothing. But that's the sound bite, and the sound bite obscures the entirely genuine and legitimate goals that the South Carolina legislature had in mind—to prevent harms to the public, which are not trivial concerns.

My goal in this debate is to convince you that once you get past the sound bite of the impact on Lucas, you'll understand that the Supreme Court should and will conclude that there was no taking in this case. Before I get into it though, ... I want to try to correct the sound bite by reciting to you the facts of a case the Supreme Court dealt with in 1987. That case involved a similar kind of regulation and raised the same fundamental issues of principle but leads to quite a different sound bite. I am referring to *First English Evangelical Lutheran Church v. County of Los Angeles.* The church had set up a camp for handicapped children in a flood plain, and a fire occurred in the watershed upstream from the camp. The county recognized immediately that there was enormous danger, since the vegetation had been removed, that flood waters could come down the river and wipe out the camp. In fact, a storm did occur, a flood did occur and the camp was completely wiped out. In response, the county put in place an interim ordinance that said there could be no inhabitable structures, which could be wiped out once again, within the flood plain. When the Supreme Court got the case it did not resolve it on the merits. Instead, it used that case to reach the conclusion that a temporary taking is compensable under the Fifth Amendment. But in the dissenting opinion, several of the justices said there was no question that the ordinance was a valid public health and safety regulation and there was no taking. And Chief Justice Rehnquist said that the Court didn't have to touch that issue and would leave it to the lower courts to find out whether there had been a taking. The case was sent back to the lower courts. No taking was found, and

From John Echeverria, "Property Rights and Environmental Protection," *Cato Policy Report* (May/June 1992). Copyright © 1992 by The Cato Institute, Washington, DC. Reprinted by permission.

when the case went up for review, the Supreme Court, which probably has some understanding of sound bites itself, declined to review it.

Lucas, as it was actually presented to the trial court, is actually a fairly easy case, in my view. The Supreme Court should conclude that Lucas did not establish a taking because he presented his claim based on the completely preposterous theory that if he suffered economic harm, that alone, regardless of any other consideration, entitled him to compensation under the Fifth Amendment. The fact of the matter is that the Supreme Court has never held, and I predict will never hold, that economic injury, standing alone, is sufficient grounds for a Fifth Amendment claim. The Court has consistently rejected that way of thinking for several reasons. First, the Court has recognized that every piece of property held in the United States is subject to the condition that it can't be used to harm others. That goes back to common law. Property rights are not absolute. They're conditional upon a responsibility to the community in which one resides.

The Department of Justice recommended initially that the United States in its brief take the position that economic harm, standing alone, constitutes a taking. Happily, wiser heads prevailed, and the solicitor general filed a brief that specifically repudiated that theory.

Richard Epstein, in his amicus brief, admits that a complete wipeout does not, by itself, make out a taking. We disagree about the range of activities in which the government can engage to prevent public harm without providing compensation. But we agree that within that range of activities, the government can act to prevent harm and no compensation is due regardless of the impact. I think it's

on that issue that this case will basically turn.

Epstein's point, at least as I understand it from his brief, is that the burden of proof is on the government to show the legitimacy of the regulation, to show that it is in fact a public harm–prevention measure. But again, one doesn't have a property interest in harming others, and if the government is trying to prevent a landowner from harming others, then there's simply no taking.

I think that Epstein and I agree that there is a line between private property and the ability of people to impose external harms on others and to harm the general public by the use of property. The question is, where is that line drawn and on what side of the line does this particular regulation fall?

I submit that the harm the South Carolina legislature was trying to deal with here was both very real and very substantial. Barrier islands are not like other real estate. They literally migrate; they move. They're unconsolidated sandy sediments that migrate laterally up and down the shore and landward in response to the action of waves and winds. They are unstable areas that are very hazardous for construction. Barrier islands in the natural state provide the most important defense for coastal areas against the effects of storms, high winds, and storm surges associated with hurricanes. Building on the beach dune system, which destroys the dune, or trying to stabilize the dune fundamentally undermines the integrity of the system. Sand naturally moves from a dune down to the beach area, replenishing the beach and allowing it to serve as a barrier to storms. If the beach dune system is stabilized, its natural function is destroyed.

It is not simply a question of harm to somebody who builds on such an unstable area, although I think there are some reasons to support paternalism in some circumstances. It is also a question of harm to others. Landward properties depend on the defense provided by the beach dune system. If that system is destroyed, those properties are exposed to storm damage. Epstein belittled what the coastal geologists refer to as projectile damage, but it's a very real phenomenon. Buildings that are on the ocean shore in front of or on top of the dunes are particularly exposed to the effects of wind and storms. After Hurricane Hugo in South Carolina, the primary adverse effects on landward structures were found to be due precisely to exposed properties that were hurled landward. All of those risks also have to be considered in light of global warming and a consequent sea level rise—again, exacerbating the hazardous nature of construction on the ocean shore and the dangers to other property owners posed by such construction.

The South Carolina Beachfront Management Act is an entirely rational, thoughtful, well-tailored response to a public hazard. The first purpose of the act, and clearly the primary purpose as recited in the act itself, is to protect the public. The act recites the fact that beaches are important recreational areas and identifies other public purposes that are served by the beaches. But what is most clear is that the regulation at issue here is specifically tailored to address a public-hazard problem.

My final point, and perhaps the most important, is that the statute specifically provided that Mr. Lucas, if he believed the line drawn pursuant to the legislative scheme was unfair, could present evidence to the coastal council and explain that the line on his property should be drawn at a different point. He never took advantage of that opportunity. He simply said, "I've been hurt and I am entitled to compensation." I believe the Supreme Court will disagree.

POSTSCRIPT

Should Property Rights Prevail Over Environmental Protection?

Political conservatives and liberals tend to divide along different lines at different points in history. In the early nineteenth century, the conservatives believed that the right of the community came before the right of the individual, while the liberals championed individual liberty over community control and democratic equality over the traditional hierarchy. With regard to the current debate, this earlier terminology has been abandoned largely because the focus of ethical debate has changed from the *political* to the *economic* questions—from questions of community governance to questions of resource management. In short, the United States has moved from an era of *political philosophy* to an era of *business management*, where the entire nation is seen as a collective resource to be managed by those with authority over it. However, if the more political terms are applied, the roles of Epstein and Echeverria may be seen in this way: Echeverria is the conservative businessman, conserving resources and letting nature take its course, while Epstein is the defender of the strategy of instant consumption.

If you were the judge who had to decide the *Lucas* case, how would you rule? Do you believe that Lucas is entitled to compensation, as argued by Epstein, or that there was no instance of compensable taking involved in the legislation, as argued by Echeverria? Does your response reflect the conservative or the liberal position?

SUGGESTED READINGS

Robert M. Andersen, "Technology, Pollution Control, and EPA Access to Commercial Property: A Constitutional and Policy Framework," *Boston College Environmental Affairs Law Review* (Fall 1989).

Rogene Buchholz, *Principles of Environmental Management: The Greening of Business* (Prentice Hall, 1993).

John Campbell and Leon N. Lindberg, "Property Rights and the Organization of Economic Activity by the State," *American Sociological Review* (October 1990).

Rachel Carson, *The Edge of the Sea* (Houghton Mifflin, 1955).

Arthur Chan, "The Changing View of Property Rights in Natural Resources Management," *American Journal of Economics and Sociology* (April 1989).

G. Tyler Miller, *Living in the Environment*, 7th ed. (Wadsworth, 1992).

David E. Mills, "Zoning Rights and Land Development Timing," *Land Economics* (August 1990).

ISSUE 18

Are Market Incentives Sufficient to Clean Up the Water?

YES: Robert W. Hahn, from "Clean Water Policy," *The American Enterprise* (November/December 1993)

NO: Jeffery A. Foran and Robert W. Adler, from "Cleaner Water, But Not Clean Enough," *Issues in Science and Technology* (Winter 1993/1994)

ISSUE SUMMARY

YES: Robert W. Hahn, a resident scholar at the American Enterprise Institute, advocates a market-based approach to ending water pollution as a more effective replacement for the inefficient "command and control" approach to water regulation that is presently in use.

NO: Jeffery A. Foran, executive director of the Risk Science Institute, and Robert W. Adler, director of the Clean Water Project at the Natural Resources Defense Council, argue that the goal of zero discharge of toxic pollutants is achievable and should be required but that only enforceable legislation—not the free market—can accomplish this task.

How clean should our drinking water be? The question sounds preposterous; obviously, we want pure water and nothing else! But relatively few countries in the world have access to water that will not make people sick. We are among the lucky few. What may be *more* preposterous is that we use our pure drinking water to take showers, bathe our pets, and water our lawns. Very few nations can afford that kind of profligacy.

Let us examine a slightly different question: What kinds of additives to water, in what amounts, should be considered "contaminants"? What levels of what kinds of pollutants are unacceptable? Remember that "natural" water — water that is untouched by any human endeavor—is not necessarily safe to drink. Without artificial chemical additives (especially chlorine), our water supply would not be safe to drink. Nature provides more than enough natural contamination of the water, in the form of diseases and parasites, as any resident of a developing nation can attest. So the debate is not between what is "natural" and what is "chemical pollution"; the debate is between what is safe and what is not. Also at issue here is what the best way is to meet our standards of safety.

Manufacturing has a long history of heavily using water in its processing of raw materials into products for the market. The wastes from this processing are often flushed back into the water supply. Many of these wastes are highly toxic due to chemical changes that have taken place during the process and to chemicals that linger in the by-products. The poisons so created often go undetected for decades. In fact, it was not until epidemiological research uncovered unusually high cancer rates and unexplained "fish kills" in certain areas around lakes and streams that anyone began to pay attention to the causes.

Since the middle of the 1950s, agriculture has also become a major pollutor of the water supply. From the 1950s to the 1970s, the green revolution—an international attempt to grow crops more quickly and on smaller parcels with the use of fertilizers and a new generation of pesticides—further burdened the water supply with rain run-off containing those chemicals. The old farming methods of rotating crops, "resting" the land, and allowing weeds and grasses to recycle naturally had prevented most of that run-off from entering the water supply.

It has been shown that creative incentives by the government at local, state, and federal levels, including economic encouragement to both industry and the farmers, can lead to the successful cleanup of our water supplies. Dramatic improvement sparked by such incentives has already been observed in U.S. bodies of water formerly characterized by lethal pollution, such as the Hudson River and Lake Michigan. But is government involvement the most efficient way to clean up the water? This is the essence of the debate that follows.

In February 1995 the U.S. House of Representatives passed a bill designed to weaken the protections of the water supply delineated in the Clean Water Act of 1987. The U.S. Senate has declined to act on that bill, so there has been no substantial change. As you read the following selections, remember that every improvement made toward environmental cleanliness costs money and that every improvement not made may be costly in terms of human health and welfare. Ask yourself what resources should be allotted for what risks.

YES

Robert W. Hahn

CLEAN WATER POLICY

The first major piece of environmental legislation to reach President Clinton's desk is likely to be the reauthorization of the Clean Water Act, last amended in 1987. Over the past two decades, water pollution regulation has been aimed at cleaning up municipal waste and reducing industrial water pollution. This effort has successfully reduced pollution and improved water quality in some circumstances. For example, between 1972 and 1988, there was a 69 percent increase in the population being served by technically sophisticated sewage treatment plants. The overall trends in water quality are less clear, however. Between 1978 and 1987 no significant progress was made in traditional measures of quality such as the levels of dissolved oxygen and bacteria in the water. Water in many parts of the country, moreover, is still priced well below its economic value, leading to excessive consumption and, in some cases, to lower levels of water quality. In addition, agricultural and other sources of water pollution such as runoff from urban areas (called nonpoint sources because of their diffuse nature) remain largely unregulated.

Three bills are presently circulating in Congress to strengthen clean water regulation, all of which focus primarily on water quality. Senators Max Baucus (D-Mont.) and John Chafee (R-R.I.) have recommended expanding the bureaucracy that enforces current laws, increasing the funding for sewage treatment, and adding toxic substances and nonpoint sources to existing regulations. Congressman Jim Oberstar's (D-Minn.) bill focuses on the regulation of nonpoint sources of pollution. Finally, a bill introduced by Congressman Gerry Studds (D-Mass.) calls for a system of user fees on toxic discharges and products known to contribute to water pollution, and for an excise tax on ingredients in pesticides and fertilizers. The revenue from these taxes would be invested in clean water infrastructure such as stormwater controls.

All of these bills would increase regulation with little regard for the economic consequences. Moreover, none of them promotes innovative approaches to regulation that could achieve better water quality at a cost lower than traditional methods of regulation.

From Robert W. Hahn, "Clean Water Policy," *The American Enterprise* (November/December 1993). Copyright © 1993 by The American Enterprise Institute. Reprinted by permission. *The American Enterprise* is a Washington-based magazine of politics, business, and culture, (800) 562-1973.

There is an alternative to traditional water quality regulation. We now can achieve improved levels of water quality at lower cost to the public, provided that Congress is willing to embark on a new approach.

DIRECTIONS FOR REFORM

The great British economist Joan Robinson once asked: "Why is there litter in the public park, but no litter in my back garden?" The answer, of course, involves incentives—we have clear incentives to keep our backyards clean. And while each of us would like to see the park kept clean, we would prefer that other people do it.

The same problem arises in managing water resources. Because we collectively own most of our major water bodies, none of us has an incentive to take care of these resources the way we would our own homes and yards. Congress should therefore change the incentive structure so that individual consumers, governments, and businesses have a direct stake in taking better care of our precious water resources.

There are basically two ways to change the incentive structure and achieve better management of water resources. The first is to sell off major public waterways, including rivers, lakes, and streams. Putting these assets into private hands would improve water quality and quantity, provided that property rights for water quality and quantity were well defined and enforceable. The new owners of these assets would have a very strong incentive to manage these water resources as well as they take care of their own backyards. Acting rationally, they would keep the water clean and allow people to use it only if they paid a price that reflected the water's value. But this approach, however meritorious, simply isn't realistic in many situations. Privatizing the nation's water resources would start a political firestorm, if not a revolution.

A less radical way to manage water resources is to apply basic economic analysis to the public management of them. This involves two steps: first, identifying appropriate goals for water quality and water use; and second, choosing appropriate methods for achieving these goals.

The level of water quality we aim for will be determined, among other things, by the economic benefits associated with consuming or using the water resource and the economic costs of providing that resource. High water quality can help preserve species habitat; allow both commercial and recreational uses of water bodies including fishing, swimming, and boating; and provide a safe drinking water supply and the satisfaction that comes from knowing waterways are clean.

INTRODUCING COST-BENEFIT ANALYSIS

According to conventional methods of cost-benefit analysis, standards should be set so that the incremental benefit of cleaning up the water just equals the incremental cost. The costs and benefits of water improvement, however, are difficult to quantify, particularly the benefits. Nonetheless, it is absolutely imperative to try to quantify them if clean water policy is to be developed in a way that leads to improvements in our standard of living.

The Environmental Protection Agency (EPA) has not devoted significant resources to developing analyses that pinpoint the areas where regulatory efforts should be best focused under the Clean Water Act. The most comprehensive analysis of the costs and benefits of current plans to achieve the objectives of the Clean Water Act was performed by economists Randy Lyon, then at Georgetown University, and Scott Farrow of Carnegie Mellon. They argue that in many current implementation plans the incremental costs of improving water quality exceed the incremental benefits. This means that many existing EPA standards and regulatory approaches are wasteful. At the same time, there are certainly heavily polluted and/or heavily used water bodies where significant improvements in water quality are well worth the cost.

Results from studies by these authors and from other studies suggest that more cost-benefit analyses should be done so that Congress and the states can concentrate on the right water problems in the right water bodies. Specifically, EPA should commission a state-of-the-art cost-benefit analysis of the current Clean Water Act so that the political debate on reauthorization can be better informed. This analysis should attempt to point out where standards should be tightened and where they should be relaxed.

The analysis should also identify key areas of uncertainty in the estimation of benefits so that more informed decisions about appropriate standards can be made. At present, relatively little is known about the relationship between the level of pollution and human health for many water contaminants, or the extent to which people value clean water that they themselves do not use.

EPA should also develop a database that permits a more accurate assessment of the benefits and costs of the Clean Water Act, and the agency should be re-quired to submit a report to Congress every two years that addresses the benefits and costs of controlling different pollutants in different waterways. (A provision in the Clean Air Act Amendments of 1990 mandates that a cost-benefit analysis be used for selected statutes in the act.) Without such information, Congress will not be in a position to make informed decisions about the economic consequences of proposed statutes.

ECONOMIC INCENTIVES

Once a standard has been chosen, the government must determine how that standard should be achieved. One way is to prescribe a technology that each company in an industry must use. This is sometimes referred to as "command-and-control" regulation. Command-and-control regulation has been criticized by economists because it does not give businesses and individuals much choice in how they achieve an environmental goal. For example, a law may require that a power plant use a scrubber to reduce air pollution, even though another technology or group of technologies might be more effective in achieving the same level of air quality. Because this approach does not take into account differing circumstances and costs, society ends up paying more.

There is a better way to meet the government's standard. The introduction of economic incentives can address many pollution problems effectively. The idea behind using economic incentives is to save resources while achieving a particular environmental goal. For example, in 1990, Congress adopted an economic incentive approach for reducing acid rain that could save as much as $1 billion annually when compared to a conventional command-and-control approach that required the largest polluters to install scrubbers.

There are, moreover, many different kinds of economic incentives. They include subsidies, taxes, deposit-refund schemes, pollution charges, marketable permits, and the removal of institutional barriers that lead to price distortions. In the interest of brevity, I will discuss only pollution charges and marketable permits.

Charge systems impose a fee or tax on pollution. For example, a chemical manufacturer would be charged for every unit of a pollutant that it discharged into a river. Several European nations, including France, the Netherlands, and Germany, currently use water pollution charge systems.

Pollution charges by themselves do not restrict the amount of pollutants that may be emitted; rather, they tax emissions. Such taxes ensure that a firm will internalize the previously external pollution costs. A firm can choose to pay the full tax or to reduce its emissions partially or completely—whichever option best fits its interests.

The advantage of the system is that all businesses face the same incentive to limit pollution at the margin. A firm will control pollution up to the point where the marginal cost of control just equals the tax it must pay. The result is that the total costs of pollution control are minimized, unlike other methods of allocating the pollution control burden across businesses. Pollution charges, like other market-based mechanisms, also provide ongoing incentives for businesses to develop and adopt better pollution control technologies.

MARKETABLE PERMIT SYSTEMS

Marketable or tradable permits can achieve the same cost-minimizing allocation of the pollution control burden as the pollution charges do, while achieving a particular environmental target. Under a tradable permit system, an overall allowable level of pollution is established for the affected area, portions of which are then allotted to businesses and government entities in the form of permits. A business that keeps its emission levels below its allotted level may sell or lease its surplus permits to others.

As with a charge system, the marginal cost of control is identical across businesses and thus the total cost of control is minimized for any given level of total pollution control. In the case of local water pollution control, for example, this approach could be substantially more efficient than current regulatory methods, both because its inherent flexibility takes advantage of differences in control costs and because it allows individual businesses to decide where and how to make desired reductions in pollution.

In the event that overall environmental targets are viewed as too strict, the government may choose to increase the supply of permits. Likewise, regulators could take the opposite stance and reduce the supply of permits in order to reduce allowable emissions.

Permit systems have been used primarily in the United States. Examples include the Environmental Protection Agency's Emissions Trading Program for reducing air pollution; the nationwide lead phasedown program for gasoline, which allowed fuel refiners to trade reductions in lead content; and the gradual phaseout of chlorofluorocarbons, where businesses are allowed to trade the right to produce or import limited quantities of these chemicals. In addition, several Western states have implemented water quantity trading in limited forms. Some states are also considering trading programs to control discharges from farms and municipal wastewater treatment plants in the least costly way.

BETTER WATER MANAGEMENT

Congress could encourage EPA to implement both pollution charge systems and marketable permit approaches. But because charges are likely to encounter political resistance, Congress should promote more widespread use of marketable permits by requiring EPA to use them as the tool of choice for improving water quality or to justify in writing why it has not chosen this alternative.

This would move the agency away from the command-and-control approach it has used for the last 20 years. A system of marketable permits could promote trading of environmental credits among a variety of sources.

Municipal treatment plants and private companies, such as chemical plants and pulp and paper plants, that can measure the amount of pollution they produce at specific points within their plants (so-called point sources) can trade permits among themselves. This approach will be effective in areas where current requirements have not succeeded in achieving water quality goals as well as in areas where load-based requirements are used, which specify a target level of pollution for a waterway. Those entities that treat their own waste and can easily reduce pollution will do so, and they will be able to make money by selling surplus permits to those who cannot cheaply reduce their own effluent. Polluters whose efflu-ent is treated at a sewage plant can also trade permits among themselves.

Nonpoint sources—farms with fertilizer or pesticide runoff, for example—can trade both among themselves and with point sources. Many current problems with water quality have arisen because nonpoint sources, such as agricultural runoff, are typically unregulated or minimally regulated. Over 18,000 water bodies will not attain water quality standards even if all point sources meet their technical requirements due to pollution from nonpoint sources. While EPA has acknowledged that nonpoint sources are a major problem, little has been done to cope with the problem.

Potentially, great cost savings can be achieved if nonpoint sources can be brought into the system. One way to do this is for EPA to develop guidelines for trading with nonpoint sources. Even if nonpoint sources remain largely unregulated, heavily regulated point sources should have the ability to trade antipollution permits with nonpoint sources provided they can show that water quality will improve as a result.

Technical uncertainties make it hard to judge how pollution levels from nonpoint sources affect water quality; there is no smokestack, for example, that can be easily fitted with a measuring device. These difficulties may initially lead to problems in determining acceptable emissions levels. Where monitoring can only be done at great cost, experts may need to rely on their practical judgment to ensure that water quality will improve. One promising application for controlling nonpoint source pollution involves the farms just north of Florida's Everglades. I have proposed a marketable permit system to limit phosphorous entering the Everglades by restricting the amount of phosphorous leaving the Everglades Agricultural Area. If a marketable permit system is not practical, it may be possible to tax a pollutant, such as phosphates in detergent, to limit its use.

Markets and permit trading can play an important role in reducing nonlocalized contaminants such as phosphorus in a cost-effective way. For example, I am working with the government in Sydney, Australia, to establish trading rules for farmers along the Hawkesbury-Nepean river system; the new rules will encourage the cost-effective phosphorus reductions needed to limit the growth of the blue-green algae that sometimes clogs parts of the river system.

The technical challenges of regulating nonpoint sources are not unique to a market-based approach, but apply to all regulatory systems including command-and-control ones. A key advantage of trading with nonpoint sources is that it will provide environmental benefits while lowering the overall cost of regulation. If regulation remains largely voluntary, a market-based approach will provide a positive incentive to limit water pollution.

Congress should also direct EPA to develop and implement rules for trading among different kinds of wetlands. Wetlands trading would provide property owners with appropriate incentives for preserving wetlands, while giving owners greater flexibility in deciding how they can develop their property. For example, Disney World agreed to restore and maintain a wetland in exchange for the right to develop its site. Because artificial wetlands can be constructed and wetlands can be restored, there is latitude for trading among wetlands. Establishing the rules for trading will be a challenge, but EPA should provide guidance on this issue.

Congress should also encourage EPA and the states to establish total maximum pollution levels for water bodies that do not meet water quality standards. The focus on environmental outcomes is likely to lead to better environmental quality at lower cost. Where there are unacceptable damages associated with pollution from specific sites, some command-and-control regulation may be necessary to set the maximum ceilings on pollution from these sites. Nonetheless, the goal of regulation should be to provide the maximum improvement in environmental quality per dollar spent. This is best achieved through making greater use of market-based approaches.

Most, if not all, of the preceding recommendations could be implemented under the existing Clean Water Act, but explicit congressional support for marketable permits will spur their use. Congress should make it clear that it is primarily concerned with making necessary improvements in water quality in a timely manner. The precise method of achieving these environmental improvements should be left to the business and government entities responsible for making the needed reductions.

WHITHER WATER REGULATION?

Integrating water quantity and water quality concerns will be a fundamental aim of the 1990s. The recommendations here have focused primarily on quality issues, but the two issues are inextricably linked. Just as water quality can be improved through the introduction of markets, so too can water quantity. Moreover, markets for water quantity can improve water quality by encouraging water conservation. While water quantity issues are generally subject to state law, the federal government could help by endorsing the use of water markets and allowing the transfer of water contracts for federal reclamation water supply projects.

We have the technical know-how to apply market-based economic methods that will improve water quality and allocation. The question is whether we have the political will. I am optimistic that more markets for improving water management will be introduced. The only question is whether Washington will lead the charge or follow. The reauthorization of the Clean Water Act provides Congress with a unique opportunity to demonstrate leadership in a way that benefits the health and welfare of the American people.

NO

Jeffery A. Foran and
Robert W. Adler

CLEANER WATER, BUT NOT CLEAN ENOUGH

The Clean Water Act has undeniably helped control and reduce pollution of the nation's surface waters. Many gross pollution problems that existed a generation ago have been eliminated. Thirty years ago, Lake Erie had deteriorated so much that an article in *Science News* declared the lake dead. In 1969, the Cuyahoga River, which was heavily contaminated with flammable oils and grease, actually caught fire. These particular problems, of course, no longer exist. In addition, more subtle but no less important pollution problems have also improved since the 1960s. For example, levels of polychlorinated biphenyls (PCBs) have declined dramatically in fish and other aquatic biota in systems such as the Great Lakes.

The Clean Water Act, which was passed in 1972, has been a critical factor behind improving water quality. Major amendments enacted in 1977 and 1987 included provisions aimed at further improving the regulation of toxic substances. But despite its many successes, the Clean Water Act (CWA) and its amendments have failed to adequately control many sources of toxic pollutants.

For example, the act required that by 1983 all surface waters should have attained a quality that "provides for the protection and propagation of fish, shellfish, and wildlife and provides for recreation in and on the water." Surface waters that achieve this level of quality are classified under the act as fishable and swimmable. Yet, according to the Environmental Protection Agency's (EPA) most recent National Water Quality Inventory, at least a third of assessed rivers, half of assessed estuaries, and more than half of assessed lakes are not yet clean enough to merit this classification.

Continuing pollution problems in surface waters have also led the U.S./Canadian International Joint Commission (IJC), a quasi-governmental body that oversees quality issues in waters shared by the two nations, to designate 42 regions in the Great Lakes basin as highly contaminated. Also, nearly all states now declare that at least some fish taken by sport anglers from contaminated lakes and streams should not be consumed. And the cost of losses in recreational fishing, swimming, and boating opportunities caused by the discharge of toxic pollutants is estimated by the U.S. General Accounting Office (GAO) to be as high as $800 million per year.

The types of pollutants that continue to cause water quality impairments are widely varied. A total of 362 contaminants, including metals such as lead and mercury, an array of pesticides, and organic industrial chemicals such as PCBs and dioxin, have been found in the Great Lakes ecosystem. Eleven of these substances have been classified by the IJC as pollutants of "critical concern."

Research conducted by the IJC and others in the Great Lakes basin has provided specific information on the loads of some highly toxic pollutants that are discharged to surface waters. For example, Lake Superior receives nearly 500 pounds of PCBs (mainly from nonpoint sources) annually, and Lakes Michigan, Huron, Erie, and Ontario receive up to 5,000 pounds annually (mainly from nonpoint sources, although over 1,000 pounds are discharged to Lakes Erie and Ontario from point sources annually). Between 1,000 and 5,000 pounds of mercury are discharged to each of the Great Lakes annually mainly from nonpoint sources, although point sources appear to contribute the major portion of mercury in Lake Erie. Large loads of lead are also contributed to the Great Lakes, mainly from point sources. Over 1,000 pounds of lead are discharged annually to Lakes Superior and Huron, over 8,000 pounds are discharged to Lake Ontario, over 30,000 pounds are discharged to Lake Erie, and over 50,000 pounds are discharged to Lake Michigan annually.

Pollutants in water are responsible for damage to wildlife that includes eggshell thinning, reduced hatching success and infertility, immune system suppression, behavioral changes, physical impairments such as crossed beaks and clubfeet as well as adverse effects on populations and communities of organisms. Similarly, the health of human populations has been affected by toxic substances in surface waters. For example, cognitive and other deficits have been documented in children born of mothers who were exposed to PCBs through consumption of large quantities of contaminated fish.

Congress is expected to reauthorize and possibly amend the CWA again early in 1994. This presents an opportunity to correct the law's flaws, which have allowed some water-pollution problems to remain. In particular, we see a need to strengthen the provisions aimed at preventing pollution rather than relying on mechanisms to treat pollution at the point of discharge.

SOURCES OF FAILURE

The objective of the CWA is to restore and maintain the chemical, physical, and biological integrity of the nation's waters. In pursuit of that objective, the act explicitly states as one goal that "the discharge of pollutants into the navigable waters be eliminated." Congress designated 1985 as the date to achieve the zero-discharge goal. A 1992 IJC report found that the United States had yet to completely eliminate the discharge of any persistent toxic substance. Failure to achieve this goal and the act's other objectives, as well as continuing water-quality problems, are attributable to inadequacies in the existing water quality regulatory process.

To understand the reasons for our failure to achieve the act's goals, it is necessary to examine the two approaches that are used concurrently under the act to control toxic substances discharged to surface waters. The first approach is the mandated use of specific treatment technology for discharges from point sources of pollution, such as industry and waste treatment plants. For each category of industry, EPA issues industrywide effluent limitations defined as the "best available technology economically achievable." However, the designated technology may not be adequate to protect all surface waters from harm.

The second approach was developed for situations where technology-based controls do not protect water quality. This "water-quality-based" approach requires EPA and the states to set maximum allowable concentrations of toxic pollutants in surface waters without regard to economic impacts or technological achievability. The concentrations are supposed to be low enough so that they pose no threat to individual organisms (including humans) or to populations, species, communities, and ecosystems. Safe concentrations of toxic pollutants are defined under the CWA by chemical-specific, numeric Water Quality Criteria (WQC). In principle, WQCs could be set at zero where necessary to protect human health and the environment. In practice, however, WQCs are set well above zero, based on often-contentious concepts of risk assessment or implicit assumptions about technological and economic attainability.

States are required under the CWA to adopt WQCs and to use them in determining how much to control the discharge of toxic pollutants from point sources as well as from nonpoint sources (such as agricultural runoff and pollutants from the atmosphere). What the states do, though it is not necessarily sanctioned by the law, is to require that pollutant concentrations meet WQC in lakes or streams only after a discharge has been diluted by mixing with water in the receiving system. Thus an industry or waste-water treatment plant is allowed to discharge toxic pollutants in its effluent at concentrations higher than WQC for those pollutants, so long as pollutant concentrations are then diluted enough in the receiving water to meet WQC.

There are two problems with this approach. First, it does not force dischargers to comply with the CWA mandate of zero-discharge of pollutants to surface waters. In fact, the entire WQC system is based on the assumption that there is an acceptable level of pollutant discharge. Second, WQC and dilution capacity are used even where the ability of the environment to assimilate pollutants has been exceeded, or where adverse impacts have occurred, particularly in receiving systems far downstream from the point of discharge. Even though a lake has unacceptable levels of a pollutant, the pollutant can be discharged into a stream that empties into the lake so long as it is diluted to acceptable levels in the stream.

Under the 1972 act, technology-based effluent guidelines were supposed to require pollution-reduction technologies that not only became increasingly more stringent until zero-discharge was achieved, but that, in theory, would progress from end-of-pipe treatment approaches to changes in manufacturing processes and other strategies that would actually prevent pollution at its sources. This progression was expected to continue to reduce pollutants while also reducing the economic burden associated with installing increasingly costly treatment technology at the point of discharge. Unfortunately, EPA has been locked into a largely end-of-pipe treatment approach to pollutant control. The result has been only partial progress toward zero-discharge under the technology-based approach, along with ever-rising costs associated with more stringent forms of waste treatment.

The water-quality-based approach to toxicant control could also force technology toward increasingly strict pollution control requirements—and, ultimately, zero-discharge. But that will not happen as long as the operating assumption is that there are acceptable levels of pollution in surface waters and that we can count on receiving systems to dilute toxic effluents.

A POLLUTION-PREVENTION STRATEGY

The most effective way to reduce the discharge of a toxic pollutant into water is to reduce the use of the chemical or its precursors. Pollution prevention can be attained by reducing the use of a chemical through changes in industrial processes (including more efficient use of chemicals), substitute chemicals, and recycling. Or reduction (and in some cases elimination) may be accomplished by the phaseout of chemicals, product changes or bans, and behavior changes that affect consumption, use, or disposal of products that create pollutants.

Each prevention strategy should result in less waste production and toxic pollutant release, not just to surface waters but to other parts of the environment as well. Thus, prevention will reduce discharges of toxic pollutants below the levels pos-sible with waste treatment alone. Ultimately, where a toxic chemical is eliminated via substitution, process change, or other mechanisms, or where environmental releases are eliminated, the discharge of that chemical will also be eliminated. The zero-discharge goal of the CWA can thus be met without risk-based arguments about acceptable pollutant levels, without the use of dilution to determine discharge limits, and without increasingly expensive treatment technologies applied at the point of discharge.

The difficulty of choosing chemical-specific pollution-prevention mechanisms and developing a schedule for their implementation is a potential obstacle to achieving pollution prevention. We therefore propose a scientific priority-setting process to determine a chemical's toxicity and assess the potential for exposure to it.

Exposure is assessed by evaluating a chemical's propensity to accumulate in the tissues of fish and other organisms, its persistence in the environment, and the amount that is released to the environment. Toxicity to aquatic plants and animals, as well as to terrestrial species (including birds and humans), is assessed by criteria that include death, impairment of growth and reproduction, and other adverse impacts, including cancer, from short- and long-term exposures.

Each toxicity and exposure component includes a set of triggers to determine whether a chemical can be classified as of high, moderate, or low concern relative to other chemicals. Once chemicals have been screened and classified, appropriate pollution-prevention activities and schedules for those activities (including the time it will take to reach zero-discharge) can be chosen.

Other factors may also influence the choice of pollution-prevention activities and the time it will take to implement them. For example, where it is determined that a hazardous chemical should be phased out of an industrial process, the pace of the phaseout may be influenced by whether there are safer substitutes, by the availability of different technologies that may not use toxic chemicals, and by the cost of developing these new chemicals or technologies. It should be generally recognized, however, that although such considerations may determine the length of time it takes to phase out a hazardous chemical, they should not affect the basic decision to phase it out.

MAKING IT LAW

Two different approaches should be taken to incorporate pollution-prevention measures into the CWA. First, the provisions of the law designed to implement technology-based and water-quality-based controls should be fine-tuned to point EPA back in the direction of zero-discharge. Fairly modest statutory changes might achieve the desired results. Second, broader changes and new requirements should be added to promote planning for pollution prevention by government and private parties.

Several requirements of the CWA should be modified to maximize the degree to which existing programs require or encourage prevention of pollution. First, the sections of the act that dictate the rules under which EPA writes categorical effluent limitations (and related pretreatment standards for dischargers to public sewers) could be modified to reinforce the original pollution-prevention philosophy, emphasizing technology-based re-

quirements for the control of toxic pollutants.

Existing provisions require EPA to "take into account" such factors as "process changes" and "non-water-quality environmental effects." The former is designed to take EPA beyond treatment applied at the discharge point and the latter to prevent impacts on other parts of the environment besides surface water. Nothing, however, forces EPA to select such options over traditional treatment methods. The act should be modified to include a hierarchy of options, under which pollution-prevention activities such as chemical substitution and process changes that reduce pollution at the source must be exhausted before point-of-discharge treatment is considered. In addition, limitations on the concentration of a toxic pollutant in a discharge could be expressed in terms of the efficiency of particular industrial processes (as efficiency relates to chemical usage), as well as the amount of reduction of the chemical in the effluent that can be achieved by pollution prevention.

Closing loopholes in the water-quality-based approach also would stimulate pollution prevention. Dischargers should be induced to adopt prevention methods through discharge permits that require the application of WQC at the point of discharge rather than allowing dilution of the effluent in the receiving water. Elimination of the dilution allowance would require reductions in the concentration and mass of pollutants that could be discharged. Industries and waste-water treatment plants could achieve these reductions by employing more expensive treatment technologies or by potentially cheaper pollution-prevention techniques.

The act should also be modified to achieve consistency among state WQC for toxicants and in the procedures used to translate criteria into discharge limits. At present, states may set their own criteria and develop their own implementation procedures, albeit with EPA guidance and authority to approve criteria and procedures. This creates an opportunity for states to use lax standards to attract business. EPA's water-quality criteria should apply nationwide, unless a state's criteria are stricter. With this change, industries and waste-water treatment plants would be forced to find ways to meet national criteria through pollution prevention. They could no longer exert pressure for lower standards by threatening to move their factories and jobs to another state.

SPURRING INNOVATION

Although amendments to existing requirements may enhance the degree to which programs encourage pollution prevention, they will not necessarily encourage or require industries and waste-water treatment plants to alter their fundamental operations to prevent pollution. We suggest two principal strategies to encourage industrial innovation. One is based on traditional "technology-forcing" for the most dangerous pollutants, and the other is designed to promote more comprehensive pollution-prevention planning by all dischargers of toxic substances.

The first approach is to identify and then ban or phase out the use and release of the most toxic, persistent, and bioaccumulative pollutants. Specific substances would be identified by the criteria discussed earlier in this article. Several hurdles must be overcome to achieve this result. The law must include a clear definition of the standards for identifying the specific toxicants subject to a ban or phaseout. A simple approach is to include a list of chemicals that warrant elimination. A specific set of criteria that EPA must use to expand the list should also be included.

Once a chemical is listed, it will be necessary to determine who decides the schedule and mechanism for phaseout. One possibility is simply to set a date and wait for technological innovation by industry, an approach that appears to have succeeded to phase out ozone-destroying chlorofluorocarbons. Another is to convene broadly representative panels that can evaluate replacements for each chemical and set reasonable deadlines for making substitutions. The least satisfactory option is to ask EPA to dictate the date and means by which processes and chemicals should change. Whatever approach is taken should be spelled out clearly in the act.

The second principal strategy is to require comprehensive pollution-prevention planning at the company, site, and production levels. At the company level, this might entail strategic decisions about how products are manufactured and sold. For example, a pesticide manufacturer might decide to phase out production of chlorinated pesticides in favor of new compounds that are less toxic to humans or that are less persistent in the environment. Or chemical pesticides might be eliminated entirely in favor of biological pest controls. At the site or plant level, pollution prevention could include covering storage areas to reduce runoff of spilled or open materials, or reuse of residues from one product or process as input into a related product or process.

At the production level, engineers are learning to substitute less-toxic input chemicals and to change the sequence, tuning, temperature, or other production conditions in ways that reduce residual toxic substances. One example of production-level pollution prevention is the replacement of elemental chlorine with chlorine dioxide or oxygen to bleach paper products. This substitution decreases chlorinated dioxins and furans as well as other highly toxic chlorinated organic compounds.

The major hook on which to hang this approach is the existing program that requires permits for all facilities that wish to discharge pollutants from point sources into surface waters. The original philosophy of this permit requirement is that no one has the right to discharge pollutants unless there is a need to do so—that is, unless it can be shown that eliminating the discharge is, for technological or economic reasons, not feasible. Over the years, this legal presumption has been implicitly reversed. Permittees can discharge until the government limits the amount and nature of the effluent. Pollution-prevention planning would help turn this presumption around.

The *Water Quality 2000* report, prepared by representatives from industry, environmental groups, academia, and government, recommended that pollution-prevention planning be conducted at all industrial facilities but that the facilities themselves decide on pollution-reduction goals and methods. Facilities would have to disclose the results of their planning to the public, stating their goals for reducing pollution and reporting on their success in achieving those goals. Such an approach could readily be included by requiring pollution-prevention plans as a condition for receiving a permit. This would take an important step back toward the direction of the original law because facilities would have to evaluate all alternatives to pollution creation and discharge as part of the permit process.

NONPOINT SOURCES

Preventing pollution may be particularly important for dealing with runoff and other nonpoint sources of toxicants, such as atmospheric deposition and contaminated sediments. The problem is extensive and in many ways more difficult to control than point sources. Furthermore, the time may be right to push for pollution prevention for nonpoint sources because this approach does not carry the political baggage of the established (and inadequate) regulatory process that governs point sources of toxic pollutants.

The 1987 amendments to the CWA require states to identify which waters are impaired by polluted runoff and other nonpoint sources and to describe measures to control these sources. Most states have met these requirements, and many have recommended voluntary implementation of "best management practices," which include approaches to pollution prevention. Therefore, there may be less resistance to mandatory implementation of newer prevention-based strategies, particularly when pollution prevention is cheaper—as it can be, for example, with the substitution of biological pest control for the use of expensive pesticides in farming.

Although we have yet to make significant progress in reducing nonpoint-source pollution from agriculture, numerous opportunities to do so exist.

These include changes in crop rotation patterns, which result in more efficient use of chemicals; substitution of less hazardous for more hazardous pesticides, along with phaseout of particularly hazardous chemicals; product changes, such as selection of disease- and pest-resistant crops that require smaller quantities of pesticides; and persuading consumers to change their behavior—by, for example, being more willing to buy cosmetically imperfect (but perfectly nutritious) produce. We do not have quantitative estimates of their pollution-prevention potential, but there is widespread agreement that concurrent implementation of a mix of them will reduce polluted runoff. And at least some of them—especially reduced use of pesticides—will probably also save money.

One promising approach that might encourage use of pollution-prevention techniques in agriculture and other land uses is site-specific planning, as incorporated in the 1990 amendments to the Coastal Zone Management Act (CZMA). This legislation requires EPA and the National Oceanic and Atmospheric Administration to publish detailed guidance on pollution-prevention measures for nonpoint sources. Each coastal state must, as a condition of its programs under both the CWA and the CZMA, develop enforceable mechanisms to ensure that such practices are employed on a site-specific basis by all major sources of polluted runoff affecting water quality in coastal areas. The *Water Quality 2000* report recommended a similar strategy for agriculture. Under this proposal, the CWA would be amended to require major landowners in impaired watersheds to develop, with EPA and state guidance, site-specific pollution-prevention plans designed to help restore the health of disturbed watersheds. This could provide the incentive for farmers to implement available pollution-prevention techniques.

CAN WE AFFORD IT?

No one has conducted a comprehensive analysis of the costs of implementing pollution prevention. Some preventive strategies may indeed entail high upfront costs. However, at least in some cases, pollution prevention can also be profitable. According to a recent GAO report, the installation of a $50,000 system to recover waste at a Clairol haircare products plant resulted in savings of about $240,000 a year. The report also describes how a campaign in Palo Alto, California, to encourage industrial users of silver to deliver their wastes to a silver reclaimer and to urge hobbyists to dispose of their silver solutions at hazardous waste-collection sites made it possible to avoid a $20 million per year expenditure for installing and operating new equipment to remove silver from the waste stream of its waste-water treatment plant.

Uncertainty about the economics of various pollution-prevention strategies is only one of the complexities with which the CWA must deal. The large number of toxic pollutants that are entering the nation's surface waters, the wide array of point and nonpoint sources of these pollutants, and the broad diversity of possible pollution-prevention activities are challenges for lawmakers considering reauthorization of the CWA. We believe that our proposals incorporate the flexibility and the scientific rigor necessary to continue the critical work of protecting our rivers, lakes, and streams.

POSTSCRIPT

Are Market Incentives Sufficient to Clean Up the Water?

Both sides of this debate may be right. As Foran and Adler argue, further progress on cleaning up the water will likely depend not on better end-of-pipe solutions (filters and decontaminants) but on preventing the pollution from the start. This, they argue, can best be accomplished by making the companies that do the polluting change the raw materials and manufacturing processes that they use. But such changes will likely be in the interests of the industries that adopt them. After all, industrial waste has to go somewhere, and no law will allow indefinite amounts of toxic materials in the water. And this interest fulfillment is a basic tenet of the free-market ideology that Hahn endorses.

Corporations can save themselves a good deal of money, in raw materials and in waste disposal costs, by adopting any effective measures to minimize the waste stream. Farmers, manufacturers, the government, and all affected parties should cooperate in planning effective solutions to this most costly and pressing problem.

SUGGESTED READINGS

Robert Adler, *The Clean Water Act: Twenty Years Later* (Island Press, 1993).

Jonathan King, "Something in the Water," *The Amicus Journal* (Fall 1993).

Debra S. Knopman and Richard A. Smith, "Twenty Years of the Clean Water Act: Has the U.S. Water Quality Improved?" *Environment* (January/February 1993).

Peter Nye, "Clean Drinking Water Becomes a National Problem," *Public Citizen* (July/August 1993).

William F. Pederson, Jr., "Turning the Tide on Water Quality," *Ecology Law Quarterly* (vol. 15, no. 1, 1988).

Julie St. Onge, "Runoff Runs Amok," *Sierra* (November/December 1988).

PART 6

Operating in the International Arena

What do we want, or expect, of our business partners abroad? This section takes on the ethical problems that arise when we find ourselves doing business with people who do not act the way we expect business associates—customers, colleagues, and industrialists—to act, given the written or unwritten rules by which our business is usually conducted. The debates in this section question some common assumptions about business and its dealings. For example, if a customer buys a perfectly good product from a reputable dealer, it is often assumed that it is none of the manufacturer's concern whether the customer should or should not have done so. Likewise, most people view the payment of any bribe, no matter whom it is paid to, as a forbidden act, punishable by law.

- Did Nestlé Act Irresponsibly in Marketing Infant Formula to the Third World?

- Is Bribery Ever Justified?

ISSUE 19

Did Nestlé Act Irresponsibly in Marketing Infant Formula to the Third World?

YES: Doug Clement, from "Infant Formula Malnutrition: Threat to the Third World," *The Christian Century* (March 1, 1978)

NO: Maggie McComas, Geoffrey Fookes, and George Taucher, from "The Dilemma of Third World Nutrition: Nestlé and the Role of Infant Formula," *Paper prepared for Nestlé, S.A.* (1985)

ISSUE SUMMARY

YES: Doug Clement, formerly the coordinator of the National Infant Formula Action (INFACT) coalition, argues that Nestlé has caused the deaths of countless infants by marketing infant formula to the Third World. INFACT brought this issue to world attention and called for the boycott of Nestlé products to protest the formula promotions.

NO: Maggie McComas, a public affairs analyst, Geoffrey Fookes, vice president of Nestlé Nutrition, and George Taucher, a professor of business administration, present Nestlé's response to its attackers and the company's view of its present and future role in protecting infant nutrition in the Third World.

The Nestlé Company has been involved in infant nutrition since the late 1800s. It has always been known for producing high-quality products. In late 1973, however, a book appeared on the market entitled *Nestlé Kills Babies*, which described what some felt were questionable business operations in certain developing nations. Here were the makings of a public relations disaster. What had gone wrong?

American birthrates and Nestlé's market for infant formula had expanded comfortably through the 1950s and 1960s. Toward the end of the 1960s, American birthrates began to decline, so Nestlé went farther afield in search of markets. (Note: the branch of the Nestlé company that was actually involved in the Third World infant formula dispute was based in Switzerland and is independent of the American branch.) Birthrates are highest in developing nations, so Nestlé took its promotional campaign to several Third World countries. As it happened, the company's employees were able to accomplish some social good while making a profit. Not only did their product have the potential to enhance the nutrition of sparse diets, but the sales representatives that were sent to distribute product samples in the maternity hospitals volunteered to teach new mothers how to bathe and care for their babies. They were called "mothercraft nurses," and they were a help to overworked medical and nursing staffs. In addition to issuing samples in the hospitals, Nestlé employed the usual promotional tools to move the infant formula—broadcasts, billboards, and leaflets—all of which associated its product with fat, happy babies.

Then babies started to get sick, and when their mothers brought them to their pediatricians, the pediatricians noticed a correlation: many of the sick babies—too many of them—were on infant formula instead of mother's milk. An ominous pattern appeared in the poverty-level formula users: impressed by the convenience of formula feeding, as taught by the mothercraft nurses in the hospitals, new mothers would opt not to nurse their babies. Whether or not these mothers had their milk supplies chemically stopped, their milk would dry up after a short period of nonuse. Once home from the hospital, they would discover just how much of the expensive formula they would have to buy, especially as the baby's appetite grew, and they would try to save money by stretching the formula—using less than instructions called for and increasing the amount of water. Worse, the water was often polluted. The instructions on the package strictly warned mothers to boil the water, but many of them could not read. Deprived of the antibodies found naturally in mother's milk, the babies were more susceptible to waterborne diseases; deprived of sufficient nutrition as the formula was stretched thinner and thinner, the babies began to starve.

Who is at fault in this? Nestlé has a proven product, legally sold, readily available, moderately priced for the middle-class household, with clear directions for use. Mothers systematically do not follow the directions, do not use enough formula, and mix it with polluted water, and the babies get sick. How can it be said that "Nestlé kills babies"?

As you read these selections, ask yourself which comes first, maintaining the freedom to choose on the market or protecting the health of infants? Also ask: Who should decide which comes first? How shall we assign liability and blame in cases where people get hurt by perfectly good products? To what extent must a business modify its activities because of the presumed ignorance of its audience? And finally, should marketing techniques that have been developed in and for highly industrialized Western societies be modified in consideration of the cultural differences of Third World nations? Or is that a form of paternalism that can lead to racial stereotyping and oppression?

YES

Doug Clement

INFANT FORMULA MALNUTRITION: THREAT TO THE THIRD WORLD

CARACAS, VENEZUELA, July 1977—In the emergency room of the Hospital de Niños lie 52 infants. All of them suffer from gastroenteritis, a serious inflammation of the stomach and intestines. Many suffer from pneumonia as well. According to the doctor in charge, roughly 10,000 Venezuelan infants die each year from gastroenteritis and pneumonia. The doctor explains that these 52 babies—like the many who preceded them and those who will follow —have one thing in common: they have all been bottle-fed with artificial milk formulas. Surveying the room with a weary frustration, he adds: "A totally breast-fed baby just does not get sick like this."

THE RISKS OF BOTTLE-FEEDING

It is an episode that recurs increasingly throughout the developing world: bottle-fed infants turn up in clinics and hospitals, malnourished, dying of gastroenteritis, dehydration and respiratory illnesses. Few scenes can more vividly depict the outcome of what one prominent physician, R. G. Hendrickse, has called "probably the most significant change in human behavior in recorded history": the move from breast to artificial feeding of infants.

In most of the world, breast-feeding is on the decline. In 1951, roughly three out of every four babies in low-income Singapore families were being breast-fed at the age of three months. Twenty years later only 5 percent were still at the breast at three months. In the Philippines, 31 percent fewer mothers nursed their babies in 1968 than in 1960. Such trends are in contrast with the recent increases in breast-feeding rates in western Europe and the United States. But it is in the Third World, where breast-feeding rates are declining rapidly, that bottle-feeding is so dangerous.

Artificial milk formulas can be used safely only if a number of conditions are satisfied. For proper use, a family must have:

1. *Sufficient income* to purchase the amount of formula required for adequate infant nutrition. But the cost of bottle-feeding in Egypt and Pakistan

exceeds 40 percent of the minimum wage, if the baby is three months old; for a six-month-old, almost two-thirds of the family's income would have to go to formula purchases.

2. *Reasonable access to clean water* that can be mixed with the formula and used to wash bottles, nipples and other equipment. In Indonesia, however, only 10 percent of all families have "reasonable" access to "safe" water, as defined by the U.N.

3. *The ability to read* and follow the fairly complex instructions for formula preparation. Barely 16 percent of women in Haiti are literate, and then usually in Creole or French. On the shelves of many Haitian grocery stores are formula cans with instructions in English and Spanish only.

4. *Access to refrigeration facilities* for storage of unused formula mixture. But fewer than 54 percent of all Brazilian families have electricity, let alone refrigerators. In rural areas of Brazil, only 11 percent of the people have electricity.

Using United Nations data for a large number of developing countries, one recent statistical study estimated that since *all* four conditions must be met before infant formulas can be properly used, only 20 percent of the people of these countries can safely feed artificial milks to their infants.

Breast-feeding, on the other hand, is a physiological possibility for well over 95 percent of all mothers. Breast milk is sterile and inexpensive, and requires no time-consuming preparation. Moreover, it contains antibodies that protect infants against a wide range of common diseases. So bottle-feeding not only presents high risks; it also replaces a virtually perfect

and readily available food. Developing countries cannot afford to lose such a resource.

PROMOTING THE PRODUCT

Yet it is in these countries that the multinational corporate producers of infant formulas have begun to sell their wares. Nestlé, Bristol-Myers, Abbott Laboratories, American Home Products, Borden, Carnation and others have realized that the high birth rates of the Third World offer a profitable alternative to the stagnating baby-food markets of the industrialized countries.

Mass-media advertising is one way that these formula producers create a market for infant formula in the developing countries. Huge advertisements appear on the sides of panel trucks in Nigeria or station wagons in Thailand. In Barbados, advertisements for Bristol-Myers's "Enfamil" were on the back covers of the 1975 and 1976 telephone books. Some companies hold "baby shows," awarding large supplies of free formula to the cutest, healthiest babies, who are then used in future promotion efforts. In the maternity wards of Philippine hospitals there are full-color calendars and posters depicting bright, healthy babies next to large cans of Nestlé's "Lactogen" and "Pelargon" formulas. And in Uruguay, newspaper ads display a new Nestlé formula: "Eledon."

Even illiterate and rural populations can be reached by the spoken word, so radio, too, has become an extensive advertising medium for formula marketers in the Third World. In Kenya, for example, infant formula ads made up almost 13 percent of all Swahili radio advertising in 1973; nine-tenths of this advertising was for Nestlé's Lactogen. In Malaysia, where the poor and rural tend to listen to the radio while the relatively rich and urban watch television, Nestlé ran three and a half times as many formula ads on radio as on TV in 1976.

"Mothercraft nurses," hired by the companies to talk to new mothers about infant care and feeding, are perhaps an even more effective influence in persuading mothers to bottle-feed. The mothercraft nurses bring cans of their company's formula when they visit mothers on the maternity wards or in their homes, and often leave samples behind. In their crisp white uniforms, the nurses are seen as medical authorities, and their explicit endorsement of bottle-feeding is a powerful reinforcement of the media message.

Such advertising persuades Third World women that formula is the modern, healthy and Western way to feed babies. Bottle-feeding becomes a status symbol; breast-feeding, a vulgar tradition. In addition, these promotion techniques plant doubts in mothers' minds about their ability to breast-feed. A typical Nestlé radio advertisement tells listeners: "When mother's milk is not enough, baby needs a special milk... Lactogen Full Protein." That message reinforces the unproven notion that breast-feeding will not be sufficient. Furthermore, such words can become a self-fulfilling prophecy. By stimulating doubts about breast-feeding ability, the sales pitches create anxiety. Doctors have long recognized that anxiety and lack of confidence strongly inhibit the "let-down reflex" which allows milk to flow successfully. Thus, unsuccessful lactation and a "need" for formula.

By playing upon fear—fear of losing status by appearing "primitive," fear of maternal inadequacy, or fear of not feeding one's baby the "scientific" and healthy way—the marketing efforts of formula corporations have contributed to, if not created, the drastic decline in breast-feeding rates in the Third World.

When this large-scale increase in bottle-feeding is coupled with the inability to bottle-feed safely, the inevitable consequence is increased infant malnutrition and disease. In a tragic attempt to save money, poor mothers "stretch" the formula by adding too much water, or by mixing in cornstarch and rice powder. In a 1969 Barbados survey, 82 percent of the mothers who were fully bottle-feeding their babies were found to be making four-day formula supplies last anywhere from five days to three weeks. In addition, without clean water and refrigeration, baby bottles and formula become perfect breeding grounds for bacteria; researchers in rural Chile found that almost 80 percent of the bottles examined showed high bacterial contamination.

The result of this overdilution and contamination is disease and often death. A study of three Arab villages revealed that while only .5 percent of totally breast-fed infants were hospitalized for gastroenteritis, almost 25 percent of the bottle-fed babies had to be treated for that disease. In 13 Latin American countries, a 1972 study conducted by the Pan American Health Organization found that whereas diarrheal diseases were responsible for roughly 52 percent of the deaths of bottle-fed infants, they accounted for only 32 percent of the deaths occurring to breast-fed babies. Researchers in Chile discovered that death rates for bottle-fed infants were three times as high as those for completely breast-fed children. Countless other studies reveal the same tragic relationship.

ADDRESSING THE ISSUE

These problems have not gone unnoticed. During the early 1970s, a few nutritionists and physicians began to warn against the use of formulas. In 1972, the Protein-Calorie Advisory Group (PAG) of the United Nations issued a statement which stressed "the critical importance of breast-feeding under the sociocultural and economic conditions that prevail in many developing countries."

Several European social-justice groups became involved in the issue, and in 1974 Mike Muller, a British journalist, published *The Baby Killer*, an important exposé of the formula problem. The issue got front-page headlines throughout Europe when Nestlé sued a Swiss action group in 1974 for translating *The Baby Killer* into German and retitling it *Nestlé Kills Babies*.

For two years the Nestlé lawsuit received a great deal of European media coverage as testimony was given and evidence gathered about the harmful effect of bottle-feeding. But because it could not be proved that Nestlé had *directly* killed babies, in June 1976 the judge found the Swiss group guilty on one count of libel (of the four originally filed by Nestlé), served its members with minimal fines and, stating that "this verdict is not an acquittal of Nestlé," called on the company to fundamentally rethink its promotion practices.

Infant-formula malnutrition became an American issue through the work of concerned church groups. In late 1974 the Interfaith Center on Corporate Responsibility (ICCR), a National Council of Churches agency which coordinates the stockholder actions for 14 Protestant denominations and more than 140 Roman Catholic orders, raised the issue of formula abuse with several U.S. formula manufacturers. Meetings with corporate management and stockholder resolutions were the major strategies used by ICCR over the next two years in its efforts to uncover information about the companies' role in the problem and to press for changes in formula promotion practices.

BRISTOL-MYERS SUED BY NUNS

Negotiations with Bristol-Myers provide a most interesting example of ICCR's work. In 1975 a stockholder resolution was filed with Bristol-Myers by members of ICCR. The resolution asked for complete and accurate information on the company's formula sales and promotion practices. In response, Bristol-Myers's public relations department issued a 20-page report which medical authorities and church representatives found to include little specific information and a number of inaccuracies.

In 1976 another resolution was filed, asking again for a complete and accurate report on Bristol-Myers formula activities. To the surprise of ICCR members, the inaccuracies of the 1975 report were repeated in the management's proxy statement in opposition to the new resolution. Moreover, this statement was provided as "proof" that the 1975 report had been "totally responsive" to previous requests for information. Believing that the Bristol-Myers statements violated a Securities and Exchange Commission (SEC) law which prohibits misstatements in proxy materials, one ICCR member, the Sisters of the Precious Blood, filed suit against Bristol-Myers in April 1976.

The Bristol-Myers lawsuit began to generate the same kind of attention in America that the Nestlé lawsuit had in

Europe. ICCR and the Sisters gathered massive amounts of evidence from 18 countries, with the help of an international community of concerned doctors, nutritionists and church-related investigators. Over 40 affidavits documented the problems caused by the promotion and sale of Bristol-Myers infant formulas.

But in May 1977 the judge handed down his decision in favor of Bristol-Myers. Surprisingly, he based his decision not on whether Bristol-Myers had made "misstatements" in its proxy statement but on the question of how such alleged lies might have affected stockholders. He decided that while the Sisters may possibly have proved that Bristol-Myers's proxy statement did contain misstatements (that the company does, in fact, sell its formulas to people who do not have the means to use them safely), the Sisters had *not* shown that they, as shareholders, had been caused "irreparable harm" by such misstatements.

The Sisters decided to appeal the decision immediately, stating that the ruling "does not address the merits of the case and makes a mockery of Securities and Exchange Commission laws requiring truth in corporate proxy statements." Other church and institutional investors agreed to file friend-of-the-court briefs for the appeal, and the SEC submitted its own brief in support of the Sisters' demand for stockholder rights.

Under pressure from the appellate court, however, the Sisters and Bristol-Myers again entered into negotiations. Early this year a settlement was reached when Bristol-Myers agreed to publish a report to stockholders including some of the Sisters' evidence from Third World countries as well as company statements on planned policy changes. The changes in Bristol-Myers's promotion practices included the prohibition of *all* direct consumer-oriented advertising, including posters, calendars and name tags in hospitals, and a stop to milk nurses in Jamaica where they had violated government regulations. The settlement is viewed as an important landmark in the infant-formula controversy, but further restrictions on promotion will be necessary, according to ICCR staff.

During this same time period, U.S. congressional representatives were beginning to consider hearings and legislation on the infant-formula issue. Representative Michael Harrington (D., Mass.) introduced a resolution in August 1976 calling for an investigation of the problem. By the following summer, Congress had passed a bill encouraging the president —through the Agency for International Development—to carry out an extensive infant and maternal nutrition program in partnership with the developing nations, with special emphasis on breast-feeding. In early 1978, Senator Frank Church's foreign economic policy subcommittee and Senator Edward Kennedy's antitrust and monopoly subcommittee considered holding hearings on the infant-formula industry.

Concerned about the infant-formula problem and seeking solutions to it, a number of church and secular groups from around the country have recently joined together in the Infant Formula Action (INFACT) coalition. On July 4, 1977, the Minnesota chapter of INFACT called for a national boycott of Nestlé products, believing that a boycott is the most effective way to put pressure on a Swiss-based company in which few Americans hold stock. At a National INFACT conference in November, INFACT representatives from around the country agreed that the boycott would become a major INFACT strategy. A national office was established in Minneapolis to coordinate local and regional boycott efforts. INFACT members also agreed to support shareholder, legislative and research efforts dealing with the infant-formula problem. With the advent of the Nestlé boycott, the infant-formula controversy has stirred more action at the local level. And as the National Council of Churches debates whether or not to endorse the boycott, church leaders note that this is the first issue in a long time that has generated such a high level of concern among the people in the pews.

THE PRODUCERS FIGHT BACK

Such intense criticism has evoked a variety of responses from the various formula producers, but a few basic principles usually underlie a company's reaction to criticism about formula sales:

1. Although they will agree that breast milk is best, they say there is a sizable need for infant formulas—above and beyond the 1-to-5 percent of mothers who are physically unable to breast-feed. Nestlé and American Home Products, for example, claim that many mothers run out of sufficient amounts of breast milk after a few months and that formula is then needed as a "supplement."

2. While admitting that formula abuse may occur in some areas, they claim that their products are not responsible. First of all, their formulas are of high quality: scientifically designed and prepared under the most stringent sanitary conditions. They also stress that they cannot be held responsible for the poverty, illiteracy and poor sanitary conditions of the Third World. And, of course, their products are said to be responsibly promoted and sold only to people who can use them safely. Each company claims that its competitors are responsible for product abuses.

3. They may make some changes in company policy, usually restricting mass-media advertising or milk-nurse activity.

4. If they were to restrict their formula promotion greatly, and give out information about their marketing overseas, they claim, they would lose their competitive position, and smaller, less ethical companies with lower-quality products would take over the market.

Critics don't take issue with the claim that the products—while inferior to breast milk—are usually of high quality. But they do disagree with the unproven theory that breast milk is not sufficient for the first four to six months of life; the great body of medical research supports the opposite conclusion.

Furthermore, they disagree with the notion that a company should not be held responsible for the social consequences of its corporate practices. While it is not held that the companies have necessarily created the poverty that exists, critics do believe that formulas should not be advertised and sold where existing socioeconomic conditions make safe formula use impossible. The promotion of formulas—whether through the mass media or the hospital system—will inevitably lead to formula misuse in such an environment. It is the ethical responsibility of the companies, in cooperation with local health workers and government agencies, to ensure that formulas are used only in cases of clear-cut medical need and/or when it is certain that the formulas can be used safely.

SUPERFICIAL CHANGES

Critics also believe that policy changes made to date by most companies have been largely superficial. It is important to end mass-media advertising, but this is just the visible tip of the promotional iceberg. A halt to promotion through the health system is equally important. Formula companies are now distributing their products through hospitals in developing countries, offering free medical equipment and other inducements to persuade doctors and administrators that they should give mothers free samples of the company's formula. Until this promotion strategy is halted, a company has not made an adequate response to the problem.

Restrictions on milk-nurse activity have been minimal. Nestlé, for instance, has taken its milk nurses out of white uniforms, only to put them into blue ones. Abbott Labs has gone so far as to take theirs out of uniform and to call them "company representatives," but the nurses still promote formula in the same deadly efficient manner.

Moreover, critics point out, there is little assurance that the new policies, weak as they are, are being enforced. Nestlé says that it has never done mass-media advertising in Latin America, but as recently as December 1977, Uruguayan newspapers published ads for "Eledon," a Nestlé formula. Bristol-Myers claims that its milk nurses operate only with the express permission of local health authorities, but during summer 1977, a Bristol-Myers nurse was found on the maternity ward of Jamaica's largest public hospital. Jamaica's Ministry of Health has long prohibited such visits.

Finally, in response to the industry argument that regulating the big companies will simply encourage the smaller ones, critics argue that only the large companies can afford the massive promotion campaigns that are so persuasive. Small companies which ride the crest of this promotional wave will find their markets considerably smaller when promotion is halted. Also, criticism of the well-known formula sellers has alerted Third World governments to the problem and led to local efforts to solve it.

Papua New Guinea, for example, has passed a law requiring a doctor's prescription in order to buy any sort of formula-feeding equipment. Guinea-Bissau has enacted a similar law. Algeria has prohibited advertising of processed baby milk, and all infant-formula trade is now under federal control. In Singapore and Malaysia, consumer groups and health professionals have begun breast-feeding campaigns, giving American and European activists credit for raising their awareness of the problem and making possible the initiation of the campaigns. In the Caribbean, significant regional efforts have been under way since 1974 to restrict bottle-feeding and encourage breast-feeding.

THE U.S. MARKET

It is ironic that the U.S. church and secular activists, who have been quite successful in illuminating the formula-abuse problem in the Third World, have devoted so little attention to the same problem at home. While extensive research on abuse problems among the American poor has just begun, there have been several reports of infant-formula malnutrition on native American reservations, in migrant labor camps, and in inner-city areas.

But restricting corporate promotion will be difficult here as well. American formula producers have a strong interest in maintaining a large domestic market, and formula promotion may be even more intense here than in the Third World. Less mass-media advertising is done, but the companies control the market more tightly and are better integrated into the health system. Abbott and Bristol-Myers together hold roughly 85 percent of the U.S. formula market. American Home Products accounts for another 10.5 percent of domestic formula sales.

These "Big Three" companies send salespeople to hospitals on a regular and frequent basis—according to one recent survey, three out of four hospitals received visits *at least* once a month. Over four-fifths of hospitals in the survey were given free formula by the companies. Doctors often get free supplies of a company's formula for their own children, presumably to persuade them to recommend that brand to their patients. In the words of one Bristol-Myers spokesperson, "If the pediatrician doesn't recommend us, we don't get the business."

The formula corporations offer hospitals substantial inducements to ensure that their formulas are distributed on maternity wards. Money for medical conferences, research grants, planning assistance for nursery additions, supplies of medical equipment and other gifts are commonly given to persuade hospitals to use a certain brand of formula. Hospitals are the perfect place to create infant-formula consumers, and the companies don't want to miss that opportunity. (It is

also significant that the directors of several major formula companies hold influential positions at large hospitals and medical schools.)

The result of this heavy promotion? Over three-quarters of the hospitals in a 1976 survey reported that they gave new mothers "gift paks" of formula when they left for home. Coincidentally, perhaps an equal proportion of American women bottle-fed their infants that year. Formula promotion by the Big Three companies has also been a major factor in the very common hospital practice of placing babies on bottles from the moment of birth on, rather than encouraging breast-feeding. Often mothers who want to breast-feed encounter strong resistance in U.S. hospitals, especially in those that serve low-income families.

Government/industry ties also seem to be rather close. A number of formula-industry employees have taken government jobs, and government programs often reflect this influence. Lobbying reinforces further the pro-industry bias. The federal Women, Infants and Children (WIC) low-cost food program, for instance, has for several years supplied infant formulas to eligible mothers. According to one doctor:

> The formula companies lobbied WIC through Congress. Ross [Abbott Labs' formula subsidiary] gave a big breakfast in Washington, D.C., invited all congressmen and their aides, and showed their film *Prescription: Food....* WIC coupons specify three formulas by name: Similac, SMA, and Enfamil.

The specified formulas are the major sellers of the Big Three.

While such intense pressure to use formulas can be viewed as a restriction of choice for American women, and one that may lead to higher rates of infant disease, the outcome is still less tragic than it is in the Third World where formula use often results in death. What is perhaps most significant about this integration of formula industry, health system and government programs in the United States is that it provides a model for future marketing efforts in the Third World.

Following the U.S. model, formula companies in developing countries use every means available to persuade doctors and hospitals to use their formulas. Abbott Labs—because it is a pharmaceutical company and knows how to sell its products via health systems—has been able to stop its direct advertising of formulas in Third World countries, and can now criticize other companies for persisting in such practices. Meanwhile, Abbott promotes heavily through the hospitals and pediatricians.

Bristol-Myers has also learned this route. Its Venezuelan formula subsidiary is reported to have paid from $5,000 to $7,000 for medical school graduation parties. And on a Philippine banana plantation, the nursery of the workers clinic has been almost totally furnished by Bristol-Myers; according to a nurse there, every baby born in that clinic is formula-fed from the hour of birth. Unfortunately, none of the plantation workers have refrigerators or running water in their homes, and formula purchases cost roughly 20 percent of the entire family's income.

AN ONGOING STRUGGLE

The problem of infant-formula malnutrition will not be an easy one to solve. Companies will resist any efforts that threaten what appears to be a lucrative market (Brazilian figures indicate a 72 percent profit margin on infant-formula sales at the retail level), and their financial resources present a major obstacle to the efforts of concerned groups.

Some companies have—under sustained pressure from critics—marginally improved their promotion and sales policies, but further changes will be harder to bring about as the squeeze on profits begins. The companies will continue to explain that their promotion of infant formulas is just one factor among many in the decline of breast-feeding in the Third World. They will insist that they are satisfying a need, not creating one. But as long as the use of their formulas continues to fill emergency rooms like that of Hospital de Niños, the struggle of the churches, governments, health organizations and social-action groups must not end.

NO

Maggie McComas,
Geoffrey Fookes, and
George Taucher

THE DILEMMA OF
THIRD WORLD NUTRITION

NESTLÉ AND THE ROLE OF INFANT FORMULA

More than 10 years ago, Nestlé became embroiled in an emotional controversy over infant feeding in the Third World. As the debate became ever more intense and an activist-led campaign held up to scrutiny the marketing practices of the infant formula industry as a whole, Nestlé remained the focus of the most vocal of critics, who for several years solicited support for a consumer boycott of the company's products in the United States.

This debate took a different, more positive, turn in May 1981, when the World Health Organization (WHO) adopted guidelines for the marketing of infant formula. This framework is now being translated into concrete measures by the national governments of some of the countries affected. At the same time, Nestlé has on its own initiative begun to apply the code in all Third World countries except where national measures are even more restrictive.

The account that follows traces the evolution of this controversy and analyzes the issues raised, the techniques employed by the critics, and Nestlé's response to both the real issues and the public debate. It is the work of a team composed of an independent business journalist, a professor of business administration and a Nestlé executive. They were asked to examine the history of the controversy in depth, being as frank and objective as possible.

The aim of this exercise is not simply to ruminate on management's past actions or provide a defense of them. The objective, rather, is to make it possible for those with an interest in the social, economic and political aspects of the controversy to review the path of events that led Nestlé to its current

From a report prepared for Nestlé, S.A., in 1982 by Maggie McComas, Geoffry Fookes, and George Taucher. Reviewed for medical accuracy by Professor Frank T. Falkner, M.D., F.R.C.P. Additional material added in 1985 by Richard Worsnop. Reprinted by permission of The Nestlé Company. Notes omitted.

policy on infant formula marketing—and to judge for themselves whether the company is serving the best interest of consumers.

THE ISSUES AT STAKE

For as long as mothers have been feeding their babies, the need for breast-milk substitutes has existed. There have always been mothers who cannot or will not breast-feed their babies, or who cannot fully satisfy their babies' needs from the breast alone. Too, other physiological factors—disease, undernourishment of the mother, death in childbirth—as well as economic, social, historical and cultural factors, account for the need for breast-milk substitutes. Work outside the home, for example, whether it be the case of the Third World mother who goes off daily to the fields or the Western office employee, may rule out the possibility of regular breast feeding. Moreover, even breast-fed babies often need supplementary foods in order to achieve optimal growth during the first few months of life.

The quality of most commercially produced infant formula has seldom been in question throughout the public controversy which began unfolding in the early 1970s. Rather, it was the way in which these products were marketed and used throughout the Third World that advocacy groups attacked. They based a worldwide campaign against the industry on claims that companies such as Nestlé were aggressively promoting the infant formula in the Third World. As a result, they said, mothers were encouraged unnecessarily to give up breast feeding, and the product was often used in settings where it could not possibly be prepared or administered hygienically. The consequence of all this, continued the crit-

ics' argument, was grave harm to some 10 million babies annually, the effect of companies' marketing practices being disease, malnutrition and even death.

ORIGINS OF THE CONTROVERSY

Among the international organizations concerned with the study and, insofar as it is possible, the improvement of worldwide nutrition, one of the most active during the 1960s was the United Nations Protein-Calorie Advisory Group (PAG). Until its dissolution in 1977, its job was to assure the coordination of nutrition research and aid programs carried out by UN agencies such as the World Health Organization (WHO), the Food and Agriculture Organization (FAO) and the UN Children's Fund (UNICEF).

The Bogotá Meeting

In December 1969, a working group organized by PAG began to study the question of nutrition *in utero*, i.e. in the unborn child, and also during the first few months of life. The group outlined a preliminary action program addressed to the governments of UN member states, to health professionals, and to representatives of the infant food industry. As a result, a cross-sectoral meeting of minds on the subject of infant nutrition was held at Bogotá, Colombia, in November 1970. The participants, who included experts from academia, governments and industry, represented an impressive storehouse of expertise on problems of nutrition, especially those relative to Latin America and the Caribbean. PAG officials, fully appreciating the great diversity among the regions and countries that make up the Third World, thought it wise to limit this first discussion to a particular geographical region. They outlined four general topics and objectives:

- emphasis of the importance of prolonged breast feeding;
- tentative guidelines for the marketing of breast-milk substitutes;
- support of the development of low-cost protein-rich weaning foods; and
- other possibilities for public health and industry "joint action."

Underlying the discussion was the concern of many health specialists over the evidence of a worldwide decline in breast feeding. While the factors causing this trend could not be precisely identified, there was natural suspicion over the obvious presence of commercial infant formula in areas where such a decline had taken place. So, these health experts sought to secure the industry's cooperation in assuring that aggressive marketing of breast-milk substitutes and possible consequent exacerbation of the trend would be avoided. Yet even as these seeds of doubt were being sown, many of the experts acknowledged that the infant formula industry did indeed have a positive impact on infant nutrition in Third World settings.

This generally positive view of the potential benefits of infant formula use in developing countries was not held by all the participants, however. The most determined, and the most vocal, among the doubters was Dr. Derrick B. Jelliffe, a PAG consulting expert who was at the time Director of the Caribbean Food and Nutrition Institute. He claimed that industry marketing practices were the *major factor* contributing to the decline in breast feeding and the parallel growth in the consumption of products that, given the poor hygienic conditions prevalent in most developing countries, contributed to infant

disease, malnutrition and death. This was the first time that a prominent health professional claimed a direct link between infant mortality trends and the promotion and consumption of infant formula. His thesis was expressed in a dramatic fashion, offering few reservations and no apologies. Not surprisingly, it provoked a lively debate that soon went beyond the confines of the PAG meeting, to be fueled for several years after by the absence of scientific data that might have definitively answered the charges that Jelliffe made.

The Debate Goes Public

In July 1973,... Dr. Jelliffe spoke in despairing terms of the PAG's efforts over the past three years. "I don't think we shall get far with this," he told an audience of health professionals, "and some other group may have to take a more aggressive, Nader-like stance in this regard."[1]

It did not take long for the "Nader-like" stance to manifest itself, and it did so within consumer advocacy groups and organizations concerned with Third World development policies. These critics of industry practices for the most part had no experience in infant nutrition. Rather, they were simply quintessential advocates, defending the interests of others, the others in this case being continents away. In any event, these critics ushered the debate into a new phase quite different from what had gone before, as cooperation gave way to confrontation.

The critics fired the first volley in the pages of the *New Internationalist,* a British publication produced under the sponsorship of three UK-based charity organizations, Oxfam, Christian Aid and Third World First. The magazine's August 1973 issue featured a question-and-answer interview with two UK child-health specialists experienced in Third World nutrition issues. This report constituted an even harsher critique than that Dr. Jelliffe had issued. It was sprinkled with assumptions about how and why infant formula was used and went on to make many damaging claims about corporate marketing practices, citing Nestlé's in particular. Among the charges, soon to be disputed or refuted, were those that Nestlé had modified its advertising in only one African country and, in that case, only under pressure from government authorities; that infant formula producers had not attempted to develop simplified feeding instructions for illiterate mothers; that supplies of substandard infant formula were often shipped to developing countries; and that company nurses sold infant formula to new mothers even as they lay in the beds of maternity hospitals.[2]

The report lacked substantiation of these claims, ignoring even the existing scientific data on Third World nutrition which, though woefully inadequate, might have given it greater credibility. Instead, the interviews were composed primarily of anecdotes that could be neither confirmed nor denied. What troubled Nestlé management in particular was the implication that certain practices pursued within the industry were those followed by Nestlé. More distressing still was the outright misrepresentation of the company's actual marketing policies. Then there was the magazine's cover, featuring a photograph of an infant's grave, atop it the empty feeding bottle and a crumpled container of Lactogen, a Nestlé product.

In late 1973, Mike Muller, a free-lance journalist on assignment for War on Want, another British charity organization, turned up on Nestlé's doorstep. Management devoted two days to interviews with Muller, who pursued a constructive, if often tough, line of questioning. Nestlé was left with the impression that both sides would benefit from the results of the discussion, yet that was not to be so. Within a few weeks, Muller's account was published and released with the flourish of a London press conference that befitted the report's sensational title *The Baby Killer*.

Skillfully written in a thrust-and-parry style, the report gave the infant formula industry some credit for its good intentions in making available a needed product. But this faint accolade was more than offset by very harsh criticism of corporate marketing practices. An introductory disclaimer pointed out that "the object of this report is not to prove that baby milks kill babies... not to prove that the baby food industry is exclusively responsible for this trend away from breast feeding."[3] Still, *The Baby Killer* glossed over all the socioeconomic constraints on breast feeding that had been an important part of the debate, concentrating instead almost exclusively on the presumed impact of marketing and promotion. The report also ignored what both nutritionists and the industry knew to be the reality of infant feeding in developing countries, namely that breast-milk substitutes were seldom used as total replacements for mother's milk, but rather as supplements in a program of "mixed feeding," and that locally produced substitutes were even more commonly used than commercial infant formula.

Of the greatest concern to Nestlé management were the out-of-context quotes that misrepresented the company's policies and attitudes to an even greater extent than had the outright errors of the *New Internationalist* report. Nestlé had made the mistake of assuming that in telling its story to this journalist, the public would finally see the full picture. That was hardly the case. Among the glaring omissions from the published report, felt Nestlé managers, were their painstaking explanations of the advantages of a "full-protein" formula the company had developed, a product designed to offer a margin of safety that would ensure the product's nutritional value in cases where a mother might be tempted to over-dilute it in preparation. Yet *The Baby Killer* presented this development as simply another commercial gimmick to build market share. Another contribution, acidified milk, a product that is less susceptible than other formulas to bacterial contamination in tropical areas, was not mentioned at all. And more damaging still was the recitation of "unethical and immoral" promotion practices, which, the report seemed to imply, could be attributed to Nestlé. Yet the practices in question had only been *described* to the journalist by Nestlé, which had in fact been referring to its competitors' practices.

In proposing solutions to the perceived problem, the author asked for nothing less than the elimination of "all promotion" to both consumers and the health profession. Even at this early stage of the campaign, it was obvious that such critics defined "promotion" so as to encompass educational materials essential to ensuring proper feeding practices. In addition, War on Want suggested that a "more broadly based campaign involving many national organizations" could have an effect on "intransigent" corporate policies.

These terms were so harsh and dictatorial that Nestlé knew it would have a hard time continuing the dialogue with organizations such as War on Want. Yet management had to face the fact that as long as the suspicions about infant formula's relationship to infant disease and malnutrition could not be definitively cast aside, it would do well to follow even more strictly the guidelines of PAG Statement 23, ensuring that its promotional campaigns provided truly useful information and did not discourage mothers from breast feeding.

So, after an internal review of marketing practices then in effect in developing-country markets, management imposed more stringent control over the distribution of product samples, elimination of direct contact between company representatives and new mothers, and the suspension of advertising that did not meet the full approval of public authorities. Meanwhile, an extensive review of the body of scientific literature on infant malnutrition and feeding patterns in developing countries was undertaken.

Even as this policy review was in progress, however, the company found itself facing a new challenge, this one in its own backyard. *The Baby Killer* had been translated into German by a Swiss activist group, and this time the errors and flaws that had characterized the original tract were greatly exaggerated. All the allegations of too-aggressive promotion and the unproven thesis that commercial formula contributed to malnutrition were now boiled down to libelous simplicity in book's title: *Nestlé Kills Babies*.

LIBEL PROCEEDINGS IN BERN

The original version of *The Baby Killer* had directly misrepresented some of Nestlé's policies. Still, it had underscored some very real problems of which industry was aware. The German-language translation, however, went considerably further in claiming infant formula to be the direct cause of infant deaths. Moreover, the title, *Nestlé Kills Babies (Nestlé tötet Babys)* cast one firm, Nestlé, as the sole perpetrator of the alleged crime.

Legal Action

Management was caught completely off guard by the publication of *Nestlé tötet Babys*. The booklet's existence came to the company's attention concurrently with its release to the press and general public in early June 1974. This time, there was no question of pursuing a rebuttal through a letter to the editor. Nor could the company simply turn a deaf ear, for Nestlé's employees and shareholders were in effect being slandered. These constituencies, along with the wider public audience, deserved a response that matched the accusations. In management's view, legal action seemed the best, perhaps the only, recourse.

Formation of ICIFI

Away from the heat of Nestlé's legal challenge, the infant foods industry as a whole had not abandoned efforts to act upon the mandate spelled out in PAG Statement 23, the result of an intense cooperative effort among industry, governments, and health professionals. Following the release of this document in late 1973, the next PAG-sponsored meeting was held in Singapore in November 1974, and it was here that company executives first discussed the possibility of forming an industry council whose principal concern would be companies' marketing practices in developing countries. In late 1975 the International Council of Infant

Food Industries (ICIFI) was formally organized in Zurich, Switzerland, bringing together eight of the largest infant formula producers, companies based in the US, Europe and Japan, Nestlé among them. One of their first actions was to develop a code of conduct embodying the principles of PAG Statement 23.

DEVELOPING INTERNATIONAL RECOMMENDATIONS

The October 1979 conference on infant feeding, sponsored jointly by WHO and UNICEF, represented the convergence of several different forces. The industry wished to shift the discussion on infant formula marketing back to the sphere of relevant government authorities, health professionals and industry experts, where the responsibility for resolving the issues lay. As for WHO, this new project meshed neatly with its ongoing programs of promoting better health for mothers and children and improving public hygiene in developing countries.

Industry was hoping that WHO's assumption of leadership would depoliticize the controversy. Yet despite the organization's strong scientific orientation and generally high degree of professionalism, international political sensitivities have tended to surface whenever the 150 member countries' delegations have convened. And each of these countries in turn must take into account internal political considerations as policymakers attempt to implement internationally agreed upon policies. This is particularly challenging in the case of the developing countries, whose obviously limited national resources must be carefully allocated to meet the several objectives that are collectively defined as the "national interest." As a practical matter, the health ministers of such countries, once they have unpacked their bags following the annual gathering of delegates at the World Health Assembly, often must vie with other public officials for limited financial and physical resources in order to implement commitments made within WHO.

In Search of Consensus

As the date for the meeting approached, corporate executives were disturbed to learn that instead of the 30 or so nutrition and industry experts anticipated, more than 150 participants, including the more vocal critics of the industry such as INFACT, ADW and War on Want, had signed up. Industry's hopes for the meeting were further deflated when it was discovered that only one background document (prepared by WHO and UNICEF) was to be circulated, and that this paper repeated essentially the same assumptions and conclusions that had long been the basis of the activist campaign. In addition, the paper's sparse review of the "current knowledge" of infant feeding was criticized not only by industrialists, but also by such a credible source as The Lancet, a leading UK medical journal.[4]

Although the meeting's conclusions were labeled a "consensus," this was something of a misnomer, given that strong differences over precisely what should be considered "appropriate" marketing practices still existed. Nestlé, however, was, on the whole, satisfied with the outcome. For one thing, many of the marketing reforms suggested in the consensus document echoed policy changes that the company had already put into effect. In addition, the meeting's concluding commitment to develop a more formal marketing code for developing countries was obviously compatible with the initiatives undertaken by the ICIFI group of companies.

NESTLÉ'S RESPONSE TO THE ISSUES

Nestlé's policy of replying quietly to its critics—when it has chosen to make any sort of reply—has puzzled many who have followed the development of the infant formula controversy. The company's approach to handling the issue is less of a mystery, however, when one examines in some detail its particular corporate culture and commercial orientation. First among these elements is Nestlé's high product quality standards, which helped the firm sail through the wave of consumer advocacy in the 1960s and 1970s largely unscathed. Nestlé's long-standing policy has been to modify a product or its accompanying marketing "package" to meet changing consumer needs or to provide a higher level of quality and safety whenever technological breakthroughs have made it possible and feasible to do so.

Because of this high level of consumer protection reflected in its product and marketing policies, Nestlé was seldom in the position of having to answer to public criticism. And management was always more concerned with responding to an identified problem in a substantive way than in publicizing the fact that such efforts had been undertaken. Thus company managers responsible for press and public relations were accustomed to handling inquiries that were modest in volume and generally uncontroversial in nature. As questions over infant formula marketing developed into an intense debate, however, it became evident that what the company *said* about the issue was as important a factor in resolving the controversy as what it actually *did* to assure that the product was used in the proper manner only by those who needed it. Thus it was particularly ironic when, at the height of the US campaign, Nestlé was accused of devoting its resources to a "massive public relations campaign" to discourage support of the boycott. This simply was not the case. If anything, the company had done too little, too late in the way of public relations, failing to inform the public at large of the steps it had taken over the years to ensure that infant formula was being made available on a selective basis and that Third World consumers were being educated as to its proper use.

Contribution to Nutrition Research

Determining the consumer's needs and how these can be met most effectively is usually accomplished through traditional, commercially oriented marketing research. In the case of infant formula, however, particularly as its use applies to Third World consumers, a more scientific approach is in order, and such research could logically be expected to be the responsibility of academic or other noncommercial institutes. The severe vacuum of knowledge about Third World nutrition and infant feeding, however, underscored by the activists' practice of advertising the very limited data that appeared to support their claims, finally led Nestlé to support new basic research in infant nutrition. In doing so, the company sought to establish a research base that would help determine, once and for all, whether there was any validity to the activists' claims that:

- only 2% of mothers are physiologically incapable of breast feeding;

- less than 6% of mothers are unable to breast-feed because of work outside the home;
- even a malnourished mother can "adequately feed" her child for at least the first four months of life.

If all that were true, Nestlé would have to rethink not only specific marketing practices but also the more important strategic question of whether infant formula is really needed. For that reason, Nestlé undertook a review of the existing scientific literature on the subject of infant feeding shortly after it sued the Swiss activists for libel and then, once the information gaps were identified, developed a research program aimed at identifying who uses infant formula, how and why it is used, and the effects of infant formula feeding on infant health. In 1979 this general program began to acquire some substance as Nestlé commissioned an independent research institute to investigate such questions within the controlled scope of three developing countries, Kenya, Malaysia and Mexico, focusing on a sample population of some 6,000 mothers. Completed in 1981, this research showed that in the countries surveyed:

- more than half of the mothers introduced supplementary foods before their infants were four months old, regardless of whether commercially produced infant formula was available;
- many of the foods being used as breast-milk substitutes and supplements were not normally recommended for this purpose; and
- infant feeding patterns in general varied enormously among the countries studied, further evidence that generalizations about nutrition and feeding habits, and even "appropriate" mar-

keting practices, could not be applied to the Third World as a whole.

Nestlé is also sponsoring other research on the use of infant formula. One study currently under way is designed to determine how long breast feeding alone will satisfy an infant's nutritional requirements for normal growth. This research, conducted in the setting of a Third world community, will deal with the issue of mixed feeding and the timing of the introduction of breast-milk supplements. Finally, Nestlé has underwritten an extensive critical review of major scientific literature on infant feeding and nutrition. Prepared under the supervision of an internationally recognized expert, this review is now available to other researchers, industrialists and lay groups with a serious interest in the subject.[5]

Product and Marketing Policies
Amidst all the clamor over infant formula marketing, Nestlé has seldom had the opportunity to demonstrate to the public that its product and marketing policies have indeed undergone substantive modification over the years. Activist demands that industry promotion be designed so as to encourage breast feeding, for example, ignore the fact that Nestlé, for one, has followed such a policy ever since it first began making products for infant feeding. More than a hundred years ago, for example, a Nestlé guidebook for new mothers put it this way: "during the first months, the mother's milk will always be the most natural nutriment, and every mother able to do so should herself suckle her children."[6] Because Nestlé continued to uphold that principle over the years, the company felt that the accusation that it was actively

discouraging breast feeding was simple libel.

The developing controversy over various marketing practices underscored the need to reconsider this evolution in feeding recommendations, however. Nestlé, for its part, decided to modify its promotional and educational materials at this point so as to place greater emphasis on breast feeding. Because of the scope and complexity of this task, the process of implementation that began in 1976 was gradual, though steady, and in taking this initiative, Nestlé was running a step ahead of the move toward international policy formulation. By the time the question of industry's role in emphasizing breast feeding was raised at the WHO/UNICEF sponsored meeting in 1979, Nestlé's new policy was in effect.

Nestlé has undertaken other substantive changes in its marketing practices over the years, including the use of mass media, the role of medical representative and qualified mothercraft personnel, and the provision of samples. In 1978, for example, Nestlé decided to end all use of mass media for advertising infant formula in Third World markets, even though such messages had already undergone considerable modification to make them much more educational and less commercial in tone and content. Virtually overnight, useful nutrition education information that had not merely been tolerated, but explicitly approved, disappeared from the scene.

LOOKING AHEAD

Over recent months, several developments have signaled the end of the controversy over infant formula marketing and the start of progress in resolving the dilemma of Third World nutrition. First has been the development of the International Code of Marketing of Breastmilk Substitutes and its adoption by most WHO member states in May 1981. Nestlé has fully embraced these guidelines, and the company is now engaged in consultations with WHO member governments that are implementing the code.

In addition, Nestlé has begun to implement the code's provisions in developing countries where governments do not plan to introduce national measures. Early in 1982, the company issued to its personnel in these countries, as well as to independent agents and distributors who play a role in Nestlé's distribution system, new marketing guidelines substantially reflecting the code's provisions. Nestlé has also taken steps to ensure compliance with the code, whether implemented through national measures or upon the company's own initiative, by forming the Nestlé Infant Formula Audit Commission, a panel of prominent medical experts, clergymen, civic leaders and experts on international policy issues. Headed by Edmund Muskie, former Secretary of State and Democratic Senator from Maine, the Commission is monitoring Nestlé's performance as measured against the code, investigating complaints and allegations concerning marketing practices now considered inappropriate in Third World markets.

One of the commission's first moves was to step into its role of monitoring Nestlé's compliance with the WHO code as interpreted either through national measures (where they existed) or, alternatively, through the company's own guidelines. Members of the commission contacted approximately 100 individuals and organizations long identified with the controversy, providing copies of the company's marketing guidelines, background material on commission and—most important—forms to be used in the documentation of reported violations of the guidelines, designed to enable the commission to pursue an investigation in each such case.

Next, the commission met with representatives of WHO and UNICEF, as well as with members of various church organizations and consumer advocacy groups, soliciting their views of the company's new instructions to its marketing personnel. The response was somewhat critical, but, in general, constructively so. As a consequence, the commission set to work proposing changes in the guidelines that would respond to two areas of criticism: first, that arising from a general misunderstanding about the role of the company's own guidelines, and second, those more substantive points in the Nestlé instructions which did indeed require some adjustment in order to better conform to the WHO code.

By the time the full commission met and issued its first quarterly report in September 1982, these suggested changes had been incorporated into the company's marketing guidelines. Said Senator Muskie in the report, "In the experience of the commission, Nestlé has demonstrated a willingness to respond positively to the imperative of change in its marketing practices."[7]

As they now stand, Nestlé's marketing policy and specific instructions to personnel include the following significant points:

- elimination of baby pictures on all product labels;
- elimination of mothercraft-nurse function;
- provision of free or reduced-cost supplies of infant formula only for children

who cannot be breast-fed, and in those cases, only through health workers;

- elimination of advertising and promotion of infant formula, including "generic" promotion in which brand names are not mentioned;

- discouragement of point-of-sale infant formula promotion by retailers;

- elimination of all gifts related to product promotion, regardless of their significance in terms of value; and

- prohibition of Nestlé-initiated contact between company personnel and mothers.

Finally, the commission simplified the complaint form to be used as the basis for investigating reported violations, in response to those concerned over the original form's length and complexity.

Also at this time, new research on infant nutrition and feeding supported by Nestlé and other companies of the ICIFI group, as well as that undertaken by international organizations such as WHO, has begun to yield results that should provide the framework against which questions of infant formula marketing need to be placed. Finally, many members of the scientific community and public figures, the very people whose support of Nestlé's adversaries was earlier so crucial to their campaign, have begun to doubt the motivations of some of the critics and to be more outspoken in their criticism of the arguments and tactics employed by the activists. This attitude puts a new burden on the advocates, who have claimed to have at heart only the best interest of Third World consumers. As a leading medical journal recently observed, "Let's hope that the people who organized this campaign to condemn the baby food companies will now turn their atten-

tion to actually doing something about the major causes of infant mortality."[8]

In a similar vein, the *Washington Post*, the newspaper which had sharply rebuked Nestlé in its editorial columns at the height of the activist campaign, has had second thoughts on the issue. In an editorial published in late 1982, the *Post* said: "There is concern, however, among health professionals and researchers—including the American Academy of Pediatrics—that the role of infant formula as a threat to infants in developing nations has been blown out of proportion.... Upon closer inspection, the data linking formula marketing and infant mortality turn out to be sketchy at best."[9]

In other sectors, these words have been echoed by positive actions that indicate a new recognition of Nestlé's commitment to follow both the letter and spirit of the WHO code. In September 1982, for example, the United Methodist Church concluded an in-depth, two-year study of the infant formula issue and resolved, by a two-to-one vote, not to boycott the company, calling upon any Methodist organizations in disagreement to establish reasons for their position by April 1983. Also, in early 1983 the American Federation of Teachers, which had backed the boycott campaign for several years, decided to end its support.

This is the time to replace futile confrontation with a renewed effort to improve infant health in the Third World. The infant formula industry has never denied the role of constructive criticism, but unsubstantiated reports of corporate misconduct are quite another thing. Nestlé now welcomes responsible advocates and professional organizations who choose to assist in the implementation and continued monitoring of compliance with the WHO code.

The fact that a company staked its reputation, as Nestlé did, upon the preservation of what is only a small part —2.5%—of its total business, flies in the face of the critics' claims that Nestlé's marketing policies are based on nothing more than the profit motive. Had it been predicted that Nestlé would spend 10 long years defending its name and actions, the company might have been well advised some time ago to give up the infant formula business altogether. By this time, surely, it could have filled the commercial gap with sales of another product, one lacking the potential for controversy—but also, no doubt, lacking the potential to fill such a vital need an infant formula does. And that is precisely the point. Nestlé has spent time and effort defending its infant formula marketing policy for the Third World not out of any attachment to particular marketing practices per se, but because the needs of these very special consumers give them far greater weight on the scale of corporate priorities than mere sales figures can indicate.

The dilemma of infant formula marketing in the Third World was apparent to Nestlé well before the activist campaign came into full bloom: The more disadvantaged the circumstances of the population, the greater the need for the product, yet the greater the hazards in preparing and administering it.

Having taken the initiative of complying with the WHO code through the development and application of its own set of instructions, Nestlé now hopes that the international guidelines will be implemented in such a way that those truly in need are not deprived of either the product or the marketing support services of information and education that are crucial to ensuring its proper use. Yet there is a greater task in improving Third World nutrition, and this is to break the vicious circle of poverty, lack of education, and insufficient health services that together contribute to disease and malnutrition. This will require a much more intensive commitment of resources not only by industry, but also by the international health and development agencies, and individual governments.

REFERENCES

1. Jelliffe, D. B., remarks at Ciba Foundation symposium, "Human Rights in Health," London, July 4–6, 1973.
2. Geach, Hugh, "The Baby Food Tragedy," *New Internationalist*, No. 6, August 1973, pp. 8–12, 23.
3. Muller, Mike, *The Baby Killer*, War on Want, March 1974.
4. "Uneasy Prelude to Meeting on Infant Feeding," *The Lancet*, Vol. II, Sept. 28, 1979, pp. 680–81.
5. Ashworth, A., et al., *Infant and Young Child Feeding—A Selected Annotated Bibliography. Early Human Development*, 1982, 6. (Supplement.)
6. Translated from the German, *Ueber die Ernärurg der Kinder*, 1871.
7. Muskie, Edmund, "First Quarterly Report—Nestlé Infant Formula Audit Commission," Oct. 14, 1982, p. 4.
8. "Does a Vote of 118 to 1 Mean the USA Was Wrong?" *Pediatrics*, Vol. 68, No. 3, September 1981, p. 431.
9. "Revisiting the Formula Fight," *The Washington Post*, Nov. 5, 1982.

POSTSCRIPT

Did Nestlé Act Irresponsibly in Marketing Infant Formula to the Third World?

To protect Third World mothers from buying a product that may make life easier for them seems perverse; to ignore the deaths of infants seems callous. Faced with a conflict between the freedom of the mother and the welfare of the child, it seems in poor taste to mention the interest of the company in making a profit and the interest of the country in establishing a favorable balance of trade. Yet these, too, are valid objectives.

Some feel that the promotional devices that Nestlé used were at fault. These devices were not necessarily deceptive or coercive by American standards, but to mothers in developing nations, the promotions had different significance. The mothercraft nurses were, to these mothers, real nurses wielding medical authority. The signs that showed fat babies beside bottles of formula were taken as guarantees that using the formula yields healthy babies. The fact that powerful, professional, and rich Westerners stood behind a course of action was overwhelmingly persuasive and often left Third World mothers with little real choice.

The infant formula issue is a paradigm case for multinational issues. To what extent shall merchants of any country promote products as they like? Is it America's right or duty to decide what is beneficial for people in other countries?

SUGGESTED READINGS

William Aiken and Hugh LaFollette, eds., *World Hunger and Moral Obligations* (Prentice Hall, 1977).

Alex M. Freedman, "Nestlé Ad Claims for Baby Formula Probed in Three States," *The Wall Street Journal* (March 2, 1989).

John Marcom, Jr., "Feed the World," *Forbes* (October 1, 1990).

Barbara Presley Noble, "Price-Fixing and Other Charges Roil a Once-Placid Market," *The New York Times* (July 28, 1991).

James E. Post, "The International Infant Formula Industry," in *Marketing and Promotion of Infant Formula in the Developing Nations,* a report prepared for the Subcommittee on Health and Scientific Research, Committee on Human Resources, U.S. Senate (1978).

Leslie Savan, "Forget the Dead Babies: Nestlé's PR Firm Spins Feel-Good Line," *Village Voice* (May 2, 1989).

ISSUE 20

Is Bribery Ever Justified?

YES: Michael Philips, from "Bribery," *Ethics* (July 1984)

NO: Thomas L. Carson, from "Bribery and Implicit Agreements: A Reply to Philips," *Journal of Business Ethics* (vol. 6, 1987)

ISSUE SUMMARY

YES: Professor of philosophy Michael Philips argues that not every payment that seems to be a bribe is, in fact, a bribe. He asserts that although it is often difficult to distinguish a true bribe from other payments, there may be no *prima facie* reason to refuse the offer of a bribe.

NO: Professor of philosophy Thomas L. Carson argues that every acceptance of a bribe involves the violation of an implicit or explicit promise or understanding connected with one's office. He maintains that Philips has failed to show that acceptance of a bribe can sometimes be morally permissible.

A *bribe* is a payment made to someone in order to influence the payee to do something that the payer wants him or her to do. But that does not include every fee for service, such as the payment one makes to induce the plumber to fix the bathtub drain. If a payment is to be called a "bribe," there must be something wrong or illegitimate about the payment; at the least, the payee must accept the bribe and perform the service so obtained secretly and/or for wrong or illegitimate sorts of reasons. *Bribe,* then, is a term that does not stand alone: it always designates a payment, but it also carries normative content that simultaneously condemns the payment. The grounds for the condemnation come from the social context of the payment: the payment is against the law, the service demanded violates the rules or professional ethics of the payee, or the payee is in some position of judgment, and American culture presupposes objectivity of the judge that is incompatible with receiving money from one of the parties judged.

But then it would follow that what counts as a bribe in one social context would not count as a bribe in another. More to the point, there are times when what American law calls a bribe is not a bribe in the countries where America tries to do business.

Among the bribery scandals that shocked the United States during the mid-1970s, the Lockheed case stands out as showing both the seriousness of the problem for normal business dealings (in, for instance, the amount that changed hands over the course of the deal) and the fuzziness of the rules that

American businesses must conform to. In 1972 the president of Lockheed was A. Carl Kotchian, who, in the course of his job, was sent to Japan to sell Lockheed's new TriStar passenger plane to a Japanese airline. Kotchian found himself kept entirely uninformed by his Japanese partners, who surfaced at odd intervals with demands for odd amounts of money, the large payments all apparently bound for the office of the prime minister; he was told that all this was standard practice and that the fees were the accepted level of payment. In the months that dragged by, while the "negotiations" continued, Kotchian was constantly warned that nonpayment would lose the sale of Lockheed's TriStar planes to the national Japanese airline; he was assured that each payment would be the last one that was necessary; and he was haunted by the vision of much of Lockheed's workforce laid off if the deal somehow, through his fault, fell through. The maddening part of the deal, as for many such transactions, was that as far as Kotchian knew, the TriStar was the best plane for the purpose for which the airline wanted it and in a fair competition would have been the plane adopted. But the fair competition was not the method of choice for that Japanese government.

In the end, the story came out; Lockheed was condemned as an immoral company, and Kotchian took the heat for bribery. In a revealing piece, Kotchian wrote up his Japanese experiences for the *Saturday Review* (July 9, 1977). The case, as he wrote it, illustrates the difficulty of doing business in a country where cultural expectations, government regulations, and business practices are entirely different from those of the United States. If it is of any comfort, the Japanese officials were also punished for their role in the affair.

In the following selections, Michael Philips concludes that many instances that are called bribery are no such thing and that it is often difficult to distinguish bribery from extortion or even from legitimate practices. Thomas L. Carson responds that any acceptance of payment in which the payee is expected to violate a "tacit agreement" is bribery and is always morally wrong.

As you read these selections, ask yourself why some payments are called "bribes" and others are not. Most people agree that bribery and extortion are wrong, but how are they wrong? What would the plumber have to say to make his agreement to fix the drain in return for payment a case of extortion rather than a fee for service? What would the person paying for the service have to say to make that payment a bribe? How do our expectations of those who hold an office in American society help to define what counts as a bribe? The problems become especially acute when we try to do business abroad. Should the U.S. government dictate how the officers of multinationals should behave in foreign business, thereby telling foreign countries how to run their business transactions? Or should businesspeople be required to conform their behavior to that of the country in which they are doing business?

YES

Michael Philips

BRIBERY

Although disclosures of bribery have elicited considerable public indignation over the last decade, popular discussions of the morality of bribery have tended largely to be unilluminating. One reason for this is that little care has been taken to distinguish bribes from an assortment of related practices with which they are easily confused. Before we can be in a position to determine what to do about the problem of bribery, we need to be clearer about what count and ought to count as bribes. Unfortunately, there is as yet very little philosophical literature on this topic.[1] In this essay I shall remedy this defect by presenting an account of the concept of bribery and by employing that account to clarify matters in three areas in which there is public controversy and confusion.

At least some confusion in discussions of bribery arises from a failure adequately to appreciate the distinction between bribery and extortion. This is true, for example, of accounts of the notorious case of Lockheed in Japan. I shall attempt to show that the morality of this and similar transactions is better assessed if we are clear on that distinction.

A second problem area arises out of the fact of cultural variability. As is generally recognized, the conduct of business, government, and the professions differs from culture to culture. In some places transactions that many Americans would consider bribes are not only expected behavior but accepted practice as well. That is, they are condoned by the system of rule governing the conduct of the relevant parties. Are they bribes? Are only some of them bribes? If so, which?

A third problem arises out of the general difficulty of distinguishing between bribes, on the one hand, and gifts and rewards, on the other. Suppose that a manufacturer of dresses keeps a buyer for a catalog company happy by supplying him with any tickets to expensive shows and athletic events that he requests. Are these bribes? Or suppose that a special interest group rewards public administrators who rule in its favor with vacations, automobiles, and jewelry. May we correctly speak of bribery here?

* * *

To answer such questions we need to say more precisely what bribes are. A bribe is a payment (or promise of payment) for a service. Typically, this payment is made to an official in exchange for her violating some official duty or responsibility. And typically she does this by failing deliberately to make a decision on its merits. This does not necessarily mean that a bribed official will make an improper decision; a judge who is paid to show favoritism may do so and yet, coincidentally, make the correct legal decision (i.e., the bribe offerer may in fact have the law on her side). The violation of duty consists in deciding a case for the wrong sorts of reasons.

Although the most typical and important cases of bribery concern political officials and civil servants, one need not be a political official or a civil servant to be bribed. Indeed, one need not be an official of any sort. Thus, a mortician may be bribed to bury a bodyless casket, and a baseball player may be bribed to strike out each time he bats. Still, baseball players and morticians are members of organizations and have duties and responsibilities by virtue of the positions they occupy in these organizations. It is tempting, then, to define a bribe as a payment made to a member of an organization in exchange for the violation of some positional duty or responsibility. This temptation is strengthened by our recognition that we cannot be bribed to violate a duty we have simply by virtue of being a moral agent. (Hired killers, e.g., are not bribed to violate their duty not to kill.) And it is further strengthened when we recognize that we may be paid to violate duties we have by virtue of a nonorganizationally based status without being bribed. (I am not bribed if—as a nonhandicapped person—I accept payment to park in a space reserved for the handicapped; nor am I bribed if—as a pet owner—I accept payment illegally to allow my dog to run free on the city streets.)

Still, it is too strong to say that occupying a position in an organization is a necessary condition of being bribed. We may also speak of bribing a boxer to throw a fight or of bribing a runner to lose a race. These cases, however, are importantly like the cases already described. Roughly, both the boxer and the runner are paid to do something they ought not to do given what they are. What they are, in these cases, are participants in certain practices. What they are paid to do is to act in a manner dictated by some person or organization rather than to act according to the understandings constitutive of their practices. Civil servants, business executives, morticians, and baseball players, of course, are also participants in practices. And their responsibilities, as such, are defined by the rules and understandings governing the organizations to which they belong. At this point, then, we are in a position to state a provisional definition of bribery. Thus, P accepts a bribe from R if and only if P agrees for payment to act in a manner dictated by R rather than doing what is required of him as a participant in his practice.[2]

One advantage of this account is that it enables us to deal with certain difficult cases. Suppose that a high-ranking officer at the Pentagon is paid by a Soviet agent to pass on defense secrets. The first few times he does this we would not hesitate to say that he is bribed. But suppose that he is paid a salary to do this and that the arrangement lasts for a number of years. At this point talk of bribery appears less appropriate. But why should something that has the character of a bribe if done once or twice (or, perhaps, on a piecework basis) cease to have that character if done more often (or, perhaps, on a salaried basis)? In my account the explanation is that the frequency or basis of payment may incline us differently to identify the practice in question. Thus, if an American officer works for the Soviet Union long enough, we begin to think of him as a Soviet spy. In any case, to the extent to which we regard his practice as spying we are inclined to think of the payments in question as payments of a salary as opposed to so many bribes. A similar analysis holds in the case of industrial spies, undercover agents recruited from within organizations, and so forth.[3] We do not think of them as bribed because we do not think of them as full-fledged practitioners of the practices in which they appear to engage.

This practice conception is further supported by the fact that a person may satisfy my account of bribery on a long-term and regularized basis and still be said to be a recipient of bribes. This is so where his continued and regularized acceptance of payments does not warrant any change in our understanding of the practices in which he participates. Thus, we do not think of a judge who routinely accepts payments for favors from organized crime as participating in some practice other than judging, even if he sits almost exclusively on such cases. This may be arbitrary: perhaps we ought rather think of him as an agent of a criminal organization (a paid saboteur of the legal system) and treat him accordingly. My point, however, is that because we do not think of him in this way—because we continue to think

of him as a judge—we regard each fresh occurrence as an instance of bribery.

At least two additional important features of bribery deserve mention. The first is a consequence of the fact that bribes are payments. For, like other kinds of payments (e.g., rent), bribes presuppose agreements of a certain kind.[4] That is, it must be understood by both parties that the payment in question is exchanged, or is to be exchanged, for the relevant conduct. In the most typical and important cases, the bribed party is an official and the conduct in question is the violation of some official duty. In these cases we may say simply that an official P is bribed by R when she accepts payment or the promise of payment for agreeing to violate a positional duty to act on R's behalf. This agreement requirement is of great importance. As I shall argue in Section IV, without it we cannot properly distinguish between bribes and gifts or rewards.

Such agreements need not be explicit. If I am stopped by a policeman for speeding and hand him a fifty-dollar bill along with my driver's license, and he accepts the fifty-dollar bill, it is arguable that we have entered into such an agreement despite what we might say about contributions to the Police Benevolence Association. As I shall argue, some of the difficulties we have in determining what transactions to count as bribes may stem from unclarity concerning the conditions under which we are entitled to say an agreement has been made.

It is a consequence of this account that someone may be bribed despite the fact that she subsequently decides not to perform the service she has agreed to perform. Indeed, we must say this even if she has never been paid but has been only promised payment, or even if she has been paid but returns this payment after she decides not to abide by her part of the agreement. I see nothing strange about this. After all, if one accepts a bribe it seems natural to say that one has been bribed. Still, I have no strong objection to distinguishing between accepting a bribe and being bribed, where a necessary condition of the latter is that one carries out one's part of the bribery agreement. As far as I can see, no important moral question turns on this choice of language.

A final interesting feature of bribery emerges when we reflect on the claim that offering and accepting bribes is prima facie wrong. I will begin with the case of officials. The claim that it is prima facie wrong for someone in an official position to accept a bribe is plausible only if persons in official capacities have prima facie obligations to discharge their official duties. The most plausible argument for this claim is grounded in a social contract model of organizations. By accepting a position in an organization, it might be argued, one tacitly agrees to abide by the rules of that organization. To be bribed is to violate that agreement—it is to break a promise —and is, therefore, prima facie wrong.[5] While I concede that this argument has merit in a context of just and voluntary institutions, it seems questionable in a context of morally corrupt institutions (e.g., Nazi Germany or contemporary El Salvador). And even were it technically valid for those contexts, its conclusion would nonetheless be a misleading half-truth.

* * *

I now turn to the first of three problem areas I shall address in this paper, namely, the problem of distinguishing between bribery and extortion. Compare the following cases:

a) Executive P hopes to sell an airplane to the national airline of country C. The deal requires the approval of minister R. P knows that R can make a better deal elsewhere and that R knows this as well. P's researchers have discovered that R has a reputation for honesty but that R is in serious financial difficulties. Accordingly P offers R a large sum of money to buy from him. R accepts and abides by the agreement.

b) The same as a except that P knows that he is offering the best deal R can get, and R knows this too. Nonetheless, P is informed by reliable sources that R will not deal with P unless P offers to pay him a considerabe sum of money. P complies, and R completes the deal.

According to my analysis a is bribery and b is not.

The difference between a and b is clear enough. In a P pays R to violate R's duty (in this case, to make the best deal that R can). In b P does no such thing. Instead, he pays R to do what is required of R by his institutional commitments in any case. Moreover, he does so in response to R's threat to violate those commitments in a manner that jeopardizes P's interests. Accordingly, b resembles extortion more than it does bribery. For, roughly speaking, R extorts P if R threatens P with a penalty in case P fails to give R something to which R has no rightful claim.

If this is true it may be that American corporate executives accused of bribing foreign officials are sometimes more like victims of extortion than offerers of bribes. For in at least some cases they are required to make payments to assure that an official does what he is supposed to do in any case. This is especially true in the case of inspectors of various kinds and in relation to government officials who must approve transactions between American and local companies. An inspector who refuses to approve a shipment that is up to standards unless he is paid off is like a bandit who demands tribute on all goods passing through his territory.

It does not follow that it is morally correct for American companies to pay off such corrupt officials. There are cases in which it is morally wrong to surrender to the demands of bandits and other extortionists. But it is clear that the moral questions that arise here are different sorts of questions than those that arise in relation to bribery. The moral relations between the relevant parties differ. The bribery agreement is not by its nature an agreement between victims and victimizers. The extortion agreement is. Moral justifications and excuses for complying with the demands of an extortionist are easier to come by than moral justifications and excuses for offering bribes.

Of course, the distinction in question is often easier to draw in theory than in practice. An inspector who demands a payoff to authorize a shipment is likely to fortify his demand by insisting that the product does not meet standards. In some cases it may be difficult to know whether or not he is lying (e.g., whether the shipment has been contaminated in transit). And given the high cost of delays, a company may decide that it is too expensive to take the time to find out. In this case, a company may decide to pay off without knowing whether it is agreeing to pay a bribe or surrendering to extortion. Since the morality of its decisions may well turn on what it is in fact doing in such cases, a company that does not take the time to find out acts in a morally irresponsible manner (unless, of course, it is in a position to defend both courses of action).

What sorts of justifications can a company present for offering bribes? It is beyond the scope of this paper to provide a detailed discussion of this question. However, I have already mentioned a number of considerations that count as moral reasons against bribery in a variety of contexts. To begin with in reasonably just contexts, officials ordinarily are obligated to discharge the duties of their offices. In these cases bribe offers are normally attempts to induce officials to violate duties. Moreover, if accepted, a bribe offer may make it more likely that that official will violate future duties. Accordingly, it may contribute to the corruption of an official. In addition, the intent of a bribe offer is often to secure an unfair advantage or an undeserved privilege. Where this is the case, it too counts as a reason against bribery. To determine whether a bribe offer is wrong in any particular case, then, we must decide: (1) whether these reasons obtain in that case; (2) if they obtain, how much weight we ought to attach to them; and (3) how much weight we ought to attach to countervailing considerations. (Suppose, e.g., that it is necessary to bribe an official in order to meet an important contractual obligation.) It is worth remarking in this regard that, where officials routinely take bribes, the presumption against corrupting officials normally will not apply. Similarly, to the extent that bribery is an accepted weapon in the arsenal of all competitors, bribe offers cannot be construed as attempts to achieve an unfair advantage over one's competitors.

* * *

It is sometimes suggested that an environment may be so corrupt that no payments count as bribes. These are circumstances in which the level of official compliance to duty is very low, and payoffs are so widespread that they are virtually institutionalized. Suppose, for example, that the laws of country N impose very high duties on a variety of products but that it is common practice in N for importers and exporters to pay customs officials to overlook certain goods and/or to underestimate their number or value. Suppose, moreover, that the existence of this practice is common knowledge but that no effort is made to stop it by law enforcement officials at any level;[6] indeed, that any attempts to stop it would be met by widespread social disapproval. One might even imagine that customs officials receive no salary in N but earn their entire livelihood in this way. One might further imagine that customs officials are expected to return a certain amount of money to the government every month and are fired from their jobs for failure to do so. Finally, one might suppose that the cumulative advantages and disadvantages of this way of doing things is such that the economy of N is about as strong as it would be under a more rule-bound alternative. Are these officials bribed?

In my analysis, the answer to this question depends on how we understand the duties of the customs officer. If the official job description for the customs officer in N (and the written laws of N) is like those of most countries, the customs officer violates his official duties according to these codes by allowing goods to leave the country without collecting the full duty. The question, however, is how seriously we are to take these written codes. Where social and political practice routinely violates them, nothing is done about it, and few members of the legal and nonlegal community believe that anything ought to be done about it, it is arguable that these codes are dead letters. If we find this to be true of the codes governing the duties of the customs officials in country N, we have good reason for saying that the real obligations of these officials do not require that they impose the duties described in those written codes (but only that they return a certain sum of the money they collect to the central government each month). Anything collected in excess of that amount they are entitled to keep as salary (recall that they are officially unpaid). In reality we might say that duties on exports in country N are not fixed but negotiable.

Of course if we decide that the written law of N is the law of N, we must describe the situation otherwise. In that case, the official obligations of the customs officials are as they are described, and the system in N must be characterized as one of rampant bribery condoned both by government and by popular opinion. It seems to me that the philosophy of law on which this account rests is implausible. However, there is no need to argue this to defend my analysis of this case. My position is simply that whether or not we describe what goes on here as bribery depends on what we take the real legal responsibilities of the customs official to be. To the extent that we are inclined to identify his duties with the written law we will be inclined to speak of bribery here. To the extent that we are unwilling so to identify his duties we will not.[7]

* * *

Let us now consider the problem of distinguishing bribes from rewards and gifts. The problem arises because gifts are often used in business and government to facilitate transactions. And to the degree to which a business person, professional person, or government official is influenced in her decision by gifts, it is tempting to conclude that she is violating her duties. In such cases we are tempted to speak of these gifts as bribes.

If I am correct, however, this temptation should be resisted. A bribe, after all, presupposes an agreement. A gift may be made with the intention of inducing an official to show favoritism to the giver, but unless acceptance of what is transferred can be construed as an agreement to show favoritism, what is transferred is not a bribe.

In some cases, of course, the acceptance of what is offered can be so construed. Again, if I offer fifty dollars to a policeman who has stopped me for speeding, he has a right to construe my act as one of offering a bribe, and I have a right to construe his acceptance in the corresponding manner. If I regularly treat the neighborhood policeman to a free lunch at my diner and he regularly neglects to ticket my illegally parked car, we have reason to say the same. Agreements need not be explicit. My point is just that to the degree that it is inappropriate to speak of agreements, it is also inappropriate to speak of bribes.

It follows from this that, if I present an official with an expensive item to induce him to show favoritism on my behalf, in violation of his duty, I have not necessarily bribed him. It does not follow from this, however, that I have done nothing wrong. So long as you are morally obligated to perform your official duty, normally it will be wrong of me to induce you to do otherwise by presenting you with some expensive item. Moreover, if you have any reason to believe that accepting what I offer will induce you not to do your duty, you have done something wrong by accepting my gift. To prevent such wrongs we have laws prohibiting persons whose interests are closely tied to the decisions of public officials from offering gifts to these officials. And we have laws forbidding officials to accept such gifts.

It might be objected that this account is too lenient. Specifically, it might be argued that wherever P presents Q with something of value to induce Q to violate Q's official duties P has offered a bribe.

But this is surely a mistake. It suggests, among other things, that an official is bribed so long as she accepts what is offered with this intent. Yet an official may accept such a gift innocently, believing that it is what it purports to be, namely, a token of friendship or goodwill. And she may do so with justifiable confidence that doing so will not in any way affect the discharge of her duty.

It may be replied that officials are bribed by such inducements only when they are in fact induced to do what is desired of them. But again, it may be the case that an official accepts what is offered innocently, believing it to be a gift, and that she believes falsely that it will not affect her conduct. In this case she has exercised bad judgment, but she has not been bribed. Indeed, it seems to me that it is improper to say that she accepts a bribe even when she recognizes the intent of the inducement and believes that accepting it is likely to influence her.

There is a distinction between accepting a drink with the understanding that one is agreeing to be seduced and accepting a drink with the knowledge that so doing will make one's seduction more likely. To be bribed is to be bought, not merely to be influenced to do something.

From a moral point of view, whenever failure to perform one's official duties is wrong it may be as bad to accept a gift that one knows will influence one in the conduct of one's duty as it is to accept a bribe. And clearly we are entitled morally to criticize those who offer and accept such inducements. Moreover, we are right to attempt to prevent this sort of thing by legally restricting the conditions under which persons may offer gifts to officials and the conditions under which officials may accept such gifts. Nonetheless, such gifts ought not to be confused with bribes. If P accepts a gift from R and does not show the desired favoritism, R may complain of P's ingratitude but not of P's dishonesty (unless, of course, P led him on in some way). If P accepts a bribe from R and does not show the desired favoritism, P has been dishonest (perhaps twice).

This point is not without practical importance. People who work in the same organization or in the same profession often form friendships despite the fact that some of them are in a position to make decisions that affect the interests of others. Here, as everywhere, friendships are developed and maintained in part by exchanges of favors, gifts, meals, and so forth. Were we to take seriously the inducement theory of bribery, however, this dimension of collegial and organizational existence would be threatened. In that case, if P's position is such that he must make decisions affecting R, any gifts, favors, et cetera from R to P should be regarded with at least some suspicion. To guard against the accusation that he has been bribed by R, P must be in a position to offer reasons for believing that R's intent in inviting him to dinner was not to induce him to show favoritism. And for R to be certain that he is not offering P a bribe in this case, R must be certain that his intentions are pure. All of this would require such vigilance in relation to one's own motives and the motives of others that friendships in collegial and organizational settings would be more difficult to sustain than they are at present.

Since decision makers are required to show impartiality they must in any case be careful not to accept gifts and favors that will influence them to show favoritism. Moreover, if they are required by their position to assess the moral character of those affected by their decisions, they may be required to assess the intent with which such gifts or favors are offered. Most officials, however, are not required to assess character in this way. In order to avoid doing wrong by accepting gifts and favors they need only be justly confident of their own continued impartiality. Thus, they are ordinarily entitled to ignore questions of intent unless there is some special reason to do otherwise. If the intent to influence were sufficient for a bribe, however, they would not be at liberty to bestow the benefit of the doubt in this way.

Again, there are cases in which impartiality is so important that decision makers should be prohibited both from accepting gifts or favors from any persons likely to be directly affected by their decisions and from forming friendships with such persons. And they should disqualify themselves when they are asked to make a decision that affects either a friend or someone from whom they have accepted gifts or favors in the reasonably recent past. Judges are a case in point. In other cases, however, institutions and professions should be willing to risk some loss in impartiality in order to enjoy the benefits of friendship and mutual aid. For these are essential to the functioning of some organizations and to the well-being of the people within them. Consider, for example, universities. The practical disadvantage of the inducement account is that it may require us to be unnecessarily suspicious of certain exchanges constitutive of mutual aid and friendship (at least if we take it seriously).

* * *

An interesting related problem arises in cultures in which a more formal exchange of gifts may be partly constitutive of a special relationship between persons, namely, something like friendship. In such cultures, so long as certain other conditions are satisfied, to make such exchanges is to enter into a system of reciprocal rights and duties. Among these duties may be the duty to show favoritism toward "friends," even when one acts in an official capacity. Moreover, the giver may be expected to show gratitude for each occasion of favoritism by further gift giving. On the face of it, this certainly looks like bribery. Is that description warranted?

To begin with, we need to distinguish between cases in which the special relationships in question are genuine and cases in which they are not. In the latter case certain ritual or ceremonial forms may be used to dress up what each party regards as a business transaction of the standard Western variety in a manner that provides an excuse for bribery. I shall say more about this presently. But let me begin with the first case.

Where the relationships in question are genuine and the laws of the relevant society are such that the official duties of the relevant official do not prohibit favoritism, this practice of gift giving cannot be called bribery. For in this case there is no question of the violation of duty. All that can be said here is that such societies condone different ways of doing business than we do. Specifically, they do not mark off a sphere of business and/or bureaucratic activity in which persons are supposed to meet as "abstract individuals," that is, in which they are required to ignore their social and familial ties. Their obligations, rather, are importantly determined by such ties even in the conduct of business and governmental affairs. Favoritism is shown, then, not in order to carry out one's part of a bargain but, rather, to discharge an obligation of kinship or loyalty. Failure to show favoritism would entitle one's kinsman or friend to complain not that one reneged on an agreement but, rather, that one had wronged him as an ally or a kinsman.

This is not to say that one cannot bribe an official in such a society. One does this here, as elsewhere, by entering into an agreement with him such that he violates his official duties for payment. The point is just that favoritism shown to friends and kinsmen is not necessarily a violation of duty in such societies. Indeed, one might be bribed not to show favoritism.

The official duties of an official, of course, may not be clear. Thus, the written law may prohibit favoritism to kin and ally, though this is widely practiced and condoned and infrequently prosecuted. This may occur when a society is in a transitional state from feudalism or tribalism to a Western-style industrial society, but it may also occur in an industrial society with different traditions than our own. To the extent that it is unclear what the official duties of officials are in such cases it will also be difficult to say what count as bribes. Indeed, even if we decide that an official does violate his duty by showing favoritism to kin and allies who reciprocate with gifts, we may not be justified in speaking of bribery here. For the official may not be acting as he does in order to fulfill his part of an agreement. Rather, he may be acting to fulfill some obligation of kinship or loyalty. Again, his failure so to act may not entitle his kinsmen or allies to complain that he had welched on a deal; rather, it would entitle them to complain that he wronged them as kinsmen or allies.

Of course, all this is so only when the relationships in question are genuine. In some cases, however, the rhetoric and ceremonial forms of a traditional culture may be used to camouflage what are in fact business relations of the standard Western variety. To the extent that this is so, the favoritism in question may in fact be bribery in ethnic dress. The relationships in question are not genuine when they are not entered into in good faith. It is clear, moreover, that when American executives present expensive gifts to foreign businessmen or foreign government officials they do so for business reasons. That is, they have no intention of entering into a system of reciprocal rights and duties that may obligate them in the future to act contrary to their long-term interest. Rather, they perform the required ceremonies knowing that they will continue to base their decisions on business reasons. Their intention is to buy favoritism. And the foreign officials and companies with whom they do business

are typically aware of this. This being the case, the invitations of the form "First we become friends, then we do business" cannot plausibly be construed as invitations to participate in some traditional way of life. Typically, both parties recognize that what is requested here is a bribe made in an appropriate ceremonial way.

* * *

On the basis of this analysis it seems clear that American officials are not always guilty of bribery when they pay off foreign officials. In some cases they are victims of extortion; in other cases, the context may be such that the action purchased from the relevant official does not count as a violation of his duty. The fact that American executives engaged in international commerce are innocent of some of the charges that have been made against them, however, does not imply that those who have made them are mistaken in their assessment of the character of these executives. One's character, after all, is a matter of what one is disposed to do. If these executives are willing to engage in bribery whenever this is necessary to promote their perceived long-term business interests, whatever the morality of the situation, it follows (at very least) that they are amoral.

NOTES

1. At the time this paper was written there were no references to bribes or bribery in the *Philosopher's Index*. Since that time one paper has been indexed—Arnold Berleant's "Multinationals, Local Practice, and the Problems of Ethical Consistency" (*Journal of Business Ethics* I [August 1982]: 185–93)—but, as the title of this short paper suggests, Berleant is not primarily concerned with providing an analysis of the concept of bribery. However, three presentations on the topic of bribery were made at the 1983

"Conference for Business Ethics" (organized by the Society for Business Ethics at DePaul University, July 25–26) and have subsequently been accepted for publication. These are: Kendall D'Andrade's "Bribery" (... in a special issue of the *Journal of Business Ethics*, devoted to the DePaul conference, 1984); John Danley's "Toward a Theory of Bribery" (... in the *Journal of Business and Professional Ethics*, 1984); and Tom Carson's "Bribery, Extortion and the Foreign Corrupt Practices Act" (... in *Philosophy and Public Affairs*, Summer 1984). Where my position on substantive questions differs significantly from D'Andrade's, Carson's, or Danley's, I shall discuss this in the notes.

2. Danley defines "bribing" as "offering or giving something of value with a corrupt intent to induce or influence an action of someone in a public or official capacity." Carson defines a bribe as a payment to someone "in exchange for special consideration that is incompatible with the duties of his position." Both go on to discuss bribery as if it were restricted to officials of organizations. Since these are the most typical and important cases of bribery, their focus is understandable. But it does have at least one unfortunate consequence. For it leads both Danley and Carson to think that the question of whether it is prima facie wrong to offer or accept bribes reduces to the question of whether officials have obligations to satisfy their positional duties. Danley argues that they do not if the institutions they serve are illegitimate. Carson argues that they do on the ground that they have made a tacit agreement with their institution to discharge those duties (accepting a bribe, for Carson, is an instance of promise breaking). Whatever the merits of their arguments concerning the responsibilities of officials, both approach the question of the prima facie morality of bribery too narrowly. For different issues seem to arise when we consider bribery outside the realm of officialdom. Clearly it is more difficult for Carson to make his tacit consent argument in relation to the bribed athlete. For it is not clear that a runner who enters a race tacitly agrees to win it (if so, he would be breaking a promise by running to prepare for future races or by entering to set the pace for someone else). Nor is it clear that a boxer who accepts payment not to knock out his opponent in the early rounds violates a tacit agreement to attempt a knockout at his earliest convenience. Danley must expand his account to accommodate such cases as well. For it is not clear what it means to say that a practice such as running or boxing is legitimate.

3. Such cases present a problem for the accounts of both Danley and Carson. At the very least they must expand their accounts of positional duties such that we can distinguish between a bribe, on the one hand, and a salary paid to a spy recruited from within an organization, on the other.

4. Carson fails to recognize the significance of this feature of bribery. This view of bribery, moreover, is inconsistent with Danley's account. Danley understands a bribe as an attempt to induce or influence someone. In this matter he appears to have most dictionaries on his side (including the OED). However, as I argue in more detail in Sec. IV he is mistaken.

5. This is Carson's argument.

6. In D'Andrade's account bribes are necessarily secret, so these could not count as bribes.

7. A corresponding point holds in relation to bribery outside the realm of officialdom. Consider the case of professional wrestling. Most of us believe that the outcome of professional wrestling matches is determined in advance. Are the losers bribed? (To simplify matters let us assume that they are paid a bit of extra money for losing.) The answer here depends on how we understand their practice. If we take them to be participating in a wrestling competition, we must say that they are bribed. In that case, by failing to compete they violate an understanding constitutive of their practice. It is reasonably clear, however, that professional wrestlers are not engaged in an athletic competition. Rather, they are engaged in a dramatic performance. This being the case the losers are not bribed. They are merely doing what professional wrestlers are ordinarily paid to do, namely, to play out their part in an informal script.

NO

Thomas L. Carson

BRIBERY AND IMPLICIT AGREEMENTS:
A REPLY TO PHILIPS

In a paper that appeared recently in *Ethics*, Michael Philips defends at some length an analysis of the concept of bribery.[1] He also attempts to give an account of the moral status of bribery. Philips attacks several views defended in my paper, "Bribery, Extortion and the 'Foreign Corrupt Practices Act,'" *Philosophy and Public Affairs*, Winter 1985, pp. 66–90. In my paper, I argue that accepting a bribe involves the violation of an implicit or explicit promise or understanding associated with one's office or role and that, therefore, accepting a bribe is always *prima facie* wrong. Philips offers two separate criticisms of this position. (1) He argues that in at least some cases of bribery the person who accepts the bribe does not thereby violate any agreements or understandings associated with any offices or positions that he holds. (2) He argues that in "morally corrupt contexts" there may be no *prima facie* duty to adhere to the agreements or understandings implicit in one's role or position. I shall offer replies to both of these criticisms, although I make some concessions to the first.

(1) Standard cases of bribery involve paying an official of an organization to do things contrary to the obligations of his office or position. The following examples all fit this model of bribery: (1) paying a judge or juror to decide in one's favor, (2) paying a policeman not to give one a traffic ticket, and (3) paying a government official not to report violations of health and safety standards. Philips concedes that in cases in which a bribe is paid to an official it is plausible to suppose that the official's acceptance of the bribe constitutes the violation of a "tacit agreement."[2] However, he claims that there are cases of bribery in which the person being bribed is self-employed and in which his acceptance of the bribe cannot be said to constitute the violation of an agreement or understanding between himself and some other party. (Philips seems to imply that in such cases there is no identifiable party *with whom* one can be said to have made an agreement.) Philips gives the example of bribing a self-employed professional athlete. In such cases, he claims, the acceptance of the bribe cannot be said to constitute the violation of a tacit agreement.

From Thomas L. Carson, "Bribery and Implicit Agreements: A Reply to Philips," *Journal of Business Ethics*, vol. 6 (1987), pp. 123–125. Copyright © 1987 by D. Reidel Publishing Co., Dordrecht, Holland, and Boston, U.S.A. Reprinted by permission of Kluwer Academic Publishers.

Clearly it is more difficult for Carson to make his tacit consent argument in relation to the bribed athlete. For it is not clear that a runner who enters a race tacitly agrees to win it (if so, he would be breaking a promise by running to prepare for future races or by entering to set the pace for someone else). Nor is it clear that a boxer who accepts payment not to knock out his opponent in the early rounds violates a tacit agreement to attempt a knockout at his earliest convenience.[3]

But, Philips to the contrary, athletes, even self-employed athletes who are not members of teams or any other organizations, compete in *public competition* (as opposed to private matches or exhibition matches) on the understanding that they will do their best to win. This understanding constitutes an implicit promise or agreement between the athlete and (i) the sponsors or promoters of the competition, (ii) the spectators, fans, gamblers, and others who follow the competition (they take an interest in the competition only on the assumption that it is serious competition in which each athlete does his best to win), and (iii) his fellow competitors. The runner who enters a public competition tacitly agrees to do his best to win. To run the race with only the intention to 'warm up' for a future race is to violate an implicit agreement. Running so as to 'pace' a teammate violates no understanding, provided that one is competing as a member of a team. In such cases, we can say that one competes on the understanding that one will do the best one can to promote the victory of one's team. The boxer who accepts a bribe not to knock his opponent out in the early rounds violates a tacit agreement to try his best to win. For him to forego early opportunities to knock his opponent out is for him to fail

to do his best to win. An athlete who participates in public competition tacitly agrees to do his best to win, short of injuring himself or others or breaking the rules of the sport. The promoters and/or sponsors of the competition, the spectators, and his fellow athletes all act on the assumption that the athletes will do their best to win. Of course, the fact that others *expect* one to do something does not suffice to show that one has consented or agreed to do it. However, there are other features in addition to the mere expectation that the athlete will do his best to win, which permit us to conclude that a tacit agreement exists in this case. The athlete knows that the others expect that he will do his best to win. Further, he knows that they play their roles in this competition only on the basis of this expectation. They would not do what they are doing (or even take an interest in the competition) if they came to believe that the athletes were not attempting to win.

Philips briefly mentions a somewhat different example that poses serious problems for my position. The case that he mentions is one in which a slave is bribed to lose a boxing match promoted by his master.[4] I find it a bit odd to refer to this as a bribe and am tempted to conclude that a necessary condition of bribery is that the person who receives the bribe accepts the payment in exchange for actions contrary to the duties associated with a position or role that he has accepted voluntarily. However, there are other cases of paying individuals to violate duties attached to positions or roles that they have not accepted voluntarily which we would not be hesitant to describe as bribes. Ordinary usage would allow that it makes sense to speak of bribing a conscripted soldier, even though he has not voluntarily accepted the duties attached to his position. Understandings or agreements entered into by slaves with their masters (or conscript soldiers with the armies of which they are a part) are not voluntary and thus do not create *prima facie* duties in virtue of implicit promises. (Perhaps some conscript soldiers do have a *prima facie* duty to fulfill the obligations of their positions, but these are not duties that they have in virtue of any promises or agreements.) I must, therefore, concede that in such cases the person accepting the bribe has not entered into any agreements or understandings of the sort that could generate a *prima facie* duty not to accept the bribe. However, it is well to note that my account still holds for the vast majority of cases of bribery. In almost all ordinary cases of bribery, the person who accepts the bribe violates duties associated with roles or positions that he has voluntarily assumed. The only exceptions are bribery of conscripted soldiers, some prostitutes, and others held as virtual slaves. The vast majority of us freely choose the roles and offices that we occupy.

(2) Philips argues that, even in those cases of bribery in which the recipient of the bribe is a member of an organization and can be plausibly said to be taking the bribe in violation of some implicit agreement or understanding, this understanding does not necessarily generate a *prima facie* duty not to accept the bribe.

> By accepting a position in an organization, it might be argued, one tacitly agrees to abide by the rules of that organization. To be bribed is to violate that agreement—it is to break a promise—and is, therefore, *prima facie* wrong. While I concede that this argument has merit in the context of just and voluntary institutions, it seems questionable in a context of morally corrupt institutions

(e.g., Nazi Germany or contemporary El Salvador). And even were it technically valid for those contexts, its conclusion would nonetheless be a misleading half-truth.... Thus, for example, it does not seem to me that, if I join the Mafia with the intention of subverting its operations and bringing its members to justice, I have thereby undertaken a *prima facie* obligation to abide by the code of that organization. Of course, one could say this and add that the obligation in question is typically overridden by other moral considerations. But this seems to me an *ad hoc* move to defend a position. We use the expression "*prima facie* duty" to point to a moral presumption for or against a certain type of action. And surely it is strange to insist that there is a moral presumption, in the present case, in favor of carrying out the commands of one's Don.[5]

I fail to see the force of this argument. Philips thinks it 'dangerous' to suppose that we have a *prima facie* duty to keep all implicit agreements, lest we fail to see that it would be wrong to fulfill our institutional duties in many morally corrupt situations (see Philips' footnote 7). But surely this is not a convincing argument. In general, it is not a valid argument to claim that since it is very clear that S ought to do x (all things considered), it cannot, in any sense, be his *prima facie* duty not to do x. Conflicts of duties aren't necessarily cases in which it is difficult to determine what one ought to do, all things considered. Nor is it an "*ad hoc* move" to say that *prima facie* duties can be overridden by other more important duties. The concept of a *prima facie* duty is derived from Ross. Ross is perfectly prepared to allow that some *prima facie* duties create only a very *weak moral presumption* for certain kinds of acts. He would have no hesitancy to say that implicit promises in the context of morally corrupt institutions create *prima facie* duties—albeit duties that can sometimes be easily overridden by other considerations. If we accept Ross' view that breaking promises (or breaking voluntary promises) is *prima facie* wrong, then we should have no reluctance to say that it is always *prima facie* wrong to accept bribes to do things that are contrary to implicit agreements or understandings into which one has entered *voluntarily*.

NOTES

1. Michael Philips, 'Bribery', *Ethics* 94 (July 1984), pp. 621–636.
2. Philips, p. 623, n.2.
3. Philips, p. 623, n.2.
4. Philips, p. 625.
5. Philips, p. 627. Philips attributes this argument to me in his footnote [5].

POSTSCRIPT

Is Bribery Ever Justified?

There are many points of view with regard to bribery. Where do you stand? Should the view of the moralists prevail, which insists on fair salaries, fair competition, and never a need to slip a payment into the outstretched hand of the customs official, dock supervisor, maitre d', purveyor of licenses, or rubber-stamper of documents? Is there a need to define with more precision what constitutes a bribe rather than a fee, license, reward, or gift?

Should governments regulate business operations more or less? Or should government remove itself from the position of regulating business payments? What group or agency should oversee any accusations or disputes regarding bribes, fees, and licenses? Should such disputes be the jurisdiction of the nation in which the transaction takes place or the nation of incorporation for the multinational? Or should a world court, UN committee, or some other international agency decide the issue?

There are further ethical dimensions that need to be kept in mind while considering this issue. First, we ought to have compassion for the poor. In many countries the bureaucracy is made up of low-status, poorly paid individuals who simply cannot survive without charging a fee to complete the paperwork and official procedures that a company needs to operate in those countries. What virtue is there in refusing to pay these usually inconsequential fees? Second, there is the troublesome status of hypocrisy. Sometimes a corporation operating in a corrupt atmosphere will hire a local "agent" who "takes care of the paperwork" and pays all the "fees." This agent is given a salary or consultant's fee for doing this task. The corporate officers probably know that the agent's "job" is to pay out bribes in their name; are *they* guilty of bribery?

SUGGESTED READINGS

David Bulton, *The Grease Machine* (Harper & Row, 1978).

Kendall D'Andrade, Jr., "Bribery," *Journal of Business Ethics* (August 1985).

Jeffrey A. Fadiman, "A Business Traveler's Guide to Gifts and Bribes," *Harvard Business Review* (July–August 1986).

John B. Matthews and Kenneth E. Goodpaster, *Policies and Persons: A Casebook in Business Ethics*, 2d ed. (McGraw-Hill, 1991).

John Tsalikis and Osita Nwachukwu, "A Comparison of Nigerian to American Views of Bribery and Extortion in International Commerce," *Journal of Business Ethics* (February 1991).

CONTRIBUTORS
TO THIS VOLUME

EDITORS

LISA H. NEWTON is a professor of philosophy and the director of the Program in Applied Ethics at Fairfield University in Fairfield, Connecticut. She received a B.S. in philosophy, with honors, from Columbia University in 1962 and a Ph.D. from Columbia in 1967. She was an assistant professor of philosophy at Hofstra University in Hempstead, New York, from 1967 to 1969, and she began teaching at Fairfield University in 1969. Professor Newton's articles have appeared in *Ethics* and the *Journal of Business Ethics*, among other publications. She is a member of the American Philosophical Association, the Academy of Management, and the American Society of Law and Medicine. Professor Newton currently serves as president of the Society for Business Ethics.

MAUREEN M. FORD is an associate for the Program in Applied Ethics at Fairfield University in Fairfield, Connecticut. She received a B.S. in business management and applied ethics from Fairfield University. Active as a consultant to community agencies, Mrs. Ford is a former president of the YWCA in Bridgeport, Connecticut, and was for several years vice president–secretary for JHLF, Inc., a marketing and consulting firm in Westport, Connecticut.

STAFF

Mimi Egan Publisher
David Dean List Manager
David Brackley Developmental Editor
Brenda S. Filley Production Manager
Libra Ann Cusack Typesetting Supervisor
Juliana Arbo Typesetter
Lara Johnson Graphics
Diane Barker Proofreader
Richard Tietjen Systems Manager

AUTHORS

ROBERT W. ADLER is a senior attorney for and the director of the Clean Water Project at the Natural Resources Defense Council in Washington, D.C., a national nonprofit organization staffed by attorneys, scientists, and resource specialists dedicated to the protection of public health and the environment. He is also an adjunct professor at the University of Virginia School of Law.

GEORGE J. ANNAS is the Edward R. Utley Professor of Law and Medicine at Boston University's Schools of Medicine and Public Health in Boston, Massachusetts. He is also the director of Boston University's Law, Medicine, and Ethics Program and the chair of the Department of Health Law. His publications include *Judging Medicine* (Humana Press, 1988) and *Standard of Care: The Law of American Bioethics* (Oxford University Press, 1993).

SISSELA BOK is a faculty member of the Center for Advanced Study in the Behavioral Sciences in Stanford, California, and a former associate professor of philosophy at Brandeis University in Waltham, Massachusetts. Her publications include *Lying: Moral Choice in Public and Private Life* (Random House, 1979), *Secrets: On the Ethics of Concealment and Revelation* (Vintage Books, 1983), and *A Strategy for Peace: Human Values and the Threat of War* (Pantheon Books, 1989).

THOMAS L. CARSON is an associate professor of philosophy at the Loyola University of Chicago in Chicago, Illinois. He has written numerous articles on ethical theory and business ethics, and he is the author of *The Status of Morality* (Kluwer Academic Publishers, 1984).

CITIZENS' RESEARCH EDUCATION NETWORK is a nonprofit policy watch organization based in Hartford, Connecticut.

DOUG CLEMENT is a former coordinator of the National Infant Formula Action (INFACT) coalition.

ROGER CRISP received a B.A. and a B.Phil. at Oxford University in Oxford, England. He has published several articles on practical ethics.

MARK DOWIE is general manager of *Mother Jones's* business operations. He has published articles in *Social Policy, Folio*, and *The Outlaw*. He has received numerous journalism awards for his investigative reporting, including the National Magazine Award from the Columbia University School of Journalism for his article "Pinto Madness." His interests are in investigating and exposing business and government practices that are legal "but nonetheless reprehensible." He is a regular contributor to *American Health* magazine and the author of *We Have a Donor: The Bold New World of Organ Transplants* (St. Martin's Press, 1988).

WILLIAM R. EADINGTON is a professor of economics and the director of the Institute for the Study of Gambling and Commercial Gaming at the University of Nevada, Reno.

JOHN ECHEVERRIA is chief legal counsel to the National Audubon Society in New York City. A 1981 graduate of the Yale Law School and the Yale School of Forestry and Environmental Studies, he has also been a legal counsel and conservation director of American Rivers, Inc., and he has served as a law clerk to U.S. district judge Gerhard A. Gesell.

FRIEDRICH ENGELS (1820–1895), a German socialist, was the closest collaborator of Karl Marx in the foundation of modern communism. The "official" Marxism of the Soviet Union relies heavily on Engels's contribution to Marxist theory. After the death of Marx in 1883, Engels served as the foremost authority on Marx and Marxism, and he edited volumes 2 and 3 of *Das Kapital* on the basis of Marx's incomplete manuscripts and notes. Two major works by Engels are *Anti-Duhring* and *Dialectics of Nature*.

JON ENTINE is an investigative reporter and TV news producer formerly with ABC and NBC. His reporting over 20 years has won him many awards, including two Emmys and the 1995 National Press Club Award. Entine has served as an adjunct professor of journalism at New York University and lectured at Columbia University.

RICHARD EPSTEIN is the James Parker Hall Distinguished Service Professor of Law at the University of Chicago in Chicago, Illinois, where he has been teaching since 1972. He has been a member of the American Academy of Arts and Sciences since 1985 and a senior fellow of the Center for Clinical Medical Ethics at the University of Chicago Medical School since 1983. He has written numerous articles on a wide range of legal and interdisciplinary subjects, and he is the author of *Forbidden Grounds: The Case Against Employment Discrimination Laws* (Harvard University Press, 1992) and *Takings: Private Property and the Power of Eminent Domain* (Harvard University Press, 1985).

HUGH M. FINNERAN (d. 1985) was the senior labor counsel for PPG Industries, Inc., a *Fortune* 500 company based in Pittsburgh, Pennsylvania, that manufactures paints, glass, printing inks, paper coatings, varnishes, and adhesives, as well as many other products.

GEOFFREY FOOKES is vice president of Nestlé Nutrition. He has been intimately involved in the infant formula controversy since 1973, having had extensive field experience in Third World infant formula marketing.

JEFFERY A. FORAN is executive director of the Risk Science Institute in Washington, D.C., and a former associate professor and director of the Environmental Health and Policy Program at George Washington University.

MARK GREEN is New York City's commissioner of Consumer Affairs. He has published 14 books on government, business, and law, including *There He Goes Again: Ronald Reagan's Reign of Error* (Pantheon Books, 1983), coauthored with Gail MacColl.

ROBERT W. HAHN is a resident scholar at the American Enterprise Institute in Washington, D.C., a privately funded public policy research organization. He is also an adjunct research fellow of Harvard University in Cambridge, Massachusetts.

LaRUE TONE HOSMER is a professor of corporate strategies in the Graduate School of Business Administration at the University of Michigan in Ann Arbor, Michigan.

ROBERT A. LARMER is an associate professor of philosophy at the University of New Brunswick in Fredericton, New Brunswick, Canada. His research interests focus on the philosophy of religion, the philosophy of the mind, and business ethics. He has written numerous articles in these fields, and he is the author of *Water into Wine: An Investigation of the Concept of Miracle* (McGill-Queens University Press, 1988). He received a Ph.D. from the University of Ottawa.

CHARLES G. LEATHERS is a professor of economics in the Department of Economics, Finance and Business Law at the University of Alabama in Tuscaloosa, Alabama.

JOHN C. LUIK is a senior associate in the corporate values and ethics programs of the Niagara Institute in Niagara-on-the-Lake, Ontario, Canada. He has also served as an ethics consultant to a number of government institutions, professional organizations, and corporations. He received degrees in politics and philosophy from Oxford University, and he has held academic appointments at the University of Oxford, the University of Manitoba, and Brock University. In addition to the ethics of advertising, his research interests include business ethics, medical ethics, environmental ethics, political philosophy, and the philosophy of Immanuel Kant.

KARL MARX (1818–1883), was a revolutionist, sociologist, and economist, from whom the movement known as Marxism derives its name and many of its ideas. Together with Friedrich Engels he published *Manifest der Kommunistischen Partei* (1848), commonly known as *The Communist Manifesto*. His most important theoretical work is *Das Kapital*, an analysis of the economics of capitalism. He also became the leading spirit of the International Working Men's Association, later known as the First International. His works became the intellectual basis of European socialism in the late nineteenth century.

MAGGIE McCOMAS is a business writer and a public affairs analyst. She first developed an interest in the Third World infant formula controversy while conducting research for the study "Europe's Consumer Movement: Key Issues and Corporate Responses," published by Business International S.A. (Geneva).

TIMOTHY MIDDLETON is a contributing editor of *Nest Egg* and a regular contributor to *Individual Investor* and *Worth*. He also hosts a weekly business radio program on WCBS in New York City.

JENNIFER MOORE is a former assistant professor of philosophy at the University of Delaware in Newark, Delaware. She has done teaching and research in business ethics and business law, and she is the coeditor, with W. Michael Hoffman, of *Business Ethics: Readings and Cases in Corporate Morality*, 2d ed. (McGraw-Hill, 1990).

JAMES NEAL has served as a lawyer in many mass disaster and product liability cases, including the Ford Pinto suit and *The Twilight Zone* movie accident trial.

JOHN O'TOOLE is the president of the American Association of Advertising Agencies in New York City. He has had a long career in advertising, and he remained with the firm of Foote, Cone and Belding Communications, Inc., for 31 years, serving 5 of those years as chairman of the board.

FRANK A. OLSON is the chairman of the board and the chief executive officer of the Hertz Corporation in Park Ridge, New Jersey, and a former John M. Olin Fellow of the Olin Papers/Olin

Fellows Program at Fairfield University in Fairfield, Connecticut. He is also a director of the UAL Corporation, Becton Dickinson and Company, and Cooper Industries, and a member of the Board of Visitors of Berry College.

PHARMACEUTICAL MANUFACTUR-ERS ASSOCIATION, founded in 1958 and located in Washington, D.C., is an association of 93 manufacturers of pharmaceutical and biological products that are distributed under their own labels. It encourages high standards for quality control and good manufacturing practices, research toward the development of new and better medical products, and the enactment of uniform and reasonable drug legislation for the protection of public health.

MICHAEL PHILIPS is a professor of philosophy at Portland State University in Portland, Oregon. A member of the Society for the Study of Business and Professional Ethics, he is a contributor to such publications as *Philosophical Studies*, the *Canadian Journal of Philosophy*, the *Journal of Business Ethics*, and *Ethics*.

J. PATRICK RAINES is an associate professor of economics, and he holds the F. Carlyle Tiller Chair in Business at the University of Richmond in Richmond, Virginia.

ARNOLD S. RELMAN is a professor of medicine and of social medicine at Harvard Medical School and a senior physician at Brigham and Women's Hospital in Boston. He was the editor in chief of *The New England Journal of Medicine* from 1977 to 1991.

GORDON RODDICK is chairman of The Body Shop and the business partner as well as the husband of The Body Shop founder, Anita Roddick.

ADAM SMITH (1723–1790) is a Scottish philosopher and economist. He is the author of *An Inquiry into the Nature and Causes of the Wealth of Nations* (1776).

RICHARD A. SPINELLO is associate dean of faculties and an adjunct assistant professor of philosophy at Boston College in Chestnut Hill, Massachusetts. He has published numerous articles on business ethics and ethical theory and on the social implications of new information retrieval technologies, and he is the author of a textbook on computer ethics entitled *Ethical Aspects of Information Technology* (Prentice Hall, 1994).

GEORGE TAUCHER is a professor of business administration at the International Management Development Institute in Lausanne, Switzerland, and a visiting fellow at the Oxford Management Center.

MICHAEL T. TUCKER is an associate professor of finance at Fairfield University in Fairfield, Connecticut; the personal finance editor at *Black Elegance* magazine; and a business consultant to the Ensign Oil and Gas Company, with specific emphasis on mergers and acquisitions. His current publishing and research interests are in the area of international finance and global ecology, and he has published many scholarly articles in finance and business. He is a coeditor of *The Northeast Journal of Business and Economics*.

MICHAEL A. VERESPEJ is a writer for *Industry Week*.

RICHARD WASSERSTROM is a professor of philosophy at the University of California, Santa Cruz, and the chair of the California Council for the Humanities.

He has published in the areas of moral philosophy, social philosophy, law, and race relations, and he is the author of *Today's Moral Problems*, 2d ed. (Macmillan, 1979) and *Philosophy and Social Issues: Five Studies* (University of Notre Dame Press, 1980).

ANDREW C. WICKS is an assistant professor in the Department of Management and Organization at the University of Washington School of Business. He has a Ph.D. in religious studies, and his interests are in normative business ethics and the connections between medical ethics and business ethics. His articles have been published in such journals as *Soundings* and *Journal of Business Ethics*.

FORD S. WORTHY is an associate editor at *Fortune* magazine.

GLENN YAGO is a faculty fellow of the Rockefeller Institute of Government at the State University of New York at Stony Brook, and he is the author of *Junk Bonds: How High Yield Securities Restructured Corporate America* (Oxford University Press, 1991).

INDEX